MW00562623

The Ketamine Papers

Welcome to an awakening to a jewel of opportunity for spacious mind, clarity and a relief from pain and suffering. Like all jewels, the ketamine space has its luster, facets, and its flaws. Ketamine journeys can be healing of trauma and depression, transformative of mind and heart, lessen the tension of ego and attachment, and enlighten and support connection and love. This book is as diverse in its presentations as are the range of ketamine applications, dosages and routes of administration. Ketamine is not for everyone. Not everyone responds. Not everyone finds it an easy medicine. For some, there are immediate awakenings. For most, it takes time for effects to manifest. In the moment of its influence and often afterwards, it may well be the most profound internal experience of mind.

—Phil Wolfson, M.D.

The Ketamine Papers
Science, Therapy, and Transformation

MAPS
Multidisciplinary Association for Psychedelic Studies

Proceeds from the sale of this book support MAPS' non-profit research into the benefits and risks of psychedelics and medical marijuana.

An earlier version of some chapters in this book appeared as articles in the *International Journal of Transpersonal Studies* (transpersonalstudies.org).

The Ketamine Papers: Science, Therapy, and Transformation
ISBN-13: 978-0-9982765-0-2
ISBN-10: 0-9982765-0-2

Multidisciplinary Association for Psychedelic Studies (MAPS)
PO Box 8423, Santa Cruz, CA 95061
Phone: 831.429.6362, Fax 831.429.6370
Email: askmaps@maps.org

Published in 2016 by MAPS.

Cover art: Reproduction of original painting (date and artist unknown).
Book and cover design: Sarah Jordan
Copyediting: Linda Stephenson
Indexing: Kelly Burch
Printed in the United States of America by McNaughton & Gunn, Saline, MI

Dedication

For Noah, who always guides and inspires.
For Eric, who always loves and exceeds all expectations.
For all those who have taught me by being themselves and more.
—*Phil Wolfson, M.D.*

For my mother, Grethe Hartelius, who passed from this world on
November 20, 2015. May she find rich contentment on her journey.
—*Glenn Hartelius, Ph.D.*

May this bit of knowledge and exploration
enter the cultural stream
to benefit all beings.

Acknowledgements

If not for my dearest friend, Joel Alter, deceased now for some years to my great loss, and his wife, Cheri Quincy, this book would not have happened. Shot into the cosmos, feeling as if I now knew death's format, and in the absence of my Phil form—that I was indeed energy itself—I took the stance that once was definitive and I would not return as there was nothing more to be learned. I had experienced what ketamine was about. Quite some years later I thought, maybe … and from there, we are now here with this book.

My great good fortune has been to be a member of a medicine circle, now for over 16 years. My brothers have been my friends and teachers and this book has been greatly influenced by their contributions and critical input. With such a long and sustained history—we have the same composition as when we began—there has come into being a sense of "group mind" that makes our individual beings seem much more connected and larger than the containers of self—a bit of the ecstatic to be sure. I am with deep gratitude for their love and mindfulness.

My partner, Julane Andries, has been my colleague and co-therapist in the development of a ketamine therapeutics. As a team that emanated from our MAPS-sponsored MDMA study of anxiety in subjects with a life-threatening illness, her patient work, support and conscious collaboration has had a major impact on the nature of our work as therapists. I am deeply grateful for her contributions.

My colleague and friend, Glenn Hartelius, is co-editor of *The Ketamine Papers,* and as the main editor of the peer-reviewed *International Journal of Transpersonal Studies,* published the forerunners of a number of the articles included herein. Glenn has been steadfast in his work for the book and has been of great support for its creation.

Rick Doblin has been a great benefactor and his support for publication of *The Ketamine Papers* has been unflinching. We thank Brad Burge and Sarah Jordan of MAPS for their work, guidance, and assistance in structuring the form of the book.

My great thanks to Richard Yensen and Donna Dryer for personal support and critical input. Michael Broffman and Michael McCulloch have been warm and unwavering in facilitating our presence at The Pine Street Clinic, where we do the ketamine work. Terry Early generously invited us into his clinic to sit in at his sessions for a memorable day that facilitated our own development of the ketamine work.

Sasha Shulgin was my great facilitator, mentor, and friend. Not a therapist himself, nor ever intending to act as one, his human wisdom, singular devotion to the truth, and his constant search for awakened, expanded mind were and are exemplary for me—and for all of us.

For the love that sustains the effort, my son Eric is my great benefactor.

—*Phil Wolfson, M.D.*

Contents

continued

The Ketamine Papers

Introduction to The Ketamine Papers

Ketamine:
Its History, Uses, Pharmacology, Therapeutic Practice, and an Exploration of its Potential as a Novel Treatment for Depression

Phil Wolfson, M.D.

IT HAS BEEN GIVEN THE ROLE of the new potential savior in the psychiatric medicine bag that is generally recognized as having gone stale. With a putative, and disputed, novel mechanism of action (MOA) in the much more widely brain dispersed glutamatergic neurotransmitter system, it has been promoted as a key to relief of treatment-resistant depression (TRD) and an increasingly wide range of other maladies for which drugs such as SSRIs and SNRIs have had limited results and for which virtually nothing new has been added for over a decade (Duman & Aghajanian, 2012; Nemeroff, 2007; Little, 2009). Ketamine has come to be well regarded for the immediate or rapid relief of depressive symptoms; for potentially providing an acute interruption of suicidal intent; and for the control of agitated, suicidal, and aggressively psychotic individuals in the ER setting. This new ketamine awareness has added to the drug's more traditional stock as a widely used dissociative anesthetic and analgesic in human and veterinary medicine. Respectfully, and not to be minimized and dispensed with, is ketamine's long history as a rapid-onset, relatively short-acting powerful psychedelic, with a reputation for fantastic mental journeys, transformative experiences, and alas, a potential for addiction (Jansen, 2004; Kolp et al., 2014). Ketamine is the only legal potentially psychedelic medicine in use—as a Schedule III substance with an indication as a dissociative anesthetic—and recently in the emergence of extensive and validated off-label usages.

This book represents a diverse but shared excitement for the development of a ketamine therapeutics.

Antidepressant responses to ketamine's administration for other reasons such as analgesia and anesthesia were known, if not widespread, before researchers at National Institute of Mental Health (NIMH) in the late 1990s began to assess ketamine's potential at low-dosage levels, attempting to exclude or at least limit the psychedelic effects of the drug (Collins et al., 2010; Krystal et al., 1994; Zarate et al., 2006). Prior, relatively early on in ketamine's use in anesthesia, descriptions arose of a disturbing "emergent syndrome," confusing and troublesome experiences having been reported by some patients exiting the ketamine space. Researchers suspected that there might be a boundary where those effects would be minimal while the novel effect as an antidote to depression would manifest.

In fact, rapid impact on TRD was found in this early NIMH research with single-session intravenous administrations of ketamine over time—40 minutes of a 0.5mg/kg solution becoming the standard, though this formula appears to have been arrived at somewhat arbitrarily from its inception. What resulted was a trance-like altered state with generally less dissociative effects, these having been deemed disturbing and undesirable—psychedelic. The resultant antidepressant effect was transitory, however immediately beneficial for those who had a positive response, and therefore unreliable and unsustainable. Generally, single sessions did not produce prolonged remissions. Extending duration with other agents has proved elusive. Extending the work to other diagnoses, such as Bipolar II, resulted in similar transitory results (Zarate Jr. et al., 2012).

It would take time and experimentation with routes of delivery, frequencies of administration, and dosages to reach the current view that there can be a cumulative ketamine effect based on multiple administrations (Katalinic et al., 2013; Zarate et al., 2013); this, regardless of route.

An overview of the present state of responses across various methodologies—there is no standardization—indicates about 70% of TRD patients responding positively, however transitorily, to one to three administrations of ketamine; and 30–60% of TRD patients having a remission of their depression for some varying length of time. This appears to be the case especially after a positive response to six or more sessions, generally administered over a two-week period. What we also have learned in this relatively short time of ketamine experience is that for some people the response is quick, even miraculous; often durable with a short series of treatments; for others it needs to be reinforced regularly on an ascendant curve of increased well-being; for still others, when depression threatens to relapse, it can be used, in essence, as a "booster"; and for some others ketamine's efficacy as an anti-depressant wears off and they become refractory to further administration.

We have also learned that other psychiatric medications have an adjunctive role as ketamine is generally not a particularly good anxiolytic; that there may be repeated resort to ketamine administration even over prolonged periods of time; and that there is at least a minimal level of mind alteration necessary for its effect—what I refer to as a "trance state." This psychological mechanism of action appears to be a necessity, whatever the pharmacological MOA may turn out to be.

While ketamine's limitations are palpable, to have a new agent that has positive pluripotentiality for a growing number of difficult psychological conditions is a most welcome development—one that deserves to be explored and amplified. Most studies put the failure rate for treatment of depression with conventional antidepressants at about one-third of patients no matter how many agents are tried (Fekadu et al., 2009; Goldberg, Privett, Ustun, Simon, & Linden, 1998; Kessler et al., 2003; Kiloh, Andrews, & Neilson, 1988). To have a new treatment that can effectively treat about half of those who are unresponsive and continue to suffer with depression is a boon indeed. Can we improve on response rates with ketamine? Can we go further? This and other key questions will be examined in the important collection of papers, experiences and views that make up this book.

In essence there are two separate strands to the ketamine story. The first and initial powerful thrust was as a new and novel psychedelic medicine that had transformative power. Either on its own or in various combinations with other psychedelics such as LSD timed for administration differentially based on practitioner experiences and preferences, ketamine became part of the available *materia medica* for journeys of the mind that often created spiritual, emotional and relational growth. The original and early work with ketamine using low to moderate transformational medication levels with psychedelic impact noted antidepressant responses related to an overall psychological benefit and an "afterglow" that could last for up to two weeks, similar and apparently longer than single-dose IV drip administration with the current dominant application (Golechha, Rao, & Ruggu, 1985; Khorramzadeh & Lofty, 1973). This was a great hint for exploring antidepressant effect. From the psychedelic perspective, my observation has been that no one comes back from a ketamine journey quite the same, that such rearrangement and novelty is beneficial, has been demonstrated repeatedly, and is a product of the escape from and transcendence of "ordinary" mind with its dysphoria, and obsessions. Ketamine provides a break with troubled usual mind and the possibility of relief and positive transformation. This transcendent movement into transpersonal experience has a unique fingerprint for ketamine.

When the NIMH protocol studies began the demonstration of ketamine as a potential psychiatric tool for the treatment of depression, and before additional studies expanded ketamine's use into frequent, multiple and near successive sessions with successful prolongation of effect, I and others familiar with the power of ketamine as a potent transcendent experience doubted and criticized the attempt to negate the mind-altering effect and still yield persistent positive antidepressant effects. While there was anecdotal support for ketamine's ability at sub-anesthetic but moderate doses to create an anti-depressant response—and though this had been noted in the earlier psychedelic literature—there were no studies to support this hypothesis for the benefit of psychedelic amplification. There still aren't, save for some hints referenced herein (Luckenbaugh et al., 2014), though some of us have begun studying this carefully and will collect data and publish results.

Much of the current research focused on depression has appeared to be an attempt to administer ketamine intravenously at rates that are slow enough and doses that are low enough to avoid much of the psychedelic effect that occurs at higher but still moderate dosages. Such an approach would be sensible if an experience of psychedelic or dissociative effects interferes with an antidepressant outcome. On the other hand, if higher dosages or the psychedelic experiences that they typically produce are both entirely safe and also associated with greater antidepressant effect, it is difficult to understand the logic of attempting to avoid psychedelic dosages. Surely it is time to set aside the old War on Drugs narrative, and embrace the use of ketamine for depression if there is evidence that it can have significant efficacy in treatment resistant depression and other indications without concern for the fact that a psychedelic experience may be inseparable from effective therapeutic dosages, and may well contribute to the therapeutic effect. Chapters in this book by Kolp et al. and Hyde include reviews of the numerous new ketamine related substances being examined for human use—substances that are based on the same mechanism of action as ketamine but without its psychedelic effects. Yet, as Ryan, Marta, and Koek (2104) note, thus far no new relative of ketamine that lacks its dissociative effects has yet to show antidepressant efficacy. Still, research is in an early stage, and more such work is planned or in process at pharmaceutical houses. It remains to be seen whether the glutamate/NMDA hypothesis that has emerged around the antidepressant effects of ketamine will be separable from its psychedelic effects. This also applies to newer rodent studies of ketamine's metabolites reputed to be free of the psychedelic but still effective as antidepressants—maze and reward behaviors. It has been generally wise to avoid thorough imputations from rats to humans, especially in the realm of psychoactive drug discovery.

Can a single chemical have remarkably dissimilar effects at different concentrations, or is there a continuum? Certainly with regards to dose related anesthetic effect, an escalation of effect corresponds to increasing dosage. Could there be an anti-depressant effect at very low ketamine dosages that disappears as psychedelic effects occur? This does not seem very likely! If dosage is reduced in an attempt to preclude psychedelic effects, at what level is that achieved, and how does benefit, such as anti-depressant effect, wane or somehow, paradoxically increase? Where, if there is such a thing, does a boundary lie between anti-depressant effect and interference by psychedelic effect—a question implied by much of the research that promotes antidepressant efficacy? Does investigator bias, the War on Drugs, the desire for status and acceptability affect research and promulgation? Whatever the answer to that may be, what is presented herein is evidence for ketamine's ability to create antidepressant and transformational experiences at low to moderate, pre-anesthetic dosages—on its own as a drug—and potentially with greater efficacy. For when embedded in a psychotherapeutic approach, ketamine-assisted psychotherapy (KAP) has great potential for emotional healing and the amelioration of human suffering and confusion.

Until an important practitioner conference took place in October 2015, it was my argument that psychedelic effects to some extent or other, were necessary for a robust antidepressant remission. I recently published a small study of experienced practitioners who participated in a single IV session to assess their experiences and view of the power of the induced state (Wolfson, 2014b). I used the results to support the view that psychedelic effects mostly absent at this dose made for trivial experiences equivalent to those encountered in the NIMH work and hence not particularly sustainable as an antidepressant effect. This was before an awareness of more sustained benefits with many ketamine sessions in various formats for succession of administration.

At the October conference, practitioners from Australia, the United Kingdom and the United States presented data from hundreds of patients with successful treatment at low doses that created trance states, but generally not with major psychedelic effects, this by the IV method, and most interestingly by oral and sublingual routes. These practitioners reported unequivocally excellent results regardless of the method of administration. As ketamine treatment for depression was spreading, and particularly with the entry of anesthesiologists administering the IV infusions in carefully prepared medical settings, the demonstration of the equivalence of outcomes of the more easily administered oral and sublingual ketamine in psychiatric office settings had a profound impact for future practice.

Ketamine has a proven safety record as a dissociative anesthetic, and there are now thousands of patients and many thousands of experiences demonstrating that it is a safe and effective treatment for depression and other psychiatric problems. The assertion that ketamine treatment needs to remain a medical procedure requiring stringent safety precautions is highly questionable. Safe and effective use in non-medical, psychiatric settings in which psychotherapeutic methods can further the effects of ketamine sessions is now well established. Stephen Hyde, in his ground-breaking 2015 book, *Ketamine for Depression*, had expressed his view that the IV route is cumbersome and unnecessary for treatment. He reiterates this in a chapter in this book. And to make this as controversial as possible, Steven Levine's chapter demonstrates the power of the ketamine IV experience as he practices this in his many clinics across the United States. No doubt this will sort out with more time and experience.

Considerations on Depression, Antidepressants, and Transformation

Depression is as old as mammalian life itself. Grief, the sensations of loss, alone-ness, frustrated desire, hopelessness, resignation, despair come along with mother-ing—as do attachment, affection, education, empathy, protectiveness, and connec-tion. These are inherent to nurturing and raising young to adulthood. They are the heart—positive and consequent—of live birthing of young—of children—who cannot survive on their own. From this perspective, the negative emotional conse-quences of a particular individual's life are systemic—culturally and situationally conditioned within a matrix of local and disparate social formations—family, band, tribe, species, interrelated and interacting other species in the broad sense of the biological community, and its resources—embedded in nature and its individual and group potentialities for creative engagement. The vectors and interactions—the symbioses, dependencies, obligations, potentialities, adaptations and threats go in all directions.

Human consciousness has tended towards an individual orientation as a distor-tion—connections and connectivities being more unconscious and built into the stored complexes that are the substrates of our interactive capacities, what in earlier times were inadequately termed "instincts." We look out from our insides and in-terpret our inputs inside. This inevitably leads to self-absorption and ego formation. But life, our life, is far more complex and interrelated than we appreciate—and much of our sensational realm never makes it to consciousness, whether it is about our own complex multicellular integrations or our relationships externally. What is exciting about the evolution of systemic thought and exploration is that it has opened us to the vast web of integrations and affecting influences and relationships, and our awareness of this is growing exponentially, ever-widening the complexity of our understanding, yielding new conceptual schemas that are continually being updated, expanded, or abandoned.

Psychiatry, as an evolving solidifying guild, now too coupled with Big Pharma and compensation through the insurance industry, has rubricized and rigidified its schema step by step. Emphasizing consensuality through the DSMs to enable a replicable conceptual and compensable diagnostic framework, it has tightened its grip on how mental health practitioners think and afflicted the public's consciousness as well. How often does one use the word "depression" mindlessly to compress feelings, or hear, "She's bipolar," as if that expresses the essence of a person. We have become all too comfortable and accepting of diagnostic terminology as if it were real and expressive of our realities. This extends to how depression is measured and formalized into a few codes that are supposed to cover the vast array of human responses (Greenberg, 2010; Greenberg, 2013; Whitaker, 2010; Wolfson, 2013).

Such an approach tends to understate the overlap between conceptually discrete DSM entities that are really not separable. Take, for example, a continuum of anxiety-grief-trauma-poverty-gender-ethnic-racial-oppressions-depression-torpor-fatigue-insomnia-agitation-confusion-interpersonal struggle-divorce-child abuse-hopelessness-lovelessness and many more linkages. These are all embedded in the term depression but not visible, as is so much of what occurs to cause depression. Far more frequently than we have acknowledged, depression is not "endogenous and not brought on by those who suffer with depression" (Wolfson, 2014a). Trauma, failed or limited attachment, neglect, and abuse of all sorts underlie depression and are too often not addressed as causative and creative of depressed states of mind (van der Kolk, 2014). Generally, this is not in the diagnostic format, for in this respect causation is linked directly to culture and outside the dominant culture's acceptable boundaries for change—and therefore of psychiatrists' / psychotherapists' responsibilities.

Antidepressants may reduce suffering and improve functionality to some degree for some people and may have an impact on their perspectives as well, but going to the "shrink" often has little impact on the chain of interlinked contributors to depression. Spuriously rigid diagnostic entities do not help the matter, as if, for example, PTSD were not a form of depression/agitation, and as if most depressions were not trauma-driven or PTSD-driven and were not linked to anxiety. They are. Psychiatric drugs are not all that specific, nor at times that helpful, yet they have been tied to the development of this constricted view. One only has to recall the relationship between certain drug companies' push for the Bipolar II category linked to the anticonvulsant Lamictal. With the patent expired and the availability of the generic lamotrigine—without all the hype and the profits—promotion of attention to Bipolar II has largely gone away.

Adding to this tendency to confine views of depression is its measurement as per the indices that give the diagnosis—a circularity to be sure—such as the Beck Depression Inventory (Beck, Steer, & Carbin, 1988), the Hamilton (Hamilton, 1959), and the MADRS (Montgomery & Åsberg, 1979). Those measures that are used to assess the effect of drugs that are in development are constrained by the instruments themselves to narrow measures of change. Yet even when administered by blinded researchers, assessment is generally obtained by self-report, since subjective reporting is truly the only means to obtain information on consciousness outside of guesswork by observation, or questioning, which are again inevitably based on self-report. The instruments used tend contain narrowing and often confusing questions about how the person feels within a very circumscribed framework. One doesn't ask, for example, how they feel about going back to their difficult circumstances; or how they feel about living with that person with whom they may be having difficulties; or about their careers; or about being laid off; or about sexuality—the latter being especially conspicuous as an omission when most of the drugs in use tend to suppress it (Fournier, DeRubeis, & Holton, 2010; Gueorguieva, Mallinckrodt, & Krystal, 2011; Hendrie et al., 2013; Kirsch & Sapirstein, 1998; Kirsch et al., 2008; McKenna, 2005; Moncrieff, 2007; Moncrieff & Cohen, 2006; Moncrieff & Kirsch, 2005; Murray & Lopez, 1997; Souery et al., 1999).

This book's papers on ketamine and its use in therapeutic contexts tends to represent a bit of defiance of all that conventionality, for its use challenges one to understand on a broader level what we are truly about as practitioners and human beings. There are those who practice psychiatry/psychotherapy to improve symptoms, which may well improve lives. There are also those who practice psychiatry/psychotherapy to change lives. Invariably, practitioners do both, or certainly the latter group must do both. At this game, in true modesty, mental health practitioners are partly successful at best. Our aspiration in producing this book is to assist practitioners a bit in improving the practice of helping humans to grow, connect, prosper, and reduce their suffering.

Ketamine Considerations—Tools for the Read and the Reader

- *Impact on consciousness: With increasing drug dosage of ketamine, the sensory inputs and perceptual integrations of the senses are turned off at the cortical level, leaving consciousness as internal and more and more subject to its own view, experience and creativity—this state of mind separated from external input, much as in a dream state, or as in a near death experience—so, an experience of heightened internal consciousness with its own particular linkages fostered by ketamine. As dosage increases, penultimately, this unique consciousness itself diminishes (hence the limits on the amount of ketamine that is evocative of this state and that increasingly causes memory loss of the experience), then is turned off, and then unconsciousness occurs.*

- *Generally, ketamine's antidepressant effect is short-lived if given in only a single administration. Repeated administration, whatever the route, tends to extend the effect and gives rise to what can be termed a cumulative effect, and is complemented and most likely further extended by being a component part of an extended psychotherapeutic modality.* **Ketamine is a Treatment.**

- *The rapid action of ketamine is due to its disruption of ordinary consciousness and its anesthetic properties. Comparisons have been made between ketamine for depression and electroconvulsive therapy (ECT), yet this juxtaposition seems less than apt since consciousness/awareness/our monitor of experience is maintained with psychiatric applications and not obliterated as in ECT. As a minimum, a trance state must be obtained for effect. Dissociative effects may well be part of the experience, differing in extent between patients even with the same dosage as mg/kg.*

- *Body weight and effect are not linearly correlated, but related—humans have a range of sensitivities irrespective of their actual size and hence only a correlation with peripheral levels of drug concentration. Brain effects are the result of multiple factors in addition to circulating concentrations of the substances applied—this being the general case with psychedelics and other psychoactive substances. In general, the greater the dosage, the greater the intoxication, but one human's point of intoxication is another human's neutrality or another human's profound experience.*

- *The mechanism of action of ketamine as an antidepressant has not been elucidated with full clarity inasmuch as the complexity of the state of depression is enormous and varied and there are undoubtedly many mechanisms at work as there are many states and ways of being depressed. No chemical treatment for depression has been fully successful thus far. And all explanations for MOAs, for SSRIs, etc., have been contradicted or found inadequate. For ketamine, other mechanisms than the glutamatergic one have been proposed—all of this coming from animal models with uncertainty as to application to humans. Of interest, and adding to the uncertainty as to ketamine's actual MOA, other agents lacking the dissociative effects of ketamine but acting as NMDA antagonists have thus far been ineffective in producing antidepressant effects. More to come for sure.*

Antidepressant substance treatments can be thought of in categories according to the schema below:

- Interruption of consciousness and breakage of the stream—usually repeated—e.g., ECT, narcoanalysis, and induced sleep in a continuum to coma.

- Disruption of consciousness—IV protocol of ketamine, sublingual, nasal, and oral low- dose regimens.

- Disruption, egolysis, and transformation—with ketamine, toward the K-Hole (the transpersonal state), in the K-Hole, and with other psychedelics.

- Direct shifting of mood and new experiences of affect—MDMA and other empathogens.

- Slow shifting of affective and anxious-/obsessional states—antidepressants like SSRIs, SNRIs, etc.

- Potential affective smoothing, refocus and obsession release as with marijuana.

From this perspective, one-time IV ketamine administration at 0.5mg/kg, or its relative equivalent, results in a mild disruption of consciousness, with a temporary release from a depressed affective and obsessional state, that state not persisting much beyond the immediate effect of the experience—save for a few people—and followed by ordinary mind and the habitual state of depression resuming. This is in part because we tend to ruminate and obsess, because character is hard to shift, because we have an ongoing but changing experience of external conditions, because external conditions don't change because we are having a ketamine session, and because we live in our own history and the history and culture of the external environment. Repeated administrations tends to assist in breaking the mental path and may well have a cumulative brain effect, if speculation on mechanisms such as neural plasticity, or chemically mediated pathways for depression hold up and are further elucidated.

And with a bit of help from Buddhist philosophy, which can be viewed as the greatest collective effort to study mind and its nature, from the Abhidharma, the philosophical/analytical "basket" of the canon, there is another schema to conceptualize this (Guenther, 1974). I invoke this because the Buddhist study of mind and the obstacles to mindfulness and clarity, as well as the development of an analysis of the mechanisms of perception, sensation, and consciousness are penetrating and applicable. Buddhism employs the subjective to penetrate to its roots, as far as anyone has gone, and validates its views by practitioners' applying theory for its corroboration generally based on direct experience.

Table 1. Ketamine as a Dissociative Anesthetic—Based on Abhidharmakosha

Capacity	Field/Object	Integrational Function	Ketamine Dose Effect
Body	Touch	Tactile perception	Analgesia @ 0.5mg/kg IV drip; 30–40mg IM
Eye	Form	Visual perception	Visual perception disruption @ 0.5mg/kg IV; 30–40mg IM
Nose	Smell	Olfactory perception	Olfactory perception disruption @ 50mg IM and higher
Mouth	Taste	Gustatory perception	Taste perception disruption @ 50mg IM and higher
Ear	Sound	Auditory perception	Auditory perception disruption @ greater than 0.5mg/kg; greater than 100mg IM
Mind	Affective and Cognitive Capacities	Consciousness	Cs disruption @ greater than 3mg/kg IV and 300mg IM

Based on these considerations, the goal of ketamine-assisted psychotherapy can be conceptualized as an egolytic transformative experience that potentially would have as its effect the reduction of obsessions and dysphoria—this occurring by breakage to some degree of the continuity of afflictive mind—allowing for reformation of consciousness, reevaluation of the past and its traumas, and hence the awakening of future prospects with the newness, flexibility, and openness of an improved experiential state. This state tends to produce a relaxation of that sense of control against the often entertained fearful possibility of one's mind going aberrant. As a result, this may well lead to a more robust and enduring antidepressant response.

Ketamine's successful entry into psychiatry calls forth a series of further explorations of ketamine's effects, in addition to its potential antidepressant property—personality transformation, relief from tormenting obsessional mind, and release from trauma, among others. With time and experience, these effects may well prove more robust and sustained than our current and highly varied formulations permit. Higher dosages will certainly include a more psychedelic component than generally occurs in the NIMH IV protocol administration. With positive preparation and administration in a safe and comfortable environment, given the physiological safety of ketamine, we can expect patients to be able to emotionally handle and benefit from experiences that include the psychedelic. This has certainly been the case with the psilocybin work being done at Johns Hopkins by Griffiths (2015; Griffiths et al., 2011), with the Heffter Research Institute, and in the MDMA-assisted psychotherapy work reported by Mithoefer et al. (2013) and MAPS.

The Ketamine Papers

This book includes papers from the core of investigators who have used ketamine in a variety of therapeutic contexts, some for over 40 years, and whose experience with the transformative and therapeutic properties, risks, and clinical successes and failures constitutes what is likely the largest body of information available on the subject. The reader is invited to take time moving through the long and detailed contours of this comprehensive undertaking. Much as there are different views and controversy, there is the opportunity for formulation of your own take on the ketamine experience. As always, there is the difference between intellectual and direct knowledge.

Beginning on a personal and anecdotal level, we offer first-person experiential reports. Off-label use of ketamine as a mind-altering substance did not begin in the laboratory, but in the psychedelic culture that grew out of the 1960s counterculture movement. Whatever the risks and limitations of such experimentation, without them the remarkable therapeutic effects of the drug might well have gone unnoticed and unresearched. The following personal accounts—both inspiring and cautionary—offer glimpses into the cultural contexts that found ketamine to be much more than a reliable anesthetic.

Ken Ring, one of the great progenitors of research on the near-death experience (NDE), regales with an account of his first powerful ketamine experiences in a way that also recollects the culture of Esalen Institute in the 1980s. In fact, there was a significant underground use of ketamine—though ketamine at the time was not yet scheduled—that paralleled on a smaller scale the then-legal exploration of MDMA for psychotherapy and peaceful transformation of interpersonal relationships. Ken's personal account serves as an in-depth exemplar of the feel of a first-time experience—though certainly not the only feel, as the breadth of ketamine experience is not subject to compartmentalization.

Stan Grof's remarkable capacity for internal experience is presented in a chapter that has been excerpted from his book, *When the Impossible Happens,* and augmented with new material. It serves as a reference for journeying on ketamine—with both the spectacular and the "dud" exemplified. Grof continues to document the amplification of the effect that Salvador Roquet had on psychedelic psychotherapy with his introduction of ketamine and his particular psychosynthesis methodology. Grof was one of Roquet's first recipients and sponsors in the United States.

This was also the era when John Lilly made his appearance in the Esalen circles, and Ralph Metzner shares a brief account of Lilly as he both exhilarated us with the possibilities of ketamine's psychedelic properties for transformation and transpersonal experiences, and horrified us at its addictive potential.

Viewing ketamine's potential for dependency through John Lilly, I provide brief closing remarks as a warning of the possibility of the poison path arising from ketamine use. Ketamine's putative mechanism(s) of action does not reside in the usual self-reward dopaminergic path; instead, its allure may well be of a different nature, a possibility that is discussed.

We begin our view of the Salvador Roquet legacy with Stanley Krippner's remarkable (and ongoing at age 84) Mexican odyssey. Krippner is the Alan Watts Professor of Psychology at Saybrook University, Oakland, California. His interest in psychedelics was sparked by a photo-essay about María Sabina, the Mazatec shaman, in 1951. At that time, he had no idea that he would meet the legendary shaman in 1980, during an expedition arranged by Salvador Roquet, another legendary figure in the annals of psychedelic studies. Krippner was one of the last participants in the Harvard University Psilocybin Research Project, ingesting the chemical in 1962 at the invitation of Timothy Leary. Robert Masters and Jean Houston asked him to write a chapter on his studies of artists and musicians who had been influenced by psychedelics for their 1967 book, *Psychedelic Art*. For various anthologies, he has written chapters on psychedelics and creativity, ecology, language, parapsychology, religion, shamanism, and social change. As a member of the pioneering group Right-A-Wrong, and a subsequent group, the Marijuana Policy Project, he gave several presentations on the futility of marijuana prohibition, and his essays on the topic date back to 1972. In collaboration with his Saybrook University student Jose Sulla, he wrote the first psychological study of spiritual experiences associated with ayahuasca, a substance he first heard about from his Northwestern University professor William McGovern, author of *Jungle Paths and Inca Ruins*. He had a long-standing friendship with Albert Hofmann and gave four presentations at Hofmann's centennial celebration in Basel, Switzerland, in 2006. Krippner is a certified drug abuse counselor, and has long taken the position that psychedelic usage should be limited to research and psychotherapy.

A conversation with Richard Yensen brings the reader into the realms of Carlos Castaneda, as well as Salvador Roquet, with whom he had a close and enduring relationship. In dialogue with me (Wolfson), Yensen shares rich accounts from the history of ketamine therapy in the piece, "Psychedelic Experiential Pharmacology: Pioneering Clinical Explorations with Salvador Roquet." Roquet left his mark on psychedelic psychotherapy in which ketamine came to play a significant part as an egolytic and then reconstitutive agent along with other psychedelics. It was Roquet who principally introduced ketamine practice into the small world of psychedelic practitioners, of which Richard Yensen was a part along with such luminaries as Stanislav Grof and Stanley Krippner. Yensen provides the details of Roquet's art form, which to this day influences many practitioners.

The realm of the psychonauts has always had a bell shape to it: There are the heroic take-it-as-far-as-you-can-go dissollusionists, or psychotomimetists bent on crushing ego and then reassembling; and the step-by-step cautionists who build the experience and practice a more classical psychotherapy approach. In between, there are those of all stripes. Over time and with experience, practitioners will shift positions and modify their practices.

A second continuum of interest is the "hard-head to vulnerable" spectrum—on the one hand a sense of anxiety about going too far, and on the other a sense of loss from not going far enough. There are two aspects: Each person is built differently with different tolerances and physical vulnerabilities. Each tends to either exaggerate or understate these. Most have a fear of losing their minds; of their minds betraying them; of madness lurking if they do too much of something or other; of a distrust of their core sanity. These too change with time and experience, albeit we humans are often best served by recognizing our limits and limitations. Yensen offers an intimate view of Roquet as a man who pushed limits, and seemed without fear of going too far.

"Ketamine Psychedelic Psychotherapy: Focus on Its Pharmacology, Phenomenology, and Clinical Applications," by Eli Kolp, Harris Friedman, Evgeny Krupitsky, Karl Jansen, Mark Sylvester, M. Scott Young, and Ana Kolp, offers a comprehensive overview of the development of psychedelic ketamine therapy. Eli Kolp's work with ketamine in a full program that he unabashedly entitles Ketamine Psychedelic Psychotherapy (KPP) is a thorough approach to working with many different diagnoses, addictions, and trauma. Kolp's treatment experience is extensive and his use of a variety of supportive and essential techniques and methodologies including MAOIs, diet, meditation, and an orientation toward the successful induction of transpersonal experiences as healing and transformative is unique, daring, and well worth understanding. Evgeny Krupitsky began groundbreaking work with ketamine in the former USSR, focusing on alcoholism and addiction in inpatient settings using first one and later two and three administrations of ketamine embedded in an intensive abstinence/therapy program (Krupitsky & Grinenko, 1997). Krupitsky has remained in Russia and has had his singular and promising work disrupted by a change in the scheduling of ketamine to the equivalent of Schedule I, claimed to be due to a dangerous accelerating street use of the drug. As a co-author of this article, Krupitsky brings the perspective of his extensive and pioneering experience. Karl Jansen is the author of *Ketamine: Dreams and Realities,* published in 2000, which remains the single most thorough and intelligent overview of the ketamine experience. Harris Friedman is senior editor of *The International Journal of Transpersonal Studies* and a significant contributor to the understanding of altered states and psychedelic psychotherapy. The remaining authors each bring an additional facet of expertise to this compelling perspective on ketamine psychotherapy.

Mikhail Zobin has continued Krupitsky's work outside of Russia, having created a clinic in Montenegro, where he has treated now over 7,000 patients with ketamine, most of them for addictions (M. Zobin, personal communication, October 2015).

What to date is the most thorough review in the literature of the use of ketamine for the treatment of depression is provided by Wesley C. Ryan, Cole J. Marta, and

Ralph J. Koek's paper, "Ketamine and Depression: A Review." They analyze and segregate studies into meaningful categories that enable a thorough review of this new field, its claims, and its limitations. From this perspective, it is more feasible to evaluate that which appears to be plausible, or overstated, or an indication of a vector for further exploration. Additionally, the tendency to strip ketamine practice of its psychedelic actuality—through adjustment of dosage and administration—is also made clear.

Born and bred in New Zealand, the second of six boys, Stephen Hyde is an experienced psychiatrist currently working in private practice in Launceston, Tasmania. In addition to raising a family, establishing a vineyard, co-writing a book about the pubs of Tasmania, songwriting, making biochar (this 2,000-year-old practice converts agricultural waste into a soil enhancer that can hold carbon, boosts food security, increases soil biodiversity, and discourages deforestation) and looking after a lively border collie, he has a special interest in the management of treatment-resistant depression. His seminal work *Ketamine for Depression* was published in 2015 and provides an extensive history, current practice, and prospects ahead. His use of sublingual ketamine has been pioneering and influential on the evolving nature of ketamine clinical practice.

Our interest in providing the reader with ketamine treatment approaches from which to reference and develop therapeutic strategies includes very different, yet also complementary, methodologies. We begin with Steven Levine, whose work with large numbers of ketamine patients make him the most extensive of practitioners in the field.

Since 2010, Steven Levine has been practicing the intravenous method of ketamine administration and most likely has had the largest number of patients and sessions in the United States, now with five centers in various cities across the country. As such, he is an excellent exponent of this method, which he extols for its reliability, consistency, as well as effect. Providing us with his introduction to the experience that is given to his patients, he clearly handles the potential for dissociative experiences. Levine's approach—as is the case with many psychiatrists, anesthesiologists and physicians practicing with ketamine in this manner—is to provide a comfortable, nonintrusive setting in which the session and the drug may enable a healing in interaction with the patient's own vector toward health and quality of life. A post-session is held and adjunctive psychotherapy from outside providers is recommended. In this chapter, Levine also provides us with a useful assessment tool for response to ketamine in the first three sessions.

Terrence S. Early offers an in-depth look into his practice using ketamine, along with a discussion of its history, political issues, and relationships to other treatments, in his paper, "Making Ketamine Work in the Long Run: The Basics." Early's practice model involves primarily the use of intramuscular ketamine—often with multiple sessions over time—embedded in an extensive therapeutic program. His comprehensive psychiatry practice, situated on the interface between psychiatry, anesthesiology, and psychotherapy, had its origins in academia and has continued in an intensive clinical practice in the Santa Barbara area that is most likely unique in the United States and internationally. His work may serve as a guide to the possibilities for using this substance, and as a specific reference manual for others interested in entering this field of practice. Often treating the most damaged and suffering individuals with commitment and heart, Early is one of those rare lions of medicine who exemplify for all practitioners the best efforts to assist and heal those in need.

Jeffrey Becker practices psychiatry/psychotherapy in the Los Angeles and Santa Barbara areas. His paper, "Regarding the Transpersonal Nature of Ketamine Therapy: An Approach to the Work," describes his use of ketamine as an enfolded part of an overall therapeutic method. Combining Edinger's ego-Self axis with aspects of Jungian thought, Becker has created his own approach to treating depression with intramuscular ketamine and its attendant experiences. He offers an explicitly transpersonal perspective for practitioners in this clinical field.

My paper on KAP is intended to offer an in-depth explication of our methodology with both sublingual and IM administration of ketamine as an explicit psychotherapeutics with its own possibilities for interventions. I had begun working in the early 1980s with MDMA and was developing a psychotherapy using that substance when the DEA, by placing MDMA in Schedule I, outlawed its use and clinical exploration (Wolfson, 1986). The work with KAP takes off from there and, as this is an evolving practice, it is meant to serve as an encouragement for development of strategies for psychotherapy utilizing ketamine as medicine and opportunity for health and change.

Included is "Ketamine (IM) Assisted Psychotherapy (KAP): A Model for Informed Consent," which potentially may serve others as they consider including ketamine in their own clinical work. This sample informed consent form is intentionally comprehensive and lengthy. Though it builds on the prior work of Eli Kolp, Terry Early, Stephen Hyde and others, this consent form reflects my own engagement with the challenges of effectively providing informed consent for KAP and is my responsibility.

The final piece presents my own schema for conceptualizing transformation—a topic of some relevance since a major claim of this section is that ketamine-assisted psychotherapy's value can be linked with the psychedelic experiences that ketamine induces—experiences that are often reported as psychologically transformative processes. My hope is that this piece will serve as a fulcrum for discussion, amplification, and healthy controversy. Included in the paper is a taxonomy offered as a meta-structure for examining transformation with psychedelics, the formats presented being derived principally from ketamine experiences, but also having wider applicability. A "transformation codex" is included as a matrix for characterizing one's own personal histories of transformational experiences.

As you read these papers, here are some points to consider:

- The complexity of our evolved brain / mind / consciousness / connectivity makes reductionist and narrow concepts and explanations for complex and varied states of mind like depression unhelpful, off the mark, and superficial. DSM diagnoses are circular and tautological, defining depression as a cluster of the symptoms that in turn define depression. They take the complexity of human beings out of the analysis and create deep mystification in all of us as we think about ourselves and others.

- The concept of antidepressants is at its core complex and varied, and the restriction in thinking primarily about drug interventions serves the pharmaceutical industry and the officials who are in charge of the self-interested fabrication of depression as disease.

- Within the realm of psychiatric medicine there are many types of drugs said to be antidepressants, and the fact that 30% to 50% of people do not respond to these drugs based on the neurotransmitter model of depression strongly suggests that this approach has serious flaws. The chemical imbalance that is theorized as the source of depression is elusive, and though it sounds empirical, there is no actual evidence that such an imbalance exists in actual individuals.

- A very partial list of antidepressants includes multiple types of chemical antidepressants with very different neurotransmitter actions and myriad other means to obtain antidepressant effects: anticonvulsants, stimulants, marijuana, exercise, meditation, hedonism, temporary satisfaction of cravings, elimination of cravings, oxytocin, sexuality, spiritual practice, money, love, children, activism, justice, a good job, respect, friendship, education, a good book, a bad book, and so on.

- Most depressive episodes come to an end without psychiatrists and without therapy. Some depressions begin with psychiatrists and psychotherapists.

- There appears to be a continuum between anxiety, trauma, and depression, and most often they are mingled.

- There are so many aspects of being and being in the world, and they all reflect and infect mood. All evaluations are oversimplifications. Even a partial evaluation of related parameters and aspects must include energy-enthusiasm-motivation-sexuality-engagement-learning-intellect-spirit-love / hate-trauma-grief / loss-failure / success-pleasure / displeasure-hopefulness / hopelessness-health-age-intelligence-blocks / phobias-social / environmental context-the cultural affect-religion-gender-education-origins and history of oppression-parenting-grief and loss-responsibilities-family-addictions, and so on.

Humans are complex, and "character," though it is tempting to see it as evanescent, not essential, and malleable, has its rigidity and implacability in all of us. After all, being a "shrink" is really a scholarship to watch oneself, as well as others. The argument here is that transformative work generally trumps symptom relief—and contains the latter within its effect size. Embedded in a repetitive psychotherapy format, the success rate for treatment of depression increases.

In most studies, it appears impossible to reliably strip ketamine of some element of mild dissociative experience, as if it were merely some undesirable "side effect." Even at a low dose, its effect is felt as being mildly "stoned." If even that minimal change of consciousness does not occur or is deliberately stripped from administration of ketamine, I believe there is then no therapy and no possibility of even a modest antidepressant effect. After all, this is not homeopathy!

This book sets out the history, the practice, the pharmacology, the effects, various therapeutic contexts, and the literature on ketamine as a psychedelic and as an antidepressant.

I hope you enjoy the controversy. You are the judge.

References

Beck, A. T., Steer, R. A., & Carbin, M. G. (1988). Psychometric properties of the Beck Depression Inventory: Twenty-five years of evaluation. *Clinical Psychology Review, 8*(1), 77–100. doi:10.1016/0272-7358(88)90050-5

Collins, K. A., Murrough, J. W., Perez, A. M., Reich, D. L., Charney, D. S., & Mathew, S. J. (2010). Safety and efficacy of repeated-dose intravenous ketamine for treatment-resistant depression. *Biological Psychiatry, 67*(2), 139–145. doi:10.1016/j.biopsych.2009.08.038

Duman, R. S., & Aghajanian, G. K. (2012). Synaptic dysfunction in depression: Potential therapeutic targets. *Science, 338*(6103), 68–72. doi:10.1126/science.1222939

Fekadu, A., Wooderson, S. C., Markopoulo, K., Donaldson, C., Papadopoulos, A., & Cleare, A. J. (2009). What happens to patients with treatment-resistant depression? A systematic review of medium to long term outcome studies. *Journal of Affective Disorders, 116*(1), 4–11. doi:10.1016/j.jad.2008.10.014

Fournier, J. C., DeRubeis, R. J., & Holton, S. D. (2010). Antidepressant drug effects and depression severity: A patient-level meta-analysis. *The Journal of the American Medical Association, 303*(1), 47–53. doi:10.1001/jama.2009.1943

Goldberg, D., Privett, M., Ustun, B., Simon, G., & Linden, M. (1998). The effects of detection and treatment on the outcome of major depression in primary care: A naturalistic study in 15 cities. *The British Journal of General Practice, 48*(437), 1840–1844

Golechha, G. R., Rao, A. V., & Ruggu, R. K. (1985). Ketamine abreaction—Two case reports. *Indian Journal of Psychiatry, 27*(4), 341–342

Greenberg, G. (2010). *Manufacturing Depression: The secret history of a modern disease* (2010). New York, NY: Simon & Schuster.

Greenberg, G. (2013). *The book of woe—The DSM and the unmaking of psychiatry.* New York, NY: Blue Rider Press / Penguin Random House.

Griffiths, R. R. (2015). Phase I study characterizing effects of hallucinogens and other drugs on mood and performance. Retrieved from http://www.clinicalconnection.com/exp/EPVS.aspx?studyID=355992&slID=13163552

Griffiths, R. R., Johnson, M. W., Richards, W. A., Richards, B. D., McCann, U., & Jesse, R. (2011). Psilocybin occasioned mystical-type experiences: Immediate and persisting dose-related effects. *Psychopharmacology (Berlin), 218*(4), 649-665..

Guenther, H. V. (1974). *Philosophy and psychology in the Abhidharma.* Delhi, India: Motilal Banarsidass.

Gueorguieva, R., Mallinckrodt, C., & Krystal, J. H. (2011). Trajectories of depression severity in clinical trials of duloxetine—Insights into antidepressant and placebo responses. *Archives of General Psychiatry, 68*(12), 1227–1237. doi:10.1001/archgenpsychiatry.2011.132

Hamilton, M. (1959). The assessment of anxiety states by rating. *British Journal of Medical Psychology, 32,* 50-55.

Hendrie, C., Pickles, A., Stanford, S. C., & Robinson, E. (2013). The failure of the antidepressant drug discovery process is systemic. *Journal of Psychopharmacology, 27*(5), 407–416. doi:10.1177/0269881112466185

Hyde, S. J. (2015). *Ketamine and depression.* Bloomington, IN: Xlibris.

Jansen, K. (2004). *Ketamine: Dreams and realities* (2nd ed.). Sarasota, FL: Multidisciplinary Association for Psychedelic Studies (MAPS).

Katalinic, N., Lai, R., Somogyi, A., Mitchell, P. B., Glue, P., & Loo, C. K. (2013). Ketamine as a new treatment for depression: A review of its efficacy and adverse effects. *Australian and New Zealand Journal of Psychiatry, 47*(8), 710–727. doi:10.1177/0004867413486842

Kessler, R. C., Berglund, P., Demler, O., Jin, R., Koretz, D., Merikangas, K. R., … & Wang, P. S. (2003). The epidemiology of major depressive disorder: Results from the National Comorbidity Survey Replication (NCS-R). *JAMA, 289*(23), 3095–3105. doi:10.1001/jama.289.23.3095

Khorramzadeh, E., & Lofty, A. (1973). The use of ketamine in psychiatry. *Psychosomatics, 14,* 344–346. doi:10.1016/S0033-3182(73)71306-2

Kiloh, L. G., Andrews, G., & Neilson, M. (1988). The long-term outcome of depressive illness. *The British Journal of Psychiatry, 153*(6), 752–757. doi:10.1192/bjp.153.6.752

Kirsch, I., & Sapirstein, G. (1998). Listening to Prozac but hearing placebo: A meta-analysis of antidepressant medication. *Prevention and Treatment, 1*(2). doi:10.1037/1522-3736.1.1.12a

Kirsch, I., Deacon, B. J., Huedo-Medina, T. B., Scoboria, A., Moore, T. J., Johnos, B. T. (2008). Initial severity and antidepressant benefits: A meta-analysis of data submitted to the FDA. *PLoS Medicine, 5*(2), e45. doi:10.1371/journal.pmed.0050045

Kolp, E., Friedman, H., Krupitsky, E., Jansen, K., Sylvester, M., Young, M. S., & Kolp, A. (2014). *International Journal of Transpersonal Studies, 33*(2), 84–140.

Krupitsky, E. M., & Grinenko, A. Y. (1997). Ketamine psychedelic therapy (KPT)—A review of the results of ten years of research. *Journal of Psychoactive Drugs, 29*(2), 165–183. doi:10.1080/02791072.1997.10400185

Krystal, J. H., Karper, L. P., Seibyl, J. P., Freeman, G. K., Delaney, R., Bremner, J. D., … & Charney, D. S. (1994). Subanesthetic effects of the noncompetitive NMDA antagonist, ketamine, in humans: Psychotomimetic, perceptual, cognitive, and neuroendocrine responses. *Archives of General Psychiatry, 51*(3), 199–214. doi:10.1001/archpsyc.1994.03950030035004

Little, A. (2009). Treatment-resistant depression. *American Family Physician, 80*(2), 167–172.

Luckenbaugh, D. A., Niciu, M. J., Ionescu, D. F., Nolan, N. M., Richards, E. M., Brutsche, N. E., … & Zarate, C. A. (2014). Do the dissociative side effects of ketamine mediate antidepressant effects? *Journal of Affective Disorders, 159,* 56-61. doi:10.1016/j.jad.2014.02.017

McKenna, M. T., Michaud, C. M., Murray, C. J., & Marks, J. S. (2005). Assessing the burden of disease in the United States using disability-adjusted life years. *American Journal of Preventive Medicine, 28*(5), 415–423. doi:10.1016/j.amepre.2005.02.009

Mithoefer, M. C., Grob, C. S., & Brewerton, T. D. (2016). Novel psychopharmacological therapies for psychiatric disorders: Psilocybin and MDMA. *The Lancet Psychiatry, 3*(5), 481–488.

Mithoefer, M. C., Wagner, M. T., Mithoefer, A. T., Jerome, L., Martin, S. F., Yazar-Klosinski, … & Doblin, R. (2013). Durability of improvement in post-traumatic stress disorder symptoms and absence of harmful effects or drug dependency after 3,4-methylenedioxymethamphetamine-assisted psychotherapy: A prospective long-term follow-up study. *Journal of Pharmacology, 27*(1), 28-39.

Moncrieff, J. (2007). Are antidepressants as effective as claimed? No, they are not effective at all. *Canadian Journal of Psychiatry, 52*(2), 96–97.

Moncrieff, J., & Cohen, D. (2006). Do antidepressants cure or create abnormal brain states? *PLoS Medicine, 3*(7), e240. doi:10.1371/journal.pmed.0030240

Moncrieff, J., Kirsch, I. (2005). Efficacy of antidepressants in adults. *British Medical Journal, 331*(7509), 155–157. doi:10.1136/bmj.331.7509.155

Murray, C. J., & Lopez, A. D. (1997). Global mortality, disability, and the contribution of risk factors: Global Burden of Disease Study. *The Lancet, 349*(9063), 1436–1442. doi:10.1016/S0140-6736(96)07495-8

Montgomery, S. A. & Åsberg, N. (1979). A new depression scale designed to be sensitive to change. *British Journal of Psychiatry, 134,* 382–389.

Nemeroff, C. B. (2007). Prevalence and management of treatment-resistant depression. *Journal of Clinical Psychiatry, 68*(8), 17-25.

Ryan, W. C., Marta, C. J., & Koek, R. J. (2014). Ketamine and depression: A review. *International Journal of Transpersonal Studies, 33*(2), 40–74. Updated version in this book.

Souery, D., Amsterdam, J., De Montigny, C., Lecrubier, Y., Montgomery, S., Lipp, O., … & Mendlewicz, J. (1999). Treatment resistant depression: Methodological overview and operational criteria. *European Neuropsychopharmacology, 9*(1), 83–91. doi:10.1016/S0924-977X(98)00004-2

van der Kolk, B. (2014). *The body keeps the score.* New York, NY: Penguin.

Whitaker, R. (2010). *Anatomy of an epidemic: Magic bullets, psychiatric drugs and the astonishing rise of mental illness in America.* New York, NY: Crown.

Wolfson, P. E. (1986). Meetings at the edge with Adam: A man for all seasons? *Journal of Psychoactive Drugs, 18*(4), 319–328.

Wolfson, P. E. (2013). Hark! The psychiatrists sing, hoping glory for that revised DSM thing! [web-only article]. *Tikkun.*

Wolfson, P. E. (2014a). Ketamine—Its history, uses, pharmacology, therapeutic practice, and an exploration of its potential as a novel treatment for depression. *International Journal of Transpersonal Studies, 33*(2), 33–39.

Wolfson, P. E. (2014b). Ketamine for depression—A mixed methods study. *International Journal of Transpersonal Studies, 33*(2), 75–83.

Zarate, C. A., Singh, J. B., Carlson, P. J., Brutsche, N. E., Ameli, R., Luckenbaugh, D. A., … & Manji, H. K. (2006). A randomized trial of an *N*-methyl-D-aspartate antagonist in treatment-resistant major depression. *Archives of General Psychiatry, 63*(8), 856–864. doi:10.1001/archpsyc.63.8.856

Zarate Jr., C. A., Brutsche, N. E., Ibrahim, L., Franco-Chaves, J., Diaz-Granados, N., Cravchik, A., … & Luckenbaugh, D. A. (2012). Replication of ketamine's antidepressant efficacy in bipolar depression: A randomized controlled add-on trial. *Biological Psychiatry, 71*(11), 939–946. doi:10.1016/j.biopsych.2011.12.010

Zarate, C., Duman, R. S., Liu, G., Sartori, S., Quiroz, J., & Murck, H. (2013). New paradigms for treatment-resistant depression. *Annals of the New York Academy of Sciences, 1292*(1), 21–31. doi:10.1111/nyas.12223

Ketamine Explorations:
Accounts of First Person Journeys

Ketamine Days

Kenneth Ring, Ph.D.

MY ADVENTURES WITH KETAMINE BEGAN WITH a fateful phone call over 30 years ago. In August of 1984, I was in California to give lectures and meet with professional colleagues in connection with my recently published book on near-death experiences, *Heading Toward Omega.* The last of my talks on that visit was to a San Francisco Bay Area medical society, which had been arranged by my cousin Cliff, a cardiologist. That evening, while I was still at Cliff's house in Orinda before leaving for Los Angeles the next day, I received a phone call from another Orinda resident who was, but would hardly remain, a stranger to me. Her name was Therese.

It turned out that Therese had read my first near-death experience (NDE) book, *Life and Death,* and wanted to talk to me about a professional matter related to that book. Since she had discovered that I was serendipitously staying near her house in Orinda, she wondered whether I could come over to meet her while I was still in town. I explained that it would not be possible, because I had to pack and leave the next morning. Therese countered by asking whether it might be possible for me to take some time on the phone right then, so that she could explain just a bit of what she had in mind. She had a very pleasant and gracious manner of speaking—there was certainly something very appealing, almost seductive, about her voice—so I readily consented. She then had a bombshell to drop concerning another invitation altogether.

Therese told me that she had been working with an oncologist, and that they were both concerned with trying to find ways for terminal patients to die with less fear and with a sense of transcendent revelation similar to that which near-death experiencers often reported. In fact, they wanted to try to induce something like an NDE, and the means they proposed to use for this purpose was the anesthetic ketamine. Because Therese had read my first book on NDEs, she regarded me as an expert on the subject. She suggested to her oncologist colleague that she ask me to be a professional subject who would take ketamine under supervision in order to see the extent to which this drug might mimic an actual NDE.

Whoa! In my mind I remember thinking, "Oh, God, wait just a minute." I already was familiar with work that had been done with terminal cancer patients along these lines using LSD, which Stan Grof and Joan Halifax had described in their book, *The Human Encounter with Death*. They had indeed shown that LSD employed in this way sometimes induced an experience that shared many of the same components and after-effects of an actual NDE, including, in most cases, a reduction of the fear of death and an increased expectation for some form of life after death.

But ketamine was another story. I knew something about this drug from having read about John Lilly's experiments with it and from some other sources, and what I had heard had certainly made me wary of it. I definitely had never had any interest in trying it—if anything, I was averse to doing so, particularly because I knew that it was administered by injection. Thoughts of heroin addiction flickered in my mind. Besides, my days of using psychoactive drugs were by then long past. I had experimented with LSD, peyote, and psilocybin for a while during the 1970s, but I had taken them only about once a year, and had stopped for good in 1977. I had no desire to try anything new along those lines, and certainly not anything like ketamine, which for me was a drug associated with real risk and danger.

"Ah, I don't think this would be for me, Therese."

Therese had an alternative proposal ready. "Well, you don't have to make up your mind now, Ken. Just think about it, and let me send you a little literature on the subject, OK?" She then mentioned that the following spring, she would be coordinating a conference on psychedelics at Esalen Institute in Big Sur, and wondered whether I would have an interest in being there—particularly because John Lilly himself would be attending. She added that it would be held during the first half of June 1985.

Now here's the kicker. Therese did not know, when she tendered this invitation, that I would actually be at Esalen exactly at that time. I had first visited Esalen in 1983 when its co-founder, Michael Murphy, had asked me to give a program on NDEs. It was successful, and Michael and I hit it off. He had recently been in touch to invite me again, this time for a much more extensive engagement at the institute.

He wanted me to come for three weeks in the late spring of 1985 as a scholar-in-residence so that I could conduct a workshop on NDEs and present my work in other workshops and seminars that would follow mine, including a monthlong workshop that would be conducted by none other than Esalen's then-permanent scholar-in-residence, Stan Grof. I had loved being at Esalen on my first visit, so naturally I jumped at the chance. So I already knew what Therese didn't—that I would be there at the same time her conference would be held.

It is a cliché among people in my world to say, "there are no coincidences." Being contrary, I usually reply, "except for accidents and chance events." In this case, however, I couldn't help feeling a little unnerved when she invited me to attend. It already seemed like destiny had decided to take a hand in my affairs.

Naturally, I told her I would love to come. Naturally, she was delighted. We agreed to put aside the whole business about ketamine for now. In due course, however, she would send me some materials pertaining to the conference. That, for the moment, was all.

Fast forward to June 1985. By then I had already spent a very engrossing week at Esalen, and had become very involved with a woman I'll simply call L., with whom I was staying. One morning, several days before Therese's conference was scheduled to begin, L. told me that Therese's roommate, S., would be arriving in order to set up things for the event. Since L. and S. were already good friends, L. invited me to come along to meet her.

That evening, the three of us met and slipped into a warm pool together, sans clothes of course—Esalen style. We were alone except for one fellow at the end of the pool. At some point, S. whispered to L., but in my hearing, "Would you like to do a little K tomorrow?"

"What's K?" I asked.

"Ketamine," L. whispered in my ear.

"Uh-oh," I thought.

Of course, I was supposed to be "saving myself" for a possible ketamine experience, which I hadn't ruled out. It had been on the agenda for Therese and me to discuss after she arrived.

L. quickly expressed her enthusiasm for having a ketamine session the following evening. She knew that a grand house on her property was temporarily vacant and L. had the key and permission to use it.

I was very conflicted, and more than a little afraid. I explained all the reasons for my hesitation, but briefly, urgently, and sotto voce so that the fellow who was still at the other end of the pool couldn't hear. Not only was I concerned about violating an implicit understanding about remaining a "ketamine virgin" for Therese, but I was really worried about having to take it by injection.

S. said to me, "Ken, I have taken it about 200 times. It's perfectly safe. I know how to give injections. Meet me for breakfast tomorrow and I'll answer all your questions."

By now, I was virtually living with L.—things happen fast at Esalen, and now I was already on the verge of taking ketamine with her and S.—so the following morning I had to hustle to meet S. for breakfast.

"I have a lot of questions," I began.

"I'm sure I can answer them all," S. replied. She did give me the feeling I could trust her. That was something I had quickly learned during my short stay at Esalen. You had to trust. If you were going to take a leap in the dark, you had to assume that someone would be there to catch you. S. radiated confidence; I felt I would be safe with her and that she would answer my questions truthfully based on her own extensive experience with ketamine. In the end, after she had explained a great deal to me, I felt reassured. But there was still one problem: Therese. I mentioned this to S.

"Call her," she said.

When later that morning I was able to reach Therese, who would be leaving for the conference in just a couple of days, she was very upset. She really didn't want me to do it—it would bias my reaction to the kind of ketamine test under controlled conditions that she was still hoping I would assent to. She urged me to decline. There was also some evident bad feeling between L. and Therese, as if they were rivals of sort (which was indeed the case, as I soon learned).

I neither consented to Therese's request, nor rebuffed it. I just didn't commit myself one way or the other. I think I evaded the whole matter and simply told her I would consider it and think it over. The conversation ended on a note of irresolution. I didn't think Therese was happy with me or the prospect I might be doing ketamine with L.

By that time, however, I had come to feel very comfortable not only with S., but also very close to L. Because there was already a strong bond of friendship between S. and L., and a growing sense of camaraderie among the three of us, I rather resented Therese's attempt to place a block of sorts in the path of what seemed a natural progression.

I decided to follow the call of my desire rather than to honor what wasn't exactly a pledge to Therese. I would do it. What the hell! This was Esalen. At Esalen, you took chances, trusting you would land on your feet.

That evening, after dark—for it was still early June—the three of us made our way down to the large house L. had commandeered for our session. Immediately I was struck by its burnished beauty. I remember a very ornately designed banister with a series of balusters that led down to the lower portion of the house, where there was a bedroom in which we would stay once we had received our injections of ketamine. In the nearby bathroom, S. got out the syringes and the little vials of ketamine, but before she began the injections, L., who was always the most eloquent of the three of us (she had a gift for spontaneous flowery incantations), took a few minutes to do a kind of ceremony, asking blessings for a safe and fulfilling journey. Now we were ready to begin.

S. had explained that even at the subanesthetic levels we would be taking, once the injection had taken place, we had to immediately go to the nearby bed, lie down, and wait. She also said she had to be careful in order to make sure that there were no bubbles in the syringe because that could cause problems. I began to feel very nervous.

She would first inject L., then me (in my thigh), and finally herself. Were we ready?

Gulp.

Once S. had injected me, I made my way to the bed. L. was already supine to my left, I was in the middle of the bed, and S. would soon join us, and lie to my right.

I waited.

After only a few minutes, I began to see swirling colors—beautiful oranges and glowing peaceful reds. I was no longer aware of my body. It was as if I were gliding on a river of color, and then I was the colors, I had merged with them.

But next, I found I was holding L.'s hand with my left hand and S.'s with my right, and I was blending into them. I could feel their energies, their essence in me, because seemingly my own boundaries had dissolved. I said—we never forgot this—"The L. of Us and the S. of Us."

L. hissed softly but with emphasis, "Yes!"

We lapsed into silence.

I continued to ride the waves of ecstasy, but this was entirely different from what I had previously experienced on MDMA, which I had taken several days earlier with L. There were peaceful, floating, beautiful colors. Then at one point, everything went black—very black. I grew frightened; I thought I might be dying. Then, a radiant exfoliating burst of new colors and another level of the trip had begun. I was no longer aware of anything but beauty—no body, no Ken, nothing but being merged with the very sensations of the experience itself from which I was not separate, there being no "I."

Eventually—because I had no sense of time I had no idea how much time had elapsed—I became aware that I was feeling the energies of L. and S. again. I was still holding their hands. But then—I remember this distinctly—my left hand began "making love" with L.'s hand. It was in the way our fingers were moving together. She responded. This was love. I felt a little bad not doing the same with S., but it was L. I was drawn to.

It turned out about 45 minutes had gone by. I was still very woozy and had to continue to lie there for a few minutes while the two of them got up.

There was a large, beautifully designed blue stone-inlaid circular hot tub nearby. Someone—probably S.—turned it on. Eventually, we all got into it and began talking softly about what we had experienced. We laughed over my phrase, "The L. of Us and the S. of Us." But it still seemed true—we had bonded, we had blended, we had become one. One in three persons, the Esalen trinity. (By the way, 20 years later, we are all still very deep and loving friends with one another.)

I spent the next day recovering—and reflecting on what I had experienced the night before. I had never taken anything like ketamine before—the experience was so qualitatively different from anything I had encountered with any of the psychedelics I had used during the '70s or with MDMA. I wasn't hooked, but I was exceedingly intrigued. Now I was really looking forward to doing it again, this time with Therese.

Speaking of Therese, she was now due the next day. The people for the conference were already arriving, S. was now busy at work preparing the conference room and making various arrangements, and Therese was scheduled to arrive that evening. I needed to get the ketamine out of my head, so to speak, and ready myself for my meeting with Therese. I hoped she wouldn't be angry with me when she learned I was no longer a ketamine virgin.

She wasn't. During the time of her conference, we quickly were on our way to becoming good friends, particularly because of another deep MDMA session we had together the night of the first day of the conference.

Therese, however, still wanted me to do ketamine with her and invited me to come up to her home in the San Francisco Bay Area once my stint at Esalen was over. Now I agreed with alacrity. I was on a ketamine roll.

The day after I had arrived, she proposed that we try an experiment. At that time,

Therese was interested in exploring various combinations of drugs. In this case, she suggested that we start with MDMA and use it as a kind of booster. When that drug had reached its peak intensity after about two hours, I would then be injected with ketamine. (S., who was in the area but had vacated the apartment temporarily so that Therese and I could remain there together, would be summoned to do the injection.) Was I game?

"But what about that ketamine session with that oncologist of yours?"

"Oh, we can put that off for a while."

I had a little hesitation, but not for long, since I had already bonded so much with Therese at Esalen. Therese's apartment had obviously been set up for such sessions. My impression was that this was the way she conducted some of her work with her clients. Since I had already come to feel very comfortable there, I was ready to relax with her, be close to her physically, and begin my second MDMA encounter with her. S. came in to wish us well, and then went elsewhere, presumably into her bedroom.

Therese and I lay down on one of her very plush rugs and waited for the MDMA to take effect. By this time, I was familiar enough with the drug to know how it would affect me. Once more, I felt myself bonding with Therese, with her essence, and the feelings just built and built with waves of love lifting me into a world of pulsating ecstasy.

At some point, S. quietly came in and injected me, but not Therese, with ketamine, but this time the dose, by agreement, was much higher than that I had taken at Big Sur. This, too, was part of the experiment. Not surprisingly, my experience was radically different. Although it started in the same way, with those beautiful shimmering colors into which I soon merged, I then found myself—although I could only recall this afterward—experiencing what I subsequently came to label "the creation of the universe." Somehow, I seemed to be an indissoluble part of "the Big Bang," except it was a soft feeling of being, not seeing, something like an expanding balloon that contained the germ of all the galaxies that were then first forming. It was as if, encoded into the star-stuff of which I was composed, was information about the very origins and evolution of the universe, which I was now tapping into. (Afterward I couldn't resist the admittedly wild speculation that this information must somehow be contained in our very cellular structure, but I had no such thoughts then. I was not capable of thinking at all.) I remember that the energy of this soft expansion was not neutral—this creation was infused with a feeling of love. (Again, afterward, I was inclined to feel that this was probably due to the effect of MDMA.)

At this point, there was no "I." There was only the experience of oneness with the nascent universe as it was in the process of formation. Any sense of time had completely disappeared. Not only that, any sense of being human, much less a particular human called Ken Ring, had also vanished. There was only this experience, but no one was observing it.

At some point—it must have been perhaps a half hour later from what Therese, who had been observing me, told me—I began to have a faint inkling of a kind of descent through an array of what seemed to be galaxies all around me, as if some invisible force, a kind of gravity, was causing a sense of downward motion—although in fact, there was still no sense of "I" or anything human—just this feeling of a descent through star systems.

After a time, I had the first intimation that there was something called "Earth," which appeared to be my destination, and with that came the slow realization that I was something—a person! That I was human, that I was heading back toward Earth. But my identity was still not clear to me.

I later learned that S. had been there during this whole session, and that she had had a tape-recorder handy in case I said anything of interest. It's good that she did because what happened next surprised everyone.

I didn't come back as myself, Ken Ring.

I returned with another identity altogether. I was a Dutch tugboat captain who appeared to have lived in the 19th century, and I spoke English with a distinct accent (that later seemed to be like that of the famous Austrian comic film actor, S. Z. "Cuddles" Sakall, a staple in films of the forties, most famously Casablanca). When I started talking in this accent, I heard Therese hiss to S. "Is the tape recorder going? We have to get this!" I have a very clear memory of what I was experiencing at this time.

First, it was as if in my final descent toward Earth—as I was slowly parachuting down, as it were—I had landed not on the ground, but had got stuck in the branches of a tree. On the ground was Ken Ring, and I, as the tugboat captain, was aware of him. But Ken Ring was no longer who I was.

Second, I remember saying and repeating, "this is a distinct personality, a distinct personality." I could not just see this man; I was him. I could feel him as if I indeed lived inside of him. I knew that he was a "cold man" (not at all like Ken)—that he was lonely, and somewhat embittered—and that he was actually envious of Ken Ring. About him he said, "Yah, Ken Ring, the guy that likes the ladies."

I knew what he looked like. I could see his face, his sideburns and whiskers. I could see him on his boat, and I could see him in a tavern where he made his remark about Ken Ring's fondness for ladies. I knew he was Dutch, even if his accent was more like that of an Austrian—and I knew I was him, not me.

You know how when you are driving in a car listening to the radio and you begin to lose the signal? Well, something like that began to happen next. I felt that the tugboat captain, whom Therese later labeled "the immigrant," was beginning to fade out and as he did—to continue the metaphor I used earlier—it as if I was now being sucked out of the tree and down into the body and person of Ken Ring.

Plop! I was back. I recognized—with relief—that I was Ken Ring again. But I remembered everything about "the immigrant," and Therese had recorded my words and accent.

In all, over the next year, I wound up doing ketamine nine times, including my first experience in Big Sur. In five of those sessions, "the immigrant" was present during the penultimate stage I passed through on my way to myself. He was always the same, and he always, as far as I can now recall, spoke in the same accent and had the same personality—cold, unfeeling, somewhat cruel, and lonely. I leave it to you to interpret who—or what—he was, and why he was so often a part of my ketamine experiences as they terminated.

My subsequent experiences with ketamine, sometimes with Therese, but mostly with others, were similar, but on the whole, not quite so intense as my initial ones had been—though still full of marvelous and enthralling sensations and periods of ego-dissolution. Whenever I would enter the k-state, I would recognize it immediately as distinctively sui generis. It represented a world of its own, radically different from any of my other experiences in altered states of consciousness and utterly beguiling. I might have used words such as "captivating" or "enchanting" were it not for one further experience I had under Therese's aegis the next year.

Remember her wish to have me become a volunteer for a ketamine session with her oncologist colleague? Well, even though I was no longer a ketamine "virgin," but almost a ketamine veteran by now, she still wanted me to undertake this journey, if only for the sake of satisfying her colleague's professional interest in my report.

So one day in the winter of 1986, at this doctor's office in the hospital, I would be given the anesthetic with a special infusion that would allow the doctor to titrate me—that is, he could control the amount of ketamine to be administered so that it could slowly be increased to its maximum. During this process, he would tape-record any utterances that I might emit and afterward, once I had recovered, he would interview me. His main interest would be to determine the extent to which I felt my experience mimicked that of an actual NDE. Therese, of course, had accompanied me there, and she would remain at my side during the entire session.

In going through my boxes of memorabilia recently, I was surprised to come across a cassette tape of this session and a two-page letter from the doctor summarizing my experience and what he felt he had learned from it. I didn't have the patience to re-listen to the tape, but I did read his letter. It brought back some aspects of the experience for me, though it was one that I remember very well, with horror.

Although some of the excerpts from the tape that the doctor's letter includes make it clear I was again experiencing vivid colors at the onset, when the dosage was increased, I was already indicating that I was "farther out now … whirling in the cosmos … like part of a galaxy … moving through vast, vast, vast spaces … like floating nebulae … going further out into space … scintillating. I see more light … ."

Then there was nothing for a long time, but what I remembered afterward was something that gave me a sense of profound metaphysical fright. What I became aware of when the dosage was apparently at or near its maximum was that human beings were not real. It was as if they were mere projections, like the images on a screen. But people were deluded because they had come to identify with the images in the same way that, when we watch a movie, we see people, not images. But only the images are real, not the people. We were no more than simulacra—the whole of existence was not as we supposed. Instead, it was empty—just full of moving images. Who or what was behind the projector? Nothing.

I am certain that I have never experienced anything more unnerving and psychologically destabilizing in my life. I felt that all points of ordinary reference and meaning had dissolved and that it left me, or what I had thought of as me, completely void.

The doctor wrote, "At this level, the process of ego-dissolution appeared to start. Pertinent comments included the statement 'I'm gone … gone … gone' and somewhat later repetitions of the word 'collapsing.' Later [there were] long howling vocalizations. During this period the speech was very dysarthric, but there was a plaintive and possibly dysphoric quality to it … . The first sign of recovery was a chuckle or laugh which sounded almost like crying. Then the first clear vocalization, 'I'm alive … I'm alive.' "

What I remember at this point was seeing Therese's elbow. I reached out for it the way a man drowning in an ocean and overcome by fear reaches for the edge of a raft. Although I obviously felt I had in a sense returned from death, what I had experienced was in no way like a transcendent radiant NDE. If anything, it was the opposite, and it left me with a feeling of something close to dread. What if what I had perceived was somehow a kind of ultimate truth about the nature of things that was blessedly veiled from us during states of ordinary consciousness?

Certainly, I had never before experienced anything like that on any of my previous trips with L. or Therese, nor would I experience anything remotely like it in any of my subsequent ketamine sessions. In fact, I've never known what to make of it. It occurred to me afterward that maybe I had never had so much ketamine in my system, that perhaps I had had too much this time. Or perhaps I had been given a glimpse of something that was an essential, if unutterably frightening, part of our universe. All I know is that the experience haunted me for days afterward and that I have never forgotten it.

Years later—almost three decades now—what do I make of these experiences? To be sure, I can't draw any generalizations about ketamine experiences on the basis of my own idiographic encounters with this drug. I don't want to claim that they have any ontological significance either. Mine were what they were, and while others may have had experiences that seemed to mimic at least some aspects of NDEs, that certainly was not true for me.

Nevertheless, I still regard ketamine as providing the means of access to a distinctive world of revelatory experiences that usually left me in a state of rapturous wonder even if upon recovering it was hard to retain much of the contents of these extraordinary voyages, which were in any event almost impossible afterward to capture in the net of language.

I remember that at the time of Therese's Esalen conference that John Lilly, one of the participants, was hardly ever present. Dressed in a kind of brown monk's robe, he seemed mostly to be in his VW microbus (if memory serves) injecting himself, as I was later told, every 15 minutes or so with ketamine. I remember thinking at the time thoughts along the lines of, "How sad—such a brilliant man," and so on.

But after my own experiences with ketamine, I was inclined to see things very differently. At least on the basis of my own experiences, ketamine gives you access to a world that is so fantastically alluring and full of wonders that to me it makes perfect sense to want to explore it, just as adventurous naturalists of previous centuries were keen to travel to unknown and exotic lands. I'm glad I took the journey.

My Ketamine Journeys

or

Ketamine and the Enchantment of Other Worlds

Stanislav Grof, M.D.

IN THE FALL OF 1972 I was introduced to the strangest psychoactive substance I have ever experienced in the 50 years of my consciousness research. The effects of this compound are so extraordinary that they stand out even in the group of psychedelics, drugs for which the German pharmacologist Louis Lewin coined the term "phantastica." This substance was ketamine.

The person who brought the remarkable psychoactive properties of ketamine to the attention of our staff at the Maryland Psychiatric Research Center was Salvador Roquet, a controversial Mexican psychiatrist known for his wild experimentation with psychedelics. Roquet used to conduct session with large groups of people, to whom he administered a variety of psychoactive substances (LSD, psilocybin, peyote, datura, and others) while exposing them to movies with shocking aggressive and sexual content. His intention was to induce in his clients profound experiences of ego death followed by psychospiritual rebirth. The purpose of his visit in Baltimore was to participate in our LSD training program for professionals.

Ketamine was discovered by Cal Stevens of Wayne State University in 1961. It has the reputation of being an unusually safe anesthetic because it has minimal suppressive effects on circulation, breathing, and the cough reflex. It gained great popularity among medical personnel as an anesthetic that was heavily used on the battlefields of Vietnam. Today, ketamine continues in widespread use as an anesthetic and analgesic in human and veterinary practices despite what has been termed "the ketamine-induced emergence syndrome," which some patients have reported as they awakened from surgery. In other words, these are the same effects as when given deliberately at subanesthetic doses to elicit psychedelic experiences.

Those members of our staff who had heard about ketamine before Roquet's visit knew that it was a substance used as a general anesthetic and had heard about the "emergence syndrome" as an untoward complication of ketamine administration that was sometimes treated by administration of tranquilizers. In his presentation to our staff, Roquet introduced an entirely new perspective; he explained that the "emergence syndrome" was not a side effect of ketamine, but part of its fascinating principal effect. Ketamine was a "dissociative anesthetic," and its mechanism of action was radically different from commonly used anesthetics, other than nitrous oxide. At subanesthetic doses, administration of this substance did not lead to loss of consciousness, but to a dose-related progressive reduction of sensory awareness of the body. He helped us to understand that as anesthesia wore off, patients were experiencing fantastic voyages through a wide range of other realities—extraterrestrial civilizations and parallel universes, the astrophysical world and the micro-world, the animal, botanical, and mineral kingdoms, other countries and historical periods, and archetypal domains of various cultures. This was the nature of the unbidden and confusing emergence effect that patients were not prepared to experience coming out of anesthesia. In contrast, Roquet's clients, who had not taken ketamine as an anesthetic but as a therapeutic agent and a vehicle for philosophical and spiritual quest, had profound mystical experiences, and many of them believed that they had encountered God. Some of them were also convinced that they had visited the bardo, the intermediate realm between incarnations, and claimed that they had lost fear of death.

For several members of our staff, including myself, Roquet's lecture generated intense curiosity and a strong desire to have a personal experience with ketamine. Roquet happened to have with him an adequate supply of the substance and offered to conduct training sessions with those of us who were interested. Our personal experiences fully confirmed Salvador's report. Ketamine clearly was a fascinating substance that was of great interest to anybody seriously interested in consciousness research. Although its effects were very different from LSD, there was no doubt that it was an important contribution to the armamentarium of psychedelic substances. The astonishing nature of ketamine experiences required lying down and journeying for periods of time without much interpersonal contact or ability to be in sensory contact with external reality because the sensory modalities were very diminished— particularly the visual, proprioceptive and tactile.

Over the years, I continued my personal experimentation with ketamine and did not cease to be astounded by the extraordinary nature of the experiences and the profound insights that they provided concerning the relationship between consciousness, the human psyche, and matter. The effects of ketamine have always been utterly unpredictable, even in the broadest sense. In my experimentation with other psychedelics, I usually had at least a rough idea where I was in my self-exploration and what might come (biographical exploration, reliving of birth, archetypal experiences, etc.). The ketamine experiences were like visits to a Cosmic Disneyland; I never knew what might come, what the "ride" would be about. And the experiences covered a wide range from the most sublime and astonishing to the completely banal and trivial. I will give at least a few examples to illustrate what I mean.

A good point of departure is ketamine's great potential to mediate astral projection. Some of these experiences are fairly straightforward, others have certain features that are bizarre and absurd, as we will see from the following examples. One evening I took ketamine in our house in Big Sur at a time when we were conducting one of our monthlong seminars at Esalen. At one point during this session, I realized that the experience had taken me to the Big House, a part of Esalen about a mile from our house, where all the group activities of the monthlong seminar took place. I saw in great detail several of the group members involved in social interaction. The next day I was able to verify the accuracy of my perception. But at the time when I was witnessing these events, I experienced myself as a pillow in the corner of the room in the Big House, my body image taking on completely the shape of this object. On another occasion, I had a similar experience, only even more extraordinary, since this time Christina shared it with me. In the middle of a joint ketamine session we were having in the bedroom of our Big Sur house, I found myself suddenly in the Esalen bath and realized that I had become a wet towel hanging over the railing overlooking the ocean. From this perspective, I was able to witness in detail what was happening there and correctly identify the people who were in the bath at that time. Toward the end of the session, I described this bizarre episode to Christina and was astounded to find out that she had exactly the same experience. The following morning, we were able to verify the accuracy of our joint experience by talking with the people involved.

As the above examples indicate, one of the extraordinary and characteristic aspects of the ketamine experience is the surprising possibility to identify experientially with various material objects and processes that we ordinarily consider unconscious because they are inorganic and we associate consciousness with higher forms of life. And yet, experiences of this kind are very frequent in ketamine sessions, and when they happen, they seem very authentic and convincing. They make it easy to understand the animistic worldview of many native cultures, according to which, not only all animals and plants, but the sun and the stars, the oceans, the mountains and rivers, and other parts of inorganic nature are all conscious.

Among my many memorable experiences of this kind were identification with the consciousness of the ocean, of the desert, of granite, of an atomic reactor in a submarine under the Arctic ice, of a metal bridge crossed by heavy trucks, of wooden stakes being driven into the earth by hits of giant mallets, of burning candles, of the fire at the end of a torch, of precious stones, and of gold. My list includes even identification with a ski boot on the foot of a cross-country skier, attached to a ski and experiencing all the shifting tensions associated with the movements involved. Equally frequent are experiences of identification with various other life forms. In one of my ketamine sessions, I became a tadpole undergoing a metamorphosis into a frog, and in another one, a giant silverback gorilla claiming his territory.

On several occasions, this mechanism provided for me extraordinary insights into the world of dolphins and whales. An additional example was what seemed to be absolutely authentic and believable experiential identification with a caterpillar building a cocoon and dissolving into amorphous liquid from which then emerged the form of a butterfly.

A particularly impressive experience of this kind was becoming a Venus flytrap, a carnivorous plant in the process of catching and digesting a fly, complete with gustatory perceptions that my human imagination could not possibly have conjured up.

The above examples of fantastic experiences contrast sharply with several of my ketamine sessions that were absolutely trivial and outright boring. I spent them by seeing endless images of brick walls, cement surfaces, and asphalt streets in the suburbs of a large city, or displays of ugly fluorescent colors, questioning why I had ever taken this substance. There was a period in my life when I had several consecutive ketamine sessions that were so horrible and disgusting that I was determined never to take the substance again. They revolved around the problem of fossil fuels and the curse they represent for life on our planet. Here is the account of one of these sessions:

The atmosphere was dark, heavy, and ominous. It seemed to be toxic and poisonous in a chemical sense, but also dangerous and evil in the metaphysical sense. Initially, I experienced it on the outside, as part of my environment, but gradually it took over and I actually became it. It took me a while to realize that I had become petroleum, filling enormously large cavities in the earth. While I was experiencing identification with petroleum as physical material, including its penetrating smell, I realized that I was also an evil metaphysical or archetypal entity of unimaginable proportions. I was flooded with fascinating insights, combining chemistry, geology, biology, psychology, mythology, history, economy, and politics. I suddenly understood something that I had never thought about before. Petroleum is fat of biological origin that got mineralized; it meant that it had escaped the mandatory cycle of death and rebirth, the recycling that the rest of the living matter is subjected to. However, the element of death was not eliminated in this process, it was only delayed. The destructive Plutonic potential of death continues to exist in petroleum in a latent form as a monstrous time bomb awaiting its opportunity to be released into the world.

While experiencing what I felt was consciousness of petroleum, I saw the death intrinsic to it manifesting as the evil and killing resulting from the greed of those who seek the astronomical profits that it offers. I witnessed countless scenes of political intrigues, economic scams, and diplomatic shenanigans motivated by petrodollars. I saw countless victims of wars fought for oil laid on the sacrificial altar of this evil entity. It was not difficult to follow the chain of events to a future world war for the dwindling resources of a substance that had become vital for the survival and prosperity of the industrialized countries. It became clear to me that it was essential for the future of the planet to reorient the economy to solar energy and other renewable resources. The linear policy of plundering the limited deposits of fossil fuels and turning them into toxic waste and industrial pollution was so fundamentally wrong that I could not understand that economists and politicians did not see it. This shortsighted policy was obviously totally incompatible with the cosmic order and with the nature of life, which is cyclical. While the exploitation of fossil fuels was understandable in the historical context of the Industrial Revolution, its continuation once its fatal trajectory was recognized seemed suicidal, murderous, and criminal.

In a long series of hideous and most unpleasant experiences, I was taken through states of consciousness related to the chemical industry based on petroleum. Using the name of the famous German chemical industrial complex, I referred to these experiences as IG Farben consciousness. It was an endless sequence of states of mind that had the quality of aniline dyes, organic solvents, herbicides, pesticides, and toxic gases, all hostile to life.

Beside the experiences related to various industrial poisons *per se,* I also identified with the states of consciousness associated with the exposure of various life forms to petroleum products. I became every Jew who had died in the Nazi gas chambers, every sprayed ant and cockroach, every fly caught in the sticky goo of the flytraps, and every plant dying under the influence of the herbicides. And beyond all that lurked the highly possible ominous future of all life on the planet—death by industrial pollution.

It was an incredible lesson. I emerged from the session with deep ecological awareness and a clear sense as to which direction the economic and political development had to take should life on our planet survive.

The series of sessions exploring the pitfalls of the industrial age, like this one, brought me to the point when I decided not to have any more ketamine experiences. But the session that was supposed to be my last attempt at ketamine self-exploration took me to the other side of the spectrum. It was so ecstatic and extraordinary that I decided to keep this door open. Here is a brief account of this experience:

I had a sense of the presence of many of my friends with whom I share interest in transpersonal psychology, values, and a certain direction or purpose in life. I did not see them, but was somehow strongly perceiving their presence through some extrasensory channels. We were going through a complex process of identifying areas of agreements and differences among us, trying to eliminate friction points by an almost alchemical process of dissolving and neutralizing. At a certain point, it seemed that we succeeded in creating a completely unified network, one entity with a clear purpose and no inner contradiction.

And then this collective organism became what I called "Spaceship in Consciousness." We initiated a movement that combined the element of spatial flight with an abstract representation of consciousness evolution. The movement was becoming faster and faster, until it reached what seemed to be some absolute limit, something like what speed of light is in the Einsteinian universe. We felt that it was possible to push beyond this limit, but that the result would be completely unpredictable and potentially dangerous. In the highly adventurous spirit that characterizes this group of our friends, we decided to go ahead and face the Unknown.

We succeeded to push beyond the limit, and the experience shifted dimensions in a way that is difficult to describe. Instead of moving through space and time, there seemed to be immense extension of consciousness. Time stopped and we entered a state that I identified as consciousness of amber. This seemed to make a lot of sense, since amber is a material representation of a situation in which time is frozen. It is a mineralized organic substance (resin), and various life forms, such as plants and insects, are preserved in it unchanged for millions of years.

What followed seemed to be a process of purification, through which any references to organic life were eliminated. The experience became crystal clear and incredibly beautiful. It seemed that we were inside of a giant diamond; countless subtle lattices intersecting in a liquid medium of incredible purity were exploding into all the colors of the spectrum. It seemed that it contained all the information about life and nature in an absolutely pure, abstract, and infinitely condensed form, like the ultimate computer. It seemed very relevant that diamond is pure carbon, an element on which all life is based, and that it originates in conditions of extreme temperatures and pressures.

All the other properties of diamond seemed to point to its metaphysical significance—its luster, beauty, transparence, permanence, exchangeability, and the capacity to separate white light into a rich spectrum of colors. I felt that I understood why Tibetan Buddhism is referred to as Vajrayana, the Diamond vehicle. The only way I could adequately describe this ecstatic rapture was to call it "diamond consciousness." This state seemed to contain all the creative energy and intelligence of the universe existing as pure consciousness beyond space and time.

I was floating in this energy as a dimensionless point of consciousness, maintaining some sense of individual identity, yet being completely dissolved and one with all of it. I was aware of the presence of my friends who had made the journey with me; they were also completely formless, mere dimensionless points. I felt that we had reached the state of ultimate fulfillment, the source of existence and our final destination, as close to Heaven as I could imagine.

What I have described above were just a few examples of my experiences with the strangest and most extraordinary psychoactive substance I have ever come across. Another property of ketamine deserves notice in this context. Christina and I have taken ketamine on several occasions in foreign countries—in Peru, Brazil, India, and Bali—and discovered that the experiences connected us to the archetypal worlds associated with these cultures, with their mythologies, with the psyche of their people, with their artifacts, and their art.

John Lilly and Ketamine:
Some Personal Recollections

Ralph Metzner, Ph.D.

I FIRST MET JOHN LILLY IN the late 1960s when I was living in Southern California near Idyllwild, teaching at an alternative residential high school for disturbed adolescents. I was aware of his early research with dolphins and also that he had written a serious analysis of the potentials of psychedelic drug experiences to open up new avenues for scientific investigations of the mind-body interface. I had read and heard about his involvement with the Arica school of meditation founded by Oscar Ichazo and his subsequent disillusionment with the esotericism and power politics of that school. From the late 1960s to the late 1970s I had been involved in a different esoteric meditation group, the School of Actualism. I was impressed by the fact that John Lilly drove up to Idyllwild in the van he was living in at the time, and took several of the meditation lessons that our group was learning. He became one of my models for his relentless devotion to the search for scientific truth—regardless of the social status and official credibility of the particular methodology involved.

I connected with John Lilly again in the early 1970s in Northern California, where I was working as a psychotherapist and teaching at the California Institute of Integral Studies in San Francisco. I attended several talks and seminars he gave on the extreme altered states induced by sensory isolation environments—to which he had added the refinement of inducing a sense of weightlessness by floating in heavily salted warm water. This particular methodology of inducing profoundly relaxing states has become incorporated into psychophysical health culture through what is commonly known as samadhi tanks.

Subsequently, in the mid-to-late 1970s I met John and Toni Lilly several times through the monthlong residential seminars at the Esalen Institute. These events were conducted by Stanislav Grof, fellow explorer of the potentials of psychedelic and other non-ordinary states of consciousness, who was then Fellow-in-Residence. My friend, the Basque anthropologist Angeles Arrien, accompanied me on several of these journeys to Esalen. It was on one of these occasions that Stan Grof offered me the opportunity to experience the state of consciousness induced by intramuscular ketamine injection—a state that was significantly different than other psychedelics I had been exploring for the past 20 years. Classified as a dissociative anesthetic—ketamine expanded my consciousness into an abstract realm of thoughts and images, but without any of the sensory fireworks of the classic psychedelics and without their potential for dramatic emotional upheavals. Ketamine brought me to a realm even more difficult to translate into verbal descriptions than the classic hallucinogens, but was uniformly pleasurable in a kind of even-tempered ecstasy. The notoriously spectacular "bad trips" of the classic hallucinogens seemed distant from this experience.

Living, teaching, and practicing in the San Francisco Bay Area in the 1980s, I conducted a few trials using intramuscularly injected ketamine, under medical supervision, as an adjunct to psychotherapy. I remember one client, who was heavily occupied with obsessive ruminations; these stopped for the hour or so of the ketamine state, which he enjoyed, but resumed afterward. I also collaborated with a couple of medical doctor friends, one of them an emergency physician. We conducted a study in which we wanted to see if we could stay in verbal communication with each other while both being under ketamine's influence. The experiment was a total failure. Each of us got caught up in attempting to decode and describe the strange abstract thought-forms we were individually experiencing.

It was from the emergency physician that I learned of John Lilly's increasingly addictive use of ketamine. At first he had collaborated with John, impressed by his seriousness in trying to scientifically map and describe interior landscapes. But after some weeks, he gradually came to realize that John was using him as a drug connection for what had become a daily or multiple daily use of ketamine. My friend stopped all contact. He told me that John claimed he was "channeling" extraterrestrial and extra-dimensional entities—but also occasionally a Los Angeles TV station reporting the evening news.

A few times on trips to Southern California during the 1980s, I connected with John, as well as Toni, ever his warm-hearted and high-spirited companion. However at social gatherings he would often leave the party and retreat to his van parked outside, apparently preferring to explore his interior states to socializing with others. I heard from one of our mutual friends concerned about his excessive abuse of ketamine that John had said he liked being in out-of-body states, because he had been raised by puritanical parents from whom he learned to dislike or even hate his body.

The German-born innovative video-artist known as Brummbear, with whom I had connected a few times during the 1980s and who was close to Lilly, sent me an e-mail message in 2001, on the occasion of John's funeral, at which he gave a eulogy. As of 2013, Brummbear was dealing with his own cancer—but gave me permission to quote from his talk at John's memorial. This is what he said:

> *John Lilly was a close friend of mine—for over 10 years we were fellow ketamaniacs, even though I also added MDMA, 2CB and other Shulgin-products in my research. The last time I shot up was a couple of years ago in Hawaii and already then it took quite a toll on my body and even more on John's. Taking ketamine is not just a flirt with death—it's a tantric fuck with death—all nine holes of your body participating—and it's not free! (Price of admission, like in Steppenwolf—your mind.) So when we saw each other last week he asked what had become a ritual between us: "Got some K, Brummbear?" And we confided with each other that we hadn't taken any psychedelics for some time—but also didn't seem to miss it that much. A day without pain is such a nice gift, as you probably understand very well.*

For myself, I will always remember John Lilly's ferociously fearless explorations of the further reaches of the mind—even at great cost to his body and to his social connections.

Ketamine Dependence:
John Lilly as Explorer and as Caveat

Phil Wolfson, M.D.

FOR MY OWN PART, I FIRST was exposed to John Lilly and ketamine at Esalen in the mid '80s when he pulled up to our weeklong ARUPA colloquium in a giant white RV and gauntly strode forth, a very altered dude indeed. During those days with him, I felt disappointed with his lack of coherence and Messianism, which he boldly presented as his personal exploration of the cosmic consciousness that he was performing solo for all of our benefit. He was unabashed about putting needles into various parts of his body that were not suppurating or scarred from recent and long-term use—and he was running out of corporeal space. He shot up intramuscularly and it seemed subcutaneously as well—and frequently—it seemed every couple of hours or so, but of that I am not certain.

When I was a young man, Lilly had impressed me with his towering intellect and fearlessness in seeking altered states and the source of consciousness. His metaphysical autobiography, *The Scientist*, was eccentric, tendentious and fascinating, and it also seemed just too out of here, on the edge of paranoia and world egress. The person who arrived at Esalen had both feet in the stratosphere and nothing on the ground. I was not alone in my disappointment and sense even of repugnance. Yet, there was also that curiosity that is inflamed when a brilliant person turns to a path that must therefore have some great depth and allure, perhaps novel wisdom making, even realization. Addiction is generally not attractive, no matter the substance, or the rationalization. In fact, Lilly's ketamine dependence was both a warning and a turn-off, and my sense was that many of the others who watched him did not feel induced at that time to try the drug.

But addiction is another one of those words—dismissive, full of judgment, too encompassing—and while that is to some extent on the mark, a cautionary on many levels, there are other aspects. Lilly was an exemplar in many respects. He had developed single-mindedness to his own exploration of consciousness that preceded ketamine and included intense brain exploration and study, psychedelics, Samadhi states and meditation, isolation tank development and countless immersions in various states. Ketamine was a means to further that exploration and he felt its power to carry him to greater depths on his particular version of his journey.

So, how do we get out there and lose it? That is an important question for those of us who use and advocate psychedelics as mind manifesting and transformational— inter- and intra-personally. Anyone doing this work as a therapist will come across those folks who become too attached to a drug or drugs, who make broad mistakes, lose their relationships, even themselves. This is neither a rarity nor a commonality. And it is always a matter of balance—and losing that balance. Or being in an unbalanced state and trying to gain balance by consuming drugs that give us relief from ourselves; or give us a sense of purpose and attainment; or our ego driving us to a singularity of view that resembles hypo-mania/mania in the sense of the loss of the monitor that overrides and guides us through the labyrinth of life, as best as it can.

From my view, Lilly exemplified the latter, losing himself in his sense of mission as a self-appointed psychonaut heading for the cosmic reaches. That seems to me to be the ego guiding the unfolding journey, entrained in the quest for the grail, single-mindedly, as all else falls away to the perceived need to be in the state itself, and the arising of an inability to let go—a kind of OCD-ness—a capture of the soul in a particular repetitive labyrinth that still seems fresh and expanding. Ketamine can have that allure—a sense of ever-differing experience that is unpredictably alive in ever-varying ways, and even programmable for a search for the source. For Lilly, at some point, he was not really able to, or perhaps not committed to bringing back the information from his roving—to Earth and its peoples, to whom he was inextricably connected and whom he came to disregard. Ketamine has that potential—allure, envelopment, cosmic contact, entry into the great mysteries.

That is a formulation, not a certain condemnation. In any event, it behooves us to keep our mind's eyes trained on balance and balancing, on helping to overcome bad paths as they begin, and to recognize that the life of the spirit and community, of education, love, connection and sharing hold us in balance and are in constant need of attention and growth.

Salvador Roquet
and the Introduction of Ketamine:
A History and Appraisal

Remembering Salvador Roquet

Stanley Krippner, Ph.D.

SALVADOR ROQUET, MD, BEGAN HIS MEDICAL career in the field of public health and later became a psychiatrist. Roquet began using mind-altering substances as an adjunct to psychotherapy in 1967 (Clark, 1977). Initially he employed these substances as a tool for shortening the time involved in psychoanalysis, employing the "psycholytic" approach, which administers small does during the course of treatment. These sessions lasted about eight hours with dosages of LSD, ketamine, psilocybin mushrooms, and ololiuqui (morning glory seeds) from plants such as *Rivea corymbosa* and *Ipomoea violacea*.

The Albert Schweitzer Cultural Association was a nonprofit organization that maintained several programs, most notably the Instituto de Psicosintesis, a private clinic located in the Popocatepetl section of Mexico City. Other programs included the Albert Schweitzer Integral School, which provided an alternative educational approach for young children. These affiliates were part of the Albert Schweitzer Cultural Association, named after the famed physician because of his work in reducing yellow fever and similar diseases in West Africa. Salvador had been inspired by Schweitzer and is given credit, by some, for virtually eliminating yellow fever in Mexico as head of a national commission.

An Invitation from Mexico

In 1969 I received a letter from Salvador telling me about his work and inviting me to visit him in Mexico City. In March 1970, I served as one of several chaperones for a high school science class that was heading to Michuatlan to view a total eclipse of the sun. Our first stop was Mexico City, and I wrote Roquet to see if we could meet. I had no response, but upon my return I found a letter from him informing me that he had been in Santa María Asunción de Matamoros, Oaxaca, laying the groundwork for a medical clinic that would serve the local populace. However, he reiterated his desire to meet me and discuss his work.

This opportunity presented itself in 1971 when I was invited to speak at the Fifth World Psychiatry Congress in Mexico City. My presentation focused on the famed statue of the Aztec mother goddess Coatlique, which I had seen the previous year in the national Museum of Anthropology. Coatlique, in Nahuatl, means "serpent skirt," a term that describes the goddess's apparel. Indeed, her head is composed of two serpents, using a juxtaposition similar to a technique Picasso, centuries later, employed in some of his paintings. The two serpent heads probably represented Coatlique's roles as both creator and destroyer, a paradox too subtle for the Spanish invaders to appreciate, and who branded the goddess as evil, burying the statue. It was rediscovered in 1790 and was put on display in the hopes of persuading the native people that the dethroned pagan deities were demonic. However, the Indians were not persuaded. They bedecked the statue with flowers and adoration, prompting a reburial. The statue was unearthed at the request of the Prussian geographer von Humboldt, but was reburied after his departure from Mexico. Eventually, the Coatlique statue became one of Mexico's cultural treasures.

Following the Congress, my wife and I visited Salvador; my secretary, Irene Lozano, served as interpreter for our discussion of his psychotherapeutic procedures. We accepted his invitation to observe a group therapy session and were cordially received by Salvador's patients, even though we did not ingest any of the several mind-altering substances that he administered that evening. As his patients began to feel the effects of the drugs, Salvador's staff projected a violent film on one wall of the room, and an erotic movie on the other wall. I thought that this was very much in the tradition of Coatlique, whose seemingly contradictory roles had not been appreciated by the Spanish invaders who failed to fathom their underlying unity. Salvador's goal was to assure his patients that a discussion of both their aggressive and sexual impulses were acceptable in this milieu.

There were some 20 patients seated on the carpet or cushions of the room. Some began to dance. Others cried or sobbed, turning to each other for support and consolation as they revealed intimate details about their life conflicts and traumas. Salvador moved among his patients, orchestrating their experiences and deftly forming small groups of patients with similar issues. Irene did her best to translate salient snatches of the conversations, but even without her help it was apparent that the group had bonded in a way that provided both insight and comfort.

We were sitting near one male patient, an artist who told his group how his father had rejected him because of his sexual orientation. During his harangue, he stated, "In fact, I can see my father coming toward me right now, even though I know it is a hallucination." In actuality, Salvador had persuaded the young man's father to attend the session and to confront his son. Once his son realized that he was not hallucinating, he wasted no time in telling his father how much the rejection had hurt him. At this point, the father apologized, said that he loved his son regardless of his sexual orientation, and the two of them embraced and wept. They continued their conversation for the duration of the all-night session. The three of us returned to our hotel, realizing that we had seen a master psychotherapist at work.

Upon my return to the United States, I notified my colleagues at the Maryland Psychiatric Research Center about Salvador's work. They immediately invited him to Baltimore, where he gave a number of well-received lectures about his approach to psychotherapy. He was allowed to participate on one of their "psychedelics for professionals" sessions, during which he received LSD under the staff's supervision. This allowed Salvador to have a first-hand view of how the Maryland psychotherapists utilized psychedelics. In December 1972, John Rhead, a research psychologist at the Center, wrote me, "I just put Salvador Roquet on a train for New York after his second visit here at the Center. He had a session with Bill Richards and Rich Yensen and we all had a nice visit. Thank you once again for getting us all together." Subsequently I discovered that Stanislav Grof was also present during the session and that Yensen, who spoke fluent Spanish, did most of the facilitation. Yensen also facilitated two additional sessions for Salvador at the Center.

Psychosynthesis Psychotherapy

In 1973, I received a letter from Salvador stating, "We are happy to have you officially on our team as Honorary Vice President and Advisor to the Instituto de Psicosintesis." He also sent me a long description of the Institute's work, noting that its incorporation of psychedelic substances into psychotherapy began in 1967. The report also noted that expeditions to remote Indian villages had been organized to study the ritual use of natural psychedelic substances. Among the findings of these investigators was the major focus of the session, namely the recovery of their "lost spirit." They also observed that dosage was carefully measured, as was the size of the group. Roquet reported that he decided to call this type of psychotherapy "psychosynthesis" (in Spanish, *psicosintesis*) because it interlaces conventional psychoanalysis with psychedelic drugs. Roquet knew nothing about the transpersonal psychotherapy, also named "psychosynthesis," formulated by the Italian psychiatrist Roberto Assagioli (1971), and which continues to be practiced several decades after its founder's death.

The report was in English, borrowing from an accurate portrayal of the group process presented by Yensen at the 1973 convention of the Association for Humanistic Psychology in Montreal, Canada. It mirrored the activities that I had personally observed the previous year. A two-hour "pre-drug" meeting takes place and group members express their expectations and fears. Those who have taken part in previous sessions share their experiences after which the group enters the treatment room. After a Yoga or meditation session, the mind-altering substances are administered. They are listed as psilocybin mushrooms, morning glory seeds, peyote cacti, datura, and ketamine hydrochloride. The report states, "Ketamine is an anesthetic drug which produces a dissociative anesthesia…. We have found that ketamine in subdissociative doses produces profound changes in psychological functioning and is helpful in therapy."

As these substances are taking effect, sensory stimulation is employed to facilitate psychotherapy. "The sensory overload show uses slides, movies, three stereo sound systems, and colored floodlights that flash intermittently. The elements included in the slides and films are as varied as possible. Within what seems a confused barrage of unrelated images and sounds, there is a main theme, life. Among the themes found useful are death, birth, sexuality, religion, and childhood. Each show is carefully assembled so that in addition to the main theme of the evening, there are slides of particular importance for each patient: scenes from childhood, family pictures, etc. These are accompanied by music of importance to that patient. During the sensorial overload show, a full-length feature film is also shown. During the session that I viewed, the film was *The Dirty Dozen,* a 1967 war movie containing several episodes where characters are attacked or killed.

The sensory overload portion lasts about eight or nine hours, after which each patient receives pictures from his or her folder. Portions of patients' previous sessions may be played back to them. They may be asked to read passages from letters or accounts from sessions they had written. They may read statements by relevant philosophers or have these materials read to them. This is followed by another session of Yoga or meditation, after which group members are allowed to sleep.

This rest period lasts only about three hours before an "integrative session" begins. Each patient discusses his or her experience, often accompanied by abreaction or catharsis. The report states that "during this session the personality of each participant is reintegrated around the insights gained during the first stage of the session…. The tone of the session is confrontation with ongoing problems in the individual's life situation." Family members or significant friends may visit patients at this time.

The course of therapy consists of 10 to 30 monthly sessions, although more sessions may be given to problematic patients. The report states that "The patient population consists mostly of neurotic out-patients as well as alcoholics and drug addicts, though antisocial personalities and schizophrenics have been treated successfully."

The monthly group sessions are supplemented by group sessions and individual sessions without drugs. Individual drug sessions may be held when patients are further along in their treatment. The report continues, "Since the personality is a self-contained, self-validated system, in order to reorganize the structure of this belief system, it is necessary to disrupt it. The element of surprise is felt to be very useful in disrupting the normal flow of interpretations that form the personality." This is the role of psychedelic agents. "The patient's unconscious contents are made conscious" and he or she is urged to confront their true selves with their customary distortions. Salvador claimed to find ketamine especially useful in facing and resolving conflicting aspects of the personality. This report was later elongated and published in book form (Roquet, Favreau, Ocana, & Velaso, 1975).

Roquet as Provocateur
Salvador's patients found his provocations very helpful in their psychotherapy. However, they overlapped into his professional and personal life. I was told that he once invited a group of Mexican physicians and psychotherapists for a dinner at which he would discuss his work. Unbeknownst to them, Salvador had "spiked" their food with psilocybin mushrooms, thinking that the experience would make them more receptive to his work. The plan backfired, and many members of the Mexican psychiatric community turned against him. When helping to write a proposal for a film treatment of Salvador's work, Harvey Cox, an esteemed American theologian, asked, "Is Salvador Roquet a charlatan, a misled do-gooder, or a modern prophet?" The film was never made, but the questions remain.

In an article for the *San Francisco Examiner,* Barney (1977) observed that Salvador ran his controversial sessions for seven years, from 1967 to 1974, under an "informal agreement with the Mexican government to overlook that country's laws against psychedelics. But then the political power shifted and Roquet went to jail for five months."

When I found out about Salvador's imprisonment, I wrote letters and articles on his behalf. Many other letters were forthcoming, some from distinguished physicians and psychotherapists who had never met Salvador but who admired his work. In June 1975, Salvador wrote me that he had been released in April, expressing his gratitude for my support. In July 1975, I received another letter from Salvador stating, "I thank you very much for the article you wrote about my imprisonment and the problems we are facing presently to work with psychodysleptics in psychosynthesis. I feel it is only with such attitude and kind of articles that we will be able to produce concern and interest for our colleagues to [reconsider their] use.... Throughout my professional work, which I have recommenced, I can see with more clarity all the time the benefits that the psychosynthesis therapy provides to the patients. And this certainty gives me strength to keep my standpoint and face the absurdly conservative and reactionary attitude of our colleagues."

In 1976, Salvador was imprisoned again, this time in the United States following a psychosynthesis session arranged by his friend Walter Houston Clark. One of my friends was a member of this group and described to me the pandemonium that resulted when the police broke into the room where the session was being held, right at the time when the drug effects were at their peak. Some of the group members thought that the raid had been arranged by Salvador to provoke abreaction! Nonetheless, the case went to trial and Salvador admitted to a misdemeanor offense of practicing medicine without a U.S. license. All the other charges against him and his U.S. hosts were dropped.

A year later, at the annual convention of the Association for Humanistic Psychology in Berkeley, California, Salvador told Barney (1977) that political pressure evoked his release from the Mexican jail and that "to this day, I don't know how I got in or how I got out." Despite the intensity of the drug experience, he claims that no patient was hurt by it. "We have 2,000 case histories and recordings of over 900 group sessions. I can say that 85 percent of them had very positive results.... The 15 percent who were not helped had at worst 'indifferent' reactions. There were no cases of people failing to make the return trip to sanity."

Taking no chances, Salvador curtailed his use of mind-altering substances in his psychosynthesis sessions. He told Barney (1977), "After I left jail, I began to travel, giving workshops and lectures. We started doing simulated sessions, with the lights and sounds without the drugs.... We found that 90 percent of the people had reactions similar to those of people who had taken the drugs.... We found that the psychedelics were nothing more than the launching pad, the nature of the sessions was conditioned by the other techniques we used." Referring to the common themes evoked in psychosynthesis—madness, death, chaos, birth, and mystical union—he remarked, "They are all terrible and all extraordinary. In death you can feel love, and when you feel love, death is conquered and ceases to exist."

An Encounter with Don Ricardo

Although Salvador no longer used psychedelics with clients in Mexico City, he occasionally took groups to distant parts of the country to work with indigenous healers. One of my students, Carl Z. (a pseudonym), joined one of these groups in January 1960 on what he described as a "death-defying drive" to Xochitenalco, in a rain forest, a three-hour drive from Mexico's capital city. For several additional hours, the dozen members of the group were guided by a Mazatec woman who led them to a house where they could stake out the space for their sleeping bags. The mushroom ceremony was to be held that very evening, despite the lateness of the hour, and the sanctuary and its altar had been festooned with a statue of Jesus, a picture of Mother Mary, candles, flowers, and incense. Roquet asked everyone to complete the Hartman Value Inventory, a psychological test he often used in his psychotherapeutic work. The inventory had been designed by Robert Hartman, a distinguished psychologist who fled Nazi Germany, became a U.S. citizen, and spent many years in Cuernavaca, Mexico, where he died in 1973 (Ellis, 1994). Salvador named his clinic on Avenida Mexico after him, The Robert S. Hartman Institute for Psychosynthesis.

Don Ricardo, an indigenous healer who often worked with Salvador, made his appearance and prayed at the altar while members of the group ingested psilocybin mushrooms in a leaf-wrapped container. Don Ricardo completed his prayers and collected the empty packages, anointing the elbows of each participant. The candles were extinguished and only the shadows of Don Ricardo's assistants remained visible.

Don Ricardo circulated among the participants, ably handling the difficulties that arose. Eventually, participants crawled into their sleeping bags for a few hours of rest. They were awakened by Don Ricardo, who proceeded to use pieces of amber resin for individual cleansings and blessings. These pieces, thought to contain impurities that had been absorbed from each participant, were burned. Group members then linked arms, rocked in unison, joined a brief group discussion, and returned to their sleeping bags.

Again, the rest period was very brief. No food had been provided and most participants were exhausted from the three-day journey, both the outer and inner pilgrimages. Salvador appeared and provided paper and colored pens, asking participants to draw relevant people and themes from a list given to them while background music was played on a battery-powered sound system. Carl was asked to lead a group meditation that would help unite and focus the group.

Salvador's daughter appeared with a collection of files, one file for each participant, and selected appropriate music based on material in the files that was played at this time. Salvador used background data from the files as well as the drawings to make statements about the participants. Carl thought that the statements tended to be excessively opinionated and psychoanalytical in nature. For example, one man was told, "An Oedipus complex is shown by the pictures you drew of your parents."

Carl concluded that Don Ricardo was an effective guide who was gentle, loving, and effective. However, he found Salvador to encourage dependence on him, to be overly interpretive and directive, and to be unresponsive to criticism. However, Carl observed that the other participants were patients of Salvador and that segment of their therapy that he observed might have been one part of a larger schema.

An Encounter with María Sabina

In 1980, I was invited to join Salvador on an expedition to Huatla de Jiminez to meet the legendary Mazatec shaman, María Sabina (Estrada, 1981). Five longtime friends joined me—Richard Yensen, a clinical psychologist and psychedelic research psychotherapist; Michael Winkelman, a cultural anthropologist; Walter Houston Clark, a comparative religions scholar; Clark's wife, Ruth; and Bonnie Colodzin, a photographer. María Sabina had been discovered by Gordon Wasson (1957), a banker and amateur mycologist (mushroom specialist). I had read the subsequent *LIFE Magazine* story about their first encounter, never imagining that I would meet Doña María, some 25 years later. Roquet knew of my longtime fascination with María Sabina, with whom he had collaborated for several years; he said that this journey would be a gift from him to me. I also discovered that even though "Doña María" is term of respect, the shaman preferred to be referred to by her given name. Wasson used neither term in his article, calling her "Eva Mendez" to disguise her identity. Of course, the subterfuge didn't work and the case can be made that Wasson launched ethnopharmacology as a discipline, and his later work of a scholarly nature, in atonement for the invasion of privacy that followed the revelation.

After a particularly hazardous drive into the Oaxaca hills, we arrived at the hamlet where María Sabina lived with her two daughters. Her son had been killed by the villagers who did not approve her invitation of Wasson to a *velada*, or sacred mushroom ceremony. Born about 1894, María Sabina had originally eaten the mush-rooms to ward off hunger. But on another occasion, she saw the image of Death standing near her ill sister, who subsequently died. Eventually, María Sabina became a *sabia*, or shaman, believing that Jesus Christ or some other spiritual entity spoke to her through the mushrooms helping her to diagnose and treat sick members of her community.

Nicolás Echevarría, creator of the 1978 documentary *María Sabina. Mujer Espiritu* had built a small house for María Sabina, affording her a splendid view of the mountainous landscape. She used the house as a dressing room preceding her veladas. On our way to this house we observed datura flowers in full bloom. I remembered that Roquet often used datura seeds in his work, usually in combination with ketamine, which modulated the effects of datura, a substance that can prove fatal if not properly administered.

When we asked permission to photograph her, María Sabina excused herself, went into her house, and reappeared wearing a *huipul,* a colorful ceremonial robe. Bonnie Colodzin was so moved by María Sabina's charisma that she began to weep uncontrollably. María Sabina took her aside, caressing the younger woman's body with fresh flowers. Bonnie recovered, took the photographs, and reported a state of well-being that endured the rest of the trip (Krippner & Winkelman, 1982).

Salvador had brought several of his patients with him, hoping that a mushroom velada would be pivotal in their ongoing psychotherapy with him. María Sabina acknowledged that the maladies of age had terminated her use of the mushrooms, but Roquet had located another practitioner named Doña Clotilde. We located this curandera and arranged a velada for the following night. Roquet asked this patient to fill out the Hartman Value Inventory and said he would return in the morning.

Doña Clotilde met us at the door to her sanctuary, dressed in a huipul. Sadly, she informed us that it was the dry season and there were not enough *hongitos* ("the little mushrooms") to go around. I told her that I had already experienced the mush-rooms and so I would not need to take them again. Her face lit up and she said, "Well, then you can be my assistant!"

Doña Clotilde's sanctuary was adjoined to her house. It was a small room with a concrete floor, one covered with pine boughs, which emitted a pleasant odor. My first act was to help Doña Clotilde stick the candles to the floor. She deftly let a small amount of melting candle wax drop to the floor, and then placed the candle in the wax until it cooled. I tried to do the same, but my candles kept falling down. I noticed that the curandera had given me candles with a rough bottom while keeping the smooth bottomed candles for her own use. I realized that this made her look adept while her assistant looked clumsy. I was only too willing to enhance her image. I simply let a larger amount of wax drip from the candles before trying to affix them. It worked quite well.

But I made my own contribution to the velada. Doña Clotilde had trouble lighting her matches, which had been stored in a container that was not waterproof. I had brought along a package of waterproof matches, which lit the candles very easily. I left the remainder of the matches with Doña Clotilde, knowing that she would now have some "magic" not available to other curanderas and curanderos.

Once the *hongitos* began to take effect, there was the usual laughing and crying, smiling and wailing. Two of Salvador's patients were having an especially difficult time, and were vomiting profusely. One was a concert pianist who had become too overcome with stage fright to continue performing. Another was a former Miss Kentucky whose looks were fading. Thrown back on using her inner, rather than her outer, resources to make her way in the world, she panicked. There were few inner assets for her to draw on. I went to a far corner of the room and asked them to tell me what was going on. First one and then the other spoke about their messages from the *hongitos*, positive messages of encouragement and hope. The advice was quite specific and very meaningful. They were so delighted with my help that they began to hug me and kiss me, one on my left side and one on my right side. Ordinarily, this would have been a pleasant experience but the stench of the vomit was so severe that I had a hard time keeping from being asphyxiated. And then I realized the function of the pine boughs. I knelt close to them and inhaled their fresh scent. This strategy allowed me to keep focusing on the revelations, doing my best to reinforce the ones that made sense.

Walter Houston Clark was also affected by the *hongitos*. The veteran of several psychedelic trips, both as a guide and as a participant, he was upset with the negative imagery that came into his field of inner vision. Walter described a stream of vampire bats hovering over him. I told Walter that vampire bats are actually admirable creatures, piercing their skin so that their babies can suck their blood for nourishment. Walter was astonished; what often seems negative can be quite positive once the larger picture is envisioned. He remarked, "And I should have realized that." I responded that even the most capable of us sometimes needs a little help from our friends. At the end of the night, it was apparent that I had learned much more being an assistant than being a participant.

The following morning, Salvador joined us. He was bright and cheerful, while the rest of us were in various stages of fatigue. Nonetheless, his patients completed their drawings and engaged in his typical group therapy procedures. I simply went back to my hotel room and collapsed.

Most of my friends and I left the Oaxaca expedition at that point, believing that nothing could surpass our encounter with María Sabina. Richard Yensen stayed with the group and told us that he had participated in an incredible mushroom velada with Don Ricardo. This was the same journey that Carl had written me about, even though Yensen's evaluation was more complimentary to Salvador. Perhaps Carl was not used to the chaos that Salvador deliberately cultivated in his role as a provocateur.

Requiem

That journey was the last time I would see Salvador in Mexico. Whenever he came to San Francisco, we would get together for lunch, dinner, or a visit to the Kabuki Hot Springs, a spa that he enjoyed. I recommended that people join his non-drug "convivials" or *convivencias*, which he directed with considerable gusto until his death in 1995.

In 2006, I was invited to make several presentations in Zurich, Switzerland, at the centennial celebration for another dear friend, Albert Hoffman, the brilliant chemist who synthesized LSD-25. I had visited Albert and his wife Anita at their home only two years earlier. None of us had any idea that the city of Zurich would plan what turned out to be a lavish international event. I was upset that Salvador's work was not included in the program and so I asked Richard Yensen and one of Salvador's assistants, Linda Rosa Corazon, to share the stage with me during one of my presentation time slots. We each mentioned Salvador and his innovative use of LSD-type drugs, as well as ketamine.

There are still lessons to be learned from Salvador's legacy. His iconic stature in the story of psychedelic psychotherapy is finally emerging. I expect history will be kind to him.

References

Assagioli, R. (1971). *Psychosynthesis: A manual of principles and techniques.* New York, NY: Viking Press.

Barney, W. (1977, September 5). Mexican therapy: "Like the end of the world." *San Francisco Examiner*, 24.

Clark, W. H. (1977). Art and psychotherapy in Mexico. *Art Psychotherapy, 4,* 41–44. doi:10.1016/0090-9092(77)90021-7

Ellis, A. R. (Ed.). (1994). *Freedom to live: The Robert Hartman story.* Atlanta, GA: Rodopi Press.

Estrada, A. (1981). *María Sabina: Her life and chants.* Santa Barbara, CA: Ross-Erikson.

Krippner, S., & Winkelman, M. (1982, January), María Sabina: Wise lady of the mushrooms. *Association for Humanistic Psychology Newsletter,* 5–7.

Roquet, S. (1973). *Psychosynthesis.* Mexico City, Mexico: Albert Schweitzer Association. (In English)

Roquet, S., Favreau, P. L., Ocana, R., & Velaso, M. R. (1975). *La existencial a través de psicodyslepticos: Una nueva psicoterapia.* Mexico City, Mexico: Asociacion Albert Schweitzer, Instituto de Psicosintesis. (In Spanish)

Wasson, G. (1957, May 13). Seeking the magic mushroom. *Life,* 100–102; 109–120.

Yensen, R. (1973). *Group therapy with a variety of hallucinogens.* Paper presented at the Annual Convention of the Association for Humanistic Psychology, Quebec, Montreal, Canada.

Z., C. (1980). *A study of the combined work of Dr. Salvador Roquet and Don Ricardo, a Mazatec Indian brujo.* Unpublished manuscript.

The author would like to thank the Saybrook University Chair for the Study of Consciousness for its support in the preparation of this chapter.

Psychedelic Experiential Pharmacology: Pioneering Clinical Explorations with Salvador Roquet

(How I Came to All of This: Ketamine, Admixtures and Adjuvants, Don Juan and Carlos Castaneda Too)

An Interview with Richard Yensen

Phil Wolfson, M.D.

RICHARD YENSEN WAS A RESEARCH FELLOW at the Maryland Psychiatric Research Center from 1972 to 1976. He studied psychedelic psychotherapy with Stanislav Grof, M.D. and other senior staff. During this time he treated patients with substance abuse disorders, cancer, neurosis, and other health professionals seeking a training experience. Dr. Yensen did his PhD dissertation on the use of MDA in psychotherapy with neurotic outpatients and conducted his research at the MPRC. Through many years of experience in government-sanctioned psychedelic research, he has evolved a non-drug shamanistic psychotherapy called Perceptual Affective Therapy. In the 1990's Richard was co-holder of IND 3250, an investigational new drug permit issued by the U.S. Food and Drug Administration to study LSD and psychotherapy until 2006. He is currently a licensed psychologist in California and director of the Orenda Institute in Vancouver and Cortes Island, British Columbia, Canada and president of the Salvador Roquet Psychosynthesis Association. He has served on the faculties of Harvard Medical School, Johns Hopkins University and the University of Maryland Medical School in Baltimore.

Phil Wolfson: *Please tell us about your background.*

Richard Yensen: I am a Latino at heart and by heritage. My mother was Panamanian, and I have deep roots in the soil of America Latina. A portion of my childhood was spent in the Panamanian isthmus, that bit of land that connects the two vast continents. There I learned Spanish and came to a certain sensitivity that would lead me to a lifelong embrace of Latin culture and people. This inspired me to bring northern and southern cultures into an inner amalgam of my own making.

PW: *When and where did you become interested in psychedelic therapy and plant medicine?*

RY: The desire to incorporate ancient healing practices with sacred plants into modern medicine has been a central passion of mine, as a clinician and psychedelic researcher, for over forty years. I was first ignited to study plant medicine during trips to Mexico, a country that offered me friendship, collegiality, and adventure. Mexico has been blessed with a wide variety of psychedelic plants and ancient traditions that have a great deal of healing potential to contribute to modern psychotherapy. I have often felt, when visiting the First Nations of Mexico, as if I were stepping back into ancient times. The wonder and honor of knowing Maria Sabina, Don Ricardo, Niuweme, and other healers and shamans, has transformed my outlook on the practice of psychedelic medicine.

PW: *What role did your contact with indigenous communities play in unfolding your passion?*

RY: My experience among native peoples has taught me that human beings tend toward a meaning-seeking and meaning-making journey during their lives. As individuals, we feel best when we are in touch with our story, our purpose, our unique nature, and can envision with some clarity a meaningful path to guide us. It is truly remarkable that native peoples, from a wide variety of indigenous nations within Mexico, are willing to share the precious keys that open doors to meaning and belonging, to spirit and wonder. The same people offering this forgotten wisdom are descendants of those who were conquered, decimated, and traumatically oppressed by invaders from Europe.

PW: *How do you think the use of plant and psychedelic medicines relates to healing trauma?*

RY: Used wisely, sacred plants and psychedelic drugs can offer an opportunity for a deep remedial healing experience, one that repairs despair and annihilates hopelessness with the most meaningful experiences possible. The effects of trauma can persist for up to seven generations after the original insult. Trauma injures the capacity to weave meaning into our lives, it decontextualizes us, injects a capricious or diabolical element into our consciousness. In the course of losing the ability to create meaning, the individual may well prepare to die of hopelessness, and in so doing, surrender their cultural and personal histories—the very source of their precious vitality. I have come to believe that such trauma lies at the core of addiction, post-traumatic stress disorder and some depressions.

PW: *Do you think native wisdom can help us adapt to our current planetary challenges?*

RY: Absolutely. We live in a world with excessive environmental stress, collapsing ecosystems, diminishing cultural diversity, loss of languages and ways of being, and the dangerous creation of a global monoculture. At this point in history, it is essential for us to pursue an awareness of, and openness to, prior successful adaptations. In order to gain the perspective necessary to adopt new treatments for trauma, we need to carefully examine the organization of cultures and societies that are able to integrate the effects, insights, and experiences of sacred plants. Indigenous cultures are sophisticated and elegant in their adaptation to the environment: their adaptation is, in my opinion, more complete than our own. The consequences of our poor adaptation are catching up with us. The pressures of expanding populations threaten humanity, as we face the same end story as a colony of bacteria that blindly consumes all available resources on a Petri dish until it collapses.

PW: *What are your thoughts on ayahuasca?*

RY: Ayahuasca is an ancient example of the power of an admixture: in pre-Columbian times the Amerindian peoples of the Amazon were perhaps the first to develop an admixture strategy in relation to psychedelic substances. Their exotic two-plant mixture, called ayahuasca, was developed without benefit of any modern psychopharmacology or laboratory instruments to monitor purity and without modern understandings of the nervous system. These pioneers were working through visionary intuition, guided by the effects of the different plants they were experimenting with. They came to the idea that one must take the leaves of a bush *(Psychotria viridis)* and combine these leaves with large chunks of a jungle liana *(Banisteriopsis caapi)* and boil them for hours. *Banisteriopsis caapi,* the vine or liana, contains a monoamine oxidase (primarily MAO-A) inhibitor. The properly prepared combination makes this otherwise inactive combination of plants blossom into a psychedelic. Ayahuasca has been used for centuries as an aid to healing (Yensen, 1988). Since the mixture is key to the presence of the desired effects, rather than a modifier of already ongoing psychedelic effects, this example is embryonic or prototypical in relation to the subsequent uses of admixtures in psychedelic psychotherapy.

PW: *You met Carlos Castaneda while he was still a student. What do you remember about his debut as a best-selling author?*

RY: Yes—I met Carlos early on my path, as he was still "unknown" as a graduate student at UCLA. He had just published a remarkable little book, *Teachings of Don Juan: A Yaqui Way of Knowledge.* My first psychedelic enchantment was with that little rogue. To me, he always insisted that his name was pronounced and spelled Castaneda, not Castañeda.

His subsequent fame and fortune were followed by academic attack and denouncement. The details of sacred plant use in Carlos's books were inaccurate at best. Perhaps the Yaqui Indian sorcerer/shaman Don Juan may have been a figment of his imagination. Amidst cries of academic fraud, Castaneda's books persisted on the bestseller lists; his bank accounts grew past the bursting point. This phenomenal success was all the more remarkable because with one notable exception (for *Time* magazine), Carlos Castaneda did not give interviews to the press, did not permit portraits, did not make television appearances, and overall laughed at the antics of journalists and influence peddlers who pretended to know what was going on in the world. Efforts to bury the popularity of Carlos Castaneda and his books remain unsuccessful to this day.

PW: *How do you perceive Carlos Castaneda's influence in the West?*

RY: Academics focusing on errors and guessing at the location and tribal identity of the sage in Castaneda's accounts ignore the most important aspect of his books, which is his consummate shamanic act. The details of sacred plant use in Carlos's books were inaccurate, and whether Don Juan actually existed or was a product of Castaneda's extraordinary imagination is not even the point. In his books, Castaneda addressed the children of those who won World War II and struggled with Korea. He addressed young men who were being asked to give their lives in a meaningless war in Southeast Asia. He captivated the imagination of a generation that grew up watching cowboys and Indians in movies and television. He took the well-established sense of cultural superiority, the illusion of progress and the notion that material plenty would address all human ills and turned them on their ear. Through his captivating portrayals of dialogs with Don Juan, he craftily suggested that this old Yaqui gentlemen knew something about how to live a meaningful life, about the inner struggles of being human. He intimated that overlooked shamanic wisdom could only be had if one gained membership in another culture. In these accounts, Carlos himself appears an utter fool and thus portrays for us the foibles of a person confronting an entirely new and different worldview. What was most important and improbable, coming from the cultural darkness of the fifties, was the worldwide arousal of an entire generation's hunger to know these secrets!

In Don Juan's own terms, Carlos shifted our assemblage point, the place in our mind where we construct reality: he shifted his readers out of a semiconscious, culturally self-centered stance. The view that native people are primitive, dimwitted, helpless and violent was transformed by Carlos, and replaced by a sense of mystery, curiosity and wonder. Now, the natives were suddenly folks who might have the secret of how to live a life of meaning and profound purpose.

After reading Castaneda's accounts, I and many others were influenced to pursue careers in anthropology, in psychology, in medicine, in literature—often in pursuit of this hidden knowledge and depth held by romantic and inaccessible Amerindians. Mexico was invaded by readers looking for Don Juan, searching for the Mazatecs, the Huichols and the Tarahumara, trying to find the lost meaning of their lives. Later, the search spread to South America.

The effects of the hunger and passion elicited by Castaneda have been mixed. Ethno-tourism has become a major industry and is tending to undermine the very societies it seeks to appreciate. Yet, can we imagine a greater shamanic success than the complete rending asunder of the blind conquest of the native peoples of America? In place of the Conquest, there came to be an extraordinary, successful restoration of a sense of wonder and esteem for native people's nobility, as well as their botanical, philosophical, and pharmacological knowledge. He transformed the contemporary children of the conquerors into determined seekers of native wisdom. This was his stroke of true mastery, his great contribution!

PW: *How would you describe the psychedelic therapy methods that were developed at the Maryland Psychiatric Research Center in the 1970s?*

RY: Experiential psychedelic pharmacology is informed and guided by the subjective experience of the drug recipient rather than relying solely on an objective understanding of drug action. Our psychedelic therapy technique involved creating the safest, most homelike atmosphere: unthreatening, peaceful and kind, a completely supportive field within which to administer a psychedelic drug. Our clinical emphasis was on encouraging the patient/subject to let go into whatever experience arose in the drug-induced altered state. Since our patients were utterly safe, un-threatened in the therapy milieu and relationship, they could be conveyed toward transcendence with the aid of carefully selected music (Bonny & Pahnke, 1972). Art was just beginning to be used as well, to facilitate integration (Kellogg, Mac Rae, Bonny, & di Leo, 1977). We felt that our approach would enhance the possibility for the occurrence of a peak or mystical experience!

It was also likely that patients/subjects might experience events that could repair emotional wounding from past life trauma. In our most advanced study we were involved with a combined psychedelic and psycholytic technique: cleaning out early emotional conflicts and difficulty using one to three, sometimes up to five drug experiences and aiming for a mystical experience to reintegrate the personality. We were working with LSD, DPT[1], and MDA as adjuncts to psychotherapy in separate studies. Our ultimate goal was to create an integrative, healing, and mystical experience for our patients and subjects.

Our subjects included inpatient alcoholics, professionals in training, outpatient neurotics, and terminal cancer patients. We also had a referral program to which lo-cal therapists could refer patients they were having difficulty treating. The program offered an opportunity for the referring therapist to become part of the treatment team, joining with our psychedelic intervention (Bonny & Pahnke, 1972; Grof, Pahnke, Kurland, & Goodman, 1971; Kurland, Pahnke, Unger, Savage, & Good-man, 1968; Kurland, Savage Pahnke, Grof, & Olsson, 1971; Pahnke, 1963; Pahnke & Richards, 1966; Pahnke, Kurland, Goodman, & Richards, 1969a, 1969b; Pahn-ke, Kurland, Unger, & Savage, 1970; Pahnke, Kurland, Unger, Savage, & Grof, 1970, 1971; Pahnke et al., 1970; Tijo, Pahnke, & Kurland, 1969).

PW: *Were drug admixtures commonly used in psychedelic psychotherapy at the time?*

RY: The dawn of psychedelic mixtures in the West took place in the late 1950s, after clinicians were already successfully using LSD in psychotherapy (Ling & Buckman, 1960). Ling and Buckman, in the UK, observed interesting interactions when they combined a new drug, labeled as a psychic energizer, with LSD. Ritalin (or meth-ylphenidate) was the name of this compound and, at the time, it was available in injectable form. They administered the drug intravenously to patients receiving low doses of LSD. They observed that Ritalin created a valuable sense of well-being in their patients, similar to the effect of amphetamines.

In the LSD sessions, their patients often regressed and entered a process that could uncover traumatic events from childhood. For example, a difficult memory or one that had been intentionally forgotten or unconsciously repressed might emerge, such as a memory of being beaten. In this process the patient might become frightened and disoriented. They noted that often patients would project elements of a scene from the past onto their therapists and/or the immediate setting. Far too often, their patients became too frightened to face this emotional flooding. The panic thus ignited would block the evocative effects of LSD. As a result, the therapeutic alliance could be diminished or threatened. But if the therapist administered Ritalin® at this time, the admixture could foster a sense of well-being and the patient might realize: "I'm really okay, even though I feel awful and I'm crying and I'm frightened and I'm running away from something. Whatever it is that I'm avoiding, it's okay to face it now. I am safe and in the presence of my doctor who wants to help me to understand what happened." The example of LSD and Ritalin demonstrates the value of a synergetic mixture: the ability of a drug combination to modify the emotional experiential quality of an ongoing psychedelic journey and to facilitate psychotherapy.

In Ling & Buckman's clinic, an effective strategy emerged for administering an additional drug that facilitated their patients feeling sufficiently safe, thus pharmacologically inducing sufficient safety to face their most frightening emotions. This ability to bring insight, catharsis and resolution was a tremendously valuable innovation in psychotherapy. Ling and Buckman deemed the discovery worthy of a book (Ling & Buckman, 1963). Betty Eisner and Hanscarl Leuner among quite a few other clinicians later incorporated stimulants as mixtures in their psychotherapy research and treatment with LSD.

PW: *What was your experience with MDA?*

RY: In 1967, Claudio Naranjo reported using MDA as an adjunct to psychotherapy (Naranjo, Shulgin, & Sargent, 1967; Naranjo, 1973). MDA is a substituted methylenedioxy-phenethylamine. MDA has some structural resemblances to both mescaline and amphetamine, and its subjective properties also seem to be a blend of the effects of these long-known and long-studied drugs.

Our team at Maryland Psychiatric Research Center (MPRC) studied the subjective effects of MDA by administering the drug in our carefully prepared psychedelic treatment suites using the techniques we had perfected for safely conducting LSD sessions. At that time, the MPRC was the last federal and state government funded research group doing clinical studies of the efficacy of psychedelic drugs in psychotherapy.

First we administered MDA to the clinical staff as a training experience. We found that where LSD demands internal exploration, MDA seemed to suggest or invite it. It also tended to foster a sense of well-being that was subjectively pleasant and quite useful in psychotherapy (Turek, Soskin, & Kurland, 1974).

At the Institute, in my own personal MDA training session, I started out frightened. It was, after all, my first official psychedelic experience. Then I became elated as the drug took hold and I transformed with it. I noticed that my left hand became freezing cold, yet my right hand remained warm. I began to warm my left hand with my right and as I was doing this self-soothing, I started to recount the story of my life to the therapists that accompanied me. I recounted many traumas of my childhood. As I narrated the memories I felt I was reliving them with only modest intensity—this included my parents' verbal fights and their subsequent noxious parental events. I continued comforting myself with my right hand. It occurred to me that in a sense my hands were illustrating the effect of the two aspects of the drug action. One side was the psychedelic—bringing up all this stuff regardless of its emotional valence without regard for how undesirable some of the emotions were—the psychedelic brought forth the traumas and fostered regression. The other side, the euphoric warm side, brought forward the soothing sensations. When the experience ended, I felt gratified at having successfully run a difficult gauntlet to arrive at my goal—to be on the road to becoming a psychedelic therapist.

Our research team's efforts were a molecular evolution. What began as a clinical technique that used a two-drug mixture (LSD and methylphenidate), with fine control over the exact timing of the second drug administration and consequently the euphoric effect it created, was transformed into a single drug. MDA was, at that time, the one drug that incorporated two previously separate functional aspects into a single molecule that exhibited both subjective qualities[2].

Subsequently, I became involved in further research to assess the use of MDA in individual psychotherapy with neurotic outpatients and ultimately used that project for my PhD dissertation. (Yensen, 1975; Yensen et al., 1976).

PW: *How did you meet Salvador Roquet? What was his influence in the field of psychedelic psychotherapy at the time?*

RY: I was a research fellow at MPRC in 1973 when the Clinical Sciences Division received a phone call from Stanley Krippner, a well-known parapsychology researcher with interests in psychedelics. Dr. Krippner had attended the recent World Psychiatry Conference in Mexico City, where he discovered the work of Salvador

Roquet, a Mexican psychoanalyst. He assured us that it was imperative that we invite this gentleman to offer grand rounds at the MPRC.

Roquet was a giant of innovation in psychotherapy and psychopharmacology, as well as a physician and high order public health official and executive in the Mexican ISSSTE[3]. He was a pioneer in the development of psychedelic admixtures. He was among the early explorers of ketamine as an adjunct to psychotherapy, and he co-discovered ketamine as an admixture to classical psychedelics in psychotherapy.

PW: *What made you feel that you could trust him?*

RY: Roquet was a man humble and open enough to ask native people how they viewed and used their sacred plants. He not only asked the questions, but took their answers seriously, even when he was uncertain of the reasons behind certain principles, like holding mushroom veladas (vigils) at night rather than in the daytime. He chose to respect centuries of ritual use and usually opted for tradition over convenience. He took what he learned from native healers and combined it with his training as a Western psychoanalyst in the tradition of Eric Fromm. Through these wide-ranging sources of inspiration and his unique awareness as a public health doctor, he forged a group psychotherapy process that could effectively address the longing for meaning and connection that is characteristic of humanity today.

PW: *What was Roquet's method? How did it differ from MPRC's?*

RY: Whereas our group in Maryland was focused on scientifically establishing the effectiveness of the experimental administration of various psychedelic drugs as adjuncts to psychotherapy, Roquet was freely combining naturalistic research and experimentation in consultation with shamanic practitioners with his unrestricted psychotherapy practice. He told us he had blanket permission to use psychedelics that had been issued through his political connections with the attorney general's office of the federal government of Mexico.

In a freewheeling, openly experimental, naturalistic mode he quickly developed an involved multilevel polytherapy. He worked with both individual sessions and group sessions and utilized a wide variety of psychoactive drugs and plants. Whereas our work was methodical and linear, he seemed to be doing everything at once! This was especially striking because our work had sometimes been criticized for being too multivariate, as we evaluated simultaneous psychotherapy and drug administration. Any experiment that involves both drugs and psychotherapy is far more complex in terms of careful scientific design and the validation of the results obtained.

Dr. Roquet practiced a kind of group therapy he called psychosynthesis[4], in groups that ranged from ten to twenty-eight patients. It was his claim that through this process he synthesized what most analysts would analyze. He envisioned his therapy as a round-trip out of normal consciousness into the world of the madman and the mystic and then back to normal. He used a plant delirogen in this approach to produce toxic psychoses in the course of a multisession, psychedelic, transpersonally oriented therapy. He viewed mystical experiences as the sine qua non of successful treatment in this sensory overload setting.

Each group was carefully selected for composition, balance and heterogeneity, not only with respect to age and sex but also length of time in treatment. Patients would receive whatever psychoactive plant or medicine was prescribed by Roquet, from a wide variety of possibilities.

Psychosynthesis sessions took place at night, mirroring shamanic practice in Mexico. Before the psychoactive session itself, the participants met in a large room for a leaderless group discussion. This allowed each patient the opportunity to meet new members and review his or her expectations, fears, and previous experiences with the group. An important function of the pre-drug meeting was to allow projections and transferences to take place between group members. There was a self-organizing quality to this therapy prelude, one that smoothly introduced a new patient to the process through descriptions from veterans. The deep candor and openness of these groups set the tone for what would ensue.

The pre-drug meeting lasted about two hours. The group then entered the treatment environment, a large room decorated with an array of paintings and posters selected for their evocative quality. Toward the rear of the room there was a large table with a variety of audiovisual equipment. In the main part of the room, mattresses were arranged along each wall. The central part of the room was kept clear so that patients could walk freely if they wished.

As soon as all the patients entered the room and settled into their spots, the sensory overload would begin. The overload used slides, movies, two stereo sound systems, and colored floodlights that could be flashed intermittently. The elements included in the slides and films were as varied as possible. Within what seemed a confusing barrage of unrelated images and sounds, there would be a main theme. Among the themes Roquet found useful were death, birth, sexuality, religion, and childhood. Each evening's stimuli were assembled so that in addition to the main theme, there were slides of particular importance for each client: scenes from childhood, family pictures, and so forth. These pictures, when projected, would be accompanied by music of importance for that particular patient. During the overload show, a full-length feature film with an evocative and conflictual theme was also projected[5]. The two stereo sound systems were used with a wide variety of music from all over the world combined with sound effects in order to modulate the depth and intensity of the group's emotional reactions. When maximum stimulation was desired a chaotic effect could be achieved by playing both stereo systems at the same time at high volume with different records.

After approximately fifteen minutes of moderately intense sensory stimuli, the psychedelic substances were administered. The substances used as therapeutic adjuncts were quite varied, including the seeds of two types of morning glory: *Rivea corymbosa* and *Ipomea violacea.* The outer coat on these seeds has an emetic effect. The vomiting, combined with a mild degree of psychedelic action, can facilitate the disruption of character armor, particularly armoring against sadness, grief, and involuntary sobbing. This in turn assisted the recovery of early childhood memories. The complex reliving of childhood trauma greatly enhanced the therapeutic alliance and increased trust in the ongoing therapy process.

In subsequent sessions, any of a variety of psilocybin-containing mushrooms[6] could be administered. In the next session, *Lophophora williamsii* (the peyote cactus) would be used to deepen the recollective-analytic process. The deepening experiences and emergence of underlying dynamics related to presenting symptoms would strengthen the therapeutic alliance, likely one key among many that unlocked the success of this therapy.

Finally, *Datura ceratocaula* (an anticholinergic delirogen with hyoscyamine, atropine, and scopolamine as active ingredients), and subsequently, ketamine hydrochloride (Ketalar) would be introduced as the last part of a repeating sequence of psychoactive adjuncts. Ketamine was used in three serial intramuscular injections of 1.5mg/kg dosage per administration.

Roquet, through consultation with an anesthesiologist colleague, had discovered that ketamine in sub-anesthetic doses produced profound changes in psychological functioning that could be helpful in his psychotherapy process. One of the important specific ways that ketamine was useful was to facilitate reintegration of Datura experiences. Following a Datura session, overwhelming anxiety was a typical response to the complete loss of control that occurred due to the acute psychotomimetic effects of this anticholinergic plant. Roquet would encourage patients to experience this anxiety for as long as they could tolerate it between sessions. Then, in the next session, he would use a triplet of ketamine administrations in a series to "bring them out of the Datura."

The compelling quality of the ketamine experience would assist his patients in confronting the conflictual material that presented itself in psychotic form during the Datura experience. This began the synthesis aspect of Roquet's analytic work.

The sensory overload portion of the drug session lasted for about six hours. After this, pictures from each patient's chart were passed out. Bibliotherapy, psychodrama, and other techniques would be blended into this multidimensional psychotherapy marathon. Passages from philosophers might be read by Roquet, and tape recordings of emotional moments from patients' previous sessions might be played back. This reflective phase was conducted without sensory overload or music. Patients might be given letters they had written to important figures in their life to read aloud for the group. Other participants might read from their descriptions of previous sessions or relevant passages from literature. This phase lasted two to three hours, ending around sunrise. At the end of this phase all participants and the therapist would sleep or rest for about an hour.

Then, the integrative phase would begin. This session lasted from four to twelve hours. Each patient would discuss his or her experience with the group. Greater abreaction and more intense catharsis than had occurred during the pharmacological drug peak were characteristic of this phase. During this session, the personality of each participant was reintegrated around insights gained during the drug session. Members of the patient's family could visit at this time as the therapeutic milieu expanded toward the everyday world. The tone of the session was confrontational, with the therapist presenting patients with ongoing problems in their life situation. The staff audiotaped every session for documentary purposes and for possible use in future sessions.

The course of therapy consisted of ten to fifteen drug sessions, although as many as twenty could be necessary for less-responsive individuals. The patient population consisted mostly of neurotic outpatients, but antisocial personality disorders, character neuroses, and even schizophrenia were also treated successfully on occasion.

The contrast between Roquet's methods and approach and ours was evident. At MPRC, we occupied a multimillion-dollar facility and conducted fairly linear clinical studies in a very focused manner according to rigorous scientific method. Suddenly we were confronted with Dr. Roquet, a single clinician, doing a much more complex treatment in an immediately relevant therapy[7] using innovative techniques we had never heard of before. He appeared to be breaking many of the rules established for successful psychedelic therapy, and yet he was reporting and illustrating remarkable results. For example, the fact that the staff wore white coats in a psychosynthesis session seemed directly at odds with our homelike atmosphere where therapist and nurse wore informal street attire.

PW: *How did the MPRC staff respond to Roquet's methods?*

RY: There was shock, denial, and disbelief on the part of many researchers at the MPRC. We had never heard of such procedures. We had never heard of ketamine. Dr. Roquet showed artwork created by his patients during and after the therapy process. Some of these folks were professional artists of enormous skill and accomplishment. Slides of these world-class pictures depicted all aspects of the psychedelic mindscape, from mystical resolution of major life conflicts to provocative cartoons illustrating sexual conflicts. There were intricate multilayered oil paintings of spiral galaxies, one with a gossamer depiction of a blissful embryo radiating from white light, shining through from behind a huge crashing breaker at the shore. The art was stunning and clearly represented deep emotional and transpersonal experiences as well as the artists' remarkable skill and acumen.

PW: *Did you personally experience ketamine in the presence of Roquet?*

RY: Absolutely. On a memorable evening, the head of our department joined me and a young medical student to experience the effects of ketamine firsthand. As far as we knew, at that time, we were the first in the United States to have the experience of ketamine intentionally administered as a psychedelic drug rather than an anesthetic.

I was concerned as Roquet injected our chief with this, until then, unknown psychedelic drug. Usually poised and thoughtful, almost contemplative, our leader was blithering. He made repeated, high-pitched, staccato sounds, rather like stuttering, except the utterances were complete gibberish. One of the most brilliant individuals I ever met was suddenly behaving rather like the village idiot! My own thoughts turned paranoid, "Is this guy trying to hurt us? What's happening here?" And just then, Roquet gave me an injection! Within three minutes it felt like a cosmic wringer washer had painlessly caught my little finger. With increasing speed I was wrung out of my body and out of my paranoid thoughts. I was melted through the floor of the session room! Actually I melted out of the room and into the universe, where I became a spiral arm in a galaxy. Then, I slowly came back to the room. These transformations were simply stunning, so much more than anything I'd ever experienced. And at the same time, they were so matter-of-fact, because the effects of ketamine were totally compelling. The drug's effects overwhelmed me. It was not polite—it didn't ask: "Would you like to go this way?" but rather it was: "Here we go!" Out and back in about an hour.

PW: *What is it about ketamine that makes it a potent adjunct to psychotherapy? How was Roquet capitalizing on those effects?*

RY: At the time I first encountered him in 1973, Roquet was using ketamine in two ways: 1) as a major psychedelic experience in its own right, and 2) as the resolving and grounding agent in a series of other sessions. He had been using it in a stepwise series: three administrations over a 24-hour group process were considered to constitute one session. Some of his approach, especially the use of Datura, had been derived from knowledge gathered through contact with indigenous healers and shamans. He would blend this traditional indigenous knowledge with his own elements, such as the use of ketamine (contemporary) following a Datura (indigenous) session.

Ketamine has a quality that might best be conveyed by personifying it, as though the effects of ketamine are saying, "Take my hand and gently but firmly let's go out of your body." The journey can be gentle, but is absolutely definite—there is no way to resist and in fact resistance is not usually a thought. Now, free of corporeal restraints and identifications, there is apparently no limit to where the mind may wander! "You are going to do this!"

Through this process, patients in Roquet's psychosynthesis would begin their journey of understanding. The ketamine session would follow a Datura-provoked toxic psychosis in a prior session (a month earlier). I will carry my personification into the inner dialog of the patient, "So that was the whole process! That is what the hallucination was referring to, that is why life was so frightening." Having lost any semblance of sanity through the effects of Datura, now this other substance would begin a process of confrontation, cathartic release and reintegration into a more insightful sense of self.

Roquet used ketamine to foster a synthesis of the raw elements that arose in the Datura session. He likened the effects of the Datura to a steam shovel. This shovel dug through the mind rather than the earth. It dredged up repressed conflicts from the unconscious. The repressed material was experienced in psychotic hallucinatory episodes. There would be huge amounts of fear and anxiety when the patient realized that they had been completely out of control, totally insane under the effects of the Datura! After a month of anguish or when the state was absolutely unbearable, ketamine was given. The ketamine journey fostered insight that the chaotic Datura experience was not simply crazy. The drug effects said, "No postponing this one, let's have a look at it right now! You, come with me!" The process with ketamine could also take on a symbolic quality, but usually more refined than the strange journey with Datura, one more likely to flow toward a conclusion. With sufficient resolution of some of their conflicts, a patient could survive to the next psychedelic session without overwhelming anxiety or depression[8]. The task of further insight and integration would then continue with a series of monthly sessions with "classical: psychedelics: mescaline from peyote, LSD, psilocybin mushrooms, and morning glory seeds (amides of lysergic acid).

PW: *What do you know about the pharmaceutical background and current use of ketamine?*

RY: Ketamine was originally developed by Parke-Davis (a subsidiary of Pfizer) as a dissociative anesthetic in the 1960s and marketed as Ketalar. Ketamine was developed in response to complaints from anesthesiologists about "emergence reactions" when using their premier dissociative anesthetic product, phencyclidine, which was marketed as Sernyl.

Fifty years later, ketamine has become the hot emerging medicine in psychiatry. Recent reports of virtually instantaneous antidepressant effects have cast ketamine as the holy grail of antidepressant development. A major drawback for pharmacologically oriented clinicians is that ketamine, at sub-anesthetic doses, can still exhibit psychedelic effects[9]. This historical review of psychedelic mixtures and ketamine will clarify the potential of ketamine as a medicine for psychedelic psychotherapy rather than as a conventional pharmacological antidepressant.

PW: *What are the psychodynamic effects of ketamine? How do they affect one's worldview?*

RY: Over the years 1973 to 1975, as I got to know Roquet more deeply, we began to speak in more detail about what ketamine actually does on an experiential and psychodynamic level. I was enthralled that ketamine helps you out of your body, so that you experience consciousness without a body. You begin to realize that it's possible to have a conscious experience with no body. This subjective experience is often exhilarating. The psychological, philosophical and ontological consequences of such an experience are profound in terms of their effect on worldview.

I mentioned to Roquet that Freud held that the ego is, first and foremost, a body ego. Wilhelm Reich was Freud's first colleague in charge of training. As a young psychiatrist he was the analyst in charge of training for the Vienna Circle. Reich noticed that as humans grow up, we develop a style of being. This style of being is character and it's based on our reaction to the supportive and noxious events in our early environment. So, if our parents would beat us every time we reached for the matches, then we learned not to grasp. Perhaps we would cringe inwardly when our curiosity was aroused in later life. The defensive stance toward early trauma, the desperate survival measures taken to protect oneself, become part of who we are, part of our character through repetition. Character is that set of repeatable and predictable responses that allow us to know a person through their behavioral repertoire. Ketamine affects character, by taking people out of their body, and out of their body-armor. Reich realized that character armor was not just a mental set of defenses, but a set of chronic tensions in the body that affect posture and stance (Reich, 1980).

PW: *Did you ever try mixing ketamine with other drugs, besides those that Roquet was already using?*

RY: We spoke of what innovations might be possible, given the enormous freedom with which Roquet was able to practice at that time. We began to discuss the idea of combining drugs and I described Ling & Buckman's work. As our dialog continued, I wondered, "What would happen if we gave ketamine as a prelude to LSD?" The experience would take the patient out of their armor and then the LSD would take effect in a preconditioned, more permeable and open psyche. The chance for a deeper response would be enhanced. The ability to more fully enter, surrender and stay with an experience might be fostered by this combination. We agreed that timing might prove as important with ketamine as it had when Ling & Buckman were using Ritalin.

Roquet wanted me to immediately inject him with a dose of ketamine and then give him LSD. I was cautious and concerned about possible complications. Roquet was a diabetic and, to me at that time, his 55 years represented close to old age! His physique resembled that of a kwashiorkor victim due to his distended abdomen. His slightly bowed legs suggested a history of malnutrition. So, instead I experimented with myself as the subject by having a colleague administer ketamine and LSD at the same time. The rationale was that ketamine would take effect in a minute or so after an intramuscular injection. The LSD would take roughly 20 minutes to have an effect. I had not counted on the speed with which sublingual LSD could be absorbed. My experience was that both compounds took effect in a quick sequence, much closer together than I had imagined they would.

The effects of the two compounds were synergistic, each enhancing the effect of the other, but completely beyond our imagining. I had an extraordinary experience that took me deeper into altered consciousness than I had ever been. The ego death was so convincing that I became certain the mixture was toxic and feared I had unintentionally administered a fatal combination.

Ketamine fosters emotional release when the patient/subject is struggling with the containment of emotional discharge in a major psychedelic experience or ego death. Ketamine assists in the softening and surrendering of the usual tonic set of energetic and connective tissue correlating to specific character body holding. The softening occurs in this practiced habitual set of muscular constrictions developed as a reaction to past insults to personal integrity; these were held in place by fear of death, suffering, and annihilation.

Subsequently, we tried other sequences and timing, and slowly developed a technique of using ketamine with other major psychedelics—in sessions with LSD, mescaline, or psilocybin. The ketamine was injected at a time when the patient was past the peak of the effects of the long-acting psychedelic, maybe past some order of an ego death, surrender, and transcendence.

Ketamine would be given at a time when the ego was reestablishing itself, in a phase where childhood memories might be accessible and emotional conflicts might be activated. The patient might be having a little trouble or they might have opened their heart a lot and now were closing down on the vulnerability. This can be observed in the body, in movement, and by direct verbal inquiry, because at this point in the session the person is oriented enough to be able to speak with you. They can recount a little bit of what's happened.

PW: *What makes ketamine an effective adjunct to other psychedelics like LSD?*

RY: When ketamine is administered, it immediately imposes an out of the body experience, and this disrupts the return to the ordinary self. It disrupts the assertion of bodily tensions that constitute character armor, so that they cannot tighten up in the ways they were tight before and cannot hold back emotionally in the ways they were holding back before, or at least not as quickly as they would otherwise. Ketamine takes patients out of their body orientation and they are opened again; then many of the feelings behind the armoring can come pouring out with a softening, cathartic release and the upwelling of deeply held emotion.

When patients start coming back from the ketamine admixture, sometimes they may start closing down again. If you observe them closing down again, you can give them a second ketamine injection, and they will go out again. We found it feasible to give them up to three ketamine sessions during the tail of diminishing LSD effects. We used a setting and timing that was ample enough so as to have a 24-hour therapeutic window for working with the person in psychotherapy.

The goal of this process is to reopen the sensitivity and sensibility of the individual, to reinstate their vulnerability and their openness and their love. Their humanity is, in this way, rescued from beneath their character armor. It is the emotional armor that restricts affect, restricts expression, restricts the love they can give themselves and others. Habitual defenses are melted, as consciousness is dissociated from the body. Without the psychophysical restraint of rigid character armor the experiential horizon expands and brims with all kinds of possibilities.

This collaboration with Roquet added a third technique to his prior methods for using ketamine in psychotherapy. I call this the Roquet-Yensen procedure. Administering ketamine as an admixture toward the end of a major psychedelic session is perhaps the best use of this drug in my experience, as it can foster the most dramatic changes in character, and also ease the difficulties that can follow complex reliving of traumatic memories.

After our discovery of the synergism between ketamine and classical psychedelics, Roquet went on to many years of practice using this safer and more manageable approach, in preference to the use of Datura as a conduit to psychosis.

PW: *How was Roquet perceived in Mexico? What happened to him after the changes of climate in Mexican politics in the 1970s?*

RY: Roquet was quite a character. On the one hand, he was admired as a lone clinician heading up a nonprofit institute, with a multifaceted approach to effectively address human suffering. There were many unique parts to his offering. At his Institute there was a Summerhill[10] inspired primary school for children. Additionally, another school taught how to be an effective parent. The psychiatry clinic, in effect, taught how to live a loving and full life. Indeed, Roquet seemed larger than life, resembling some of his heroes, a combination of Albert Schweitzer and Mother Theresa.

However, he was also, and undisputedly, a controversial figure. He shared wild exploits ranging from his ethically questionable participation in psychedelic interrogation by the Federal Police, to giving a young revolutionary named Mario Falcon a therapeutic psychedelic experience that convinced him to surrender, in the midst of the subsequent, nonviolent student protest and occupation of the University of Mexico—UNAM. That nonviolent occupation resulted in the murder of as many as 300 students and civilians by the Mexican police, which has come to be known as the Tlatelolco Massacre. Falcon subsequently decided to emigrate to Chile and become an artist. Roquet negotiated his release. Roquet's participation remains controversial and for some stained his reputation in Mexico.

Robert S. Hartman, the well-known philosopher and axiologist from University of Tennessee and UNAM, described the work at Roquet's Institute as meaning making of the highest intrinsic order. This was not entirely realized by the Mexican Constabulary. Roquet's benefactor at the Department of Justice (Procuraduria), the originator of his "blanket" permission to practice psychosynthesis with psychedelics, had presidential ambitions in the forthcoming election. Soon, the winds of fate changed direction. Roquet knew it was coming and thought he had accepted his fate.

The headline that led to Roquet's arrest was, "24 hours in Hell." The article appeared in the popular magazine *Tiempo*. It was part of a carefully orchestrated press blitz designed to discredit him and portray his work in the most outrageous way. The journalist, the author of the article, was so terrified in his psychosynthesis session that he locked himself in the bathroom the entire time!

The federales burst into the institute expecting to catch the doctor dispensing the prohibited elixirs of freedom, the condemned sacred plants, sacraments to the first people in this land. When the Conquistadors arrived in the New World full of the Spanish Inquisition, they brought with them the mysterious un-healing evil wounds of trauma. There was no tolerance for direct experience of the sacred. They preferred symbols of spirit mediated through corrupt priests deeply involved with power and royalty. That first horse of the Apocalypse, who initially waded ashore in the New World disguised as a Conquistador, now arrived in the form of a federale, policeman of the Federal District of Mexico.

After his arrest, Roquet was interrogated in the room in which he had interrogated others. He knew of the existence and the location of the two-way glass but that made the dismantling of his identity perhaps more brutal. He was broken completely!

They imprisoned him in a former palace called Lecumberri, then transformed into an inescapable prison. Its history is somehow fitting for a country of such passion and struggle, as is Mexico. The sprawling building that was at once magnificent and humiliating represented the power of the state to annihilate the gift of freedom that is life, to incarcerate those who would dare to challenge the ultimate authority and reign of the great static archetype of government. This palace turned penitentiary had an illustrious list of unwilling tenants that included the great revolutionary Pancho Villa and the impassioned muralist David Alfaro Siqueiros. Jaime Ramón Mercader del Río Hernández, murderer of Leon Trotsky, had lingered there after his famous act of assassination. Only the prominent revolutionary general, Pancho Villa had ever escaped the clutches of this enslaving dungeon alive. No wonder they called it The Black Palace of Lecumberri! The powerful tendrils of royalist domination contained those yearning revolutionary urges to liberation more effectively that day than they did in the time of Pancho Villa.

PW: *How did you react to Roquet's persecution?*

RY: Roquet and I shared a vital wound throughout our lives. Both of us had been abandoned by our fathers at birth. We danced a transferential tango in our emotional relationship. I was both his father and his son and he mine. I was his LSD guide in training sessions at the Maryland Center; he was mine in sessions when I visited him in Mexico. We felt admired, loved, acknowledged, and abandoned by each other throughout 22 years or more of collegial friendship.

At the time of his imprisonment, I was only 23 years old and a PhD candidate, but I had to set him free! His defense team had told me that the key to success was humiliation of those who condemned him. Letters from world famous people, powerful icons from abroad, would immeasurably aid his case. I raced to Mexico City to testify before the House of Deputies and the Supreme Court. I brought with me two psychiatrists, Kenneth Godfrey and James Davis. Dr. Godfrey was a well-established psychedelic researcher at the Veterans Administration Hospitals, and he bore a letter of support from perhaps the most illustrious psychiatrist in the United States, Dr. Karl Menninger, who was co-founder of the famous Menninger Clinic in Topeka, Kansas. Dr. Davis was co-founder of the fledgling Davis Psychiatric Clinic in Indianapolis, Indiana. He came to describe how impressed he and his U.S. Air Force–trained psychiatrist brother Larry were with Roquet's therapy process. Dr. Walter Houston Clark, psychologist of religion, also joined us in the struggle to liberate this pioneer of psychedelic medicine from the clutches of denouncing political expediency. The administration of my own Maryland Psychiatric Research Center was not willing to risk the political consequences of supporting Roquet against the gathering forces of the great wave of prohibition, although he was one of our LSD professional training program participants.

A U.S.–born lawyer practicing in Mexico City told me that the CIA had approached Roquet about "treating" a few special patients for them. If he would turn his art once again to interrogation, as he had been willing to do for the Mexican government at one point, the U.S. spy agency would establish a clinic where he could practice as freely in the U.S. as he had in Mexico. Roquet turned them down, and they began fueling the process that led to his arrest and imprisonment as a political football in the forthcoming presidential election.

PW: *There is something about Salvador Roquet that brings to mind Carlos Castaneda. Do you see any parallels between these two figures?*

RY: Roquet was charismatic in his actions, commanding and compelling in his therapy. Carlos Castaneda was charismatic and compelling in his writing. The sticking point for both was charisma, the illusive and compelling quality that completely seduces followers. The charm that completely seduces the place in each of us that wants to be led by a superior individual. A double-edged sword, charisma can be a tremendously positive quality. Certainly these two men would not have occupied the place they occupy in history were it not for their charismatic qualities. Yet, in a way, the undoing of each of them was precipitated by their charisma, by their compelling popularity with some, and by the jealousy that was engendered in others.

PW: *Do you foresee any hope of continuing the project of investigating ketamine's potentials for expanding consciousness and healing?*

RY: Currently, ketamine is being studied as an *instant antidepressant* (Maeng & Zarate, 2007; Maeng et al., 2008; Aan Het Rot, Zarate, Charney, & Mathews, 2012; Laje et al., 2012). Researchers have isolated the antidepressant effects they have observed, and are attempting to engineer molecules that will separate antidepressant effects from psychedelic effects. Having a new source of powerful antidepressants is, of course, very valuable. Yet, what I have described in terms of ketamine's psychedelic effects is both so complicated and so advanced that we do not have, as yet, an appropriate way to measure what is actually happening. We are getting closer to that with recent work by Robin Carhart-Harris and David Nutt in the United Kingdom with brain scans and magneto encephalography (MEGs; Carhart-Harris & Friston, 2010; Carhart-Harris et al., 2012).

It will take us many years in our over-regulated, drug war inhibited, logical scientific approach, to be able to develop complex and integrated approaches as Roquet and I were able to do with the clinical freedom he briefly enjoyed. All good things come to an end, and even he was beset with legal problems and imprisonment later in his career. Subsequent legal victories and clinical vindication were unable to reinstate his unique permissions and freedom to practice. I was privileged to have known and worked with Salvador Roquet. His life and unique practice have left an indelible mark on psychedelic psychotherapy, and on the broad notion of what is psychotherapy. There are many contemporary practitioners who remain influenced by him and he is an enduring part of the work that continues to attempt to understand and benefit humans and their relationships.

Notes

1. Dipropyltryptamine had a variable duration of action, approximately one hour in low doses (psycholytic doses) and four to six hours in higher doses (psychedelic doses).

2. When in the 1980s a compound with less prominent psychedelic effects and more prominent euphoria was revealed, MDMA emerged as a promising psychotherapy adjunct (Greer & Strassman, 1985)

3. Instituto de Seguridad y Servicios Sociales de los Trabajadores del Estado, Institute of Social Services and Safety for the Workers of the State.

4. Although psychosynthesis is better known as an approach to transpersonal psychotherapy pioneered by Roberto Assagioli in Italy, Roquet's approach was independently developed and is an absolutely unique style of therapy. The only commonality is the name.

5. For instance, The Bird Man of Alcatraz was one of the films used on occasion, for its dramatic portrayal of an Oedipal theme concerning the protagonist's relationship with his mother.

6. *Psilocybe mexicana, Psilocybe mazatecorum, Psilocybe cubensis,* for example.

7. Roquet had around three hundred patients engaged in his process at any given time.

8. I introduced Salvador Roquet to Richard Evans Schultes, the intrepid Harvard botanist who documented so many psychedelic plants in the Amazon during WWII. When I mentioned the use of morning glories and Datura, Schultes was immediately animated and enthused in his response: "What a wonderful idea! Perhaps when the Aztecs referred to the Ololiuqui *(Rivea corymbosa)* as the sister of Datura, they were referring to more than a floral resemblance." He found it

fascinating that they could be kept or used together. He also mentioned that Datura is a common admixture to ayahuasca prepared by shamans in the Amazon.

9. These are referred to as emergence reactions in the anesthesia literature and Parke-Davis admitted that 12.5% of patients reported this after ketamine anesthesia.

10. Summerhill School is an independent British boarding school that was founded in 1921 by Alexander Sutherland Neill in the belief that the school should be made to fit the child, rather than the other way around.

References

aan het Rot, M., Zarate, C., Charney, D. S., & Mathew, S. J. (2012). Ketamine for depression: Where do we go from here? *Biological Psychiatry, 72*(7), 537–547. doi: 10.1016/j.biopsych.2012.05.003

Bonny, H. L., & Pahnke, W. N. (1972). The use of music in psychedelic (LSD) therapy. *Journal of Music Therapy, 9*, 64–87.

Carhart-Harris, R. L., Erritzoe, D., Williams, T., Stone, J. M., Reed, L. J., Colasanti, A., ... Nutt, D. J. (2012). Neural correlates of the psychedelic state as determined by fMRI studies with psilocybin. *Proceedings of the National Academy of Sciences of the United States of America, 109*(6), 2138–2143. doi:10.1073/pnas.1119598109

Carhart-Harris, R. L., & Friston, K. J. (2010). The default-mode, ego-functions and free-energy: A neurobiological account of Freudian ideas. *Brain, 133*(4), 1265–1283. doi:10.1093/brain/awq010

Greer, G., & Strassman, R. J. (1985). Information on "Ecstasy." *The American Journal of Psychiatry, 142*(11), 1391.

Grof, S., Pahnke, W. N., Kurland, A. A., & Goodman, L. E. (1971). LSD-assisted psychotherapy in patients with terminal cancer. Presented at the Fifth Symposium of the Foundation of Thanatology, New York City, November 12, 1971.

Kellogg, J., Mac Rae, M., Bonny, H. L., & di Leo, F. (1977). The use of the mandala in psychological evaluation and treatment. *American Journal of Art Therapy, 16*(4), 123–134.

Kurland, A. A., Pahnke, W. N., Unger, S., Savage, C., & Goodman, L. E. (1968). Psychedelic psychotherapy (LSD) in the treatment of the patient with malignancy. *Excerpta Medica International Congress*, Series 180, 432–434.

Kurland, A. A., Savage, C., Pahnke, W. N., Grof, S., & Olsson, J. E. (1971). LSD in the treatment of alcoholics. *Pharmakopsychiatrie Neuro-Psychopharmakologie*, *4*(2), 84–94.

Laje, G., Lally, N., Mathews, D., Brutsche, N., Chemerinski, A., Akula, N., ... Zarate, C. (2012). Brain-derived neurotrophic factor Val66Met polymorphism and antidepressant efficacy of ketamine in depressed patients. *Biological Psychiatry, 72*(11), e27–e28. doi:10.1016/j.biopsych.2012.05. 031

Ling, T. M., & Buckman, J. (1960). The use of LSD in individual psychotherapy. *Proceedings of the Royal Society of Medicine*, *53*(11), 927–929.

Ling, T. M., & Buckman, J. (1963). *Lysergic acid and Ritalin in the treatment of neurosis.* London, UK: Lombarde Press.

Maeng, S., & Zarate, C. A. Jr. (2007). The role of glutamate in mood disorders: Results from the ketamine in major depression study and the presumed cellular mechanism underlying its antidepressant effects. *Current Psychiatry Reports*, *9*(6), 467–474.

Maeng, S., Zarate, C. A. Jr., Du, J., Schloesser, R. J., McCammon, J., Chen, G., & Manji, H. K. (2008). Cellular mechanisms underlying the antidepressant effects of ketamine: Role of alpha-amino-3-hydroxy-5-methylisoxazole-4-propionic acid receptors. *Biological Psychiatry*, *63*(4), 349–352. doi:10.1016/j.biopsych.2007.05.028

Naranjo, C. (1973). *The healing journey: New approaches to consciousness.* New York, NY: Pantheon.

Naranjo, C., Shulgin, A. T., & Sargent, T. (1967). Evaluation of 3,4-methylenedioxyamphetamine (MDA) as an adjunct to psychotherapy. *Medicina et Pharmacologia Experimentalis (International Journal of Experimental Medicine)*, *17*(4), 359–364.

Pahnke, W. N. (1963). Drugs and mysticism: An analysis of the relationship between psychedelic drugs and mystical consciousness. Cambridge, MA: Harvard University.

Pahnke, W. N., Kurland, A. A., Goodman, L. E., & Richards, W. A. (1969a). LSD-assisted psychotherapy with terminal cancer patients. *Current Psychiatric Therapies*, *9*, 144–152.

Pahnke, W. N., Kurland, A. A., Goodman, L. E., & Richards, W. A. (1969b). LSD-assisted psychotherapy with terminal cancer patients. In R. E. Hicks & P. J. Fink (Eds.), *Psychedelic drugs: Proceedings of a Hahneman Medical College and Hospital Symposium sponsored by the Department of Psychiatry*, 33–42. New York, NY: Grune & Stratton.

Pahnke, W. N., Kurland, A. A., Unger, S., & Savage, C. (1970). The experimental use of psychedelic (LSD) psychotherapy. In J. R. Gamage & E. L. Zerkin (Eds.), *Hallucinogenic drug research: Impact on science and society.* Beloit, WI: STASH Press.

Pahnke, W. N., Kurland, A. A., Unger, S., Savage, C., & Grof, S. (1970). The experimental use of psychedelic (LSD) psychotherapy. *Journal of the American Medical Association, 212*(11), 1856–1863.

Pahnke, W. N., Kurland, A. A., Unger, S., Savage, C., & Grof, S. (1971). The experimental use of psychedelic (LSD) psychotherapy. *Internationale Zeitschrift fur klinische Pharmakologie, Therapie, und Toxikologie, 4*(4), 446–454.

Pahnke, W. N., Kurland, A. A., Unger, S., Savage, C., Wolf, S., & Goodman, L. E. (1970). Psychedelic therapy (utilizing LSD) with cancer patients. *Journal of Psychedelic Drugs, 3*(1), 63–75.

Pahnke, W. N., & Richards, W. A. (1966). Implications of LSD and experimental mysticism. *Journal of Religion and Health, 5*(3), 175–208.

Reich, W. (1980). *Character analysis.* New York, NY: Farrar, Straus & Giroux.

Tjio, J. H., Pahnke, W. N., & Kurland, A. A. (1969). LSD and chromosomes: A controlled experiment. *Journal of the American Medical Association, 210*(5), 849–856.

Turek, I. S., Soskin, R. A., & Kurland, A. A. (1974). Methylenedioxyamphetamine (MDA) subjective effects. *Journal of Psychedelic Drugs, 6*(1), 7–13.

Yensen, R. (1975). The use of 3, 4 Methylenedioxyamphetamine (MDA) as an adjunct to brief intensive psychotherapy with neurotic outpatients (Doctoral dissertation). Available from ProQuest Dissertations & Theses Global. (Order No. 7607258)

Yensen, R. (1988). From mysteries to paradigms: Humanity's journey from sacred plants to psychedelic drugs. *ReVISION, 10*(4), 31–50.

Yensen, R., di Leo, F. B., Rhead, J. C., Richards, W. A., Soskin, R. A., Turek, I. S., & Kurland, A. A. (1976). MDA-assisted psychotherapy with neurotic outpatients: A pilot study. *Journal of Nervous and Mental Disease, 163*(4), 233–245.

Ketamine:
An Overview of Its History and Use

Ketamine Psychedelic Psychotherapy: Focus on its Pharmacology, Phenomenology, and Clinical Applications

Eli Kolp, M.D., Harris L. Friedman, Ph.D.,
Evgeny Krupitsky, M.D., Ph.D., Karl Jansen, M.D.,
Mark Sylvester, M.D., M. Scott Young, Ph.D., Anna Kolp, B.A.

KETAMINE IS AN EXTREMELY INTERESTING SUBSTANCE, especially from a transpersonal healing perspective, as it not only has a wide range of potential clinical applications, including through what is here called ketamine psychedelic psychotherapy (KPP), but it is the only legally available (i.e., through a physician's off-label prescription without having to go through regulatory hurdles) substance within the United States that can reliably produce psychedelic experiences. Consequently, we review the literature on the clinical application of KPP, and focus on the phenomenology of ketamine-induced psychedelic experiences in terms of possible clinical applications within a transpersonal context.

Arylcyclohexylamines: Ketamine's Family Tree

The arylcyclohexylamines (also known as arylcyclohexamines or arylcyclohexan amines) were originally developed as anesthetics by Parke-Davis. Unlike all other anesthetic agents, except perhaps nitrous oxide, the arylcyclohexylamines do not generally extinguish consciousness, but instead appear to "dissociate" mind from body (thus the name of "dissociative anesthetics"). The arylcyclohexylamines predominantly block the N-methyl-D-aspartate (NMDA) receptor, a target for the neurotransmitter glutamate in the brain, and prevent the NMDA receptor from being activated by glutamate (Ahmadi & Mahmoudi, 2005; Ahmadi, Khalili, Hajikhani, & Naserbakht, 2011). In addition to NMDA antagonism, the arylcyclohexylamines produce μ opioid receptor agonism (Itzhak & Simon, 1984) and cause dopamine reuptake inhibition (Chaudieu et al., 1989). Some of the arylcyclohexylamines also produce sigma receptor agonistic (He et al., 1993), nACh receptor antagonistic (Eterović et al., 1999), and D_2 receptor agonistic (Seeman, Ko, & Tallerico, 2005) actions.

Antagonism of the NMDA receptor generates dissociative (hallucinogenic), anesthetic, neuroprotective and anticonvulsant effects; stimulation of the sigma and D_2 receptors contributes to hallucinogenic (psychomimetic) effects; activation of the μ-opioid receptor causes analgesic and anxiolytic effects; blockade of the dopamine transporter mediates stimulant and euphoriant effects (as well as adding to psychomimetic effects in higher doses); the combination of the two last qualities confers a strong antidepressant effect; and the combination of all the above pharmacological properties make the arylcyclohexylamines powerful psychedelic drugs.

The first member of the arylcyclohexylamine class to be discovered was phencyclidine. It was synthesized in 1926, eventually patented in 1953 by the Parke-Davis pharmaceutical company for use as an anesthetic agent for humans and animals, and was marketed under the brand name Sernyl (referring to serenity). By 1965, its use with humans was discontinued as clinical studies revealed that patients experienced what was then seen as "psychotic" symptoms when emerging from the drug's effects (so-called "emergence delirium"). Today, it is rarely used even in the veterinary community. However, it continues to be legally available for research purposes in the United States, but as a Schedule II controlled substance.

Phencyclidine re-emerged as a drug of abuse in the mid-1960s due to its strong euphoriant and psychedelic qualities. The drug was relatively easy and inexpensive to manufacture in clandestine laboratories and it quickly became popular on the streets, with names such as "angel dust" and PCP. PCP can be pressed into pills or put in capsules and swallowed. When ingested orally, effects are felt in 30 to 45 minutes and last from six to 24 hours. Doses of less than 5 mg produce euphoriant effects (feelings of elation and joy, relaxation, feelings of unreality and mild dissociation from the environment), while doses of 10 mg or more produce psychedelic effects (distorted sense of one's body, a feeling of weightlessness, distorted sense of time and space, visual and auditory hallucinations).

PCP use spread in the 1970s. When PCP is snorted or smoked (for example, users dipped tobacco or cannabis cigarettes in the liquid form of PCP or sprinkled its powder form on a leafy material like tobacco or cannabis), the effects are felt within four to five minutes and last from four to six hours. PCP can also be injected, although this appears to be a less common route of administration.

PCP use may have peaked around 1978, when *People* magazine called it the country's "number one" drug problem. PCP became infamous for its recurrent binges (so-called "runs"), when chronic users would take PCP repeatedly for two to three consecutive days at a time without eating or sleeping. It was estimated that at least seven million Americans used PCP on at least one occasion between 1975 and 1983. The American Psychiatric Association (APA) Diagnostic and Statistical Manual (DSM)-IV-TR (APA, 2000) devoted a separate chapter to this substance entitled "Phencyclidine-Related Disorder." By the mid-1980s, PCP use began declining, perhaps partly as a result of the increased popularity of ketamine and crack cocaine. Eventually, PCP use slowly faded away, although there is still some manufacture by clandestine chemists. Today PCP is classified as a hallucinogen and the new APA (2013) DSM-5 places its effects in the Hallucinogen-Related Disorder category, with classical hallucinogens.

The second compound from the arylcyclohexylamines class, eticyclidine, was also developed by Parke-Davis and evaluated for anesthetic potential under the code name CI-400. Eticyclidine is very similar in effects to phencyclidine and is slightly more potent. Parke-Davis did not continue its research of eticyclidine after the development of ketamine, a similar drug with more favorable properties. Nevertheless, eticyclidine (under the name of PCE) did make its way to the streets and was briefly abused in the 1970s and 1980s. It did not become popular with recreational users due to its unpleasant taste and tendency to cause nausea. Eticyclidine was placed into the U.S. Schedule I list of illegal drugs in the 1970s and its use is unknown today.

Ketamine was the third compound from the class of arylcyclohexylamines that Parke-Davis developed as part of an effort to find a safer and more predictable anesthetic agent than its precursors. Unlike the first two creations of Parke-Davis, ketamine proved to be the most promising compound and eventually became the company's most successful anesthetic, sedative, analgesic, anxiolytic, and neuroprotective agent.

Ketamine Pharmacology

Ketamine hydrochloride, a phencyclidine derivative, was originally invented in 1962 by the American organic chemist Calvin Stevens, who initially called the compound CI-581 and later renamed it ketamine. Ketamine, like all the arylcyclohexylamines, predominantly targets the neurotransmitter glutamate, which is an excitatory messenger that turns on the brain cells and triggers an electrical impulse. Ketamine opposes this action by blocking the N-methyl-D-aspartate (NMDA receptor). It prevents the NMDA receptor from being activated by glutamate (Anish, Berry, Burton, & Lodge, 1983; Thomson, West, & Lodge, 1985). Ketamine also has direct and/or indirect effects on the μ opioid (Fink & Nagai, 1982; Fidecka, 1987; Freya, Latish, Schmidhammer, & Portoghese, 1994; Herman, Vocci, & Bridge, 1995; Latasch & Freye, 1993; Smith et al., 1980; Winters et al., 1988), dopamine (French, Mura, & Wang, 1993; Irifune, Shimizu, & Nomoto, 1991; Irifune et al., 1997; Keita, Lecharny, Henzel, Desmonts, & Mantz, 1996; Nishimura & Sato, 1999; Rao, Kim, Lehmann, Martin, & Wood, 1990), serotonin (Kim, Park, & Park, 1998; Lindefors et al., 1997; Martin, 1982; Minami, Minami, & Harris, 1997; Pallotta, Segieth, & Whitton, 1998), acetylcholine (Cohen, Chan, & Trevor, 1973; Durieux & Nietgen, 1997; Mimura et al., 1992; Morita et al., 1995; Toro-Matos, Rendon-Platas, Avila-Valdez, & Villarreal-Guzman, 1980), GABA (Drejer & Honore, 1987; Lindefors et al., 1997), cannabinoid (Richardson, Aanonsen, & Hargreaves, 1998; Stella, Schweitzer, & Piomelli, 1997), nitric oxide (Abajian, Page, & Morgan, 1973; Carroll, Lac, Asencio, & Kragh, 1990; Galley & Webster, 1996; Lin, Chiou, & Wang, 1996) and sigma (Hustveit, Maurset, & Oye, 1995) systems.

Ketamine hydrochloride may be administered via a variety of routes including oral, sublingual, rectal, intranasal, intramuscular, and intravenous routes. Ketamine is a highly lipid soluble chemical and, as a result, its clinical effects present within 45 to 50 seconds of administration when given intravenously, within three to four minutes when given intramuscularly, within five to 10 minutes when given intranasally, and within 20 to 30 minutes when given orally (Alonso-Serra & Wesley, 2003). The 1992 version of the Physicians' Desk Reference (PDR) indicated that ketamine use is usually devoid of life-threatening side effects and that several instances of unintentional administration of overdoses of ketamine of up to 10 times that usually required for surgical anesthesia have been followed by prolonged but complete recovery (PDR Network, 1992).

More than 10,000 published reports describe ketamine's high level of effectiveness and its confirmed biological safety in most cases, although like all drugs there is the possibility of some adverse effects in some people (Bauman, Kish, Baumann, & Politis, 1999; Dachs & Innes, 1997; Ersek, 2004; Reich & Silvay, 1989; Ross & Fochtman, 1995; Shapiro, Wyte, & Harris, 1972). Clinical studies have generally detected no long-term impairment of behavior or personality functioning as a result of repeated ketamine use (Siegal, 1978), but some individual case studies of ketamine dependence have raised questions at times (e.g., Jansen, 1990, 2000, summary in Jansen, 2001) and there have been some recent concerns about, for example, toxicity to the urinary system (e.g., Selby et al., 2008; Wood, 2013).

According to several in vitro and animal studies, ketamine can even have neuroprotective properties under some circumstances (Hoffman et al., 1992; Shapira, Artru, & Lam, 1992; Shapira, Lam, Eng, Laohaprasit, & Michel, 1994). Subsequently, ketamine has been used as a neuroprotective agent to prevent brain damage from head trauma, strokes, heart attacks, epileptic seizures, low oxygen levels, and low blood-sugar levels (Albanese et al., 1997; Bar-Joseph, Guilburd, Tamir, & Guilburd, 2009; Filanovsky, Miller, & Kao, 2010; Hirota & Lambert, 1996; Hughes, 2011; Mayberg, Lam, Matta, Domino, & Winn, 1995; Rothman et al., 1987; Shapira et al., 1994; Weiss, Goldberg, & Choi, 1986).

Ketamine Biochemistry and Electrophysiology

Extensive research of the biochemical aspects of ketamine has been done by one of us, a Russian researcher, Evgeny Krupitsky, and a U.S. researcher, John Krystal, who both have conducted extensive independent studies since the 1980s. Krupitsky and Krystal later collaborated in researching the biochemistry of ketamine (Krupitsky et al., 2001; Krystal et al., 2003a).

Krupitsky conducted ketamine studies at the Center for Research in Addiction and Psychopharmacology in St. Petersburg, Russia, researching the effects of ketamine administration on metabolism of biogenic amines, including dopamine, serotonin, monoamine oxidase type A (MAO-A), monoamine oxidase type B (MAO-B), GABA, ceruloplasmin, and B-endorphin. The results of these biochemical investigations show that during the ketamine session, dopamine levels were increased, serotonin and GABA concentrations were not altered significantly, ceruloplasmin activity and the B-endorphin levels were increased, and the activity of MAO-A in blood serum and MAO-B in blood platelets significantly decreased. The results provided biochemical data showing that the pharmacological actions of ketamine affect monoaminergic and opioidergic neurotransmitter metabolism (Krupitsky et al., 1990).

These changes in the metabolism of neurotransmitters allow some opinions to be formed about the underlying neurochemical mechanisms of ketamine's psychedelic action. For example, an increase of ceruloplasmin activity causes a corresponding increase in the conversion of monoamines into adrenochromes, which have hallucinogenic activity (Anokhina, 1975; Nalbandyan, 1986). This particularly takes place under the conditions of inhibited MAO activity and increased dopamine levels. This is of interest because such conditions are typical for the action of many classical hallucinogens (Hamox, 1984; McKenna, Towers, & Abbott, 1984). The fact that the pharmacological actions of ketamine affected both monoaminergic and opioidergic systems, two neurochemical systems involved in pathogenesis of alcoholism, is an important result of this biochemical investigation, as it is possible that these actions contribute to the efficacy of KPP.

Krupitsky has also used EEG computer-assisted data in studying underlying mechanisms of KPP (Krupitsky & Grinenko, 1997). EEG recordings were taken before, during, and after the ketamine session by placing 16 electrodes according to the international scheme. After analog-digital conversion, standard programs of computer assisted spectral EEG analysis and topographic mapping of EEG were employed. The data of EEG computer-assisted analysis demonstrated that ketamine increases delta activity (1.5–2×) and particularly theta activity (3–4×) in all regions of the cerebral cortex. This is evidence of limbic system activation during ketamine sessions, as well as evidence of the reinforcement of the limbic cortex interaction (Pribram, 1971). These findings can also be considered to a certain extent as indirect evidence of the strengthening of the interactions between the so-called conscious and unconscious levels of the mind during KPP (Simonov, 1987).

There are also some data indicating that the interaction between the frontal cortex and the limbic system are important for the action of ketamine on the brain. Previously, it has been demonstrated in positron emission tomography (PET) with fluorodeoxyglucose (FDG) studies that ketamine-induced disturbances of glutamatergic neurotransmission results in a specific hyperfrontal metabolic pattern in the human brain associated with psychedelic experiences, specifically visionary experience and ego-dissolution (Vollenweider et al., 1994). Also, frontal lobotomy reduces the psychedelic response to phencyclidine in schizophrenic patients (Itil, Keskiner, Kiremitci, & Holden, 1967). Ketamine activates the interaction between brain structures associated with cognitive processing of information (frontal cortex) and structures involved in the processes of emotions, motivations, memory, and subconscious experiences and perceptions (limbic structures). Such enhanced interaction may be an important neurophysiological mechanism underlying the phenomenology of ketamine psychedelic experiences and the dramatic psychological changes caused by those experiences.

John Krystal, chair of the department of psychiatry at Yale University School of Medicine, directed ketamine research at the Connecticut Mental Health Center in New Haven. He utilized ketamine primarily as a psychomimetic agent to study the neurobiology of schizophrenia, and focused on ketamine's effects on perceptual and cognitive functioning (Krystal et al., 1994, 1998a, 1998b, 1999, 2000). Krystal's group also collected a substantial body of evidence demonstrating that ketamine's major underlying mechanism of action on the brain is the blockade of the N-methyl-D-aspartate (NMDA) receptors, which are mostly located in the cortex and hippocampus and are involved in processes of integration and transmission into the cortex of incoming signals from all sensory modalities (Krystal et al., 1994). This finding was confirmed by another group of investigators (Oye, Paulsen, & Maurset, 1992), verifying that a significant reduction of sensory transmission and activation of autonomous cortex-limbic interactions may be important underlying mechanisms of the psychedelic action of ketamine.

In addition, Krystal's group completed clinical research studying the effect of ketamine's NMDA glutamate receptor antagonist response in recovering ethanol-dependent patients (Krystal et al., 1998b). Twenty male patients with alcoholism who had not consumed alcohol for 10 days to four weeks prior to the study completed three test days that involved the administration of very low (0.1 mg/kg) and low-to-medium (0.5 mg/kg) doses of ketamine or saline solution under randomized double-blind conditions. Ethanol-like subjective effects were assessed using visual analog scales to measure "high" and degree of similarity to ethanol, cocaine, and cannabis, and also employed a scale assessing the number of standard alcohol drinks producing similar subjective effects. This team concluded that ketamine produced ethanol-like effects in a dose-related way on each scale, exhibiting similarity to ethanol. However, its effects were judged more similar to the sedative, rather than stimulant, alcohol effects. Ketamine effects also were more like ethanol than cannabis or cocaine. Ethanol-like effects were more prominent at the higher ketamine dose, a dose rated as similar to greater levels of ethanol intoxication. The production of ethanol-like subjective effects by ketamine supports the potential clinical importance of NMDA receptor antagonism among the mechanisms underlying the subjective effects of ethanol in humans (Krystal et al., 1998b; Krystal et al., 2003b).

Ketamine Development

In 1964, ketamine was officially tested on the first human subjects, the inmates at the Jackson Prison in the State of Michigan. The study was done by Edward Domino, MD, an American clinical pharmacologist (Domino, Chodoff, & Corssen, 1965). Domino was the first investigator to discover that ketamine has multiple pharmacological effects, including anesthetic, analgesic, and antidepressant effects.

Domino was also the first researcher who discovered the "schizophrenomimetic" (hallucinogenic) properties of ketamine. He reported that most of his subjects described strange experiences like feeling "spaced out" and "floating" (Domino, 2010). Initially, Domino used the word "dreaming" to describe the drug's hallucinogenic effect. However, the Parke-Davis scientists did not like that name out of the company's concerns that the U.S. Food and Drug Administration (FDA) may label ketamine as "psychotomimetic," which might stop the clinical development of a very promising pharmaceutical. Domino discussed the unusual actions of ketamine with his wife and mentioned that the subjects were "disconnected" from their environment. His wife came up with the term "dissociative anesthetic" that "dissociates" so-called mind from body (Domino, 2010). From that time, the "dissociative anesthetic" name has been assigned not only to ketamine hydrochloride, but also to the entire class of psychoactive arylcyclohexylamines.

In 1966, Parke-Davis patented ketamine under the brand name Ketalar for use as an anesthetic in humans and animals. Ketamine was successfully tried on American soldiers in the Vietnam War (when it got nicknamed the "buddy drug" because it could be administered by a corpsman or a fellow soldier due to its relative safety and ease of administration). In the course of the Vietnam War, it became the most widely used battlefield anesthetic, sedative, and analgesic, giving an excellent opportunity for American anesthesiologists and surgeons to become familiar with the agent.

Ketamine rapidly became the drug of the choice used by the U.S. military for CASEVAC, a military term for the emergency patient evacuation of casualties from a combat zone to a clearing station or a nearby hospital, increasingly by helicopter in the jungle wars. In most cases a wounded soldier would be in a hospital receiving medical care within 35 minutes of being wounded. Patients were moved directly from the battlefield directly into the preoperative and resuscitation shelter while under the effects of field-administered ketamine.

Impressively, the use of ketamine as an agent for analgesia and conscious sedation during battlefield-casualty evacuations helped to decrease the mortality rate of wounded soldiers who made it to medical treatment from 4.5% during the Korean War to 2.6% during the Vietnam War. The U.S. soldiers knew that, if they were wounded, they had a better chance of surviving and quickly receiving medical care than in any other war in which the United States had previously participated, a fact that did much to boost troop morale (Vietnam Studies, Department of the Army, 1973).

Eventually, in 1970, the FDA approved the use of ketamine anesthesia with children, adults, and the elderly. Since that time, ketamine has been widely used in hospitals and for office procedures due to its rapid onset, short duration of action, and superior safety. Ketamine has now been in clinical practice for 50 years and has been continually used as a usually very safe anesthetic to evoke general anesthesia, a first line agent to induce procedural conscious sedation, a potent non-opiate analgesic to control both acute and chronic pain, a unique neuroprotective agent to prevent brain damage, a superior anxiolytic to control preoperative and end-of-life anxiety, a rapid-onset antidepressant to treat chronic depression and other treatment-resistant psychiatric conditions, and, for a period, the only legal hallucinogenic drug available to conduct psychedelic psychotherapy (although there has been some forward movement in that regard in recent years, with some work recommencing using substances such as psilocybin and DMT; Friedman, 2006).

Unsurprisingly, ketamine has also become popular on "the streets" for its strong euphoriant effects and potent hallucinogenic properties. There are some matters of relevance to therapeutic issues to be learned from its nonmedical and recreational use, so this paper also reviews some of that material.

Ketamine Pharmacotherapy

It has been proposed (Haas & Harper, 1992; White, Way, & Trevor, 1982) that the "ideal" agent for anesthesia must possess the following specific characteristics:

- Effective in inducing anesthesia
- Minimal cardiovascular effects
- Minimal respiratory effects
- Ability to titrate
- Rapid onset of action
- Predictable duration of effect
- Short elimination half-life
- Anxiolytic at subanesthetic doses
- Analgesic in subanesthetic doses
- Soluble in water
- Stable in solution
- Absence of pain on injection
- Absence of post-injection irritation.

A few classes of drugs, such as the opioids, barbiturates, and benzodiazepines, meet some, but not all, of these criteria. Today, ketamine is one of only a very few agents that regularly meets all of these criteria of an ideal anesthetic, when the dose is suitable for the patient and purpose. Certainly a large bolus dose of ketamine as a sudden intravenous push can affect respiration and intracranial pressure, but in that instance it can often be argued that the dose was not suitable for the patient and purpose. Ketamine is included in the 18th edition of the World Health Organization (2013) model list of essential medicines, promulgating its availability in a health system.

It has been a half a century since Domino administered ketamine to the first human subjects (Domino et al., 1965). Since then, ketamine has become widely accepted as an outstanding agent to reduce preoperative anxiety and facilitate induction of general anesthesia, as it appears to have virtually all of the desired properties of the ideal agent. Subsequently, ketamine has been used worldwide for an extensive range of various procedures, including preoperative sedation, intraoperative anesthesia, and postoperative analgesia (Haas & Harper, 1992).

While there are many anesthetic drugs available, internationally ketamine remains among the most popular general anesthetics, especially in the Developing World and emergency contexts, because of its low cost, ease of storage, advantageous airway and respiratory properties, hemodynamic stability, broad range of clinical applications, and excellent therapeutic index (Craven, 2007; USAARL Report, 2010). Ketamine's wide therapeutic window (Green, Clem, & Rothrock, 1996; Green et al., 1999; Strayer & Nelson, 2008) makes it the anesthetic of choice in austere or resource-poor environments where monitoring equipment may be rudimentary or absent and a single operator must provide the anesthetic and monitor a patient (Green et al., 1996; Strayer & Nelson, 2008). It can be administered via almost any route, although intravenous (IV) and intramuscular (IM) administrations are by far the most popular and best studied for surgical anesthesia (Mistry & Nahata, 2005). The initial dose of ketamine administered intravenously ranges from 1 mg/kg–4.5 mg/kg, and intramuscular doses range from 6.5–13 mg/kg (White et al., 1982). Ketamine is highly lipid soluble and, as such, clinical effects present within one minute of administration when given intravenously and within five minutes when given intramuscularly (Alonso-Serra & Wesley, 2003).

Today, the most frequent use of ketamine has been for conscious sedation for physically or emotionally painful procedures (procedural sedation) and analgesia for acute and chronic pain, both on the battlefield and in emergency departments worldwide, and also in veterinary medicine. For use in sedation only, the doses of ketamine are 0.5–0.75 mg/kg IV or 2–4 mg/kg IM; for use as an analgesic and/or anxiolytic agent, the doses of ketamine are 0.2–0.3 mg/kg IV, 0.5–1.5 mg/kg IM and intranasal, and 1–2 mg/kg sublingual, oral and rectal.

Peak plasma concentrations have been reported to occur within 1 min following IV administration, 5 to 15 minutes following IM injection, 30 minutes after oral administration and 45 minutes after rectal administration (Domino et al., 1984; Grant, Nimmo, & Clements, 1981; Pedraz et al., 1989). Elimination is primarily by the kidney, and only a small percentage is recovered in the urine as the unchanged drug (Chang, Savory, & Albin, 1970). The elimination half-life of ketamine is approximately 2 hours (Domino et al., 1984), although there are some longer estimates. Metabolites which are also active NMDA receptor blockers can sometimes be detected in urine for up to a week or more (e.g., Ebert, Mikkelsen, Thorkildsen, & Borgbjerg, 1997.)

When ketamine is administered in small (analgesic, anxiolytic, and sedative) doses, it does not usually impair spontaneous respirations and does not increase blood pressure and heart rate (Subramaniam, Subramaniam, & Steinbrook., 2004; Visser & Schug, 2006; White et al., 1982), which makes ketamine an especially desirable analgesic/anxiolytic/sedative for use on the battlefield and in evacuation procedures. Today, combat medics continue using ketamine for battlefield sedation and pain management because of its minimal impact on medic carrying capacity and ability to withstand environmental extremes. It is also much more field expedient than any other analgesic due to its low occurrence of side effects (Guldner, Petinaux, Clemens, Foster, & Antoine, 2006). In a recent review of analgesic options for pain relief on the battlefield, Black and McManus (2009) wrote that, in sub-anesthetic doses, ketamine is almost ideal as an analgesic due to providing profound-pain relief, potentiating opioids, preventing opioid hyperalgesia, and its margin of safety.

The use of ketamine by emergency physicians prior to the 1990s was infrequent (Green & Krauss, 2004a, 2004b). However, after a landmark study by Green and Johnson (1990), it has become one of the most popular agents for procedural sedation and analgesia in emergency departments. In their review of 11,589 administrations of ketamine for sedation, Green and Johnson (1990) firmly established the drug's safety and efficacy for medical use.

Since then, ketamine has been extensively used as an analgesic in intensive and acute care medicine (particularly in emergency medicine), and there has been considerable further research on the efficacy, safety, contraindications, guidelines, and dosing of ketamine (Green & Krauss, 2004a, 2004b; Lin & Durieux, 2005; Mistry & Nahata, 2005). It has been well documented that ketamine has a very low frequency of adverse effects in doses used for conscious sedation and analgesia (Alonso-Serra & Wesley, 2003; Cherry, Plummer, Gourlay, Coates, & Odgers, 1995; Howes, 2004; Jennings, Cameron, & Bernard, 2011; Porter, 2004). Today ketamine is routinely stocked in all emergency departments across the United States, Australia, New Zealand, and many other countries (Sacchetti, Senula, Strickland, & Dubin, 2007); due to its exceptional analgesic and sedative properties at low doses, ketamine has been widely used for treatment of acute postoperative pain, so-called breakthrough pain in patients with acute and/or chronic pain, and for management of neuropathic pain disorder, ischaemic limb pain disorder, refractory cancer pain, and as a pediatric sedation tool for use with acutely injured children (Bell, Dahl, Moore, & Kalso, 2006; Buvanendran & Kroin, 2009; Carr et al., 2004; Ellis, Husain, Saetta, & Walker, 2004; Green & Krauss., 2004a, 2004b; Howes, 2004; McGlone, Howes, & Joshi, 2004; Petrack, Marx, & Wright, 1996; Rakhee & Milap, 2005; Schmid Sandler, & Katz, 1999; Visser & Schug, 2006). In addition, low-dose ketamine has successfully served as an effective adjunct to standard opioid therapy, as well as an adjunct to various non-opiate analgesic agents (Schmid, Sandler, & Katz, 1999).

One of the reasons ketamine has been repeatedly studied and scrutinized is its uniqueness among all other sedatives, hypnotics, and analgesics (primarily opiates, barbiturates, and benzodiazepines). The standard definition of conscious procedural sedation is dose-dependent alterations in consciousness that result in mild to deep sedation, preserving responsiveness to verbal or tactile stimuli. Ketamine, in contrast, exerts its effect through a functional and electrophysiological dissociation or disconnect between the thalamo-neocortical and limbic areas of the brain (Green & Krauss, 2004a, 2004b; Krupitsky & Grinenko, 1997; Mistry & Nahata, 2005). Therefore, it does not have a characteristic dose-response continuum by progressive titration; the dissociation is present or absent with a very narrow transition zone (Mistry & Nahata, 2005). At doses below a certain threshold, ketamine produces analgesia and anxiolysis; however, once the critical dosage threshold of roughly 1–1.5 mg/kg IM (or 0.5–0.75 mg/kg IV) is reached, the characteristic dissociative state abruptly appears (Krauss & Green, 2006). Furthermore, dissociation is described as a "trance--like cataleptic state" of "sensory isolation" (Mistry & Nahata, 2005), meaning little or no responsiveness is present.

Most importantly, unlike other traditional sedatives, ketamine usually preserves cardiovascular stability, spontaneous respirations and protective airway reflexes, even when exerting its full effect (Green & Krauss, 2004a, 2004b; Mistry & Nahata, 2005). Because of this, the dissociative state is not consistent with the definitions of conscious sedation (Green & Krauss, 2004a, 2004b; Krauss & Green, 2000, 2006), which has resulted in a separate definition for ketamine procedural sedation, namely "dissociative sedation" (American College of Emergency Physicians, 2005). It should be noted that ketamine is a nonreversible agent; once the dissociative state is initiated, it cannot be aborted (Alonso-Serra & Wesley, 2003; White et al., 1982).

Ketamine performs as a superior fast-acting analgesic and anxiolytic in low doses (0.2–0.3 mg/kg IV, 0.5–1 mg/kg IM and intranasal, and 1–2 mg/kg sublingual and oral), as an effective reliable sedative in medium doses (0.5–0.75 mg/kg IV, 1.5–4 mg/kg IM), and a safe short-acting anesthetic in high doses (1–4.5 mg/kg IV and 6.5 –13 mg/kg IM).

Ketamine-Induced Emergence Phenomena

Although ketamine is biologically safe in most instances of medical use and has an excellent safety profile, it is not without controversy, as it generates peculiar psychological side effects (vivid imagery, visual hallucinations, excitement, irrational behavior) dubbed "emergence delirium," it has a high dependence potential when abused, and use in a drug-abuse context has recently resulted in multiple reports of harm to the kidney and bladder (cystitis) in some people (e.g., Bokor & Anderson 2014; Meng et al., 2013; Selby et al., 2008; Tam et al., 2014; Wood, 2013). This has become a fairly hot topic in, for example, Hong Kong urology, where ketamine abuse is rife, but appears not to have been specifically reported by long-term heavy users of medically-sourced ketamine such as John Lilly, and those who contributed to one of our author's (Jansen, 2001) book, *Ketamine: Dreams And Realities*. However, some of the latter did complain of mysterious "K pains" in the pelvic region, and it seems increasingly likely that these persons may have been susceptible to these urological issues as the evidence continues to mount, from multiple medical specialists in multiple countries, that some long-term heavy users are susceptible to urological side effects. There have also now been animal studies pointing to a mechanism (e.g., Gu et al., 2014), so this is unlikely to be one of those random panics that have characterized the War on Drugs (e.g., scare tactics, such as "LSD damages your chromosomes") that were later discredited as propaganda (Dishotsky, Loughman, Mogar, & Lipscomb, 1971.)

Domino was the first clinician who documented that 30% of patients had an "emergence delirium" after ketamine anesthesia (Domino et al., 1965). Subsequently, he asked Parke-Davis to contact Elliot Luby, a psychiatrist at the Lafayette Clinic, who had previously used phencyclidine (Sernyl) to induce the same phenomena in normal volunteers and psychiatric patients (Domino, 2010). The Parke-Davis researchers were concerned that Luby would conclude that ketamine was schizophrenomimetic, which would perhaps result in the Parke-Davis executives and lawyers stopping its development. It was a reasonable concern, as Luby earlier documented that phencyclidine-induced states had similarity to "schizophrenic syndrome" (Luby, Cohen, Rosenbaum, Gottlieb, & Kelley, 1959). Consequently, Parke-Davis insisted that their own psychiatrist observed the subjects recovering from ketamine anesthesia. This psychiatrist concluded the subjects had an emergence reaction quite similar to diethyl ether (Domino, 2010).

Emergence delirium is not a new phenomenon in clinical practice. Eckenhoff and colleagues (1961) had reported the signs of "hyperexcitation" in patients "emerging" from diethyl ether, phencyclidine, or cyclopropane anesthesia. This phenomenon refers to a clinical condition in which patients experience a variety of "behavioral disturbances," including crying, disorientation, sobbing, and thrashing during early emergence from anesthesia (Eckenhoff et al., 1961). Emergence delirium (a.k.a. "emergence reaction," "emergence agitation" and "emergence excitation") is defined as the disturbance of a patient's attention to and awareness of the environment accompanied by disorientation, hyperactive motor behavior, and perceptual alterations immediate postanesthesia (Sikich & Lerman, 2004).

Parke-Davis understandably selected the less frightening name of "emergence phenomenon" rather than "delirium," and seems to have underreported the frequency of this controversial side effect. For many years, Parke-Davis reported on their ketamine (Ketalar) data sheet that the frequency of emergence phenomena was only 12%. This number was too low, however, and was eventually dropped from their later data sheet (Parke-Davis Product Information Sheet, 1999-2000). The actual percentage reporting emergence phenomena after ketamine anesthesia is close to 40% in many studies (Abajian et al., 1973; Hervey & Hustead, 1972; Khorramzadeh & Lofty, 1973; Krestow, 1974; O'Neil, Winnie, Zadigian, & Collins, 1972; Overton, 1975; Sadove, Shulman, & Fevgold, 1971). One study even reported a 100% incidence range of emergence phenomenon (Garfield, Garfield, Stone, Hopkins, & Johns, 1972).

It was quickly discovered that "emergence phenomena" may occur independently of anesthesia and can be reliably generated by an administration of a sub-anesthetic dose of ketamine. Collier reported that, at one-sixth to one-tenth of the dose used for general anesthesia, ketamine can create psychedelic experiences with disconnection from surroundings, perception of floating, becoming disembodied as a mind or soul, and even dying and going to a different world (Collier, 1972). He also noted that loss of reality contact appears more pronounced than with other psychedelics. In addition, Collier reported that dissociative experiences often seemed so authentic that users were not sure whether they had or had not actually become "disembodied."

The discovery that ketamine is a powerful psychedelic drug did not end its popularity as an outstanding anesthetic agent. Instead, use of benzodiazepines (the most frequently used are midazolam, lorazepam, and diazepam) and increasingly propofol have been utilized to control emergence problems due to their strong amnestic and dream-suppressing properties. In addition, the combined use of ketamine and benzodiazepines or propofol has the advantage of providing increased sedation and anxiolysis (Cartwright & Pingel, 1984; Domino et al., 1984; Dundee, 1990; Haas & Harper, 1992; Tobin, 1982; Toft & Romer, 1987; White et al., 1982; White et al., 1988).

Ketamine as a Psychedelic Drug

The ketamine dissociative experience (emergence phenomena) is, in fact, a non-ordinary state of consciousness (NOSC) during which the individual's awareness and perception are dramatically changed and radically refocused. This psychedelic experience is often induced by IM injections of ketamine in doses that are typically used for dissociative sedation and lasts from 45 minutes to one hour. The patient completely loses contact with external reality and gets involved in a profound psychedelic experience. The ketamine-induced non-ordinary states of consciousness may include any of the following:

- Feelings of leaving one's body (i.e., out-of-body experience)
- Awareness of becoming a non-physical being
- Emotionally intense visions (e.g., of deceased relatives, "angels," "spirits")
- Encounters with archetypal beings (e.g., Christ, Buddha, Krishna)
- Encounters with nonterrestrial beings (e.g., "space aliens")
- Visits to mythological realms of consciousness
- Re-experiencing the birth process

- Vivid dreams and memories of past or future incarnations
- Experience of psychological death and rebirth of self (i.e., near-death experience)
- Feelings of ego dissolution and loss of identity
- Experience of reliving one's life
- Deep feelings of peace and joy
- Sense of transcending normal time and space
- Feelings of interconnectedness with all people and nature
- Feelings of cosmic unity with the Universe and God
- Sense of sacredness
- Profound sense of ineffability of the experience
- Intuitive belief that the experience is a source of objective truth about the nature of "absolute reality."

(Collier, 1972; Jansen, 1989a, 1989b, 1997; Khorramzadeh & Lofty, 1976; Kolp et al., 2006, 2007; Krupitsky et al., 1992; Krupitsky & Grinenko, 1996, 1997; Krupitsky & Kolp, 2007; Lilly, 1968; Moore & Alltounian, 1978; Weil & Rosen, 1983).

John Lilly, an American neuroscientist, psychiatrist, and "psychonaut" (explorer of his own mind, often with the aid of substances), began a series of self-experiments with psychedelic substances in the early 1960s. Initially, he used LSD, which he sometimes self-administered in a sensory isolation flotation tank (Lilly, 1972). Circa 1971, Lilly started an exploration of the use of ketamine by self-administering various doses of ketamine via intramuscular injections, often using an isolation tank to enhance its effects (Lilly, 1978).

Lilly documented a relationship between dosage levels and the qualities of ketamine experiences that he himself had. He reported that intramuscular injections of ketamine at 25 mg did not cause visual images, whereas over 30 mg it produced such images when eyes are closed. At above 50 mg, visual images became stronger; however, in his case there was no dissociation of the mind from the body. At above 75 mg, visual images significantly increased and feelings of detachment of the mind from the body began. At above 100 mg, visual images became intense even when the eyes were open, and feelings of complete dissociation of the mind from the body were common. At above 150 mg, the mind completely disconnected from the body and feelings of total dissolution of ego were common. The doses above 300 mg produced unconsciousness (Lilly, 1978). However, like many long-term ketamine users, Lilly developed a notable tolerance to ketamine over the years, and thus his own dose-response relationships changed (summarized in Jansen, 2001). Lilly proposed utilizing ketamine as a psychotherapeutic agent by using ketamine-induced non-ordinary states of consciousness for reprogramming the interface of brain-mind, and also described ketamine's antidepressant effects (Lilly, 1972).

Ketamine-Induced Non-Ordinary States of Consciousness

Ketamine induces at least four distinct NOSCs that depend on at least three major factors (as is the case with all other classical hallucinogenic substances): the dose of ketamine, the physical "setting" of the ketamine administration, and the mindset (often just referred to as "set") of the person prior to the ketamine administration [see table 1]. These different states of consciousness may be partly distinguished by a) the degree of a dissociation of the mind from the body; and b) the degree of ego dissolution.

In considering the effects of substances on a person, among other factors it is necessary to consider the dose taken, how it is taken, and the speed at which it is taken, the size and gender of the person, other substances taken (either before, at the same time or afterwards), the tolerance of the individual, and the set and setting. The term set includes personality, past experiences, mental health, mood, motivations, intelligence, imagination, attitudes, what is going on in his or her life, and his or her expectations. The term setting refers to the conditions of use, including the physical, social, and emotional environment, including the other people present.

The first state is an empathogenic (or "generating a state of empathy" or "heart-opening") experience. The term "empathogenic" was proposed in the early 1980s by Ralph Metzner, and is generated in response to an injection of a low sub-psychedelic dose of ketamine, the type of dose that may be used for anxiolysis and/or analgesia (0.25 mg/kg–0.5 mg/kg IM, or 25 mg–50 mg IM). This state lasts from 45 minutes to two hours and may be characterized by the following features:

- The awareness of the body remains well-preserved
- The body feels very comfortable and relaxed
- The ego functioning is well-maintained; however, the ego defenses are significantly lessened

Table 1. Ketamine-induced non-ordinary states of consciousness

State	Features	Typical Ketamine Dose	Duration
Empathogenic Experience	Awareness of body; comfort and relaxation; reduced ego defenses; empathy, compassion, and warmth; love and peace; euphoria; mind is dreamy with non-specific colorful visual effects.	Low sub-psychedelic dose similar to that used for anxiolysis and/or analgesia (0.25 mg/kg – 0.5 mg/kg IM, or 25 – 50 mg IM)	45 – 60 mins
Out-of-Body Experience (OBE)	Complete separation from one's body; significantly diminished ego defenses; visits to mythological realms of consciousness; encounters with non-terrestial beings; emotionally intense visions (e.g. deceased relatives, spirits); vivid dreams of past and future incarnations; re-experiencing the birth process.	Medium psychedelic dose such as that used for mild conscious dissociative sedation (0.75 mg/kg – 1.5 mg/kg IM, or 75 mg – 125 mg IM)	45 – 60 mins
Near-Death Experience (NDE)	Departure from one's body; complete ego dissolution/loss of identity; experienced physical (body) and psychological (mind) death; experience being a single point of consciousness simply aware of itself; reliving one's life; aware of how actions have affected others, with moral judgment of self.	High psychedelic dose such as that used for moderate to severe conscious dissociative sedation (2.0 mg/kg – 3.0 mg/kg IM, or 150 – 250 mg IM)	45 – 60 mins
Ego-Dissolving Transcendental Experience	Ecstatic state of the dissolution of boundaries between the self and external reality; complete dissolution of one's body and self (soul); transcending normal mass/time/space continuum; collective consciousness; unity with Nature/Universe; sacredness.	Rare in low doses (0.25 mg/kg – 0.5 mg/kg IM, or 25 – 50 mg IM), more common in high psychedelic doses (2.0 mg/kg – 3.0 mg/kg IM, or 150 – 200 mg IM)	45 – 60 mins

- The person experiences feelings of empathy and compassion for themselves

- The mind feels emotional warmth, well-being, and joy

- Strong feelings of love and peace are prevailing

- Feelings of euphoria, pleasure and joy are common

- Feelings of ecstasy and enhanced sensuality are frequent

- The mind is dreamy with frequent nonspecific colorful visual effects

- The person may feel they have forgiveness and understanding of themselves and for those with whom they have important relationships.

It is also entirely possible for these doses to produce marked dysphoria and other unpleasant changes in mental and physical state. This is far more likely to happen if the set and setting are negative.

The empathogenic NOSC is like the state induced by sub-psychedelic doses of classical hallucinogenic substances (LSD, psilocybin, DMT, mescaline, etc.), or regular doses of classical empathogenic substances (MDA, MDMA, 2-CB, etc.). This state can be combined with guided imagery or verbalized meditations and may sometimes be utilized to resolve long-standing intra-psychic conflicts, to treat the after effects of trauma in the victims of physical and sexual abuse or other assault, to control the symptoms of post-traumatic stress disorder (e.g., in soldiers), or to resolve interpersonal problems in spousal and family relationships. Unlike the other three NOSC, which are more intense and overpowering, an empathogenic experience is more likely to leave the patient with an ability to consciously recall this particular non-ordinary state of consciousness.

The second NOSC is an "out-of-body experience" (OBE), and may be induced in response to an injection of a medium psychedelic dose of ketamine, which is in the range used for mild conscious dissociative sedation (0.75 mg/kg–1.5 mg/kg IM, or 75 mg–125 mg IM). This state lasts from 45 minutes to one hour and may be characterized by the following features:

- Feelings of complete separation from one's body
- The ego defenses are significantly diminished; however, the rudimentary ego structure is still preserved and the experiencer is well aware of the self
- Awareness of becoming a non-corporeal being
- Apparent visits to mythological realms of consciousness
- Apparent encounters with non-terrestrial beings (e.g., "space aliens")
- Emotionally intense visions (e.g., deceased relatives, "angels," "spirits")
- Encounters with archetypal beings (e.g., Krishna, Buddha, Christ)
- Vivid dreams and memories of past or future incarnations
- Re-experiencing the birth process.

This NOSC is similar to the state that can sometimes be induced by medium doses of classical hallucinogenic substances (LSD, psilocybin, mescaline, etc.), although the visions are more realistic, well-defined, and frequently get organized into a specific "story." This type of experience can bring to the conscious awareness a plethora of unconscious material and may be utilized as an adjunct to psychodynamic psychotherapy. This state may sometimes be enhanced when combined with calm, evocative music (e.g., classical, Trance, or New Age) to assist with relaxation and immersion into the experience. Unlike an empathogenic experience, OBE leaves the person with only a partial ability to consciously recall all details of this particular NOSC after the experience, partly due to an avalanche of phantasmagoric visions and sensory overload, and partly for physical reasons as more extensive NMDA receptor blockade interferes with memory formation (Collingridge, 1987; Jansen, 1990a, 1990b).

The third NOSC is a "near-death experience" (NDE), which may be induced by an injection of a high psychedelic dose of ketamine, in the range that may be used for moderate to severe conscious dissociative sedation (2.0 mg/kg–3.0 mg/kg IM, or 150–250 mg IM). This state lasts from 45 minutes to one hour and is characterized by the following features:

- Feelings of complete departure from one's body
- Feelings of complete ego dissolution and loss of identity
- A strong belief of being physically dead
- Experience of psychological death of the mind (the self)
- Feelings of becoming a single point of consciousness (the Self, or a soul) that is simply aware of itself with no other points of reference
- Sensations of moving through a tunnel
- Experience of reliving one's entire life
- Becoming aware that one is responsible for every thought, word, and action of one's life prior to the NDE
- Awareness of how others were affected by one's thoughts, words, and actions
- Performing the moral judgment of the self based on one's own sense of right and wrong, holding one accountable for one's thoughts, words, and actions
- Experience of visiting non-physical realities (either paradisiacal or hellish realms of consciousness) based on one's own self-judgment

- Encounters with non-corporeal entities
- Experience of visiting an eternal, featureless void (nothingness)
- Experience of psychological rebirth of the ego.

This NOSC is similar to the state that is sometimes induced by high doses of classical hallucinogenic substances (e.g., LSD, psilocybin, DMT, mescaline), although the visions may be more intense, well-structured, and liable to become organized into a form of life review. Some research has found that approximately 70% of NDEs are accompanied by feelings of calm and peace, while about 30% of NDEs are very frightening (Greyson, 1983; Greyson & Stevenson, 1980). This NOSC type of experience can sometimes bring enhanced insight into one's deeds and misdeeds, and may sometimes be very beneficial as an adjunct to existential psychotherapy as well as to so-called "ego death/rebirth" psychotherapy (Krupitsky & Grinenko, 1997; Kungurtsev, 1991). This state may also be combined with non-associative, evocative music to assist with an immersion into the experience. Similar to the OBE, the NDE leaves the patient with only a partial ability to consciously recall this particular NOSC on the following day, although key features of the overall experience may be surprisingly well-remembered (i.e., surprising because ketamine's action at NMDA receptors and on neurotransmitters is likely to impede short-term memory).

Ketamine's ability to replicate NDEs is well-documented (Collier, 1972; Domino, Chodoff, & Corssen, 1965; Ghoneim, Hinrichs, Mewaldt, & Petersen, 1985; Grinspoon & Bakalar, 1979; Kungurtsev, 1991; Lilly, 1968; Rumpf et al., 1969; Siegel, 1978, 1980, 1981; Sputz, 1989; Stafford & Golightly, 1967; White et al., 1982). One of our authors (Jansen) analyzed similarities between ketamine-induced transpersonal experiences and NDEs in a series of studies, concluding that 150–200 mg of ketamine can reproduce all of the features commonly associated with NDEs (Jansen, 1989a, 1989b, 1990a, 1990b, 1991, 1997, 2001). Three of this paper's authors (Jansen, Kolp, & Sylvester) had personal NDEs from natural causes, as well as NDE-like ketamine-induced experiences, and can personally verify the striking similarities between both phenomena (e.g., a compelling sense of being dead, sensations of moving through a tunnel, one's life review, visits of non-physical realities, encounters with non-corporeal entities, an experience of the void).

NDEs can be very transformative in some people, and can induce positive changes in spiritual development and worldview (Ring, 1980, 1984; Ring & Valeriano, 1998). Ketamine-induced NDEs appear to be equivalent to natural NDEs and may facilitate stable recovery by accelerating patients' psycho-spiritual growth and broadening their worldviews (Kolp et al., 2007, 2009; Krupitsky & Grinenko, 1997; Krupitsky & Kolp, 2007). In addition to bringing an insight into one's existential problems, the NDE can also generate a spontaneous resolution of the patient's addictive illnesses, psychological problems, and personality disorders. These experiences can also generate a spontaneous spiritual conversion and a dramatic improvement in moral character (Kolp et al., 2007, 2009; Krupitsky & Grinenko, 1997; Krupitsky & Kolp, 2007).

The fourth type of NOSC is perhaps the most fascinating and sometimes the most potentially beneficial ketamine-induced experience, as it is an ego-dissolving transcendental (EDT) experience (an ecstatic state of the dissolution of boundaries between the self and external reality), which may be characterized by the following features:

- Feelings of complete dissolution of one's body
- Feelings of complete dissolution not only of ego but also the self
- Sense of transcending normal mass/space/time continuum
- Feelings of interconnectedness with all people (or sense of experiencing collective consciousness)
- Feelings of cosmic unity with nature
- Feelings of cosmic unity with the universe
- Feelings of becoming a "Unified Field"
- Feelings of becoming God, frequently experienced as an ocean of brilliant white light
- Deep feelings of love, peace, serenity, joy, and bliss
- Profound sense of sacredness of the experience
- Profound sense of ineffability of the experience
- Intuitive belief that the transcendental experience is a source of objective truth about the nature of absolute reality.

There are some indications that the EDT experience is not always dose dependent and may occur even with a low dose of ketamine (0.25 mg/kg worldviews 0.5 mg/kg IM, or 25–50 mg IM), although it is more frequent with a high psychedelic dose of ketamine (2.0 mg/kg–3.0 mg/kg IM, or 150–250 mg IM). The EDT experience may last from 45 minutes to 1 hour and may be an excellent adjunct to transpersonal psychotherapy.

Similar to the NDE, the EDT experiences sometimes generate some resolution of the patient's addictive illnesses, psychological problems, and personality disorders, including instances of spontaneous healing from chronic psychosomatic illnesses, particularly where these are dissociative/conversion in type. In addition, there are some anecdotal accounts of patients who had a spontaneous remission of some forms of serious medical disease (Fenwick & Fenwick, 1995; Grey, 1985; Morse & Perry, 1992; Ring & Valeriano, 1998; Roud, 1990). Like NDEs, EDT experiences have the advantages of potentially rapidly accelerating patients' psychospiritual growth, broadening their worldviews, and possibly generating a spontaneous spiritual change with an improvement in moral character (Kolp et al., 2007, 2009; Krupitsky & Grinenko, 1997; Krupitsky & Kolp, 2007).

Psychedelic Psychotherapy
The acute psychological effects of ketamine can be psychedelic in nature. There are many previous studies on the effectiveness of psychedelic psychotherapy (Grinspoon & Bakalar, 1979; Grof, 1980; Jansen, 1997, 2001; Khorramzadeh & Lofty, 1973, 1976; Kolp et al., 2006, 2007, 2009; Krupitsky & Kolp, 2007; Krupitsky et al., 1992, 1997, 2002; Kurland et al., 1971; Leary, Metzner, & Alpert, 1964; Roquet, 1974; Strassman, 1995) suggesting that incorporating a psychedelic experience into psychotherapy may have beneficial effects in many ways, including:

- Contributing to the cathartic process
- Stabilizing positive psychological changes
- Enhancing personal growth and self-awareness
- Catalyzing insights into existential problems
- Increasing creative activities
- Broadening spiritual horizons
- Harmonizing relationships with the world and other people.

Although the ceremonial and therapeutic uses of hallucinogenic drugs have been known worldwide for millennia (Furst, 1972; Schultes & Hofmann, 1979), scientific research of psychedelic-assisted psychotherapy began more recently. Some of the experiments of the great British chemist Sir Humphrey Davy, later president of the Royal Society, with nitrous oxide at the Pneumatic Institution at Bristol, in the late 18th and early 19th century, hinted at what was possible; unfortunately, the opportunity was entirely missed, including the opportunity to develop nitrous oxide as what would have been the first anesthetic, with Sir Davy later dismissing his experiments into the effects of nitrous oxide on the mind as frivolous. Consequently, surgical operations continued to cause terrible pain for at least another hundred years. The failure to see the opportunities was partly cultural and has been related to the 19th century cultural attitude to pain (Holmes, 2008). Cultural attitudes, rather than issues genuinely related to science and medicine, may currently play an important role in greatly restricting the use of psychedelic psychotherapy in contemporary society, but there are some signs of a thaw.

The Italian psychoanalyst Baroni (1931) started using a mixture of mescaline and *Datura stramonium* as an aid in psychoanalytical psychotherapy in the 1920s, and the work of Meduna (1950) with carbon dioxide is also worthy of note. However, psychedelic research largely began in the 1950s, after Sandoz Laboratories distributed lysergic acid diethylamide (LSD) and psilocybin to all researchers interested in hallucinogen-assisted therapy. Since then, the scientific investigation into psychotherapeutic uses of psychedelic drugs has been conducted in many countries and resulted in the release of dozens of books and more than a thousand peer-reviewed clinical papers reporting the use of psychedelic substances administered to more than 40,000 subjects (Dyck, 2005; Grinspoon & Bakalar, 1979; Passie, 1997). Numerous clinical research studies of the subjects treated with psychedelic compounds, performed from the late 1950s through the present time, repeatedly demonstrated sometimes impressive treatment outcomes (e.g., Grob, 1998, 2002; Grof, 1980; Grinspoon & Bakalar, 1979; Kolp et al., 2006, 2007, 2009; Krupitsky & Kolp, 2007; Pahnke, 1968, 1969; Pahnke, Kurland, Goodman, & Richards, 1969; Pahnke, Kurland, Unger, Savage, & Grof, 1970; Pahnke, Kurland, Unger, Savage, Wolf, & Goodman, 1970; Pahnke, McCabe, Olsson, Unger, & Kurland, 1969; Richards, 1979/1980; Richards, Grof, Goodman, & Kurland, 1972; Richards et al., 1979; Richards, Rhead, DiLeo, Yensen, & Kurland, 1977; Walsh & Grob, 2005; Watts, 1973; Yensen & Dryer, 1993/1994).

Hallucinogen-assisted psychotherapy evolved into three major methodologies: hypnodelic psychotherapy, psycholytic ("mind-loosening") psychotherapy, and psychedelic ("mind-manifesting") psychotherapy. Hypnodelic psychotherapy has its goal as being to maximize the power of hypnotic suggestion by combining it with the low (sub-psychedelic) doses of hallucinogenic substances in order to lower ego defenses without actually creating a visionary experience (Grof, 1980). Hypnodelic psychotherapy goes back to the 19th century, when ether, nitrous oxide, and chloroform were used to induce and deepen hypnotic states (e.g., Schrenck-Notzing, 1891). Later on, a procedure called "narcoanalysis" was developed to use an amphetamine/barbiturate-induced state of excitation/sedation to recall repressed conflicts (Horsley, 1943). Its use in the treatment of "traumatic combat neuroses" (one of the former names for post-traumatic stress disorder) attained some importance (Grinker & Spiegel, 1945).

Psycholytic therapy (a.k.a. "psycholysis") involves the use of medium doses of psychedelic drugs that create a powerful mind-altering experience without dissolution of ego functioning (Eisner, 1997; Eisner & Cohen, 1958; Leuner, 1967). This technique was regularly practiced in numerous European treatment centers during the 1950s and 1960s. In 1954 Sandison and Spencer reported "abreactive memory actualizations" leading to a remarkable progress of "neurotic" patients treated with LSD (Sandison & Spencer, 1954). Around the same time Leuner (1959) developed a day-dream technique in psychotherapy that became established through the present time as "guided affective imagery" (Leuner, 1977, 1984). He documented that treatment with low doses of hallucinogens predictably generated regression and catharsis experiences in his psychotherapy patients (Leuner, 1959, 1971, 1977, 1984).

The earlier investigators reported that psycholytic psychotherapy (or psycholysis) presented to psychotherapists unique opportunities to overcome rigid defense mechanisms in treatment-resistant patients (Arendsen, 1963; Leuner, 1971; Mascher, 1967). Other reported advantages of psycholysis, in addition to the amplification of psychotherapeutic process, were its capacity to increase the effectiveness of treatment and to shorten the length of psychotherapy to half of the typical time (Arendsen-Hein, 1963; Leuner, 1971, 1977, 1984; Mascher, 1967).

Psychedelic therapy involves the use of higher doses of hallucinogenic drugs, with the aim of inducing ego-dissolving transpersonal (e.g., transcendental, mystical, spiritual) peak experiences (Grinspoon & Bakalar, 1979; Grob, 1998, 2002; Grof, 1978, 1980, 1986; Grof & Halifax, 1976; Grof, Goodman, Richards, & Kurland, 1973; Pahnke, 1968; Pahnke et al., 1969, 1970; Richards et al., 1972, 1977, 1979; Walsh & Grob, 2005; Watts, 1973; Yensen & Dryer, 1993/1994). This method was initially developed by Hoffer and Osmond in the United States (Hoffer, 1967). In 1950, they observed that many alcoholic patients developed a spontaneous remission after the frightening experiences of a delirium tremens (Hoffer, 1967). Subsequently, they resolved to induce a facsimile of delirium tremens with high doses of LSD, in order to generate abstinence in alcoholic patients. To their surprise, those patients who had positive experiences, such as religious, spiritual, or mystical experiences, had even longer-lasting therapeutic effects (Hoffer, 1967). Following their original experiments, Osmond and Hoffer developed the technique of psychedelic psychotherapy based on the induction of mystical experiences. They used a quasi-religious preparation, high doses of LSD, specific surroundings, and evocative music to attempt to induce a transformative mystical state of consciousness (Hoffer, 1967).

Pahnke (1962) conducted a double-blind experiment and scientifically documented that the induction of mystical experiences ("Unio mystica") can generate rapid acceleration of psychospiritual growth. His work was further replicated by Leary, Litwin, and Metzner (1963), who came to the same conclusion.

The reports based on ethnographic observations of the ritual administration of certain hallucinogenic plants are also relevant. La Barre (1989) and Andritzky (1989) documented dramatic positive personality changes in individuals with alcoholism who participated in indigenous shamanic ceremonies (Peyote cult and Brazilian Ayahuasca religion).

During the 1960s and 1970s, the psychedelic technique was extensively studied and further optimized at the NIMH Psychiatric Research Center and Spring Grove Hospital (Grof, 1975, 1978; Pahnke et al., 1970; Richards et al., 1977; Yensen & Dryer, 1993/1994). Both hypnodelic and psycholytic psychotherapies were usually conducted repeatedly at intervals of one to four weeks, between 10 and 50 psychotherapeutic sessions, in combination with hypnotic, psychoanalytical, or psychodynamic psychotherapy (Eisner, 1997; Eisner & Cohen, 1958; Grof, 2001; Leuner, 1967). Psychedelic psychotherapy generally included one to three sessions with a psychedelic agent, greatly depended on set and setting, and was generally administered as a part of humanistic, existential, or transpersonal psychotherapy (Grinspoon & Bakalar, 1979; Grob, 1998, 2002; Grof, 1978, 1980, 1986; Grof & Halifax, 1976; Grof et al., 1973; Kolp et al., 2006, 2007, 2009; Krupitsky & Kolp, 2007; Pahnke, 1968, 1969, 1970; Richards et al., 1972, 1977, 1979; Walsh & Grob, 2005; Watts, 1973; Yensen & Dryer, 1993/1994).

Hallucinogen-assisted psychotherapy has been used for the treatment of people with a variety of psychological problems, including alcoholism and other addictive illnesses, anxiety and mood disorders, autism, psychosomatic diseases, criminal recidivism, and end-of-life issues, to name a few. The previous studies asserted that the most powerful results from treatment were induced by transpersonal (e.g., transcendental, mystical, spiritual, or religious) peak experiences (Pahnke, 1968, 1969; Pahnke, Kurland, Goodman, & Richards, 1969; Pahnke, McCabe, Olsson, Unger, & Kurland, 1969; Pahnke, Kurland, Unger, Savage, & Grof, 1970; Pahnke et al., 1970). This mystical peak experience (an ego-dissolving non-ordinary state of consciousness) induced by psychedelic substances can be in turn used to accelerate and enrich the course of psychotherapy. Depending on the therapist's school of thought, the ego-dissolving transcendental experience can be used as an adjunct to behavioral/cognitive, psychoanalytical/psychodynamic, humanistic/existential, or transpersonal psychotherapy. Each school of psychotherapy has its advantages and shortcomings. However, it seems that psychedelic-induced non-ordinary states of consciousness may be successfully used as an adjunct for several major schools of psychotherapy. It is thus understandable that, since the early 1970s through to the present time, a number of international psychiatric investigators have utilized ketamine-induced non-ordinary states of consciousness for psychotherapeutic treatment of various psychological problems, mental diseases, chemical dependencies, psychosomatic illnesses and personality disorders.

History of Ketamine Psychedelic Psychotherapy

Roquet was the first clinician to publish results from using ketamine for psychedelic psychotherapy, which occurred in Mexico (Roquet, 1975; Roquet & Favreau, 1981; Roquet, Favreau, Ocana, & Velasco, 1971). He combined traditional psychoanalytical techniques with the shamanic healing practices of indigenous Mexican Indian ceremonies and created a new approach to psychedelic psychotherapy that he called "psychosynthesis" (not the psychosynthesis developed by Roberto Assagioli, 1965). Roquet utilized ketamine 1.5 mg/kg (or approximately 125 mg IM) and treated primarily neurotic patients, although he described some success with character disorders and selected psychotic patients (Roquet, 1975; Roquet & Favreau, 1981; Roquet et al., 1971; Yensen, 1973, 1985). His therapeutic regimen also incorporated other psychedelic substances, such as LSD, mescaline, and psilocybin. Roquet used ketamine (and other psychedelic substances) in a group setting between 1969 and 1974 and applied his technique of psychosynthesis to approximately 150 patients (Yensen, 1985). He reported positive outcomes in 85% of his patients (Roquet, 1975; Roquet & Favreau, 1981; Yensen, 1985).

Roquet described four levels of possible experiences with ketamine (as well as with all other psychedelic compounds he utilized). The first and most superficial level is a level of minor perceptual distortions. The second level is a level of wish fulfillment and fantasy (as the patient merely runs from problems with pleasant fantasies). Although patients can experience certain mystical states on this level, the experience usually does not yield true insight and results in only minimum reorganization of the personality. The third level is the level of existential anxiety and is often characterized by experiences of psychological death and rebirth. This level is frequently accompanied by the feeling of intense abreaction with catharsis afterward. The fourth level is the most intense, when the personality disappears completely, all previous points of reference are lost, and profound reorganization occurs. At this level, true life-altering experiences of a mystical nature can take place. Roquet regarded this level as essential to successful therapy and aimed to synthesize a healthy personality through the integrative qualities of this experience (Roquet, 1975; Roquet & Favreau, 1981; Yensen, 1973).

In Argentina, Fontana (1974) employed ketamine as an adjunct to psychotherapy for depression to facilitate regression to prenatal levels combining disintegration and death followed by progression to rebirth. He reported that ketamine allows therapists to introduce themselves into, and to correct, primitive experience through the relationship. Fontana emphasized the advantages of ketamine as making it possible to reach deep levels of regressions that had not been observed previously. However, we could not find the specific dose of ketamine he utilized, the type of psychotherapy he applied to his clients, or the specific number of the patients he treated with ketamine psychedelic psychotherapy.

In Iran, Khorramzadeh and Lofty (1973) administered ketamine as an "abreactive agent" to patients with various psychiatric illnesses (anxiety, depression, phobias, obsessive-compulsive neurosis, conversion reaction, hypochondriasis, and hysteria) and psychosomatic disorders (tension headaches and ulcerative colitis). Subjects were chosen from the inpatient population of a psychiatric unit of a university hospital in southern Iran. A total of one hundred patients (61 males and 39 females) were investigated, ranging in age from 16 to 66. Patients with organic brain syndrome and psychoses were excluded.

Ketamine was administered intravenously in three dose ranges in Khorramzadeh and Lofty's (1973) work. The first group (25 patients) received 0.2–0.3 mg/kg body weight. Of the 25 subjects in this group, only one was reported as having a minimal response and 24 showed no response. These 24, along with 72 others, were then given a higher dose of ketamine (0.4–0.6 mg/kg body weight). A total of 95 demonstrated the abreactive response consisting of excitement, emotional discharge, verbalization of conflict, and emergence phenomena. Of the latter, all had facilitation of their psychotherapy and symptom relief. Group 3 included only one failure from the group 2 as well as three new patients. They received 0.7–1.0 mg ketamine/kg of body weight. According to the authors, all of these patients showed the abreactive response and had facilitation of their psychotherapy with symptom relief. In total, 74 subjects had intense visionary experiences; out of those, 51 patients recalled vividly painful childhood events regarding the key figures in that period. The complications were described as very minimal and included apprehension (two subjects), nausea (three subjects), and vomiting (two subjects), which were treated with perphenazine (5 mg IM) with positive response.

Khorramzadeh and Lofty's (1973) subjects were seen six months after the injection. Only nine patients were not doing well at this time, while 91 of the patients were doing quite well. After one year, 88 patients were still being observed and all except two were reported to be doing well (one had ulcerative colitis and the other tension headaches). They both requested another injection, which was given and led to relief of symptoms for an unspecified period of time. They postulated that ketamine activated unconscious and repressed memories, while it could temporarily transport the patient back into childhood, reviving traumatic events with intense emotional reaction. They also concluded that ketamine's cathartic effect was related to its mind-expanding qualities and recommended the use of this chemical as an abreactive agent.

Khorramzadeh and Lofty (1976) later conducted another study to determine the types of ketamine-induced emergence phenomena and to discover any possible correlation between these phenomena and the type of personality involved. They used Eysenck's Personality Inventory (EPI) to evaluate the three dimensions of personality (Extraversion or E, Neuroticism or N, and Psychoticism or P) in patients who undertook ketamine anesthesia during surgery. A total of 606 patients were given a Persian adaptation of EPI the night before ketamine anesthesia for operation. The maximum score accepted as normal for E and N was 11, and for P was 5. When E fell below 5, it was considered an indication of Introversion. Out of 606 patients, 394, or 65%, showed no reaction. All of them had normal scores. The remaining 212 patients, or 35%, fell into the following seven groups, according to their various scores:

- Group E. Sixty-five patients (10.7%) scored high in E (over 14). They experienced pleasant dreams, and some of them even felt they were in heaven among angels. Later questioning showed that they were all devoted Muslims. All of them expressed their willingness to undergo the experience again.

- Group N. Seventy patients (11.5%) had high scores in N (over 14). They all felt dizzy and related that to an experience of falls or rapid circular movements. They were indifferent to future use of the agent.

- Group P. Only 15 patients (2.4%) had high scores in P. They all reported body image distortions, loss of control over their limbs, and a sensation of a part of their body floating. In some the reaction was such that it had to be ended with perphenezine 5 mg IM. All refused to go through the experience again.

- Group NP. Fourteen patients (2.3%) scored high both for N and P. They had the combined experiences of groups N and P, making them feel terrified and most apprehensive. They were adamantly against future use of ketamine.

- Group PE. Ten patients (1.6%) scored high both in P and E. They screamed or laughed and had increased motor activity and some used foul language while regaining consciousness. They all stated that they had a good time and the screaming was because of losing the pleasant feeling. They were willing to undergo the experience again.

- Group NE. Eighteen patients (2.9%) had high scores in N and E, and although they had the feeling of falling or circling, it was not at all unpleasant. One male patient stated that it was like a funny orgasm without ejaculation. They did not mind the future use of ketamine.

- Group Low E. Twenty patients (3.3%) scored 5 or lower in E. They cried and used profanity mostly directed at their close friends and relatives. After regaining consciousness, 10 of them had amnesia but the rest stated that they knew they were using profanity but could not control it. None wished to go through the experience again.

Khorramzadeh and Lofty (1976) reported that the EPI was found to be reliable in predicting the type of emergence phenomena. The reported results apparently showed that the majority of the patients (65%) did not experience emergence phenomena at all (those with normal scores). Of the remaining 35%, the majority had either pleasant (those with high scores in E, EP, and NE) or indifferent (those with high score in N) experiences. Only 8% had unpleasant experiences (those with high

P and NP, and low E). This study supported that, in emergency situations requiring ketamine anesthesia, the drug may be administered without undue concern regarding the emergence phenomena, since only a small minority of patients had very unpleasant side effects. The study also documented that, in non-emergency situations, a simple questionnaire may help the anesthesiologist to select suitable candidates for ketamine induction.

Psychiatrist Stanislav Grof (1980) developed the most comprehensive theory of psychedelic psychotherapy from the transpersonal perspective. He wrote that psychedelics facilitate therapeutic experiences of symbolic death and rebirth of the ego, allowing clients to work through deep traumatic fixations in their unconscious. Grof designed a specific psychedelic psychotherapeutic approach, which he applied successfully with more than 750 patients. Although Grof primarily used LSD in his work, he acknowledged that ketamine holds great promise due to its affinity with dynamic systems. He reported that the psychoactive effect of ketamine is so powerful that it can catapult patients beyond impasses from previous LSD sessions to reach higher levels of integration (Grof, 1980).

Last in this regard, we want to mention the interesting recent work on DMT and spirituality in the United States by psychiatrist Rick Strassman (2000, 2014). We see this as very complementary to our interest in ketamine.

Present Research on Ketamine Psychedelic Psychotherapy

In Russia, one of us (Evgeny Krupitsky) conducted the most comprehensive, rigorous scientific clinical research on ketamine psychedelic psychotherapy to date (Krupitsky & Grinenko, 1997; Krupitsky & Kolp, 2007; Krupitsky et al., 1990, 1992, 1999, 2002, 2007). He began using ketamine as an agent for psychedelic psychotherapy in 1985 in the former Soviet Union. His early exploration of the use of ketamine as a psychotherapeutic agent employed a behavioral psychotherapy, specifically an aversive conditioning model for the treatment of alcohol dependence that was customary in Russia before the fall of the U.S.S.R. Krupitsky et al. (1992) combined traditional behavioristic methods of aversive therapy oriented toward creating negative associations between the use of alcohol and undesirable physical effects with earlier applications of psychedelic psychotherapy for treatment of alcoholism that sought to change an individual's attitude towards the use of alcohol but failed to imprint negative associations around the use of alcohol (Smith, 1964; Smith & Seymour, 1985). He created the affective contra-attribution (ACA) method that combined both of these approaches.

Initially, Krupitsky induced an aversive psychedelic experience by combining ket-amine with bemegride (an analeptic agent with strong anxiogenic properties) in order to generate the frightening emotive experiences and produce strong negative emotions towards alcohol in the context of a terrifying hallucinatory experience. This forms the basis of the ACA method. These negative experiences are connected with the use of alcohol and with the alcoholic's life style. Later on, Krupitsky learned that those subjects who instead had an ecstatic transpersonal experience had equally remarkable, if not greater, beneficial outcomes, and his work gradually shifted from a behavioral model to an existential and eventually transpersonal paradigm (Kru-pitsky & Grinenko, 1997).

Krupitsky initially used ketamine as an alternative treatment for alcoholism only. His original ketamine study demonstrated that KPP is highly effective in the treat-ment of alcohol dependence. Of 111 patients who received KPP in the first study, 69.8% were sober one year later, while only 24% in the control group remained abstinent during the one-year follow-up period (Krupitsky et al., 1992).

Krupitsky summarized his findings and documented that his patients became less anxious and depressed, more responsible and emotionally mature, with increased ego strength and positive changes in self-concept. His studies also showed that KPP brings about profound positive changes in life values and purposes, in attitudes to the different aspects of life and death, and rapidly accelerates psychospiritual de-velopment. Patients began to see other purposes, other values, other meaning and pleasures in their lives, grew more self-confident and balanced, more emotionally open and self-sufficient, and more responsible for their lives and the lives of their loved ones (Krupitsky & Grinenko, 1997).

Krupitsky and his team (1999) also examined the effectiveness of KPP for the treatment of heroin dependence. The team designed a double-blind randomized clinical trial comparing the relative effectiveness of a high psychedelic dose of ket-amine (2.0 mg/kg IM) to a low non-hallucinogenic dose of ketamine (0.2 mg/kg IM) for the psychotherapeutic treatment of heroin addiction. The preliminary six-month follow-up demonstrated that a hallucinogenic (psychedelic) dose of ket-amine was more effective than a non-hallucinogenic (sub-psychedelic) dose. Two-year follow-up data confirmed that the rate of abstinence in the high-dose ketamine group was significantly higher than that in the low-dose control group, while the corresponding rate of relapse was lower (Krupitsky et al., 2002).

This comprehensive study with heroin addicts, the first double-blind clinical trial of KPP conducted entirely within the evidence-based medical paradigm, clearly established that KPP significantly reduced the craving for heroin, considerably decreased the levels of anxiety and depression, markedly increased the level of spiritual development, and, to a great extent, enhanced understanding of the meaning and purpose of life. Interestingly, many of the measured change variables did not differ significantly between high and low dose groups. This suggests that the psychotherapy common to both groups played an important role in the observed effects. This could also be the effect of set and setting combined with a relatively low dose of ketamine. In addition, the study demonstrated that KPP produced few or no significant adverse reactions, and no subject participating in the study became addicted to ketamine (Krupitsky et al., 1999, 2002).

Krupitsky's most recent work employed single versus repeated sessions of ketamine-assisted psychotherapy in subjects with treatment-resistant heroin dependence who do not respond well to the initial treatment with KPP (Krupitsky et al., 2007). Fifty-nine detoxified inpatients with heroin dependence received one KPP session prior to their discharge from an addiction treatment hospital, and were then randomized into two treatment groups. Participants in the first group received two addiction counseling sessions followed by two KPP sessions, with sessions scheduled on a monthly interval (multiple KPP group). Participants in the second group received two addiction counseling sessions on a monthly interval, but no additional ketamine therapy sessions (single KPP group). At one-year follow-up, survival analysis demonstrated a significantly higher rate of abstinence in the multiple KPP group. Thirteen out of 26 subjects (50%) in the multiple KPP group remained abstinent, compared to six out of 27 subjects (22%) in the single KPP group ($p<0.05$). Once again, no differences between groups were found in anxiety, depression, the severity of craving for heroin, or their understanding of the meaning of their lives. The data from this study provide some evidence that treatment-resistant patients who did not experience a mystical state of consciousness during the initial ketamine session may benefit from a second or even a third ketamine session. It appears that two or three repeated KPP sessions may work better and provide a higher rate of abstinence in heroin addicts than one KPP session, suggesting that increasing the number of KPP sessions might increase the efficacy of treatment.

Krupitsky's comprehensive clinical research of ketamine psychedelic psychotherapy has clearly documented that KPP is a safe and sometimes very effective treatment for alcoholism and opioid dependencies. It also proved to be efficacious in the treatment of stimulant dependence, as well as a very effective modality for the treatment of comorbid psychiatric conditions, such as post-traumatic stress disorder, neurotic depression, anxiety disorders, and avoidant personality disorders. In addition, his scientific work demonstrated that KPP might be effective for the treatment of phobic neurosis, obsessive-compulsive neurosis, and histrionic personality disorder (Krupitsky & Grinenko, 1997; Krupitsky & Kolp, 2007; Krupitsky et al., 2002).

Many of Krupitsky's patients developed a more spiritual approach to life through their transpersonal experiences. These encouraging clinical results occurred because of positive changes in the life values and purposes, relationships, and worldviews of these patients. They showed a transformation of emotional attitudes, a decrease in the level of inner discord, internal tension, discomfort, and emotional isolation; improved self-assessment; and a tendency to overcome the passive aspects of their personalities. These significant changes, along with a positive transformation of the patients' system of life values and meaning, as well as changes in their worldview, created a positive attitude toward a sober life and supported patients' ongoing stable sobriety (Krupitsky & Grinenko, 1997; Krupitsky & Kolp, 2007).

Unfortunately, changes in the regulations governing ketamine research in Russia brought Krupitsky's research efforts to a halt. When Krupitsky began working with ketamine psychedelic psychotherapy in 1985, psychedelics were not widely known in Russia and ketamine was a Schedule III drug in that country. After the collapse of the U.S.S.R., all drugs, including psychedelics, became much more available in Russia, ketamine included. Subsequently, ketamine abuse among Russian youth rapidly escalated from the late 1990s. The Russian government thus moved ketamine from Schedule III into Schedule II in 2002. Ketamine remains available only for anesthesia and conscious sedation at the present time in Russia. It became unavailable for the treatment of addictive disorders and psychiatric illnesses, and Krupitsky had to abandon his innovative work with KPP.

Technique of Ketamine Psychedelic Psychotherapy

Krupitsky has developed a specific and comprehensive course of KPP that comprises three main stages: preparation, administration, and integration (Krupitsky & Grinenko, 1997; Krupitsky & Kolp, 2007; Krupitsky et al., 1990, 1992, 1999, 2002, 2007). In the preparation stage, preliminary psychotherapy is carried out with patients, who are told that the psychedelic session may induce important insights concerning their personal problems, their system of values, their notions of self and the world around them, and the meaning of their lives. Patients are educated that all of these insights may lead to positive changes in their personalities, which will be important for healing their underlying problems and shifting to a sober lifestyle.

At least five to 10 hours of psychotherapy are provided before the ketamine session in order to establish the psychospiritual goal for the transpersonal experience and prepare the subject for the session. The therapist pays close attention to issues such as the patient's personal motives for treatment, goals for a sober life, and ideas concerning the cause of the disease and its consequences. The patient and therapist together form an individually tailored "psychotherapeutic myth" during this dialogue that creates an atmosphere of confidence and mutual understanding during the first stage of KPP. This then becomes the most important therapeutic factor responsible for the psychological content of the second stage of KPP (Krupitsky & Grinenko, 1997; Krupitsky & Kolp, 2007).

The second stage of this approach to KPP is the induction of the transpersonal experience through the administration of ketamine. Breakfast is omitted on the morning of ketamine administration, and all participants refrain from food and drink for at least eight hours prior to this experience. Patients are told that they will enter some unusual states of consciousness and are instructed to surrender fully to the experience. After the patient lies down in a comfortable supine position with eyeshades, ketamine is injected intramuscularly, in doses from 2.0 mg/kg to 2.5 mg/kg. The intramuscular route is preferred because the onset is more gradual and the psychedelic experience lasts longer. With an intravenous psychedelic dose (from 0.7 mg/kg to 1.0 mg/kg), the effect lasts only about 15 to 20 minutes, but with an intramuscular injection, it lasts from 45 minutes to an hour (Krupitsky & Grinenko, 1997; Krupitsky & Kolp, 2007).

With a background of specially chosen music, generally free-floating non-associative classical or New Age, the patient typically has a powerful non-ordinary state of consciousness, frequently resembling a mystical experience. After 45 minutes to an hour, the patient slowly comes back from the experience. During the recovery period, which takes from one to two hours, the patient begins to feel ordinary reality returning. At this point in the session, the patient usually begins to describe the experience and some discussion and interpretation is begun with the psychotherapist. After the session, the patient goes to rest. The patient is asked to write down a detailed self-report of the transpersonal ketamine experience that evening (Krupitsky & Grinenko, 1997; Krupitsky & Kolp, 2007).

The third stage is the integration of the ketamine-induced experience, which is carried out after the ketamine session. It is generally done in a group psychotherapy format, because the dynamic of the shared group experience appears more powerful and therapeutic than individual therapy alone. From three to five hours of psychotherapy are provided after the ketamine session to help subjects interpret and integrate their experiences during the session into everyday life. With the aid of the psychotherapist during the integration phase of treatment, the patients discuss and interpret the personal significance of the symbolic content of their ketamine-induced non-ordinary state of consciousness. This discussion is directed toward helping the patients make a correlation between their psychedelic experience and their intra- and interpersonal problems. The therapist assists the patients in the psychological integration of the spiritual transformation that can result from the direct transpersonal experience. This uniquely profound and powerful experience often helps patients to generate fresh insights that enable them to integrate new, often unexpected meanings, values, and attitudes about the self and the world (Krupitsky & Grinenko, 1997; Krupitsky & Kolp, 2007).

It should be explicitly pointed out that a ketamine-induced psychedelic experience may have only marginal and transitory beneficial effects in and of itself, no beneficial effects at all, or may be harmful when ketamine is used in uncontrolled settings recreationally. It can sometimes lead to significant medical problems and addiction (Jansen, 2000, 2001; Jansen & Darracot-Canckovic 2001; Ricuarte, 2005). The therapeutic relationship, as well as set and setting, are paramount to the effectiveness of ketamine psychedelic psychotherapy.

In order for the KPP sessions to cause positive transformative experiences, it is of central importance to carefully prepare patients for the KPP session, to attentively supervise them during the session, and to provide extensive psychotherapy after the session to facilitate the integration of the ketamine-induced transpersonal experience and to help patients personally accept insights gained during the KPP session (Krupitsky & Grinenko, 1997; Krupitsky & Kolp, 2007).

Present Use of Ketamine Psychedelic Psychotherapy

One of us, Dr. Eli Kolp, is a bicultural psychiatrist and was originally trained in the former U.S.S.R. as a public psychiatrist. After Kolp requested that the Soviet authorities allow him to emigrate from the U.S.S.R., he was instead sent to work as an addiction specialist in the Moscow Alcohol and Drug Abuse Clinic #1, where Kolp learned how difficult the treatment of alcoholism in Russia could be. Even with the most intensive long-term treatment, which included multiple sessions of an unpleasant aversive conditioning, more than 75% of Russian alcoholics relapsed on alcohol within one year after completion of treatment.

After Kolp immigrated to the United States in 1981, he successfully re-trained as a private psychiatrist and began practicing general adult and geriatric psychiatry. Circa 1990, Kolp returned to the treatment of addictive illnesses, both in private and public sectors, where he directed various outpatient, residential, and inpatient programs specializing in the treatment of alcohol, drug, and/or food addiction. He quickly learned that efforts to treat alcoholism in the American population are costly and have a low rate of recovery, as they do in Russia.

A previous meta-analysis of outcomes of treatment for alcoholism (Nathan, 1986) showed that different treatment methods did not appear to be associated with significantly different long-term outcomes. It was reported that treatment factors, including theoretical orientation, content, locus, and intensity of treatment, revealed little or no difference in treatment outcome, despite great differences in costs. Although abstinence rates one year after treatment may reach 40% to 50% for persons with good treatment prospects (well-motivated, employed, sub-chronic alcoholics with a large network of support and substantial personal resources treated at private treatment facilities), typical abstinence rates for poorly motivated, unemployed, chronic alcoholics with a limited network of support and few personal resources seen at public treatment facilities were 25% or less. Rates of abstinence at and beyond the two-year mark are often less than 50% of the rates of abstinence at the one-year mark.

In the United States, Kolp, inspired by Krupitsky, thus began working towards utilizing ketamine psychedelic psychotherapy in 1994. His approach was explicitly meant to replicate Krupitsky's pioneering work and to extend it into another cultural context, the United States. With Krupitsky's guidance (while Krupitsky was working for one year with Krystal as a visiting scientist in the Department of Psychiatry at Yale University), Kolp designed a research protocol, entitled *The Ketamine-Assisted Therapy of Alcoholism*. The protocol was first approved by the Safety Committee of the James A. Haley Veterans Hospital in Tampa, Florida, and then by the Research and Development Committee of the Department of Veterans Affairs. It was further approved by the Research Committee of the Department of Psychiatry at the University of South Florida College of Medicine and the Institutional Review Board of the University of South Florida Health Science Center. Finally, by the end of 1996, the protocol was approved by the FDA, which issued to Kolp an Investigational New Drug permit. Unfortunately, the implementation of the protocol never materialized due to a lack of the institutional support and an absence of research funds. The Department of Veterans Affairs did not allow Kolp to use its facility and resources for this purpose, apparently because of the controversial nature of psychedelic psychotherapy at that point in time, which was somewhat prior to the recent "thaw" which has allowed some human work to be done with drugs such as psilocybin and MDMA (e.g., Friedman, 2006; Griffiths, Richards, Johnson, Mc-Cann, & Jesse, 2008; Griffiths, Richards, McCann, & Jesse, 2006).

Kolp was also unable to obtain funding for the study from multiple sources. It thus became necessary to abandon the planned, formal research study. Instead, Kolp employed ketamine psychedelic psychotherapy (KPP) in his private psychiatric practice. During the first several years (1994–1999), Kolp administered KPP to more than 70 patients. The patients were males and females, 21–64 years old, who identified alcohol as their drug of choice and satisfied the diagnostic criteria for alcohol dependence. Kolp followed all patients treated with KPP for as long as they continued the aftercare treatment, and he had individual and group sessions with them on a regular basis, from once a month to once every three months. In addition to being diagnosed with alcoholism, the vast majority of Kolp's patients (nearly 90%) had concurrent addictions (e.g., to caffeine, sugar, nicotine, cannabis, benzodiazepines, opiates, and amphetamines), and about half had coexisting psychological problems (e.g., generalized anxiety disorder, social phobias, primary insomnias, acute and repeated stress disorders, pain disorder, panic disorder, depressive disorder, post-traumatic stress disorder, tension and migraine headaches, somatization disorder, and chronic fatigue syndrome). As with Krupitsky's technique, Kolp's treatment modality explicitly relied on the transpersonal effects of ketamine to facilitate psychotherapeutic change. Kolp experimented with several different courses of treatment with KPP, ranging from a time-limited individual treatment on an outpatient basis to an intensive one- to three-week group treatment in the framework of a residential program. Kolp summarized his empirical clinical observations on KPP effectiveness for treating alcoholism and other coexisting disorders in his first report (Kolp et al., 2006).

After gaining extensive experience with KPP for the treatment of alcoholism, Kolp extended the inclusion criteria for KPP and began accepting patients with other drug dependencies and food addiction Kolp also started utilizing KPP for the treatment of end-of-life anxiety in patients with terminal illnesses. He continued utilizing group psychotherapy in a residential setting for treatment of addictive disorders and co-existing psychological problems. In addition, Kolp continued utilizing individual psychotherapy on an outpatient basis for treatment of existential anxieties in terminally ill people and selected patients with addictive disorders who did not wish to participate in a residential treatment program, or could not tolerate a group process.

During the second stage of his work with KPP (2000–2006), Kolp treated approximately one hundred patients with various addictive illnesses (primarily alcoholism, opiate dependence, and food addiction), concurrent psychological diseases (mainly anxiety and mood disorder, acute and repeated stress disorders, and psychosomatic disorders), coexisting personality disorders, and existential anxieties related to end-of-life issues. Kolp documented his empirical findings in a second report (Kolp et al., 2007). In addition, Kolp collaborated with Krupitsky, and both authors published their combined experience and accumulated data on clinical research and empirical observation of the effectiveness of KPP (Kolp, Krupitsky, Friedman, & Young, 2009; Krupitsky & Kolp, 2007).

During the third stage of his work with KPP (2007 through the present), Kolp continued treating patients with various addictive illnesses, concurrent psychological diseases, and coexisting personality disorders. He also started accepting for KPP selected clients who had already resolved their addictions and major psychological problems and were looking for growth-oriented psychotherapy and lifestyle optimization.

In addition, Kolp began treating patients with chronic treatment-resistant depression (TRD), which is presently defined as a failure to respond to an adequate trial with two or three conventional antidepressants. Interestingly, the vast majority of the patients with TRD were not psychologically minded and had no interest in KPP. Instead, they desired to undertake only pharmacotherapy with a low sub-psychedelic dose of ketamine. In total, during the past seven years, Kolp administered KPP to approximately 150 "psychologically-minded" clients with drug and food addictions, and ketamine pharmacotherapy to about 50 "pharmacologically-minded" patients with treatment-resistant chronic anxiety and/or depressive disorders.

Kolp also administered KPP in the same three-stage format as was originally designed by Krupitsky: preparation, administration, and integration. Kolp always used a high psychedelic dose of ketamine (2.0 mg/kg–2.5 mg/kg IM, or 150–200 mg IM) in order to both avoid an out-of-body experience (OBE) and to specifically induce the near-death experience or, considered by Kolp as even more desirable, the ego-dissolving transcendental experience. Kolp disfavors an OBE for the same reasons that were previously discussed by Roquet and colleagues (1971, 1975) and Yensen (1973): most of the time the OBE simply represents the patient's wish fulfillment and the patient only runs from problems with pleasant fantasies. Although the OBE may resemble certain mystical states, the experience usually does not yield true insight and, in fact, may even have a negative effect on the ego, as illustrated by the following case study:

C was a 52-year-old Caucasian female with a long history of binge alcoholism. She reported a stable childhood, with no history of physical or sexual abuse. C was raised as a Roman Catholic. However, she abandoned that denomination during her late teens, continuing as a non-denominational Christian.

C began using alcohol at age 16, started drinking on a regular basis at age 18, and developed alcohol binges at age 25. Her binges lasted from three or four days to two weeks every several weeks, with a consumption of nearly one liter of vodka a day during the binges. She undertook more than 10 various rehabilitation programs. However, she never had a stable remission (her longest remission lasted seven months, including two months in a rehabilitation program). C did not wish to participate in a group residential program and elected an individual outpatient treatment. In addition, she did not follow strict preparatory guidelines (a whole food plant-based diet, optimal hydration, daily meditation and exercise, limitation of screen time, etc.). Moreover, she continued using sugar, caffeine, and nicotine throughout the preparatory stage. Although she received 150 mg of ketamine IM, her ego remained well-preserved and she did not experience EDT, or, at least, NDE. Instead, she had an OBE that she described as "paradisiacal":

> *My mind left my body and I found myself in the Heaven … flying high above the silver and gold clouds … in the company of thousands of angels who were there to guide and protect me. The music was exceptionally lovely and we were ascending higher and higher … eventually arriving into the Garden of Eden. The angels showed me the beauty of their home and then helped me to soar directly to the throne of Jesus. His presence overwhelmed me and I started crying and laughing at the same time. I felt the Jesus' unconditional love and understood that all my sins were forgiven. He blessed me and I promised Him to never ever touch another drink of Vodka again. I then returned back into my body … feeling joyful and full of bliss … and I knew—with all my heart—that I got reformed forever.*

She attended only one follow-up session and proudly reported that she had rejoined her church and started praying again on a daily basis.

She insisted that her encounter with Jesus completely healed her from alcoholism and that she no longer needed to participate in an AA 12-step recovery program. C relapsed on alcohol eight months later and committed suicide soon after the end of her two-week binge.

Kolp quickly discovered that the OBE can be fascinating and gratifying for the ego, but it can sometimes have a rather low therapeutic potential outside of a long-term psychodynamic psychotherapy that requires repeated inductions of the OBE. Subsequently, Kolp's primary goal has been to induce the ego-dissolving transcendental experience, or at least the near-death experience, since both the NDE and EDT experiences more frequently generate not only a complete resolution of the patient's addictive illnesses and coexisting psychological problems, often after a single session, but may also cause instances of spontaneous healing from chronic psychosomatic illnesses (Fenwick & Fenwick, 1995; Grey, 1985; Kolp et al., 2007, 2009; Krupitsky & Grinenko, 1997; Krupitsky & Kolp, 2007; Morse & Perry, 1992; Ring, 1980, 1984; Ring & Valeriano, 1998; Roud, 1990). In addition to its more specific healing potentials, the NDE and the EDT experiences may also rapidly accelerate patients' psychospiritual growth, broaden their worldviews, and generate a spontaneous spiritual transformation with a dramatic improvement of moral character (Kolp et al., 2007; Krupitsky & Grinenko, 1997; Krupitsky & Kolp, 2007).

The primary factors that greatly influence the likelihood of these desirable NDE and EDT experiences are the dose of ketamine, the mindset of an individual prior to the ketamine session, and the session's setting. To reiterate, the mindset is the mental state that a person brings to the experience, such as thoughts, mood, personality structure, expectations, and worldviews. It is the most important part of KPP and basically stands for a rigorous preparation for the ketamine-induced experience. The setting is also very important and includes physical (the room's atmosphere) and social (feelings of the group's participants towards one another and toward therapist/therapists) components. The social support network is particularly important in the outcome of the ketamine-induced NOSC. The group and/or a therapist are able to control and guide the course of the experience, both consciously and subconsciously. Anxiety prior to the experience or a disagreeable environment may induce a frightening experience. On the other hand, curiosity and a positive attitude, together with a comfortable and safe place, are more likely to generate a blissful experience.

In addition to set and setting, the novelty of the psychedelic experience may be salient for successful problem resolution. Psychedelics are a unique class of drugs that produce intense effects unlike those of other drugs, and one's first "trip" can therefore be a profound and life-changing experience (as common wisdom says, "there is no second chance for the first impression"). Consequently, for those with extensive histories of psychedelic use, there is a diminished chance that a ketamine experience will be all that unique and transformative ("just another trip"), whereas for the novice psychedelic user, given proper mindset and setting, the experience can be profound.

Kolp believes that the most influential component of a successful KPP (in addition to dose, set, and setting) that can greatly increase the odds of the optimal EDT experience is vigilant preparation prior to the ketamine administration. Without a careful and laborious preparation, only about half of the patients may have an NDE (even with a dose of ketamine that is set to cause a near-death experience) and only one out of 20 or 25 patients may have an EDT experience. By attentively preparing the patients for a ketamine-induced experience through creating the spiritually oriented mindset (as well as carefully controlling the setting), the likelihood of having an NDE becomes nearly universal. Meanwhile, the likelihood of an EDT experience can be increased from only one out of 20–25 patients to three or four out of 10 patients. Unfortunately, the EDT experience is very elusive and there is no guarantee of the EDT occurrence even with the most arduous preparation.

Whether the patient elects to participate in a residential group program or outpatient individual treatment, Kolp starts the preparatory period six weeks prior to the induction of the ketamine experience. During those six weeks, all patients participate in weekly group psychotherapy (unless the patient does not want a residential treatment, or cannot tolerate a group process; in that case the patient is engaged in a weekly individual psychotherapy). During the same six weeks, Kolp strongly encourages all patients to prepare the body and mind through partial fasting following a whole food plant-based (WFPB) diet, optimal hydration, de-stressing through daily meditation, contemplation on the nature of the Self and God, limitation of "screen" time, and daily exercise. Kolp further suggests detoxifying the body from all sedatives (such as sugar, alcohol, benzodiazepines, and opiates) due to their tendency to dull the mind, and all psychostimulants (such as caffeine, nicotine, ephedrine, amphetamines) due to their tendency to aggrandize the ego.

In the experience of Kolp, fasting is a key aspect of the more acute preparatory process. The reasons why this is of assistance to the outcome remain speculative, but fasting has long been a part of the spiritual quest in many cultures and religions because it seemed to weaken the ties of the physical body to the material realm. Fasting can be total, abstaining from all food and beverages apart from water, or it can be partial. Kolp never asks patients to undergo a total fast. However, he highly recommends a partial fast and suggests abstaining prior to the ketamine session from highly refined simple carbohydrates (all sugary drinks such as soda pop and fruit juices, chocolate, doughnuts, cookies, cake, candy, etc.), highly processed complex carbohydrates (white bread, rolls, pasta, white rice, French fries, etc.), dairy products (milk, yogurt, sour cream, butter, cheese, ice cream, etc.), fatty "rich" foods (steak, bacon, salami, pastrami, hamburgers, cheeseburgers, etc.) and "junk" foods (chips, pretzels, crackers, pizza, etc.). Participants are encouraged to follow the WFPB diet, getting the majority of calories from vegetables, with some calories coming from certain whole grains, legumes, fruits, and nuts. During the fasting period, optimal hydration is strongly recommended by drinking one glass of water (no carbonated, caffeinated, or sugary drinks of any kind) every two to three hours during wakeful time.

To calm and prepare the mind, Kolp recommends taking a time out for daily meditation or mindfulness sessions. Ideally, participants would take 20 to 30 minutes each day for this practice. However, even 10 to 15 minutes daily is beneficial. Kolp also recommends spending 15 to 20 minutes every day contemplating on the nature of the Self and the nature of whatever the person understands by the word "God" or the connectivity between the Self and the rest of the Universe, or a Higher Power as in the 12-step programs. Many participants find it helpful to keep a journal during this time to document their progress, including any regressions, in order to stay on track during this phase.

In addition, Kolp strongly advises de-stressing the mind by limiting screen time beyond that which is required for each individual participant's employment. Recreational screen time should be limited to less than two hours daily. Screen time includes, but is not limited to, computer use, watching television, playing video games, watching movies, and using smartphones.

Exercise is recommended at least five days a week for a period of 45 to 60 minutes at a time. Kolp recommends low impact isotonic exercises such as deep stretching or yoga; however, any type of exercise is beneficial.

Although the preparatory guidelines may seem strict, this conscious preparation of the body, mind, and spirit prior to the administration of ketamine is seen by Kolp as increasing the likelihood of having either a classic NDE or distinct EDT experience. In Kolp's experience, after a detailed, vigilant, and focused preparation, almost

50% of participants have a classical NDE and nearly 35% participants have a highly desirable EDT experience. Unfortunately, even with the most arduous preparation, approximately 15% of participants still have a standard OBE. Most of them are the patients who had a very high tolerance to sedatives (e.g., sugar, alcohol, benzodiazepines, barbiturates, and opiates), severe control issues (they are simply unable or unwilling to surrender to the existential or transpersonal experience), persistent difficulties in maintaining long-term interpersonal relationships, and those with dogmatic beliefs in an authoritative or critical God.

After six weeks of an outpatient preparation and detoxification as well as six weekly psychotherapy sessions, the patients are placed in a structured residential setting for the second stage of treatment—the administration of ketamine-induced non-ordinary states of consciousness. The length of a residential component varies from one week (growth-oriented program) to three weeks (addiction rehabilitation program). The one-week growth-oriented residential program offers 30 hours of psychoeducational and encounter groups, existential and transpersonal group psychotherapies, and interactive classes and didactic lectures. The three-week rehabilitation program for the treatment of food and drug addiction provides the same 30 hours of analogous psychoeducational and encounter groups, existential and transpersonal group psychotherapies, and interactive classes and didactic lectures. In addition, it provides another 60 hours of various life skills training such as communication skills, problem solving skills, relapse prevention, relationship skills, anger management, and decision-making, as well as training in optimal lifestyle and advising health issues, nutrition education with food purchase and preparation, nonverbal therapies, such as art therapy and music therapy, in order to provide the patients with alternative means of self-expression, problem resolution, and motivational enhancement. Those patients who opt out of a residential component of a treatment program receive the administration of ketamine in an outpatient setting, without the benefits of an intense group process of a residential program.

Whether ketamine administration is performed in an outpatient office, or in a residential center, Kolp recommends both settings have comfortable, scenically pleasant, home-like atmospheres. Breakfast is omitted on the morning of ketamine administration, and all participants refrain from food and drink from midnight through the ketamine-induced experience. The ketamine solution is administered via a brief intramuscular injection, rather than an intravenous administration requiring the use of an IV line, adding to the comfort of each patient. After the injection, the patient wears eyeshades, is instructed to fully surrender to the ketamine-induced experience, and beautiful, evocative music starts playing to assist with relaxation and immersion into the experience.

The NOSC lasts from 45 minutes to an hour under these conditions and then the patient slowly comes back from the experience. During the recovery period, which takes from one to two hours, the background composition changes from a free-floating non-associative music to an inspirational guided imagery meditation to affirm the patient's sought after transformation. When patients return to an ordinary state of consciousness, they are asked to describe the experience, and some limited discussion and interpretation is begun with the psychotherapist. After the session, the patient goes to rest and is asked to write down a detailed self-report of the ketamine-induced transpersonal experience during the second part of the day.

The integration of a ketamine-induced experience starts on the evening after the ketamine session and continues throughout the rest of the residential program. After the end of a residential component of the treatment, all patients continue weekly group psychotherapy sessions on an outpatient basis for three additional weeks. The patients who elect to participate in an outpatient individual treatment also receive three weekly individual psychotherapy sessions during the integration part of the treatment. Afterward, Kolp provides follow-ups every six months for all patients treated with KPP for as long as they continue to participate in aftercare.

With these in-depth, challenging preparatory and aftercare guidelines, Kolp was able to increase the effectiveness of KPP from 70% reported by Krupitsky (1992, 1997) to approximately 85% previously reported by Roquet (1975) and Yensen (1985). So far, the longest observed remission has been for 12 years (the patient undertook a three-week residential treatment program in 2002), as illustrated by the following case study:

> B was a 47-year-old Eurasian male who identified himself as a food addict. He reported no childhood trauma and described his nuclear family as very loving and supportive. B was raised as a Methodist, but changed his religious identification to a non-denominational Christian during his late teens and eventually began identifying himself as "spiritual but not religious" during his early 30s. He described himself as a "steak and potato man," and was proud of himself for never having a dessert. B was 6 feet 4 inches in height and 220 pounds in weight by age 18 and remained very fit throughout his mid-20s due to a very strenuous athletic involvement (a football player in high school and six

years of active duty service in the Marine Corps). After an honorable discharge from the armed forces at the age of 26, he became employed as a manager of a fast food restaurant.

B described himself as a compulsive overeater, who never attempted to compensate for his bingeing with purging behaviors such as fasting, laxative use, or vomiting. He did exercise a good deal through his early 30s. However, he eventually stopped working out and developed a sedentary lifestyle. In addition, he became engaged in "grazing" behavior and started picking at food throughout the day.

B's food preference was for fats and flour products, which he consumed three times a day, in addition to snacking between his major meals. His tolerance slowly increased and by his late 30s, his typical breakfast consisted of one 8-ounce sirloin steak, two big baked potatoes with sour cream, four scrambled eggs, a couple of sausages or two slices of ham, and a half dozen biscuits with butter. His lunch and dinner were equally impressive, always including large amounts of meats, bread, and butter. In addition, B had three to four self-made sandwiches between his main meals, which he prepared from a slice of ham or bologna meat, a slice of cheese, and two slices of white bread with butter. Once a month he treated himself with a 30-ounce strip sirloin at a steak house. B was a participant in an April 2000 survey, who would not give up meat for a week even if he were paid a thousand dollars to do so.

By the age of 40, B's weight reached 300 pounds. He was already diagnosed with hypertension, type II diabetes, hyperlipidemia, osteoarthritis, and sleep apnea. He had to take eight medications a day and his primary physician repeatedly warned him that he was a few years away from a stroke or a heart attack,. At that point B started taking some action and began dieting, but always unsuccessfully. He would stay on a diet of the season for a few weeks and sometimes drop several pounds in weight. However, each time he resumed his compulsive overeating.

B joined Overeaters Anonymous (a 12-step recovery program based on the principles of Alcoholics Anonymous, which is also known as The Fellowship) at age of 42, but left the program after a year ("too much praying, but no spiritual awakening"). He also briefly tried

Food Addicts in Recovery Anonymous (an alternative 12-step based program) and had no problems with completely abstaining from sugar, but could not abstain from the flour products longer than several weeks. In addition, he resented weighing and measuring all his meals and could not abstain from snacking between meals. B undertook a sleeve gastrectomy at age of 44, which helped him to decrease his weight to 250 pounds. However, he managed to "re-feed" himself within two years after the surgery. By the time he applied for treatment with KPP his weight was 310 pounds.

B was willing to stop eating meat and dairy products for six weeks prior to a ketamine session and agreed to abstain from highly refined and/or highly processed food for the same period of time. He reported severe cravings for fats and flour during the first three weeks. However, he was able to remain abstinent from the prohibited items. B actively participated in all groups, meditated twice a day, and started walking for 30 minutes every other day. Unbeknownst to his therapist and the group, B sneaked out of the residential facility the evening prior to the administration of ketamine in order to have his "last supper," a veal parmigiana dish. The following morning B received 250 mg of ketamine IM and had a very frightening NDE that he described as "hellish":

I got out of the body and initially rejoiced the freedom of leaving my fat and sick body. Within a minute or two though my mind started dissipating and it scared me very much. I remember thinking: I am really dying … it is the end of my life … oh, no, no … please make it stop. The mind completely gone and all that remained was a soul … silent, sad and lonely … rapidly falling into the abyss of nothingness. At some point the movement … stopped and the soul became motionless in the middle of the void. All of the sudden, my entire life began getting replayed and the soul was despondently observing my Earthly life of a glutton … a hungry sponge devouring countless living beings out of a lust for taste. The feeling of sorrow became resilient and the last conscious awareness was terrifying—if the Hell and the Heaven do, in fact, exist, the soul definitely belongs to the Hell.

As soon as my soul came to this conclusion, it got immediately sucked deep into an infinite ocean of unconditional sorrow and became that veal calf ... taking away from the mother ... suspended in a stall ... restricted in movements ... without seeing a sky and the trees ... sensing that something is terribly wrong ... that it is not how life is supposed to be lived ... tormented and very miserable ... finally going through a cruelty of a slaughterhouse ... hanged upside down ... skinned while still being alive. The soul's suffering became repetitive ... re-living life of all animals that my body consumed and my mind adored ... again and again ... life after life ... with no end at all. It seemed like the soul has been tortured for thousands if not millions of years before the mind re-emerged and then re-entered the body. My whole essence was screaming—no more carnivorous lifestyle ... no more causing suffering and death to God's innocent creatures.

B has continued to conscientiously participate in aftercare since the completion of his treatment and completely abandoned eating any animal products, both meat and dairy. He continued meditating daily and restarted exercising on a regular basis. B did not give up eating biscuits and potatoes (no butter and no sour cream), but he started limiting the consumption of flour and starches to once a week, eating only two biscuits and one potato on the weekends. Within two years, his weight stabilized at around 200 pounds and has remained constant since. The number of the medications has decreased from eight to one, and his hypertension, type II diabetes, hyperlipidemia, and sleep apnea have completely resolved.

Although the above case is rather exceptional, the vast majority of the patients treated with KPP do develop a stable remission, lasting from two or three to five or seven years and longer. Kolp, like Krupitsky before him, has repeatedly observed a dramatic improvement in patients' overall bio-psycho-socio-spiritual functioning, including rapid optimization of a personal lifestyle, decreased levels of inner conflicts and emotional isolation, enrichment of interpersonal relationships, resolution of existential death anxiety, positive changes in the life values and purposes, broadening of the worldviews, and acceleration of psychospiritual growth, through his approach to KPP.

Possible Mechanisms of the Effectiveness of KPP

Krupitsky previously reported that ketamine increases delta and theta activity in the cortex, evidencing limbic system activation as well as limbic-cortex interaction (Krupitsky & Grinenko, 1997). It was further documented that ketamine exerts its effect through a functional and electrophysiological dissociation or disconnect between the thalamo-neocortical and limbic areas of the brain (Green & Krauss, 2004a, 2004b; Mistry & Nahata, 2005).

Therefore, the Russian group including Kolp hypothesized that ketamine's underlying mechanism of action on the brain is the blockade of the thalamo-cortical projections and the activation of the interactions between frontal cortex and limbic structures, which results in a specific hyperfrontal metabolic pattern in the human brain, associated with ketamine-induced psychedelic experience (intense visionary experience and ego-dissolution). The thalamus' primary function is to relay sensory and motor signals to the cerebral cortex; the frontal cortex is responsible for cognitive processing of information (conscious mind); and the limbic system is the brain's center of emotions (unconscious mind). Thus, ketamine blocks transmission of incoming signals from all sensory modalities, including signals from the outer world and one's own body, and reinforces the interactions between the so-called cognitive and emotional minds. In other words, ketamine appears to disconnect the self from so-called objective reality, ties self-aware and unaware levels of mind in a closed loop, and removes a filter between conscious mind and unconscious mind, resulting in a profound waking dream that bears a remarkable resemblance to OBE, NDE, or EDT experiences.

The ketamine-induced non-ordinary states of consciousness seem to generate a different level of self-identification. Kolp describes that as, during OBEs, self-identity switches from "I am Body" to "I am Mind," while during NDEs the self-identity becomes more similar to "I am Soul," and during the EDTs more like *Unio mystica* or mystical union in which self-identity further progresses to "I am God." At no time, of course, is it suggested in KPP that the Soul and/or God experiences constitute any proof of the existence of any specific theological concept. These psychedelic experiences are subjective phenomena that cannot be easily, if ever, scientifically objectified, and they certainly do not prove the existence of any transcendental reality. Nevertheless, for reasons that remain speculative, having the uniquely profound and powerful mystical experience can significantly contribute to broadening attitudes about the self and the world, positive changes in life values and purposes, resolution of existential death anxiety, and rapid acceleration of spiritual transformation.

In 1962, Pahnke (1962, 1968, 1969; Pahnke et al., 1970) conducted the double-blind "Marsh Chapel Experiment" (a.k.a. the "Good Friday Experiment") investigating whether a psychedelic agent (psilocybin) would cause a genuine mystical experience in religiously predisposed subjects. Virtually all members of the psilocybin group (graduate degree divinity students) reported having profound religious experiences, and the faculty of the Harvard Divinity School concluded that a psychedelic agent can indeed facilitate such mystical experiences.

Twenty-five years later, Doblin (1991) traced seven theological seminary students participating in the Good Friday Experiment and reported that all of the psilocybin subjects continued considering that their original religious experience had a genuineness in terms of mystical nature and characterized it as a high point of their spiritual lives. One of these students was religious scholar Huston Smith, an author of several textbooks on comparative religion, who later on described his original psychedelic experience as the most powerful homecoming he had ever experienced (Smith, 2001).

In 2002, a group of investigators at Johns Hopkins University conducted a more rigorously controlled study similar to the Good Friday experiment (Griffiths et al., 2006). The study's participants were hallucinogen-naïve adults who reported regular participation in religious or spiritual activities. The study compared psilocybin (30 mg) and methylphenidate (40 mg) using a double-blind between-group, crossover design. Thirty volunteers received 30 mg of psilocybin and 40 mg of methylphenidate in counterbalanced order. Two or three sessions were conducted at two-month intervals. To obscure the study design, six additional volunteers received methylphenidate in the first two sessions and un-blinded psilocybin in a third session. The eight-hour sessions were conducted individually. Volunteers were encouraged to close their eyes and direct their attention inward. The study's investigators documented that 67% of the participants who received psilocybin experienced powerful NOSC that had similarities to naturally occurring mystical experiences. Furthermore, those drug-induced mystical experiences were rated by volunteers as having great personal and spiritual significance that resulted in sustained positive attitudes and behavior that were corroborated by ratings from friends and family.

Sixteen months later, the same group of researchers at Johns Hopkins University completed a follow-up to their original psilocybin study (Griffiths et al., 2008). Two-thirds of the study participants continued rating the psychedelic-induced experience as among the top most meaningful experiences in their lives. Sixty-four percent of the participants reported that the experience increased well-being and life satisfaction, and 58% met criteria for having had a "complete" mystical experience. Seventeen percent indicated that it was the most meaningful and significant experience, while none of the participants rated the experience as leading to decreased well-being or decreased life satisfaction. The researchers concluded that the mystical aspect of the experience was crucial in achieving positive therapeutic outcomes, and they recommended additional therapeutic trials with hallucinogens.

Kolp thinks it is evident that an ego dissolution during psychedelic-induced mystical (transcendental, spiritual) peak experience is perceived by healthy volunteers and mentally ill patients alike as transcending their individual body restrictions and generates a psychological sense of security which extends beyond the impermanence of the finite corporeal body. Successively, the individuals can better cope with the prospect of the yet to come death and demonstrate a long-lasting resolution of existential death anxiety (Cohen, 1965; Griffiths et al., 2006, 2008; Grinspoon & Bakalar, 1979; Grob, 1998, 2002; Grof, 1978, 1980, 1986; Grof & Halifax, 1976; Grof et al., 1973; Kast, 1966a, 1966b; Kast & Collins, 1964; Kolp et al., 2007, 2009; Krupitsky & Grinenko, 1996; Krupitsky & Kolp, 2007; Krupitsky et al., 1992; Pahnke, 1968; Pahnke et al., 1970; Richards et al., 1972, 1977, 1979; Walsh & Grob, 2005; Watts, 1973; Yensen & Dryer, 1993/1994). The following case study demonstrates the efficacy of ego-dissolving transcendental experience in the treatment of a patient with chronic depression, recurrent headaches, and combined opioid and barbiturate dependence:

> M was a 34-year-old Hispanic American female who had been suffering from chronic depression since puberty. In addition, she developed recurrent headaches two years after her marriage at the age of 22. She was raised as a non-denominational Christian and changed her self-identity to "spiritual but not religious" during her early 20s. She reported no history of physical and/or sexual abuse during her childhood, but acknowledged a long history of an ongoing repeated stress due to a hapless marriage (she described her husband as a "patriarchal male chauvinist pig"), two children of ages 11 and 9 with conduct disorder and ADHD (whom she referred to as "little terrorists"), and a demanding full-time job with an "awful boss."
>
> M began psychiatric treatment at the age of 16 and had already been prescribed many antidepressants, including five SSRIs (fluoxetine, paroxetine, sertraline, citalopram, and escitalopram), three SN-

RIs (venlafaxine, duloxetine, and desvenlafaxine), one NRI (bupropion) and one NaSSA (mirtazapine). Although she responded well to the treatment with her first SSRI and first SNRI SNRIs (both times the remission lasted for 9 and 6 months respectively), the efficacy of antidepressant treatment eventually became marginal. M also started treatment with a neurologist at the age of 24 and was treated with several anti-migraine medications, including sumatriptan, metoprolol, topiramate, gabapentin, rizatriptan, and pregabalin, all with limited results.

At the time of her initial evaluation for KPP treatment, M was taking a combination of bupropion (300 mg in the morning), mirtazapine (45 mg at bedtime), and Fioricet (codeine 30 mg, butalbital [a barbiturate] 50 mg, acetaminophen 300 mg, and caffeine 40 mg), which she took as two capsules four times a day (240 mg of codeine and 400 mg of butalbital daily). She continued complaining of chronically depressed mood (she scored 28 points on the Beck Depression Inventory) and recurrent headaches (three to four times a week, lasting for several hours).

M elected to participate in a group residential program and agreed to get detoxified from the two sedatives (codeine and butalbital) and the two antidepressants (bupropion and mirtazapine) because her medications "did not work anyway." In addition, she dutifully followed strict preparatory guidelines (a whole food plant-based diet, optimal hydration, daily meditation and exercise, limitation of screen time, and contemplation on the nature of the Self and God). After successful preparation on an outpatient basis, M was admitted to a residential program where she became actively engaged in an intensive group process. She received 150 mg of ketamine IM and reported the following EDT experience:

My body became dissolved as an icicle in a hot water and my mind began steadily expanding as an inflating balloon. First, I got aware of the surrounding space around me and actually became the growing trees ... and birds ... and animals ... and other people ... in the range of 300–400 yards around me. This expansion did not stop at it and my mind continued progressively getting larger and

> *larger … until it embraced the entire Earth and I became aware that I am a part of the Great Mother Gaia. At that point my individual mind disappeared and became transformed into collective mind. The collective mind continued rapidly expanding to the entire Solar system … then to the entire Milky Way galaxy … and eventually to the entire Universe. The individual awareness shifted to the awareness of the Universal Mind and my personal Soul became a part of the Universal Consciousness. God and I are One and We are omniscient, omnipotent, omnificent and omnipresent. The experience seemed lasting for the eons … and all that time the awareness remained "everything is exactly as it should be" … "We are all One" … "everything is perfect" … "everything is perfect."*

M continued in aftercare for two and a half years until she and her family relocated to another state. She reported that her chronic depression had finally resolved and her recurrent headaches were completely gone. M also became actively engaged in ongoing family psychotherapy and reported marked improvements in her relationships with her husband and children, as well as improvements in her other interpersonal relationships. She continued exercising and practicing meditation on a regular basis, stopped consuming animal products, and began volunteering in a local charity.

M's case represents a typical KPP treatment outcome among those patients who experienced an ego-dissolving mind-expanding transcendental experience.

Antidepressant Effects of Ketamine

The low dose of ketamine used for analgesia and anxiolysis as well as the medium dose of ketamine used for conscious sedation can reliably produce brief but robust antidepressant effects. Various investigators started publishing reports documenting antidepressant effects of ketamine in the early 1970s. These earlier studies, performed from the 1970s through the 1990s, utilized ketamine in medium doses and generally attributed anxiolytic/antidepressant responses to an overall psychological improvement following the induction of NOSC, a specific phenomenon called "psychedelic afterglow." This psychedelic afterglow state consists of positive physical and psychological changes, including increased psychological clarity, feelings of being cleansed, increased confidence, feeling of happiness and well-being, state of inner peace, feelings of detachment, motivation to improve oneself, and strong feelings of empathy for everyone. The afterglow state was thought to be induced by the psychedelic peak experience and reported to last from several days to several weeks and longer (Adamson, 1985; Bolle, 1985, 1988, 1992; Grossbard, 1989; Fontana, 1974; Khorramzadeh & Lofty, 1976; Krupitsky, 1993/1994; Krupitsky & Grinenko, 1996, 1997, 1998; Krupitsky et al., 1992; Moore & Altounian, 1978; Roquet, 1975; Roquet & Favreau, 1981; Roquet et al., 1971; Yensen, 1973).

However, it was also long recognized that ketamine was likely to acutely improve mood secondary to its effects on, for example, the dopamine system, which have some commonalities with amphetamine and cocaine, and there was certainly long-standing speculation as to a neurochemical basis for ketamine improving mood for up to a week, with lack of a post-stimulant crash being attributed to such possibilities as the lingering presence of active ketamine metabolites and/or gene induction (summarized in Jansen, 2001). In this context, it is of note that the original Maudsley monograph describing amphetamine psychosis warned against attributing mental state changes to anything other than amphetamine while the metabolites could still be detected in the urine, and that the metabolites could sometimes be detected for at least a week (Connell, 1958), as is sometimes the case with ketamine.

The general trend changed with a formal study done by Krystal's group of investigators who reported that research subjects with symptoms of depression showed a dramatic antidepressant response to an administration of low sub-psychedelic doses of ketamine (Berman et al., 2000). It is interesting to note that the original purpose of this study was not to research the antidepressant effects of ketamine but to assess its cognitive effects on subjects with mental illness. The antidepressant effect of ketamine was apparently not expected by this group (Brown, 2007). Some similar studies have replicated these findings and confirmed that low doses of ketamine can produce a rapid antidepressant effect lasting from one or two days to one or two weeks (Kudoh et al., 2002; Ostroff, Gonzalis, & Sanacora, 2005). These results would probably not have been a surprise to most nonmedical and recreational users of the drug, who have long reported elevation in mood for up to a week (summarized in Jansen, 2001).

These earlier reports seemed to have only a limited impact until a study was conducted at the National Institute of Mental Health (Zarate et al., 2006). This randomized controlled trial was specifically conducted in subjects with TRD, including some patients who had not responded to electroconvulsive therapy. The study provided evidence that a single sub-anesthetic dose of ketamine may provide rapid but non-sustained relief of depressive symptoms.

Since publication of this study, further reports have confirmed the efficacy of ketamine for the treatment of major depressive disorder and the depressive phase of bipolar disorder (aan het Rot et al., 2010; Bjerre & Fontenay, 2010; Diaz-Granados et al., 2010; Ibrahim et al., 2012; Liebrenz et al., 2007, 2009; Murrough et al., 2011, 2012; Rasmussenet et al., 2013; Rot et al., 2008; Zarate et al., 2012, 2013). Most recent studies have used a low sub-psychedelic dose of ketamine (0.5 mg/kg) administered via IV infusion over 40 to 60 minutes (aan het Rot et al., 2010; Bjerre & Fontenay, 2010; Diaz-Granados et al., 2010; Glue, Gulati, Le Nedelec, & Duffull, 2011; Ibrahim et al., 2012; Liebrenz et al., 2007, 2009; Murrough et al., 2011, 2012; Rasmussen et al., 2013; Rot et al., 2008; Zarate et al., 2006, 2012, 2013), and one study utilized a low sub-psychedelic dose of ketamine (1 mg/kg) via IM administration (Glue et al., 2011). The number of ketamine administrations has varied from one to six (aan het Rot, Zarate, Charney, & Mathew, 2012).

There are also reports documenting the effectiveness of ketamine pharmacotherapy in the treatment of eating disorders (Mills, Park, Manara, & Merriman, 1998) and obsessive-compulsive disorder (Rodriguez et al., 2013). Murrough and colleagues examined the efficacy of repeated ketamine infusions on the length of post-treatment remission (Murrough et al., 2012). The study's subjects underwent a washout of antidepressant medication followed by up to six IV infusions of ketamine (0.5 mg/kg) administered three times per week over a 12-day period. Seventy-one percent of the patients developed a remission. However, the median time to relapse after the last infusion of ketamine was only 18 days. Some researchers have thus been adopting a maintenance strategy (Messer & Haller, 2010). There have been reports of oral (Irwin & Iglewicz, 2010; Paslakis, Gilles, Meyer-Lindenberg, & Deuschle, 2010) and sublingual (Lara, Bisol, & Munari, 2013) ketamine as an effective maintenance antidepressant. Since intranasal ketamine has been already used as an effective maintenance sedative and analgesic (Bahetwar, Randey, Saskena, & Chandra, 2011; Reid, Hatton, & Middleton, 2011), this technique is also being developed as both an initial and maintenance treatment of major depression (Lapidus et al., 2014). These three modalities—oral, sublingual, and intranasal—are emerging as the preferred delivery methods of a ketamine maintenance treatment.

It is unknown how many persons who take non-prescribed ketamine (i.e., non-medical and recreational users) are actually taking the drug to self-medicate what amount to depressive disorders. It is also unknown how many clinical practitioners in the United States have administered ketamine to patients with TRD, but general correspondence suggests a marked increase. An internet search identified an on-line organization (Ketamine Advocacy Network (KAN)) that has a list of "ketamine doctors" in the United States who are performing the ketamine administration procedure (www.ketamineadvocacynetwork.org). At the time of writing this paper, KAN was listing 17 physicians from three specialties, including 10 psychiatrists, five anesthesiologists, and two neurologists. All physicians are providing both the initial infusion of ketamine to rapidly relieve depression and a maintenance therapy to lengthen a remission after the symptoms of depression re-emerge. Sixteen physicians administer IV infusions of ketamine, and one psychiatrist administers IM injections. One psychiatrist is offering a post-infusion maintenance treatment with transcranial magnetic stimulation, one anesthesiologist is offering maintenance treatment with intranasal and oral ketamine, and one neurologist is offering an intranasal maintenance treatment.

It is understandable why the majority of known ketamine providers have used IV infusions. All initial research studies that reported a robust antidepressant effect of ketamine were using IV infusions of ketamine. However, IV infusions are partly the preferred delivery methods in a research setting because an IV line provides access for collecting blood samples to measure various biochemical markers before, during, and after the procedures. Outside the research setting, IV infusions may offer no particular advantage, and seem unlikely to be more beneficial than IM injections. This fact was emphasized by the initial group of formal researchers (aan het Rot, Zarate, Charney, & Mathew, 2012), who pointed out that previous research documented that IV administration of conventional antidepressants did not support increased efficacy over oral administration (Moukaddam & Hirschfeld, 2004).

From the viewpoint of a physician practicing in a clinical setting, the IV infusions have many disadvantages. They are supposed to be performed in a hospital setting and to require the presence of an anesthesiologist, decrease the duration of therapeutic NOSC from 45 to 60 minutes to 20 to 25 minutes (unless performed as a continuous drip), and can increase the procedure's cost to the patients from approximately $400 per IM administration to around $2,000 per IV infusion, or more. Meanwhile, ketamine administration for treatment of mental illnesses remains an "experimental" procedure and its cost is not yet being covered by any medical insurance company, forcing non-research patients in the United States to bear the cost. In addition, IV infusions needlessly medicalize the procedure and, consequently, may increase the chances of a frightening experience. It has been suggested that IV ketamine infusions should perhaps be reserved for emergency room treatment only, where acutely suicidal depressed patients frequently present themselves (Larkin & Beautrais, 2011), although it is likely that even in this context, IV will eventually be shown to have no powerful advantage over IM when all the costs and benefits are weighed, as has gradually been demonstrated in psychiatric ICU hospital practice for benzodiazepines and antipsychotics, in which context giving the medicines as an IV injection is fading away in English-speaking countries (e.g., Taylor, Paton, & Kapur, 2012).

Other practitioners have already started utilizing IM injections of ketamine as the preferred treatment. A leading article in the January 2013 issue of *Psychiatric Times* (Kaplan, 2013) described a ketamine treatment program at the University of California San Diego (UCSD) Medical Center, directed by David Feifel, an associate professor in the Department of Psychiatry. Feifel recommended starting with the initial infusion to assess the length of a remission. Those patients who demonstrate at least one week of a stable remission are then referred for a maintenance treatment with repeated administrations of a low intramuscular dose of ketamine (0.5 mg/kg) and no more frequently than once every two weeks. Feifel has begun utilizing an IM administration because of its practicality and cost effectiveness. He shared that when the UCSD program first started, anesthesiologists were required to give the intravenous ketamine infusions in an acute care setting, with the costs of IV procedures around $2,000 per infusion; in contrast, IM administrations are now given by nurses, with an attending physician available during the procedure, and the cost went down significantly (Kaplan, 2013).

Ketamine psycho-pharmacotherapy is rapidly gaining momentum. The FDA awarded the breakthrough therapy designation for the development of intranasal ketamine for treating depression (a definition of breakthrough therapy is a drug that treats a serious or life threatening disease and preliminary clinical evidence indicates that the drug may demonstrate substantial improvement over existing therapies on one or more clinically significant endpoints, such as substantial treatment effects observed early in clinical development). If a drug is designated as breakthrough therapy, the FDA will expedite the development and review of such a drug. All requests for breakthrough therapy designation will be reviewed within 60 days of receipt, and the FDA will either grant or deny the request. This is the first time this special designation, usually reserved for drugs targeting a lethal epidemic or a deadly form of cancer, has been awarded for the development of a medication for a mental disorder.

A key remaining question is the duration of ketamine's effect, which significantly varies not only from person to person, but also from treatment to treatment for the same person. At times, the effect only lasts a day or two and at other times, the effect lasts one or two weeks, or even a month.

The Biological vs. Psychological and Transpersonal Effects of Ketamine

As noted, some of the earlier ketamine studies attributed the anxiolytic and antidepressant post-treatment effects to "psychedelic afterglow" following the induction of NOSC. Contrary to the earlier reports, most of the recent studies ignore the psychological effects of ketamine-induced altered states of consciousness and appear to largely dismiss these psychological phenomena, particularly those of a transpersonal quality, which are presented mostly as an undesirable side effect. For example, Arun Ravindran, psychiatry professor at the University of Toronto and chief of mood and anxiety disorders at Toronto's Centre for Addiction and Mental Health, will be leading a study specifically exploring oral and intranasal routes of ketamine administration. In an interview with the Toronto Star (Ballingall, 2014), Professor Ravindran referred to ketamine-induced psychological phenomena as an unwanted side effect that he called the "relaxed dissociated state."

Virtually all scientific investigators who have recently published in this area present similar opinions in their published writings, and largely attribute the antidepressant effects of ketamine to its pharmacological properties to alter the glutamate system, which in turn modulates other systems such as dopamine (aan het Rot et al., 2010; Bjerre & Fontenay, 2010; Diaz-Granados et al., 2010; Glue et al., 2011; Ibrahim et al., 2012; Liebrenz et al., 2007, 2009; Murrough et al., 2011, 2012; Rasmussen et al., 2013; Rot et al., 2008; Zarate et al., 2006, 2012). This current biological theory proposes that, in addition to biochemical sub-types of depression caused by an "imbalance" of biogenic amines (serotonin, norepinephrine, and dopamine), there is also a separate sub-type of depression that biochemically mediates the same syndromic diagnosis of major depressive disorder due to an "imbalance" of glutamate (aan het Rot et al., 2010; Bjerre & Fontenay, 2010; Hashimoto, 2009; Ibrahim et al., 2012; Liebrenz et al., 2007; Machado-Vieira, Manji, & Zarate, 2009; Murrough et al., 2011; Rasmussen et al., 2013; Rot et al., 2008; Scolnick, Popik, & Trullas, 2009; Zarate et al., 2006, 2012).

There are complications with this theory. An existing NMDA receptor antagonist, memantine, was first developed in 1968 and has long been used as a neuroprotective agent and prescribed by some doctors for moderate-to-severe dementia. Like many other NMDA antagonists, memantine is a dissociative agent at above therapeutic doses (Morris & Wallach, 2014). It can even substitute for phencyclidine in rodent and primate drug discrimination studies (Parsons & Danysz, 1999). Although memantine has been associated in some studies with a modest decrease in the clinical deterioration of patients with moderate-to-severe dementia (Rossi, 2006), it has been reported as having only an insignificant positive effect on mood in the treated patients (Areosa, Sherriff, & McShane, 2005). There is still relatively little evidence of even a minimal effect on mild Alzheimer's disease (Schneider, Dagerman, Higgins, & McShane, 2011). Zarate and his team have also reported that memantine does not relieve depression (Brown, 2007). The claim that memantine would be effective in Alzheimer's disease was rather surprising as it is well established that NMDA receptor blockade impairs memory rather than improving it (e.g., Collingridge, 1987). Ketamine users tend to report problems with their short-term memories rather than any improvement (Jansen, 2001; Morgan & Curran, 2012).

Another available glutamate-modulating agent, riluzole (Rilutetek), a drug that inhibits glutamate release, does somewhat improve depression but no better than conventional antidepressants and with the same time delay (Sanacora et al., 2007; Zarate et al., 2004, 2005). Riluzole was also researched in patients treated with ketamine in an attempt to sustain antidepressant effects. However, the studies failed to demonstrate any benefit over placebo in maintaining response to an IV ketamine infusion (aan het Rot et al., 2012; Brown, 2007; Ibrahim et al., 2012; Mathew et al., 2010).

A recent study using sophisticated proton magnetic resonance spectroscopy has specifically investigated ketamine's effects on glutamate brain levels in depressed patients but found no association between the antidepressant effects of ketamine and any significant changes in brain glutamate levels in both immediate (three hours) and delayed (two days) response to a ketamine administration (Valentine et al., 2011).

Undoubtedly, ketamine has many direct and/or indirect pharmacological effects on the human brain that may immediately improve the subject's mood. These effects are multifactorial. In addition to affecting the glutamate system (similarly to alcohol), ketamine affects the dopamine system (similarly to NRIs and amphetamines), GABA system (similarly to benzodiazepines), serotonin system (similarly to SSRIs), mu opioid system (similarly to opiates), cannabinoid system (similarly to THC), and nitric system (similarly to nitrous oxide or "laughing gas"). All of the above compounds have been shown to rapidly generate anti-anxiety and antidepressant effects (especially when administered intravenously). The duration of their effects, however, has generally not much exceeded the pharmacological life of a particular compound and, it must be noted, its psychoactive metabolites which can be much longer.

Approximately one-third of the ketamine subjects did not maintain a remission of depressive symptoms for longer than 24 hours post-infusion. Two-thirds of the subjects did maintain a remission lasting from two days to two weeks. Why would remission last longer than one day? One possibility is some persistence of the NMDA-receptor active metabolites, with variations between people in the rate of metabolism due to genetic and lifestyle differences (Jansen, 2001). There are other psychiatric treatments where the persistence of metabolites, sometimes for many weeks, is accepted as central to the mechanism of action. The antipsychotic drug haloperidol is a good example, with the active metabolite lasting in the blood for many weeks. Thus ceasing to take haloperidol rarely results in an immediate relapse of psychosis.

However, it is also possible that the so-called "relaxed dissociated state" is not an unwanted side effect, but is actually a cause of protracted remissions for psychological reasons. This may well prove to be the correct explanation. A recent study done by the Zarate group of investigators (Luckenbaugh et al., 2014) presented data from 108 treatment-resistant inpatients who met criteria for major depression or type I and II bipolar disorder and were given a subanesthetic ketamine infusion. The group examined whether dissociation experiences, measured by the Clinician-Administered Dissociative States Scale (CADSS), correlated with improvements in the Hamilton Depression Rating Scale (HDRS). The correlations' analysis indicated that there was a significant association between increased CADSS scores and improvement in HDRS scores, while none of the other analyzed parameters significantly correlated to HDRS change. The study concluded that those patients with more dissociation are also those in whom ketamine has a greater antidepressant efficacy, while the patients who did not show the dissociation did not have antidepressant efficacy in the post-infusion period.

This paper resonates with the earlier ketamine studies attributing a post-treatment remission of anxiety and depression to the quality of NOSC experience. It may be that one-third of the experimental ketamine subjects had an alcohol-like euphoric affect and their remission thus lasted for no longer than 24 hours post-infusion. Another one-third of the subjects had an MDMA-like empathogenic experience, and their remission lasted for two to five days post-infusion. The last one-third of the patients had an OBE, and their remission lasted for one to two weeks and even longer. These odds are expected due to the fact that the standard 50 mg dose of ketamine used in the research subjects is located on the critical dosage threshold between empathogenic and hallucinogenic responses, giving many subjects a 50% chance to have either an empathogenic or a hallucinogenic experience.

It seems that reducing the experiences of ketamine to just being due to biological causes may be doing injustice to its psychological, and even transpersonal, effects. The following clinical case supports the theory that psychological factors are important:

> W was a 59-year-old Caucasian female, with a past history of sexual abuse (between ages 11 and 17) and a lifelong history of avoidant personality disorder (now reclassified as anxious personality disorder). She also developed scoliosis (a sideways curvature of the spine) during the growth spurt just before puberty and suffered from chronic pain since her mid-teens. In addition, she developed regular panic attacks, occurring one to three times a week, lasting from 10 or 20 minutes to several hours, since her late teens. W was raised as a Methodist, but converted to Hinduism at age 18, when she joined an ashram (a version of a contemporary monastery) in order to escape from her abuser (stepbrother). W embraced a Yogini lifestyle and started practicing daily transcendental meditation, two times a day, one hour each sitting.
>
> At the age of 27, during an exceptionally long 10-day silent retreat, she spontaneously developed the Samadhi experience (ego-dissolving transcendental state of consciousness of mystical union with God) that lasted for several hours. W reported that after experiencing this state of "ecstatic bliss," her anxious personality, chronic pain, and recurrent panic attacks were "gone in a blink of an eye." Her remission lasted for nine years until she was raped at the age of 36, which triggered a relapse of panic disorder, chronic pain disorder, and avoidant behavior. The rape also caused the onset of chronic depression.
>
> W continued meditating devotedly every single day and attended numerous silent retreats. However, she never had a mystical experience again. She had to start taking pharmaceuticals to control her chronic anxiety, depression, and pain, and she was treated with paroxetine, diazepam, and hydrocodone. The medications controlled her problems, but only partially. In addition, W slowly developed tolerance, which

required a periodic upward adjustment of medication dose. By the time she requested ketamine treatment, she had to take daily 60 mg of paroxetine, 80 mg of diazepam, and 120 mg of hydrocodone. Despite high doses of three pharmaceuticals, she continued having chronic depression (her Beck Depression Inventory [BDI] score was 29), chronic anxiety (her Beck Anxiety Inventory [BAI] was 36) and chronic pain (rated 7 on 0–10 scale).

W considered undertaking KPP, after discovering a description of the EDT experience on Kolp's website, in which she recognized her spontaneous Samadhi experience. She had no difficulties to prepare herself for the experience, as she already practiced a vegan lifestyle, meditated and exercised daily, contemplated on the nature of the Self and God much of her waking time, and used screen time only occasionally. For the last 10 days of the preparation, she started practicing a juice fast in order to increase a chance of the EDT experience.

The day before the administration of ketamine, W consulted her guru (a spiritual guide), who actively discouraged her from having the drug-induced EDT experience. She was apparently told that the "Creator cannot be experienced through a narcotic, you should instead double your meditation time." She accepted the guru's instruction and requested to have only 50 mg of ketamine, since W believed that this dose represented a medically recommended dose that should be used as a therapeutic agent for the treatment of chronic "treatment-resistant" depression. Her therapist supported her wish, reminded W that she had a good chance of having the EDT experience due to her outstanding preparation, and instructed W "to close her eyes, start meditating, and surrender to whatever is to come." W followed this instruction, positioned herself in a Savasana ("corpse") pose, and then comfortably remained in the pose for the next two hours. Upon her return from the journey she shared this experience:

As soon as I started breathing slowly and reciting my mantra my body started quickly relaxing and within three or four minutes the body became deeply relaxed and very comfortable. For the first time in the past 23 years the pain has disappeared. My mind was feeling very peaceful and calm … yet the mind remained fully awake and alert. Again, for the first time in the past 23 years, the sad mood and persistent anxiety have gone away. At that point I stopped meditating and started enjoying the profound feelings of empathy, compassion and love for myself. The whole experience was full of joy and peace … I only regret that I stopped meditating and did not transcend to the Soul Consciousness and then to the God Consciousness.…

W maintained a symptom-free remission for three and one-half weeks and then developed a relapse of anxiety, followed by pain, and then depression. It was suggested that she undertake a second ketamine treatment. However, her spiritual guide persuaded her against it, pointing out that it may represent a drug-seeking behavior. The guru's advice was "keep meditating." At that point, W was started on phenelzine, 15 mg daily, with only a minimum response. After four weeks of treatment, the dose of phenelzine was increased to 30 mg daily, with a good response. W maintained a partial remission and her BDI score decreased to 17, the BAI score declined to 19, and her chronic pain level reduced to 3 to 4 on a scale of 10. She required two more adjustments of the phenelzine dose, to 45 mg 10 months later, and to 60 mg 17 months later. During her two-year follow-up, W continued maintaining a steady remission: her BDI score further decreased to 14, the BAI score remained 19, and the chronic pain level became stable at 3.

As this case demonstrates, a spontaneous EDT experience can prolong the length of remission from depressive symptoms significantly longer than the best drug-induced empathogenic experience. Although all NOSCs may contribute to accelerated healing, it seems that the EDT experience may have the most healing potential.

The majority of Kolp's patients with chronic treatment-resistant depression (approximately 90%), who requested ketamine pharmacotherapy with a sub-psychedelic dose (50 mg IM), never had a trial with any MAOI antidepressants. Subsequently, Kolp began offering a trial with a MAOI antidepressant to all MAOI-naïve patients and recommended starting the trial on the day following the IM ketamine administration. Nearly 80% of the patients responded well, maintained a steady remission, and did not require a maintenance treatment with repeated IM administrations of ketamine.

Ketamine Addiction

The concerns of W's guru about drug-seeking behavior in some ketamine users do have merit, as ketamine can generate strong effects on mood (feelings), cognition (thinking), and perception (imagery) that make some people want to use it repeatedly. However, initially both the FDA and the DEA accepted the Parke-Davis testimonials and apparently agreed that ketamine has no addictive properties. It was subsequently discovered that ketamine is a substance with very significant dependence potential for multiple reasons (Jansen, 2001). In fact, the 68th edition of the *Physicians' Desk Reference* specifically warns physicians that prolonged use of ketamine may lead to tolerance and drug dependence (PDR Network, 2013). Kolp found that more than two-thirds of his ketamine patients wanted to have another empathogenic experience the following day and nearly one-third of the patients wished to promptly repeat a psychedelic experience.

Ketamine has been available to hospital staff since late 1960s, and persons working in this context were among the first ones to personally test the drug's empathogenic and psychedelic effects. The street use of ketamine hydrochloride solutions was first noted in San Francisco and Los Angeles circa 1971, while other forms of ketamine (powder and tablets) were first noticed on the street in 1974 (Ashley, 1978). Ketamine went under a variety of street names, including Special K and Vitamin K (Siegel, 1978).

One of the first reports describing the testimonials of nonprescription ketamine users came from Rumpf and his group of investigators (1969), whose subjects described ketamine hallucinations as "utopic," "fantastic," or "mysterious." Only one out of their 18 subjects considered the dream experiences normal and ordinary. The experience was termed pleasant by six subjects, unpleasant by eight, and neutral by four. Unexpectedly, Rumpf and colleagues reported that fully one-third of the group (six subjects) had "true hallucinations" with the concomitant delusions that their dreams were not dreams, but, in point of fact, real events (Rumpf et al., 1969).

The first comprehensive study examining the patterns of ketamine addiction was done by Siegel (1978), who examined 23 subjects with recreational ketamine use. His sample included 13 injection users of ketamine and 10 intranasal ketamine users. Use of ketamine was primarily experimental or social in nature, and the drug was viewed by users to be a potent yet safe hallucinogen with a short duration of action and few if any adverse effects. Ketamine users tended to titrate their use in order to achieve the desired effects of stimulation, dissociation, visual hallucinations, and transcendental experiences (Siegel, 1978). When asked to rank all drugs in terms of general recreational preference, Siegel reported that intranasal users ranked cocaine first, while injection users ranked LSD first. The users consistently described ketamine in the following ways:

- Ketamine was perceived by users to be a safe, nontoxic, potent hallucinogen with a short duration of action and few adverse reactions.

- Ketamine was perceived by most users as the only hallucinogen that did not produce anxiety or fear reactions.

- Ketamine was considered to have unique euphoric-hallucinogenic properties that enabled a user to experience, with varying dosages, effects similar to either cocaine, amyl nitrite, phencyclidine, or LSD.

Ketamine users repeatedly sought and experienced the following desirable effects: floating sensations and dissociation (87%), stimulation (83%), hallucinations (78%), increased cognitive or mental associations (74%), euphoria (26%), and transcendental or religious experiences (17%). Despite the widespread beliefs among users about the lack of adverse reactions, a number of untoward effects were also reported, including ataxia (100%), slurring of speech (70%), dizziness (61%), mental confusion (35%), hyperexcitability (26%), unpleasant imagery (26%), blurring of vision (17%), negative hallucinations, or the inability to see things that were really there (17%), decreased sociability (17%), anxiety (13%), nausea (13%), insomnia (13%), and decreased sexual motivation (9%).

Siegel (1978) documented the specific long-term effects, both positive and negative, resulting from ketamine use. Some ketamine users described a lasting elevation of mood (43%), deeper insights into self and others (35%), and positive changes in attitudes and personality (17%). Other ketamine users reported undesired long-term effects including flashbacks (57%), attentional dysfunction (22%), and decreased sociability (9%). Overall, long-term effects appeared equally divided between positive and negative experiences.

Ketamine was further popularized during the 1970s by John Lilly, and to a lesser extent by astrologer Marcia Moore, who wrote books on the subject of self-use of ketamine. Lilly published a book entitled *The Scientist* (1978) and Moore (together with her husband, Dr. Alltounian) published a book called *Journeys into the Bright World* (1978). Both books documented the unusual phenomenology of ketamine intoxication and prompted others to experiment with ketamine. Subsequently, many ketamine users in the "first wave" preferred ketamine for its psychedelic properties and administered it via IM self-injections.

The ketamine scene began changing during the late 1980s to early 1990s when lower doses of ketamine in pill and powder form, for intranasal use, became more prevalent due to its empathogenic and stimulant effects at lower doses (Tori, 1996; NDIC Bulletin, 2004). Ketamine began appearing on the club, underground party, and rave scenes, being used together with or instead of ecstasy (MDMA), cocaine, and amphetamines. By the mid-1990s, ketamine had entered mainstream dance culture, and it remains a popular dance drug today (e.g., Joe-Laidler & Hunt, 2008).

Eventually, the U.S. Drug Enforcement Agency (DEA) became alarmed by this development and changed ketamine's schedule in August of 1999, making it a controlled substance and moving the drug to Schedule III of the Controlled Substances Act of 1970. Other countries have also done so, most recently India, which had been a major source for the European market. India is now being replaced by China as the source. In 2000 the Hong Kong government placed ketamine in Schedule 1, a drastic measure in response to the recent rise in ketamine prevalence in East Asia.

As previously noted, the Russian government moved ketamine from Schedule III into Schedule II in 2002 after ketamine became popular with Muscovite teenagers. In 2005, Canada reclassified ketamine as a Schedule I narcotic. The United Kingdom moved ketamine from Class C to Class B in June of 2014. Controls were also tightened in New Zealand. These more recent changes were partly driven by the reports of binge nonmedical ketamine use being linked with damage to the urinary system in some users. In addition, ketamine is in Category 3 under Mexico's General Health Law. However, generic ketamine is still easily obtained in a "veteranaria farmacia" as "ketamina" for $15 to $20 a gram. According to a DEA report from 2004, over 80% of ketamine seized in the United States at that time, 10 years ago, was of Mexican origin (NDIC Bulletin, 2004).

Unlike phencyclidine, ketamine production is a complex and time-consuming process, making clandestine manufacturing of ketamine impractical. Meanwhile, ketamine is produced commercially in a number of countries, including (for example) the United States, Mexico, Colombia, China, India, Germany, and Belgium, where it may be diverted from legitimate sources. There have also been reports of industrial-scale illicit ketamine manufacture in China (UN Office on Drugs and Crime, 2010).

Ketamine's use as a recreational drug has been rising over the last 30 years (Copeland & Dillon, 2005; Dillon & Degenhardt, 2001; Jansen, 2000; Moore & Measham, 2008). Travis (2005) reported that ketamine was one of the six most common drugs for sale in United Kingdom cities. Stirling and colleagues (2008) published an update on recreational drug use in the UK and reported that 4% of the young adults in the study had tried ketamine at least once. Dillon, Copeland, and Jansen (2003) reported that about one in three Australian respondents in a study of a drug user culture acknowledged the use of ketamine in the previous 12 months. The 2006 National Survey on Drug Use and Health (NSDUH) reported that in the United States an estimated 2,300,000 persons aged 12 and older had used ketamine in their lifetime, and 203,000 were past year users (NSDUH Report, 2006).

There is a substantial popular literature describing ketamine dependence (e.g., Lilly, 1978; Sputz, 1989; Turner, 1994). Ketamine recurrent binges can be sustained for many days and even several weeks. The medical literature has documented the same and the number of case studies is mounting (Ahmed & Petchkovsky, 1980; Hurt & Ritchie, 1994; Jansen, 1990a, 1990b, 2000, 2001; Kamaya & Krishna, 1987; Moore & Bostwick, 1999; Morgan & Curran, 2012; Soyka, Kripinsky, & Volki, 1993). The evidence from animal studies indicates that ketamine can form a dependence syndrome (Beardsley & Balster, 1987). The multiple problems related to dependence on ketamine, including education, relationships, employment, finances, and involvement in crime, have also been documented (Lim, 2003).

In his private practice, Kolp has been handling ketamine as a Schedule II substance and has been repeatedly warning all patients that ketamine should never be used except under the direct supervision of a licensed physician. Instead of a ketamine maintenance treatment, Kolp encourages all MAOI-naïve patients to have a trial with MAOIs first, prior to commencing recurrent administrations of ketamine. To those patients who do not accept a trial with MAOI, or who failed it, Kolp offers a maintenance treatment with IM ketamine. However, he prefers limiting the frequency of ketamine IM administration to once every four to six weeks, and never more frequently than once every two weeks. Kolp does not utilize oral, sublingual, or intranasal ketamine maintenance treatment for his patients in order to minimize the potential for ketamine abuse and dependence. The procedural parenteral approach (administering IM and IV ketamine in the office) would reduce the abuse and dependence potential by strictly controlling access to ketamine. In contrast, dispensing the drug to the patients (in-home oral, sublingual, and intranasal self-administration) would likely increase the abuse and dependence potential by increasing access to ketamine, and normalizing the use rather than this being a "special event."

Potential Side Effects of Ketamine Long-Term Treatment
The previously presented data on ketamine's safety profile has been established for episodic and/or time-limited use of ketamine. Meanwhile, the side effects of acute and intermittent uses of a chemical substance and side effects of the chronic use of the same compound may have two entirely different profiles. Once ketamine (and

other similar glutamatergic compounds) are sanctioned for use as oral antidepressants, tens of millions of patients may start using this class of chemical compounds for an extended period of time. There may be value in comparing both the acute and chronic use of ketamine with another compound described as having some similar glutamatergic properties.

Ethanol, similar to ketamine, has the capacity to block glutamate effects at the NMDA receptor, which contributes to ethanol's acute behavioral effects and to the natural history and neuropathology of alcoholism (Tsai, Gastfriend, & Coyle, 1995). Ethanol decreases the NMDA-stimulated ion currents across the range of ethanol concentrations (from 5 to 100 mmol/L) that has been associated with human ethanol intoxication (Lovinger, White, & Weight, 1989; Nakanishi, 1992; Simson et al., 1991). Meanwhile, chronic long-term ethanol consumption increases the levels of NMDA receptors, up-regulates NMDA receptor-related binding, and produces cross-tolerance with other noncompetitive NMDA antagonists (Danysz, Jankowska, Glazewski, & Kostowski, 1992; Fidecka & Langwinski, 1989; Grant, Valverius, Hudspith, & Tabakoff, 1990; Iorio, Reinlib, Tabakoff, & Hoffman, 1992; Trevisan et al., 1994).

This increased NMDA receptor function produced by chronic long-term ethanol consumption contributes to alcohol withdrawal seizures (Grant et al., 1990) and ethanol neurotoxic effects (Chandler et al., 1993). The NMDA antagonists ketamine and phencyclidine substitute for ethanol in preclinical drug discrimination paradigms (Grant & Colombo, 1993; Grant, Knisely, Tabakoff, Barrett, & Balster, 1991). This biochemical data may allow extrapolation of the effects of chronic long-term ethanol consumption to some possibly analogous effects of long-term chronic administration of ketamine and other related NMDA antagonist compounds.

Ethanol has well-known anxiolytic and antidepressant effects with a robust onset of action and good anti-shock (neuroprotective) qualities when used sporadically. It usually only has a few serious side effects when used episodically. The side effects of acute ethanol use, however, are very different than the side effects of chronic use. Ethanol, a known NMDA antagonist, is notorious for its ability to trigger apoptotic neurodegeneration when used chronically (Hoffman, Rabe, Moses, & Tabakoff, 1989) and is a leading cause of dementia (Moriyama, Mimura, Kato, & Kashima, 2006).

A laboratory study conducted on primates suggested that chronic use of ketamine may induce neuronal cell death that is both apoptotic and necrotic in nature (Slikker et al., 2007). Other experimental data have confirmed this earlier study and documented that chronic ketamine exposure might produce irreversible deficits in brain functions due to neurotoxic effects, involving the activation of apoptotic pathways in the prefrontal cortex (Sun et al., 2014). A recent epidemiological study conducted on frequent and infrequent ketamine users reported that frequent ketamine use is associated with impairments in working memory, episodic memory, and aspects of executive function as well as reduced psychological well-being (Morgan, Muetzelfeldt, & Curran, 2009). The preliminary data are suggestive that once ketamine and other similar glutamatergic compounds become available on the market as oral antidepressants, chronic long-term use might cause neurodegenerative changes in the brain of some patients.

The Future of Ketamine Psychotherapy from a Pharmacological Perspective

Although there is currently a lack of scientific data supporting a glutamate "imbalance" as a primary pathophysiological cause of major depression, there is a very short duration of post-ketamine remission of depression, and there are questions regarding the long-term adverse effects of chronic use of ketamine, there is excitement in the psychiatric research community about the discovery of a new class of antidepressants with a mechanism that may be beyond the effects of biogenic amine neurotransmission.

Professor Preskorn (2012) of Kansas University School of Medicine, who has been the principal investigator on over 250 clinical trials including drug development studies of all antidepressants marketed in the United States in the last 25 years (www.preskorn.com), pointed out that all of the existing antidepressants are variations on the pharmacology of amphetamine, iproniazid (MAOI), and imipramine (TCA) and predicted that ketamine and related drugs could revolutionize psychiatry. Yale professors Ronald Duman and George Aghajanian, in a recent 2012 review of the ketamine research in *Science*, stated that the emerging ketamine treatment is the most important psychiatric discovery in recent times.

Nevertheless, it is very unlikely that ketamine will be developed for a mass market. It is an old drug that has long been off patent, so it is not currently profitable for drug manufacturers. The issue of some risk to the kidneys and bladder among some nonmedical users is not going away and affects perceptions, although the quantities involved and the circumstances for these people may differ markedly from its use for antidepressant, psychedelic, and other treatment regimens, and the risk in the latter situations will likely be minimal. Furthermore, its reputation as an abused hallucinogen may now be too firmly embedded in the public awareness for any kind of marketing campaign of the sort commonly associated with antidepressants with billions of dollars at stake.

In addition, the accepted model for all available antidepressants is oral adminis-tration. Even ECT treatment involves both an anesthetic (sometimes ketamine is used for this, and poses an important confounding variable in some ECT studies) along with the production of seizures with electricity. The intravenous and intra-muscular routes of antidepressant administration will severely limit the market size. The profit to be made from ketamine by the pharmaceutical industry from its use as an antidepressant thus appears to be somewhat limited. An aim of the present ket-amine campaign will be to encourage research and development of similar NMDA receptor antagonist compounds that may be more profitable. Ketamine on its own has eight presently known metabolites, including esketamine, arketamine, bromo-ketamine, deschloroketamine, ethketamine, fluoroketamine, methoxetamine, and methoxyketamine. Meanwhile, the entire arylcyclohexylamines group of presently known chemical compounds has nearly 60 various compounds. Reportedly, at least 30 other unscheduled analogs have been produced by clandestine sources.

As of July 2014, Johnson & Johnson is developing a nasal spray formulation of esketamine for the management of treatment-resistant depression (Wijesinghe, 2014). Esketamine (a.k.a. (S)-ketamine or S(+)-ketamine) is the S(+) enantiomer of ketamine and twice as potent as racemic ketamine. A Phase 1 clinical trial of intra-nasal esketamine is sponsored by a Johnson & Johnson subsidiary, Janssen Pharma-ceutical Research & Development, LLC. This company is conducting a clinical trial with 58 participants in Belgium; the purpose of this study is to assess the efficacy and dose response of intranasal esketamine (14 mg, 28 mg, 56 mg, and 84 mg) compared with placebo (clinicaltrials.gov/show/NCT01998958).

Another privately held biopharmaceutical company, Naurex Inc., has recently announced that it has successfully completed a Phase 2b clinical study of GLYX-13, the company's lead compound (www.naurex.com). The FDA has already granted Fast Track Designation to the research and development of this compound. The company also reported that it initiated a Phase 2a study of another orally active agent, NRX-1074, after collecting positive results from a recently completed Phase 1 study of the NRX-1074 drug. Both compounds are NMDA receptor antagonists. However, their specifics are unknown. Krystal, who may be one of the most power-ful figures today in biological psychiatry, has endorsed research and development of both compounds, and Preskorn is a study investigator (www.naurex.com).

Cerecor Inc., a Maryland-based biopharmaceutical company, is also in the process of developing a new antidepressant drug, CERC-301 (formerly known as MK-0657), as a therapy for TRD. The drug is a selective NMDA receptor antagonist and an orally active compound (Ibrahim et al., 2012). The company has initiated Phase II clinical trials in November of 2013 and this study has received Fast Track Designation from the FDA for TRD (www.cerecor.com).

AstraZeneca, PLC (AZN) is studying another NMDA receptor antagonist, lanicemine (Wijesinghe, 2014). Lanicemine was originally developed as a neuroprotective agent and then was redeveloped as an antidepressant following the report of Zarate and colleagues (2012), who documented that lanicemine has potent antidepressant effects similar to ketamine. However, the drug is claimed to have little or no psychotomimetic side-effects (Zarate et al., 2012).

Although ketamine itself will probably not become the next generation of antidepressants, it seems that numerous other members of the arylcyclohexylamines class will be presented for this purpose, and probably also presented as the next generation of anti-anxiety drugs, mood-stabilizers, and procognitive agents. Their impact on the urinary system will need to be assessed where long-term daily use is planned. It remains to be seen whether the next generation of glutamate-antagonist based pharmaceuticals will result in a growth of addiction to those that are psychoactive arylcyclohexylamines.

In addition to this flurry of activity to develop psychopharmacological applications of ketamine, especially in ways that can yield profits, there remains its psychological and transpersonal healing potential. Our position is that these offer its greatest likelihood of benefit, rather than through ketamine's biological application.

Conclusion

Ketamine is a potent substance that offers much promise for alleviating suffering due to mental health issues, but it also poses considerable danger when it is misused. As a psychiatric medication, ketamine offers a wide range of applications, from mild doses alleviating depression (at least in the short term) to psychedelic dosages offering the possibility of transpersonal healing. The fact that ketamine is the only psychedelic that can legally be prescribed in the United States makes it unique at this time, and we encourage its responsible use within medical contexts for providing access to deep and profound healing experiences that may be difficult, if not impossible, for many to achieve without the aid of such a substance.

We hope that ketamine will remain legally available for clinical applications and scientific research, including for the field of psychedelic psychotherapy. The current interest in ketamine may eventually bring psychedelic psychotherapy some-what closer to the mainstream of psychiatry and psychology. Those dismissive of its spiritual component, who are inclined to consider this as "flakey," should bear in mind that the most successful and cost-effective treatment for alcohol dependence remains the 12-step programs, such as Alcoholics Anonymous (The Fellowship; Alcoholics Anonymous World Services, 1984), and of course the spiritual component lies at the very heart of this approach (Corrington, 1989; Nathan, 1986). Spirituality retains a place in contemporary psychiatry. It is not so long ago that the Spirituality Special Interest Group became one of the nine Special Interest Groups at the Royal College of Psychiatry in London, and interest continues to grow. It would be difficult to argue that all of these psychiatrists are part of a lunatic fringe.

The United States is a country in which the overwhelming majority of the population has some spiritual beliefs. When one considers the high morbidity and mortality from disorders such as alcohol dependence and depression, it seems foolish to neglect all of the opportunities for treatment that this circumstance may offer. From a contemporary perspective, KPP is less drastic than some of its alternatives, such as ECT used for TRD and for which ketamine is sometimes used as an anesthetic (and may even be the source of much of ECT's purported effectiveness). It may be time for a cultural shift in perceptions. With billions of dollars at stake, it is understandable that some vested interests may directly and/or indirectly lobby to oppose any shift away from the culture of taking daily tablets (or perhaps nasal sprays) and the use of ECT as the ultimate psychiatric treatment. However, if protocols develop which combine innovative methods, such as KPP with ongoing maintenance alongside conventional medicines as "standard practice," some of the profit-based opposition may eventually lessen. Likewise, opposition from both conservative factions that might oppose any substance that can be seen as generating a "high," as well as by more spiritually liberal factions that might denigrate such substances as less valid than using so-called "natural" approaches (e.g., meditation), would have to be confronted in the face of the tremendous suffering that KPP could alleviate.

References

aan het Rot, M., Collins, K., Murrough, J., Perez, A., Reich, D., Charney, D., & Mathew, S. (2010). Safety and efficacy of repeated-dose intravenous ketamine for treatment-resistant depression. *Biological Psychiatry, 67*, 139-145. doi:10.1016/j.biopsych.2009.08.038

aan het Rot, M., Zarate, C., Charney, D., & Mathew, S. (2012). Ketamine for depression: Where do we go from here? *Biological Psychiatry, 72*, 537-547. doi:10.1016/j.biopsych.2012.05.003

Abajian, J. C., Page, P., & Morgan, M. (1973). Effects of droperidol and nitrazepam on emergence reactions following ketamine anesthesia. *Anesthesia and Analgesia: Current Researches, 52*, 385-389. doi:10.1213/00000539-197305000-00018

Adamson, S. (1985). *Through the gateway of the heart: Accounts of experiences with MDMA and other empathogenic substances.* San Francisco, CA: Four Trees.

Ahmadi, A., Khalili, M., Hajikhani, R., & Naserbakht, M. (2011). New morpholine analogues of phencyclidine: Chemical synthesis and pain perception in rats. *Pharmacology Biochemistry and Behavior, 98*(2), 227-233. doi:10.1016/j.pbb.2010.12.019

Ahmadi, A., & Mahmoudi, A. (2004). Synthesis and biological properties of 2-hydroxy-1-(1-phenyltetralyl)piperidine and some of its intermediates as derivatives of phencyclidine. *Arzneimittel-Forschung, 55*(9), 528-532.

Ahmed, S. N., & Petchkovsky, L. (1980) Abuse of ketamine. *The British Journal of Psychiatry, 137*(3), 303.

Albanèse, J., Arnaud, S., Rey, M., Thomachot, L., Alliez, B., & Martin, C. (1997). Ketamine decreases intracranial pressure and electroencephalographic activity in traumatic brain injury patients during propofol sedation. *Anesthesiology, 87*(6), 1328-1334. doi:10.1097/00000542-199712000-00011

Alcoholic Anonymous World Services. (1984). *The story of Bill Wilson and how the A. A. message reached the world.* New York, NY: Author.

Alonso-Serra, H. M., & Wesley, K. (2003). Position paper for the National Association of EMS Physicians Standards and Clinical Practices Committee. Prehospital pain management. *Prehospital Emergency Care, 7*(4), 482-488. doi:10.1080/312703002260

American Psychiatric Association. (2000). *Diagnostic and statistical manual-IV-TR.* Washington, DC: Author.

American Psychiatric Association. (2013). *Diagnostic and statistical manual-5.* Washington, DC: Author. doi:10.1176/appi.books.9780890425596.744053

Andritzky, W. (1989). Sociopsychotherapeutic functions of Ayahuasca healing in Amazonia. *Journal of Psychoactive Drugs, 21*, 77-89. doi:10.1080/02791072.19 89.10472145

Anis, N. A., Berry, S. C., Burton, N. R., & Lodge, D. (1983). The dissociative anaesthetics ketamine and phencyclidine, selectively reduce excitation of central mammalian neurons by N-methyl-aspartate. *British Journal of Pharmacology, 79*, 565-575. doi:10.1111/j.1476-5381.1983.tb11031.x

Anokhina, I. (1975). *Neurochemical mechanisms of psychiatric diseases.* Moscow, Russia: Meditsina.

Arendsenhein, G. (1962). Treatment of the neurotic patient, resistant to the usual techniques of psychotherapy, with special reference to LSD. *Topical Problems of Psychotherapy, 10*, 50-57.

Areosa, S., Sherriff, F., & McShane, R. (2005). Memantine for dementia. *Cochrane Database of Systematic Reviews, 2*(Art. No. CD003154). doi:10.1002/14651858. CD 003154.pub3

Ashley, R. (1978). Avant-garde highs. *High Times, 31*, 62-64.

Assagioli, R. (1965). *Psychosynthesis: A manual of principles and techniques.* New York, NY: Hobbs Dorman.

Bahetwar, S. K., Randey, R. K., Saskena, A. K., & Chandra, G. (2011). A comparative evaluation of intranasal midazolam, ketamine and their combination for sedation of young uncooperative pediatric dental patients: A triple blind randomized crossover trial. *Journal of Clinical Pediatric Dentistry, 35*, 415-420. doi:10.17796/jcpd.35.4.l43h3354705u2574

Bar-Joseph, G., Guilburd, Y., Tamir, A., & Guilburd, J. N. (2009). Effectiveness of ketamine in decreasing intracranial pressure in children with intracranial hypertension. *Journal of Neurosurgery: Pediatrics, 4*(1), 40-46. doi:10.3171/2009.1.peds08319

Baroni, D. (1931). Gestandnisse im Meskalinrausch. *Psychoanalytische Praxis, 1*, 145-149.

Bauman, L. A., Kish, I., Baumann, R. C., & Politis, G. D. (1999). Pediatric sedation with analgesia. *American Journal of Emergency Medicine, 17*(1), 1-3. doi:10.1016/S0735-6757(99)90001-3

Beardsley, P., & Balster, R. (*1987*). Behavioral dependence upon phencyclidine and ketamine in the rat. *Journal of Pharmacology and Experimental Therapeutics, 242*(1), 203-211.

Bell, R. F., Dahl, J. B., Moore, R. A., & Kalso, E. A. (2006). Perioperative ketamine for acute postoperative pain (Review). *Cochrane Database of Systematic Reviews*, *1*(Art No. CD004603). doi:10.1002/14651858.CD004603.pub2

Berman, R., Cappiello, A., Anand, A., Oren, D., Heninger, G., Charney, D., & Krystal, J. (2000). Antidepressant effects of ketamine in depressed patients. *Biological Psychiatry, 47*(4), 351-354. doi:10.1016/S0006-3223(99)00230-9

Bjerre, J., & Fontenay, C. (2010). Ketamin ved melankolsk depression. *Ugeskr Lager, 172*, 460-461.

Black, I. H., & McManus, J. (2009). Pain management in current combat operations. *Prehospital Emergency Care, 13*(2), 223-227. doi:10.1080/10903120802290778

Bokor, G., & Anderson, P. D. (2014). Ketamine: An update on its abuse. *Journal of Pharmacology Practice, 27*(6), 582-586. doi: 10.1177/0897190014525754

Bolle, R. (1985). *Dream experiences at sub-anesthetic doses of the anesthetic Ketanest* (Medical dissertation). Göttingen, Germany: Göttingen University.

Bolle, R. (1988). *At the origin of longing. Depth-psychological aspects of altered states of waking consciousness with the anesthetic Ketanest.* Berlin, Germany: Verlug fur Wissenchaft und Bilding.

Bolle, R. (1992). About the pre- and perinatal experience-space in psychotherapy. *Yearbook of the European College for the Study of Consciousness, 1992*, 151-164.

Brown, W. (2007). Ketamine and NMDA receptor antagonists for depression. *Psychiatric Times, February*, 2007.

Buvanendran, A., & Kroin, J. (2009). Multimodal analgesia for controlling acute postoperative pain. *Current Opinion in Anesthesiology, 22*, 588-593. doi:10.1097/ACO.0b013e328330373a

Carr, D., Goudas, L., Denman, W., Brookoff, D., Staats, P., Brennen, L., ... Mermelstein, F. (2004). Safety and efficacy of intranasal ketamine for the treatment of breakthrough pain in patients with chronic pain: A randomized, double-blind, placebo-controlled, crossover study. *Pain, 108*, 17-27. doi:10.1016/j.pain.2003.07.001

Carroll, M. E., Lac, S. T., Asencio, M., & Kragh, R. (1990). Intravenous cocaine self-administration in rats is reduced by dietary l-tryptophan. *Psychopharmacology, 100*(3), 293-300. doi:10.1007/BF02244596

Cartwright, P., & Pingel, S. (1984). Midazolam and diazepam in ketamine anesthesia. *Anesthesia, 39*, 439-442. doi:10.1111/j.1365-2044.1984.tb07312.x

Chandler, L. J., Newsom, H., Sumners, C., & Crews, F. (1993). Chronic ethanol exposure potentiates NMDA excitotoxicity in cerebral cortical neurons. *Journal of Neurochemistry, 60*(4), 1578-1581. doi:10.1111/j.1471-4159.1993.tb03326.x

Chang, T., Savory, A., & Albin, M. (1970). Metabolic disposition of tritium-labeled ketamine in normal human subjects. *Metabolism: Clinical and Experimental Research, 18*, 597-601.

Chaudieu, I., Vignon, J., Chicheportiche, M., Kamenka, J. M., Trouiller, G., & Chicheportiche, R. (1989). Role of the aromatic group in the inhibition of phencyclidine binding and dopamine uptake by PCP analogs. *Pharmacology, Biochemistry, and Behavior, 32*(3), 699-705. doi:10.1016/0091-3057(89)90020-8

Cherry, D. A., Plummer, J. L., Gourlay, G. K., Coates, K. R., & Odgers, C. L. (1995). Ketamine as an adjunct to morphine in the treatment of pain. *Pain, 62*, 119-121. doi:10.1016/0304-3959(95)00010-P

Cohen, M. L., Chan, S. L., & Trevor, A. J. (1973). In vitro inhibition of rat brain norepinephrine uptake and acetylcholineesterase by ketamine. *Federation Proceedings, 32*(3), 682-690.

Cohen, S. (1965). LSD and the anguish of dying. *Harper's, 231*, 69-77.

Collier, B. (1972). Ketamine and the conscious mind. *Anesthesia, 27*, 120-134. doi:10.1111/j.1365-2044.19 72.tb08186.x

Collingridge, G. L. (1987). The role of NMDA receptors in learning and memory. *Nature, 330*, 604-605. doi:10.1038/330604a0

Connell, P. H. (1958). *Amphetamine psychosis* (Maudsley Monograph). Oxford, UK: Oxford University Press.

Copeland, J., & Dillon P. (2005). The health and psycho-social consequences of ketamine use. *International Journal of Drug Policy, 16*, 122-131. doi:10.1016/j.drugpo.2004.12.003

Corrington, J. (1989). Spirituality and recovery: Relationship between levels of spirituality, contentment and stress during recovery from alcoholism in AA. *Alcoholism Treatment Quarterly, 6*(3-4), 151-165. doi:10.1300/J020V06N03_09

Craven, R. (2007). Ketamine. *Anaesthesia, 62*(Suppl. 1), 48-53. doi:10.1111/j.1365-2044.2007.05298.x

Dachs, R., & Innes, G. (1997). Intravenous ketamine sedation of pediatric patients in the emergency department. *Annals of Emergency Medicine, 29*(1), 146-150. doi:10.1016/S0196-0644(97)70321-4

Danysz, W., Dyr, W., Jankowska, E., Glazewski, S., & Kostowski, W. (1992). The involvement of NMDA receptors in acute and chronic effects of ethanol. *Alcoholism, Clinical and Experimental Research, 16*(3), 499-504. doi:10.1111/j.1530-0277.1992.tb01407.x

Diaz-Granados, N., Ibrahim, L., Brutsche, N. E., Newberg, A., Kronstein, P.,

Khalife, S., ... Zarate, C. A. (2010). A randomized add-on trial of an N-methyl-D-aspartate antagonist in treatment-resistant bipolar depression. *Archives of General Psychiatry, 67*(8), 793-802. doi:10.1001/archgenpsychiatry.2010.90

Dillon, P., Copeland, J., & Jansen, K. (2003). Patterns of use and harms associated with non-medical ketamine use. *Drug and Alcohol Dependence, 69*(1), 23-28. doi:10.1016/S0376-8716(02)00243-0

Dillon, P., & Degenhardt, L. (2001). Ketamine and GHB: New trends in club drug use? *Journal of Substance Use, 6*, 11-15. doi:10.1080/146598901750132045

Dishotsky, N. I., Loughman, W. D., Mogar, R. E., & Lipscomb, W. R. (1971). LSD and genetic damage. *Science, 172*, 431-440. doi:10.1126/science.172.3982.431

Doblin, R. (1991). Pahnke's "Good Friday Experiment": A long-term follow-up and methodological critique. *Journal of Transpersonal Psychology, 23*(1), 1-28.

Domino, E. (2010). Taming the ketamine tiger. *Anesthesiology, 113*(3), 678-684. doi:10.1097/aln.0b013e3181ed09a2

Domino, E., Chodoff, P., & Corssen, G. (1965). Pharmacologic effects of CL-581, a new dissociative anaesthetic, in man. *Clinical Pharmacological Therapeutics, 6*, 279-291.

Domino, E., Domino, S., Smith, R., Domino, L., Goulet, J. R., Domino, K. E., & Zsigmond, E. K. (1984). Ketamine kinetics in unmedicated and diazepam-premedicated subjects. *Clinical Pharmacology and Therapeutics, 36*, 645-653. doi:10.1038/clpt.1984.235

Drejer, J., & Honore, T. (1987). Phencyclidine analogues inhibit NMDA-stimulated [3H] GABA release from cultured cortex neurons. *European Journal of Pharmacology, 143*, 287-290. doi:10.1016/0014-2999(87)90546-2

Duman, R., & Aghajanian, G. (2012). Synaptic dysfunction in depression: Potential therapeutic targets. *Science, 338*, 68-72. doi:10.1126/science.1222939

Dundee, J. (1990). Twenty-five years of ketamine. *Anesthesia, 45*, 159-160. doi:10.1111/j.1365-2044.1990.tb14287.x

Durieux, M. E., & Nietgen, G. W. (1997). Synergistic inhibition of muscarinic signaling by ketamine stereoisomers and the preservative benzethonium chloride. *Anesthesiology, 86*(6), 1326-1333. doi:10.1097/00000542-199706000-00014

Dyck, E. (2005). Flashback: Psychiatric experimentation with LSD in historical perspective. *Canadian Journal of Psychiatry, 50*(7), 381-388.

Ebert, B., Mikkelsen, S., Thorkildsen, C., & Borgbjerg, F. M. (1997). Nor-ketamine, the main metabolite of ketamine, is a non-competitive NMDA receptor antagonist in the rat cortex and spinal cord. *European Journal of Pharmacology,*

333(1), 99-104. doi:10.1016/S0014-2999(97)01116-3

Eckenhoff, J. E., Kneale, D. H., & Dripps, R. D. (1961). The incidence and etiology of postanesthetic excitement: A clinical survey. *Anesthesiology, 22*(5), 667-673. doi:10.1097/00000542-196109000-00002

Eisner, B. (1997). Set, setting and matrix. *Journal of Psychoactive Drugs, 29*(2), 213-216. doi:10.1080/02791072.1997.10400190

Eisner, B., & Cohen, S. (1958). Psychotherapy with lysergic acid diethylamide. *Journal of Nervous and Mental Disease, 127*, 528-539. doi:10.1097/00005053-195812000-00006

Ellis, D., Husain, H., Saetta, J., & Walker, T. (2004). Procedural sedation in paediatric minor procedures: A prospective audit on ketamine use in the emergency department. *Emergency Medicine Journal, 21*, 286-289. doi:10.1136/emj.2003.007229

Ersek, R. A. (2004). Dissociative anesthesia for safety's sake: Ketamine and diazepam—a 35-year personal experience. *Plastic and Reconstructive Surgery, 113*(7), 1955-1959. doi:10.1097/01.PRS.0000122402.52595.10

Eterović, V. A., Lu, R., Eakin, A. E., Rodríguez, A. D., & Ferchmin, P. A. (1999). Determinants of phencyclidine potency on the nicotinic acetylcholine receptors from muscle and electric organ. *Cellular and Molecular Neurobiology, 19*(6), 745-757. doi:10.1023/A:1006905106834

Fenwick, P., & Fenwick, E. (1995). *The truth in the light: An investigation of over 300 near-death experiences.* London, UK: Headline.

Fidecka, S. (1987). Opioid mechanisms of some behavioral effects of ketamine. *Polish Journal of Pharmacology and Pharmacy, 39*(4), 353-360.

Fidecka, S., & Langwinski, R. (1989). Interaction between ketamine and ethanol in rats and mice. *Polish Journal of Pharmacology and Pharmacy, 41*(1), 23-32.

Filanovsky, Y., Miller, P., & Kao, J. (2010). Myth: Ketamine should not be used as an induction agent for intubation in patients with head injury. *Canadian Journal of Emergency Medicine, 12*(2), 154-157.

Finck, A. D., & Nagai, S. H. (1982). Opiate receptor mediation of ketamine analgesia. *Anesthesiology, 56*(4), 291-297. doi:10.1097/00000542-198204000-00011

Fontana, A. (1974). Terapia antidpresiva con Ci 581 (ketamine). *Acta Psiquiatrica Y Psicologica de America Latina, 4*, 20-32.

French, E. D., Mura, A., & Wang, T. (1993). MK-801, phencyclidine (PCP), and PCP-like drugs increase burst firing in rat A10 dopamine neurons: Comparison to competitive NMDA antagonists. *Synapse, 13*(2), 108-116. doi:10.1002/syn.890130203

Freya, E., Latish, L., Schmidhammer, H., & Portoghese, P. (1994). Interaktion von S-(+)-Ketamin mit Opiatrezeptoren. Effekte aud EEG, evoziertes Potential und Atmung am wachen Hund [Interaction of S-(+)-ketamine with opiate receptors. Effects on EEG, evoked potentials and respiration in awake dogs}. *Der Anaesthesist, 43*(Supplement 2), S52-S58.

Friedman, H. (2006). The renewal of psychedelic research: Implications for humanistic and transpersonal psychology. *The Humanistic Psychologist, 34*(1), 39-58. doi:10.1207/s15473333thp3401_5

Furst, P. (1972). *Flesh of the Gods: The ritual use of hallucinogens.* New York, NY: Waveland.

Galley, H. F., & Webster, N. R. (1996). Brain nitric oxide synthase activity is decreased by intravenous anesthetics. *Anesthesia and Analgesia, 83*(3), 591-594.

Garfield, J. M., Garfield, F. B., Stone, J. G., Hopkins, D., & Johns, L. A. (1972). A comparison of psychologic responses to ketamine and thiopental-nitrous oxide-halothane anesthesia. *Anesthesiology, 36,* 329-338. doi:10.1097/00000542-197204000-00006

Ghoneim, M., Hinrichs, J., Mewaldt, S., & Petersen, R. (1985). Ketamine: behavioral effects of subanesthetic doses. *Journal of Clinical Psychopharmacology, 5*(2), 70-77. doi:10.1097/00004714-198504000-00003

Glue, P., Gulati, A., Le Nedelec, M., & Duffull, S. (2011). Dose- and exposure-response to ketamine in depression. *Biological Psychiatry, 70,* 9-12. doi:10.1016/j.biopsych.2010.11.031

Godwin, S. A., Caro, D. A., Wolf, S. J., Jagoda, A. S., Charles, R., Marett, B. E., & Moore, J. (2005). Clinical policy: Procedural sedation and analgesia in the emergency department. *Annals of Emergency Medicine, 45*(2), 177-196. doi:10.1016/j.annemergmed.2004.11.002

Grant, I. S., Nimmo, W. S., & Clements, J. A. (1981). Pharmacocinetics and analgesic effects of im and oral ketamine. *British Journal of Anesthesiology, 53*(8), 805-810. doi:10.1093/bja/53.8.805

Grant, K., & Colombo, G. (1993). Discriminative stimulus effects of ethanol: Effect of training dose on the substitution of N-methyl-D-aspartate antagonists. *Journal of Pharmacology and Experimental Therapeutics, 264*(3), 1241-1247.

Grant, K., Knisely, J., Tabakoff, B., Barrett, J., & Balster, R. (1991). Ethanol-like discriminative stimulus effects of non-competitive *N*-methyl-D-aspartate antagonists. *Behavioral Pharmacology, 2*(2), 87-95. doi:10.1097/00008877-199104000-00002

Grant, K., Valverius, P., Hudspith, M., & Tabakoff, B. (1990). Ethanol withdrawal seizures and the NMDA receptor complex. *European Journal of Pharmacology, 176*(3), 289-296. doi:10.1016/0014-2999(90)90022-X

Green, S. M., Clark, R., Hostetler, M. A., Cohen, M., Carlson, D., & Rothrock, S. G. (1999). Inadvertent ketamine overdose in children: Clinical manifestations and outcome. *Annals of Emergency Medicine, 34*, 492-497. doi:10.1016/S0196-0644(99)80051-1

Green, S. M., Clem, K. J., & Rothrock, S. G. (1996). Ketamine safety profile in developing world: Survey of practitioners. *Academic Emergency Medicine, 3*, 598-604. doi:10.1111/j.1553-2712.1996.tb03470.x

Green, S. M., & Johnson, N. E. (1990). Ketamine sedation for pediatric procedures: Part 2, review and implications. *Annals of Emergency Medicine, 19*, 1033-1046. doi:10.1016/S0196-0644(05)82569-7

Green, S., & Krauss, B. (2004a). Clinical practice guideline for emergency department ketamine dissociative sedation in children. *Annals of Emergency Medicine, 44*(5), 460-471. doi:10.1016/j.annemergmed.2004.06.006

Green, S., & Krauss, B. (2004b). Ketamine is a safe, effective, and appropriate technique for emergency department paediatric procedural sedation. *Emergency Medicine Journal, 21*, 271-272. doi:10.1136/emj.2004.015370

Grey, M. (1985). *Return from death: An exploration of the near-death experience.* London, UK: Arkana.

Greyson, B. (1983). The psychodynamics of near-death experiences. *Journal of Nervous and Mental Disease, 171*, 376 -381. doi:10.1097/00005053-19830600000008

Greyson, B., & Stevenson, I. (1980). The phenomenology of near-death experiences. *American Journal of Psychiatry, 137*, 1193-1196. doi:10.1176/ajp.137.10.1193

Griffiths, R., Richards, W., Johnson, M., McCann, U., & Jesse, R. (2008). Mystical-type experiences occasioned by psilocybin mediate the attribution of personal meaning and spiritual significance 14 months later. *Journal of Psychopharmacology, 22*, 621-632. doi:10.1177/0269881108094300

Griffiths, R., Richards, W., McCann, U., & Jesse, R. (2006). Psilocybin can occasion mystical-type experiences having substantial and sustained personal meaning and spiritual significance. *Psychopharmacology, 187*, 268-283. doi:10.1007/s00213-006-0457-5

Grinker, R., & Spiegel J. (1945). *War neuroses*. Philadelphia, PA: Blakiston.

Grinspoon, L., & Bakalar, J. (1979). *Psychedelic drugs reconsidered*. New York, NY: Basic Books.

Grob, C. (1998). Psychiatric research with hallucinogens: What have we learned? *Heffter Review of Psychedelic Research, 1*, 8-20.

Grob, C. (2002). *Hallucinogens: A reader*. New York, NY: Tarcher/Putnam.

Grof, S. (1975). *Realms of the human consciousness: Observations from LSD research*. New York, NY: Independent.

Grof, S. (1978). LSD and the human unconsciousness: Observations from psychedelic research. In J. Fosshage & P. Olsen (Eds.), *Healing: Implications for psychotherapy* (pp. 213-259). New York, NY: Human Science Press.

Grof, S. (1980). *LSD psychotherapy*. Alameda, CA: Hunter House.

Grof, S. (1986). *Psychedelic therapy and holonomic integration*. Berlin, Germany: Verlag fur Wissenschaft und Bildung.

Grof, S. (2001). Non-ordinary states of consciousness: Healing and heuristic potential. D. Lorimer (Ed.), *Thinking beyond the brain: A wider science of consciousness*. Edinburg, UK: Floris Books.

Grof, S., Goodman, L., Richards, W., & Kurland, A. (1973). LSD-assisted psychotherapy in patients with terminal cancer. *International Pharmacopsychiatry, 8*, 129-144.

Grof, S., & Halifax, J. (1976). Psychedelics and the experience of death. In A. Toynbee (Ed.), *Life after death* (pp. 197-198). New York, NY: McGraw-Hill.

Grossbard, A. (1989). *Evaluation of a shamanic oriented psychotherapy process* (Doctoral dissertation). San Francisco, CA: California Institute of Integral Studies. (UMI No. 8926005)

Gu, D., Huang, J., Yin, Y., Shan, Z., Zheng, S., & Wu, P. (2014). Long-term ketamine abuse induces cystitis in rats by impairing the bladder epithelial barrier. *Molecular Biology Reports, 41*(11), 7313-7322. doi:10.1007/s11033-014-3616-5

Guldner, G. T., Petinaux, B., Clemens, P., Foster, S., & Antoine, S. (2006). Ketamine for procedural sedation and analgesia by nonanesthesiologists in the field: A review for military health care providers. *Military Medicine, 171*(6), 484-490.

Haas, D., & Harper, D. (1992). Ketamine: A review of its pharmacologic properties and use in ambulatory anesthesia. *Anesthesia Progress, 39*(3), 61-68.

Hamox, M. (1984). Common neurochemical correlates to the action of hallucinogens. In B. L. Jacobs (Ed.), *Hallucinogens: Neurochemical, behavioral and clinical perspectives* (Vol. 4, pp. 143-169). New York, NY: Raven Press.

Hashimoto, K. (2009). Emerging role of glutamate in the pathophysiology of major depressive disorder. *Brain Research Reviews, 61*, 105-123. doi:10.1016/j. brainresrev.2009.05.005

He, X. S., Raymon, L. P., Mattson, M. V., Eldefrawi, M. E., & De Costa, B. R. (1993). Synthesis and biological evaluation of 1-1-(2-benzobthienyl) cyclohexylpiperidine homologs at dopamine-uptake and phencyclidine- and sigma-binding sites. *Journal of Medical Chemistry, 36*(9), 1188-1193. doi:10.1021/jm00061a009

Herman, B. H., Vocci, F., & Bridge, P. (1995), The effects of NMDA receptor antagonists and nitric oxide synthase inhibitors on opioid tolerance and withdrawal. Medication development issues for opiate addiction. *Neuropsychopharmacology, 13*(4), 269-293. doi:10.1016/0893-133X(95)00140-9

Hervey, W. H., & Hustead, R. F. (1972). Ketamine for dilatation and curettage procedures: Patient acceptance. *Anesthesia and Analgesia: Current Researches, 51*, 647-655. doi:10.1213/00000539-197207000-00040

Hirota, K., & Lambert, D. (1996). Ketamine: Its mechanism of action and unusual clinical uses. *British Journal of Anaesthesia, 77*(4), 441-444. doi:10.1093/ bja/77.4.441

Hoffer, A. (1967). A program for the treatment of alcoholism: LSD, malvaria and nicotinic acid. In H. Abramson (Ed.), *The use of LSD in psychotherapy and alcoholism* (pp. 343-406). New York, NY: Bobbs-Merrill.

Hoffman, P., Rabe, C., Moses, F., & Tabakoff, B. (1989). N-methyl-D-asparate receptors and ethanol: Inhibition of calcium flux and cyclic GMP production. *Journal of Neurochemistry, 52*, 1937-1940. doi:10.1111/j.1471-4159.1989. tb07280.x

Hoffman, W. E., Pelligrino, D., Werner, C., Kochs, E., Albrecht, R. F., & Schulte, A. E. J. (1992). Ketamine decreases plasma catecholamines and improves outcome from incomplete cerebral ischemia in rats. *Anesthesiology, 76*, 755-762. doi:10.1097/00000542-199205000-00014

Holmes, R. (2008). *The age of wonder: How the romantic generation discovered the beauty and terror of science.* New York, NY: Harper Collins.

Horsley, J. (1943). *Narco-analysis.* New York, NY: Oxford University Press.

Howes, M. C. (2004). Ketamine for paediatric sedation/analgesia in the emergency department. *Emergency Medicine Journal, 21*, 275-280. doi:10.1136/ emj.2003.005769

Hughes, S. (2011). BET 3: Is ketamine a viable induction agent for the trauma patient with potential brain injury. *Emergency Medicine Journal, 28*(12), 1076-1077. doi:10.1136/emermed-2011-200891

Hurt, P., & Ritchie, E. (1994). A case of ketamine dependence. *American Journal of Psychiatry, 151*, 779. doi:10.1176/ajp.151.5.779a

Hustveit, O., Maurset, A., & Oye, I. (1995). Interaction of the chiral forms of ketamine with opioid, phencyclidine, sigma and muscarinic receptors. *Pharmacology and Toxicology, 77*(6), 355-359. doi:10.1111/j.1600-0773.1995.tb01041.x

Ibrahim, L., Diaz-Granados, N., Jolkovsky, L., Brutsche, N., Luckenbaugh, D. A., Herring, W. J., ... & Zarate Jr., C. A. (2012). A randomized, placebo-controlled, crossover pilot trial of the oral selective NR2B antagonist MK-0657 in patients with treatment-resistant major depressive disorder. *Journal of Clinical Psychopharmacology, 32*(4), 551-557. doi:10.1097/JCP.0b013e31825d70d6

Iorio, K. R., Reinlib, L., Tabakoff, B., & Hoffman, P. L. (1992). Chronic exposure of cerebellar granule cells to ethanol results in increased N-methyl-D-aspartate receptor function. *Molecular Pharmacology, 41*, 1142-1148.

Irifune, M., Shimizu, T., Nomoto, M. (1991). Ketamine-induced hyperlocomotion associated with alteration of pre-synaptic components of dopamine neurons in the nucleus accumbens of mice. *Pharmacology Biochemistry and Behavior, 40*, 399-407. doi:10.10 16/0091-3057(91)90571-I

Irifune, M., Fukuda, T., Nomoto, M., Sato, T., Kamata, Y., Nishikawa, T., ... Kawahara, M. (1997). Effects of ketamine on dopamine metabolism during anesthesia in discreet brain regions in mice: comparison with the effects during the recovery and subanesthetic phases. *Brain Research, 763*(2), 281-284. doi:10.1016/S0006-8993(97)00510-6

Irwin, S., & Iglewicz, A. (2010). Oral ketamine for the rapid treatment of depression and anxiety in patients receiving hospice care. *Journal of Palliative Medicine, 13*, 903-908. doi:10.1089/jpm.2010.9808

Itil, T., Keskiner, A., & Kiremitci, N. (1967). Effect of phencyclidine in chronic schizophrenia. *Canadian Journal of Psychiatry, 12*(2), 209-212.

Itzhak, Y., & Simon, E. J. (1984). A novel phencyclidine analog interacts selectively with mu opioid receptors. *The Journal of Pharmacology and Experimental Therapeutics, 230*(2), 383-386.

Jansen, K. (1989a). The near-death experience. *British Journal of Psychiatry, 154*(6), 883-884. doi:10.1192/bjp.154.6.883a

Jansen, K. (1989b). Near-death experience and the NMDA receptor. *British Medical Journal, 298*, 1708-1709. doi:10.1136/bmj.298.6689.1708-b

Jansen, K. (1990a). Ketamine: Can chronic use impair memory? *International Journal of Addiction, 25*, 133-139. doi:10.3109/10826089009056204

Jansen, K. (1990b). Neuroscience and the near-death experience: Roles for the NMSA-PCP receptor, the sigma receptor and the endopsychosins. *Medical Hypotheses, 31*, 25-29. doi:10.1016/0306-9877(90)90048-J

Jansen, K. (1991). Transcendental explanations and the near-death experience. *Lancet, 337*, 207-243. doi:10.1016/0140-6736(91)92215-N

Jansen, K. (1997). The ketamine model of the near-death experience: A central role for the N-methyl-D-asparate receptor. *Journal of Near-Death Studies, 16*, 5-27. doi:10.1023/A:1025055109480

Jansen, K. (2000). A review of the non-medical use of ketamine: Use, users and consequences. *Journal of Psychoactive Drugs, 32*(4), 419-433. doi:10.1080/027 91072.2000.10400244

Jansen, K. (2001). *Ketamine: Dreams and realities*. Sarasota, FL: MAPS.

Jansen, K. L., & Darracot-Cankovic, R. (2001). The nonmedical use of ketamine, part two: A review of problem use and dependence. *Journal of Psychoactive Drugs, 33*(2), 151-158. doi:10.1080/02791072.2001.10400480

Jennings, P. A., Cameron, P., & Bernard, S. (2011). Ketamine as an analgesic in the pre-hospital setting: A systematic review. *Acta Anaesthesia Scandanavia, 55*, 638-643. doi:10.1111/j.1399-6576.2011.02446.x

Joe-Laidler, K., & Hunt, G. (2008). Sit down to float: The cultural meaning of ketamine use in Hong Kong. *Addiction Research & Theory, 16*(3), 259-271. doi:10.1080/16066350801983673

Kamaya, H., & Krishna, P. R. (1987). Ketamine addiction. *Anesthesiology, 67*, 861-862. doi:10.1097/00000542-198711000-00054

Kaplan, A. (2013). New claims and findings for ketamine in severe depression. *Psychiatric Times, 1*, 1-10.

Kast, E. (1964a). Pain and LSD-25: A theory of attenuation of anticipation. In D. Solomon (Ed.), *LSD: The consciousness-expanding drug* (pp. 239-254). New York, NY: G. P. Putnam.

Kast, E. (1964b). LSD and the dying patient. *Chicago Medical School Quarterly, 26*, 80-87.

Kast, E., & Collins, V. (1964). Lysergic acid diethylamide as an analgesic agent. *Anesthesia and Analgesia, 43*, 285-291. doi:10.1213/00000539-196405000-00013

Keita, H., Lecharny, J. B., Henzel, D., Desmonts, J. M., & Mantz, J. (1996). Is inhibition of dopamine uptake relevant to the hypnotic action of i.v. anesthetics? *British Journal of Anaesthesia, 77*(2), 254-256. doi:10.1093/bja/77.2.254

Khorramzadeh, E., & Lofty, A. (1973). The use of ketamine in psychiatry. *Psychosomatics, 14*(6), 344-346. doi:10.1016/S0033-3182(73) 71306-2

Khorramzadeh, E., & Lofty, A. (1976). Personality predisposition and emergence phenomena with ketamine. *Psychosomatics, 17*(2), 94-95. doi:10.1016/S0033-3182(76)71152-6

Kim, H. S., Park, I. S., & Park, W. K. (1998). NMDA receptor antagonists enhance 5-HT2 receptor-mediated behavior, head-twitch response, in mice. *Life Sciences, 63*(26), 2305-2311. doi:10.1016/S0024-3205(98)00519-0

Kolp, E., Friedman, H. L., Young, M. S., & Krupitsky, E. (2006). Ketamine enhanced psychotherapy: Preliminary clinical observations on its effectiveness in treating alcoholism. *The Humanistic Psychologist, 34*, 399-422. doi:10.1207/s15473333thp3 404_7

Kolp, E., Krupitsky, E., Friedman, H., & Young, M. S. (2009). Entheogen-enhanced transpersonal psychotherapy of addictions: Focus on clinical applications of ketamine for treating alcoholism. In A. Browne-Miller (Ed.), *The Praeger international collection on addictions* (Vol., 3, pp. 403-417). Westport, CT: Praeger.

Kolp, E., Young, M. S., Friedman, H., Krupitsky, E., Jansen, K., & O'Connor, L. (2007). Ketamine enhanced psychotherapy: Preliminary clinical observations on its effects in treating death anxiety. *International Journal of Transpersonal Studies, 26*, 1-17.

Krauss, B., & Green, S. M. (2000). Sedation and analgesia for procedures in children. *New England Journal of Medicine, 342*, 938-945. doi:10.1056/NEJM200003303421306

Krauss, B., & Green, S. M. (2006). Procedural sedation and analgesia in children. *Lancet. 367*, 766-780. doi:10.1016/S0140-6736(06)68230-5

Krestow, M. (1974). The effects of post-anaesthetic dreaming on patient acceptance of ketamine anaesthesia: A comparison with thiopentone-nitrous oxide anaesthesia. *Canadian Anaesthetists' Society Journal, 21*(4), 385-389. doi:10.1007/BF03006072

Krupitsky, E. (1993/1994). Ketamine psychedelic therapy (KPT) of alcoholism and neurosis. *Yearbook of the European College for the Study of Consciousness, 1993/1994*, 113-122.

Krupitsky, E. M., Burakov, A. M., Romanova, T. N., Grinenko, A. Y., & Strassman, R. J. (2000). Ketamine assisted psychotherapy (KPT) of heroin addiction: Immediate effects and six months follow-up. *MAPS Bulletin, 9*(4), 21-26.

Krupitsky, E., Burakov, A., Romanova, T., Dunaevsky, I., Strassman, R., & Grinenko, A. (2002). Ketamine psychotherapy for heroin addiction: Immediate effects and two-year follow-up. *Journal of Substance Abuse Treatment, 23*, 273-283.

Krupitsky, E. M., Burakov, A. M., Romanova, T. N., Grinenko, N. I., Grinenko, A. Y., Fletcher, J., ... Krystal, J. H. (2001). Attenuation of ketamine effects by nimodipine pretreatment in recovering ethanol dependent men: Psychopharmacologic implications of the interaction of NMDA and L-type calcium channel antagonists. *Neuropsychopharmacology, 25*(6), 936-947. doi:10.1016/S0893-133X(01)00 346-3

Krupitsky, E. M., Burakov, A. M., Dunaevsky, I. V., Romanova, T. N., Slavina, T. Y., & Grinenko, A. Y. (2007). Single versus repeated sessions of ketamine-assisted psychotherapy for people with heroin dependence. *Journal of Psychoactive Drugs, 39*(1), 13-19. doi:10.1080/02791072.2007.10399860

Krupitsky, E. M., & Grinenko, A. Y. (1997). Ketamine psychedelic therapy (KPT): A review of the results of ten years of research. Journal of Psychoactive Drugs, 29(2), 165-183. doi:10.1080/02791072.1997.10400 185

Krupitsky, E. M., & Grinenko, A. Y. (1998). Ten year study of ketamine psychedelic therapy (KPT) of alcohol dependence. *The Heffter Review of Psychedelic Research, 1,* 56-61.

Krupitsky, E. M., Grinenko, A. Y., Berkaliev, T. N., Paley, A. I., Tetrov, U. N., Mushkov, K. A., & Borodikin, Y. S. (1992). The combination of psychedelic and aversive approaches in alcoholism treatment: The affective contra-attribution method. *Alcoholism Treatment Quarterly, 9*(1), 99-105. doi:10.1300/J020V09N01_09

Krupitsky, E. M., Grinenko, A. Y., Karandashova, G. F., Berkaliev, T. N., Moshkov, K. A., & Borodkin, Y. S. (1990). Metabolism of biogenic amines induced by alcoholism narcopsychotherapy with ketamine administration. *Biogenic Amines, 7*(6), 577-582.

Krupitsky, E., & Kolp, E. (2007). Ketamine psychedelic psychotherapy. In M. Winkelman & T. Roberts (Eds.), *Psychedelic medicine: Addictions medicine and transpersonal healing* (Vol. 2, pp. 67-85). Portsmouth, NH: Praeger.

Krystal, J. H., Bennet, A., Abi-Saab, D., Belger, A., Karper, L. P., D'Souza, D. C., ...

Charney, D. S. (2000). Dissociation of ketamine effects on rule acquisition and rule implementation: Possible relevance to NMDA receptor contributions to executive cognitive functions. *Biological Psychiatry, 47*, 137-143. doi:10.1016/S0006-3223(99)00097-9

Krystal, J. H., D'Souza, D. C., Karper, L. P., Bennett, A., Abi-Dargham, A., Abi-Saab, D., ... Charney, D. S. (1999). Interactive effects of subanesthetic ketamine and haloperidol in healthy humans. *Psychopharmacology, 145*, 193-204. doi:10.1007/s002130051049

Krystal, J. H., Karper, L. P., Bennett, A., D'Souza, D. C., Abi-Dargham, A., Morrissey, K., ... Charney, D. S. (1998a). Interactive effects of subanesthetic ketamine and subhypnotic lorazepam in humans. *Psychopharmacology, 135*, 213-229. doi:10.1007/s002130050503

Krystal, J. H., Karper, L. P., Seibyl, J. P., Freeman, G. K., Delaney, R., Bremner, J. D., ... Charney, D. S. (1994). Subanesthetic effects of the noncompetitive NMDA antagonist, ketamine, in humans. Psychotomimetic, perceptual, cognitive, and neuroendocrine responses. *Archives of General Psychiatry, 51*, 199-214. doi:10.1001/archpsyc.1994.03950030035004

Krystal, J. H., Petrakis, I. L., Krupitsky, E., Schütz, C., Trevisan, L., & D'Souza, D. C. (2003a). NMDA receptor antagonism and the ethanol intoxication signal: From alcoholism risk to pharmacotherapy. *Annals of the New York Academy of Science, 1003*, 176-184. doi:10.1196/annals.1300.010

Krystal, J., Petrakis, I., Limoncelli, D., Webb, E., Gueorgueva, R., D'Souza, D., ... Charney, D. (2003b). Altered NMDA glutamate receptor antagonist response in recovering ethanol-dependent patients. *Neuropsychopharmacology, 28*, 2020-2028. doi:10.1038/sj.npp.1300252

Krystal, J. H., Petrakis, I. L., Webb, E., Cooney, N. L., Karper, L. P., Namanworth, S. ... Charney, D. S. (1998b). Dose-related ethanol-like effects of the NMDA antagonist, ketamine, in recently detoxified alcoholics. *Archives of General Psychiatry, 55*, 354-360. doi:10.1001/archpsyc.55.4.354

Kudoh, A., Takahira, Y., Katagai, H., Takazawa, T. (2002). Small dose ketamine improves the postoperative state of depressed patients. *Anesthesia and Analgesia, 95*, 114-118. doi:10.1097/00000539-200207000-00020

Kungurtsev, I. (1991). Death-rebirth psychotherapy with ketamine. *The Albert Hofmann Foundation Bulletin, 2*(4), 2-6.

Kurland, A., Savage, E., Pahnke, N., Grof, S., & Olson, E. (1971). LSD in the treatment of alcoholics. *Pharmacopsychiatry, 4*(2), 83-94. doi:10.1055/s-0028- 1094301

La Barre, W. (1989). *Peyote cult* (5th ed.). Norman, OK: University of Oklahoma.

Lapidus, K., Levitch, C., Perez, A., Brallier, J., Parides, M., Soleimani, L., ... Murrough, J. (2014). A randomized controlled trial of intranasal ketamine in major depressive disorder. *Biological Psychiatry, 76*(12), 970-976. doi:10.1016/j.biopsych.2014.03.026

Lara, D., Bisol, L., & Munari, L. (2013). Antidepressant, mood stabilizing and precognitive effects of very low dose sublingual ketamine in refractory unipolar and bipolar depression. *International Journal of Neuropsychopharmacology, 16*(9), 2111-2117. doi:10.1017/S1461145713000485

Larkin, G., & Beautrais, A. (2011). A preliminary naturalistic study of low-dose ketamine for depression and suicidal ideation in the emergency department. *International Journal of Neuropsychopharmacology, 14*, 1127-1131. doi:10.10 17/S1461145711000629

Latasch, L., & Freye, E. (1993). Opioid receptors mediated respiratory effects and antinociception after (S+)ketamine. *Acta Anaesthesia (Belgium), 44*, 93-102.

Leary, T., Litwin, G., & Metzner, R. (1963). Reactions to psilocybin administered in a supportive environment. *Journal of Nervous and Mental Disease, 137*, 561-573. doi:10.1097/00005053-196312000-00007

Leary, T., Metzner, R., & Alpert, R. (1964). *The psychedelic experience: A manual based on the Tibetan book of the dead.* New York, NY: University Books.

Leuner, H. (1959). Psychotherapie in modellpsychosen. In E. Speer (Ed.), *Kritische Psychotherapie* (pp. 94-102). München, Germany: J. F. Lehmanns.

Leuner, H. (1967). Present state of psycholytic therapy and its possibilities. In H. Abramson (Ed.), *The use of LSD in psychotherapy and alcoholism* (pp. 101-116). New York, NY: Bobbs Merrill.

Leuner, H. (1971). Halluzinogene in der psychotherapie. *Pharmakopsychiatrie & Neuropsychopharmakologie, 4,* 333-351. doi:10.1055/s-0028-1094326

Leuner, H. (1977). Guided affective imagery: An account of its developmental history. *Journal of Mental Imagery, 1*, 73-92.

Leuner, H. (1984). *Guided affective imagery.* New York, NY: Wiley.

Liebrenz, M., Borgeat, A., Leisinger, R., & Stohler, R. (2007). Intravenous ketamine therapy in a patient with treatment resistant depression. *Swiss Medical Weekly, 137*, 234-236.

Liebrenz, M., Stohler, R., & Borgeat, A. (2009). Repeated intravenous ketamine therapy in a patient with treatment resistant depression. *The World Journal of Biological Psychiatry, 10*, 640-643.

Lilly, J. (1968). *Programming and metaprogramming in the human biocomputer: Theory and experiments.* Malibu, CA: Communication Research Institute.

Lilly, J. (1972). *The center of the cyclone: An autobiography of inner space.* New York, NY: Julian Press.

Lilly, J. (1978). *The scientist: A novel autobiography.* New York, NY: Lippincott.

Lim, D. (2003). Ketamine associated psychedelic effects and dependence. *Singapore Medical Journal, 44*(1), 31-34.

Lin, S. Z., Chiou, A. L., & Wang, Y. (1996). Ketamine antagonizes nitric oxide release from cerebral cortex after middle cerebral artery ligation in rats. *Stroke, 27*(4), 747-752. doi:10.1161/01.STR.27.4.747

Lin, C., & Durieux, M. E. (2005). Ketamine and kids: An update. *Paediatric Anaesthesia, 15*, 91-97. doi:10.1111/j.1460-9592.2005.01475.x

Lindefors, N., Barati, S., & O'Connor, W. T. (1997). Differential effects of single and repeated ketamine administration on dopamine, serotonin and GABA transmission in rat medial prefrontal cortex. *Brain Research, 759*(2), 205-212. doi:10.1016/S0006-8993 (97)00255-2

Lovinger, D. M., White, G., & Weight, F. F. (1989). Ethanol inhibits NMDA-activated ion current in hippocampal neurons. *Science, 243*, 1721-1724. doi:10.1126/science.2467382

Luby, E., Cohen, B., Rosenbaum, G., Gottlieb, J., & Kelley, R. (1959). Study of a new schizophrenic drug, Sernyl. *Archives of Neurology and Psychiatry, 81*, 363-369. doi:10.1001/archneurpsyc.1959.02340150095011

Luckenbaugh, D. A., Niciu, M. J., Ionescu, D. F., Nolan, N. M., Richards, E. M., Brutsche, N. E., ... Zarate C. A. (2014). Do the dissociative side effects of ketamine mediate its antidepressant effects? *Journal of Affective Disorders, 159*, 56-61.

Machado-Vieira, R., Manji, A., & Zarate, C. (2009). The role of the tripartite glutamatergic synapse in the pathophysiology and therapeutics of mood disorders. *Neuroscientist, 15*, 525-539. doi:10.1177/1073858409336093

Martin, L. L., Bouchal, R. L., & Smith, D. J. (1982). Ketamine inhibits serotonin uptake in vivo. *Neuropharmacology, 21*(2), 113-118. doi:10.1016/00 28-3908(82)90149-6

Mascher, E. (1967). Psycholitic therapy: Statistics and indications. In H. Brill (Ed.), *Neuropsychopharmacology* (pp. 441-444). Amsterdam, Netherlands: Excerpta Medica Foundation.

Mathew, S., Murrough, J., aan het Rot, M., Collins, K., Reich, D., & Charney,

D. (2010). Riluzole for relapse prevention following intravenous ketamine in treatment-resistant depression: A pilot randomized, placebo-controlled continuation trial. *International Journal of Neuropsychopharmacology, 13*, 71-82. doi:10.1017/S1461145709000169

Mayberg, T. S., Lam, A. M., Matta, B. F., Domino, K. B., & Winn, H. R. (1995). Ketamine does not increase cerebral blood flow velocity of intracranial pressure during isoflurane/nitrous oxide anesthesia in patients undergoing craniotomy. *Anesthesia and Analgesia, 81*, 84-89.

McGlone, R. G., Howes, M. C., & Joshi, M. (2004). The Lancaster experience of 2.0 to 2.5 mg/kg intramuscular ketamine for paediatric sedation: 501 cases and analysis. *Emergency Medicine Journal, 21*, 290-295. doi:10.1136/emj.2002.003772

McKenna, D. J., Towers, G. H., & Abbott, F. S. (1984). Monoamine oxidase inhibitors in South American hallucinogenic plants. Part 2: Constituents of orally active myristicaceous hallucinogens. *Journal of Ethnopharmacology, 12*, 179-211. doi:10.1016/0378-8741(84)90048-5

Meduna, L. J. (1950). *Carbon dioxide therapy*. Chicago, IL: Charles Thomas.

Meng, E., Wu, S. T., Cha, T. L., Sun, G. H., Yu, D. S., & Chang, S. Y. (2013). A murderer of young bladders: Ketamine-associated cystitis. *Urological Science, 24*(4), 113-116. doi:10.1016/j.urols.2013.09.001

Messer, M., & Haller, I. (2010). Maintenance ketamine treatment produces long-term recovery from depression. *Primary Psychiatry, 17*, 48-50.

Mills, I. H., Park, G. R., Manara, A. R., & Merriman, R. J. (1998). Treatment of compulsive behaviour in eating disorders with intermittent ketamine infusions. *QJM: An International Journal of Medicine, 91*(7), 493-503. doi:10.1093/qjmed/91.7.493

Mimura, M., Namiki, A., Kishi, R., Ikeda, T., Miyake, H., & Iwasaki, H. (1992). Central cholinergic action produces antagonism to ketamine anesthesia. *Acta Anaesthesiology Scandinavica, 36*, 460-462. doi:10.1111/j.1399-6576.1992.tb03497.x

Minami, K., Minami, M., & Harris, R. A. (1997). Inhibition of 5-hydroxytryptamine type 2A receptor-induced currents by n-alcohols and anesthetics. *Journal of Pharmacology and Experimental Therapeutics, 281*(3), 1136-1143.

Mistry, R. B., & Nahata, M. C. (2005). Ketamine for conscious sedation in pediatric emergency care. *Pharmacotherapy, 25*, 1104-1111. doi:10.1592/phco.2005.25.8.1104

Moore, K., & Measham, F. (2008). It's the most fun you can have for twenty quid: Motivations, consequences and meanings of British ketamine use. *Addiction Research & Theory, 16*(3), 231-244. doi:10.1080/16066350801983681

Moore, M., & Alltounian, H. (1978). *Journeys into the bright world.* Rockport, MA: Para Research.

Moore, N., & Bostwick, J. (1999). Ketamine dependence in anesthesia providers. *Psychosomatics, 40*(4), 356-359. doi:10.1016/S0033-3182(99)71231-4

Morgan, C., & Curran, H. (2012). Ketamine use: A review. *Addiction, 107*(1), 27-38. doi:10.1111/j.1360-0443.2011.03576.x

Morgan, C., Muetzelfeldt, L., & Curran, H. (2009). Ketamine use, cognition and psychological wellbeing: A comparison of frequent, infrequent and ex-users with polydrug and non-using controls. *Addiction, 104*(1), 77-87. doi:10.1111/j.1360-0443.2008.02394.x

Morita, T., Hitomi, S., Saito, S., Fujita, T., Uchihashi, Y., & Kuribara, H. (1995). Repeated ketamine administration produces up-regulation of muscarinic acetylcholine receptors in the forebrain, and reduces behavioral sensitivity to scopolamine in mice. *Psychopharmacology (Berlin), 117*(4): 396-402. doi:10.1007/BF02246210

Moriyama, Y., Mimura, M., Kato, M., & Kashima, H. (2006). Primary alcoholic dementia and alcohol-related dementia. *Psychogeriatrics, 6*(3), 114-118. doi:10.1111/j.1479-8301.2006.00168.x

Morris, H., & Wallach, J. (2014). From PCP to MXE: A comprehensive review of the non-medical use of dissociative drugs. *Drug Testing and Analysis, 6, 614-632.* doi:10.1002/dta.1620

Morse, M., & Perry, P. (1992). *Transformed by the light: The powerful effect of near-death experiences on people's lives.* New York, NY: Villard.

Moukaddam, N., & Hirschfeld, R. (2004). Intravenous antidepressants: A review. *Depression and Anxiety, 19*, 1-9. doi:10.1002/da.10135

Murrough, J., Perez, A., Mathew, S., & Charney, D. (2011). A case of sustained remission following an acute course of ketamine in treatment-resistant depression. *Journal of Clinical Psychiatry, 72*(3), 414-415. doi:10.4088/JCP.10l06447blu

Murrough, J., Perez, A., Pillemer, S., Stern, J., Parides, M., aan het Rot, M., ... Iosifescu, D. (2012). Rapid and longer-term antidepressant effects of repeated ketamine infusions in treatment-resistant major depression. *Biological Psychiatry, 74*(4), 250-256. doi:10.1016/j.biopsych.2012.06.022

Nakanishi, S. (1992). Molecular diversity of glutamate receptors and implications for brain function. *Science, 258*(5082), 597-603. doi:10.1126/science.1329206

Nalbandyan, R. (1986). Copper-containing brain proteins and their significance in etiology of schizophrenia. *Neurochemistry, 5,* 74-84.

Nathan, P. E. (1986). Outcomes of treatment for alcoholism: Current data. *Annals of Behavioral Medicine, 8,* 40-46. doi:10.1207/s15324796abm0802&3_7

National Drug Intelligence Center (2004). *Ketamine.* Intelligence Bulletin No. 2004-L0424-007. Washington, DC: US Department of Justice.

Nishimura, M., & Sato, K. (1999). Ketamine stereoselectively inhibits rat dopamine transporter. *Neuroscience Letters, 274*(2), 131-134. doi:10.1016/S0304-3940(99)00688-6

NSDUH Report (2006). *Use of specific hallucinogens.* Washington, DC: Substance Abuse and Mental Health Services Administration.

O'Neil, A. A., Winnie, A. P., Zadigian, M. E., & Collins, V. J. (1972). Premedication for ketamine analgesia. *Anesthesia and Analgesia, 51*(3), 475-482.

Ostroff, R., Gonzales, M., & Sanacora, G. (2005). Antidepressant effect of ketamine during ECT. *American Journal of Psychiatry, 162*(7), 1385-1386. doi:10.1176/appi.ajp.162.7.1385

Overton, D. A. (1975). A comparison of the discriminable CNS effects of ketamine, phencyclidine and pentobarbital. *Archives Internationales de Pharmacodynamie et Therapie, 215,* 180-189.

Oye, I., Paulsen, O., & Maurset, A. (1992). Effects of ketamine on sensory perception: Evidence for a role of N-methyl-D-aspartate receptors. *Journal of Pharmacology and Experimental Therapeutics, 260*(3), 1209-1213.

Pahnke, W. (1962). *Drugs and mysticism: An analysis of the relationship between psychedelic drugs and the mystical consciousness* (Unpublished doctoral dissertation). Cambridge, MA: Harvard University.

Pahnke, W. (1968). The psychedelic mystical experience in terminal cancer and its possible implications for psi research. In R. Cavanna & M. Ullman (Eds.). *Psi and altered states of consciousness* (pp. 115-128). New York, NY: Parapsychological Association.

Pahnke, W. (1969). The psychedelic mystical experience in the human encounter with death. *Harvard Theological Review, 62,* 1-21.

Pahnke, W. (1970). Drugs and mysticism. In B. Aaronson. & H. Osmond. (Eds.), *Psychedelics: The uses and implications of hallucinogenic drugs* (pp. 145-64). Garden City, NY: Anchor.

Pahnke, W., Kurland, A., Goodman, L., & Richards, W. (1969). LSD-assisted psychotherapy with terminal cancer patients. In R. Hicks & P. Fink (Eds.). *Psychedelic Drugs* (pp. 33-42). New York, NY: Grune & Stratton.

Pahnke, W., Kurland, A., Goodman, L., & Richards, W. (1969). LSD-assisted psychotherapy with terminal cancer patients. *Current Psychiatric Therapies, 9,* 144-152.

Pahnke, W., Kurland, A., Unger, S., Savage, C., & Grof, S. (1970). The experimental use of psychedelic (LSD) psychotherapy. *Journal of the American Medical Association, 212,* 1856-1863. doi:10.1001/jama.1970.03170240060010

Pahnke, W., Kurland, A., Unger, S., Savage, C., Wolf, S., & Goodman, L. (1970). Psychedelic therapy (utilizing LSD) with cancer patients. *Journal of Psychedelic Drugs, 3,* 63-75. doi:10.1080/02791072.1970.10471363

Pallotta, M., Segieth, J., & Whitton, P. S. (1998). N-methyl-d-aspartate receptors regulate 5-HT release in the raphe nuclei and frontal cortex of freely moving rats: Differential role of 5-HT1A autoreceptors. *Brain Research, 783*(2), 173-178. doi:10.1016/S0006-8993(97)01333-4

Parke-Davis Product Information Sheet (1999-2000). Ketlar®, ABPI *Compendium of Data Sheets and Summaries of Product Characteristics, 1999-2000* (pp. 1120-1122). London, UK: Datapharm.

Parsons, C., Danysz, W., & Quack, G. (1999). Memantine is a clinically well tolerated N-methyl-D-aspartate (NMDA) receptor antagonist–a review of preclinical data. *Neuropharmacology, 38*(6), 735-767. doi:10.1016/S0028-3908(99)00019-2

Paslakis, G., Gilles, M., Meyer-Lindenberg, A., & Deuschle, M. (2010). Oral administration of the NMDA receptor antagonist S-ketamine as add-on therapy of depression: A case series. *Pharmacopsychiatry, 43,* 33-35. doi:10.1055/s-0029-1237375

Passie, T. (1997). *Psycholitic and psychedelic therapy research 1931-1995: A complete international bibliography.* Hannover, Germany: Laurentius.

PDR Network (1992). *Physicians' desk reference 1992* (46th ed.). Oradell, NJ: Medical Economics.

PDR Network (2013). *Physicians' desk reference 2014* (68th Ed.). Montvale, NJ: Author.

Pedraz, J., Calvo, M., Lanoa, J., Muriel, C., Lamas, J., & Dominguez-Gil, A. (1989). Pharmacocinetics of rectal ketamine in children. *British Journal of Anaesthesiology, 63,* 671-674. doi:10.1093/bja/63.6.671

Petrack, M., Marx, M., & Wright, S. (1996). Intramuscular ketamine is superior to meperidine, promethazine, and chlorpromazine for pediatric emergency department sedation. *Archives of Pediatric Adolescent Medicine, 150,* 676-681. doi:10.1001/archpedi.1996.02170320022003

Porter K., (2004). Ketamine in prehospital care. *Emergency Medical Journal, 21,* 351-354. doi:10.1136/emj.2003.010843

Preskon, S. (2012). Ketamine: The hopes and the hurdles. *Biological Psychiatry, 72,* 522-523. doi:10.1016/j.biopsych.2012.07.021

Pribram, K. (1971). *Languages of the brain: Experimental paradoxes and principles in neuropsychology.* Englewood Cliffs, NJ: Prentice-Hall.

Rao, T. S., Kim, H. S., Lehmann, J., Martin, L. L., & Wood, P. L. (1990). Selective activation of dopaminergic pathways in the mesocortex by compounds that act at the phencyclidine (PCP) binding site. *Neuropharmacology, 29*(3), 225-230. doi:10.1016/0028-3908(90)900 05-C

Rasmussen, K., Lineberry, T., Galardy, C., Kung, S., Lapid, M., Palmer, B., ... Frye, M. (2013). Serial infusions of low-dose ketamine for major depression. *Journal of Psychopharmacology, 27*(5), 444-450. doi:10.1177/0269881113478283

Reich, D., & Silvay, G. (1989). Ketamine: An update on the first twenty-five years of clinical experience. *Canadian Journal of Anaesthesiology, 36*(2), 186-197. doi:10.1007/BF03011442

Reid, C., Hatton, R., & Middleton, P. (2011). Case report: Prehospital use of intranasal ketamine for paediatric burn unit. *Emergency Medical Journal, 28,* 328-329. doi:10.1136/emj.2010.092825

Richards, W. (1979/1980). Psychedelic drug-assisted psychotherapy with persons suffering from terminal cancer. *Journal of Altered States of Consciousness, 5,* 309-319.

Richards, W., Grof, S., Goodman, L., & Kurland, A. (1972). LSD-assisted psychotherapy and human encounter with death. *Journal of Transpersonal Psychology, 4,* 121-150.

Richards, W., Rhead, J., Di Leo, F., Yensen, R., & Kurland, A. (1977). The peak experience variable in DPT-assisted psychotherapy with cancer patients. *Journal of Psychoactive Drugs, 9,* 1-10. doi:10.1080/02791072.1977.10472020

Richards, W., Rhead, J., Grof, S., Goodman, L., Di Leo, F., & Rush, L. (1979). DPT as an adjunct in brief psychotherapy with cancer patients. *Omega, 10,* 9-26. doi:10.2190/ngub-v4rm-t7dc-xth3

Richardson, J. D., Aanonsen, L., & Hargreaves, K. M. (1998). Hypoactivity of the spinal cannabinoid system results in NMDA-dependent hyperalgesia. *Journal of*

Neuroscience, 18(1), 451-457.

Ricuarte, G., & McCann, U. (2005). Recognition and management of complications of new recreational drug use. *Lancet, 365*(9477), 2137-2145. doi:10.1016/S0140-6736(05)66737-2

Ring, K. (1980). *Life at death: A scientific investigation of the near death experience.* New York, NY: Coward, McCann, Goeghegan.

Ring, K. (1984). *Heading toward omega.* New York, NY: William Morrow.

Ring, K., & Valeriano, E. (1998). *Lessons from the light: What we can learn from the near-death experience.* New York, NY: Plenum/Insight.

Rodriguez, C., Kegeles, L., Levinson, A., Feng, T., Marcus, S., Vermes, D., ... Simpson, H. (2013). Randomized controlled crossover trial of ketamine in obsessive-compulsive disorder: Proof-of-concept. *Neuropsychopharmacology, 38*(12), 2475-2483. doi:10.1038/npp.2013.150

Roquet, S. (1974). *Operacion Mazateca: Estudio de hongos y otras plantas allucinoganas Mexicanastratamiento psicoterapeutico de psicosintesis.* Mexico City, Mexico: Asociacion Albert Schweitzer.

Roquet, S., & Favreau, P. (1981). *Los alucinogenos de la conception indigena a una nueva psicoterapia.* Mexico City, Mexico: Editiones Prisma.

Roquet, S., Favreau, P., Ocana, R., & Velasco, M. (1971). *The existential through psychodisleptics—a new psychotherapy.* Mexico City, Mexico: Asociacion Albert Schweitzer.

Ross, P., & Fochtman, D. (1995). Conscious sedation: A quality management project. *Journal of Pediatric Oncology Nursing, 12*, 115-121. doi:10.1177/104345429501200305

Rossi, S. (Ed.). (2006). *Australian medicines handbook.* Adelaide, Australia: AMH Pty.

Rot, M., Chaney, D., & Mathew, S. (2008). Intravenous ketamine for treatment-resistant major depressive disorder. *Primary Psychiatry, 15*(4), 39-47.

Rothman, S., Thurston, J., Hauhart, R., Clark, G., & Solomon, J. (1987). Ketamine protects hippocampal neurons from anoxia in vitro. *Neuroscience, 21*, 673-683. doi:10.1016/0306-4522(87)90028-5

Roud, P. (1990). *Making miracles.* New York, NY: Waener.

Rumpf, K., Dudeck, J., Teuteberg, H., Münchoff, W., & Nolte, H. (1969). Dreamlike experiences during brief anesthesia with ketamine, thiopental and propanidid [Dreamlike experiences during brief anesthesia with ketamine, thiopental and propanidid]. In H. Kreuscher (Ed.), *Ketamine* (pp. 161-166). Berlin, Germany:

Springer-Verlag. (German) doi:10.1007/978-3-642-999 58-1_22

Sacchetti, A., Senula, G., Strickland, J., & Dubin, R. (2007). Procedural sedation in the community emergency department: Initial results of the ProSCED registry. *Academic and Emergency Medicine, 14*(1), 41-46. doi:10.1111/j.1553-2712.2007.tb00369.x

Sadove, M. S., Shulman, M., Hatano, S., & Fevold, N. (1971). Analgesic effects of ketamine administered in subdissociative doses. *Anesthesia and Analgesia, 50*(3), 452-457. doi:10.1213/00000539-197105000-00037

Sanacora, G., Kendell, S., Levin, Y., Simen, A., Fenton, L., Coric, V., & Krystal, J. (2007). Preliminary evidence of riluzole efficacy in antidepressant-treated patients with residual depressive symptoms. *Biological Psychiatry, 61*(6), 822-825. doi:10.1016/j.biopsych.2006.08.037

Sandison, R., Spencer, A., & Whitelaw, J. (1954). The therapeutic value of lysergic acid diethylamide in mental illness. *Journal of Mental Science, 100*,(419) 491-507. doi:10.1192/bjp.100.419.491

Schmid, R. L., Sandler, A. N., & Katz, J. (1999). Use and efficacy of low-dose ketamine in the management of acute postoperative pain: A review of current techniques and outcomes. *Pain, 82*, 111-125. doi:10.1016/S0304-3959(99)00044-5

Schneider, L., Dagerman, K., Higgins, J., & McShane, R. (2011). Lack of evidence for the efficacy of memantine in mild Alzheimer disease. *Archives of Neurology, 68*(8), 991-998. doi:10.1001/archneurol.2011.69

Schrenck-Notzing, F. (1891). Die bedeutung narcotischer mittel fur den hypnotismus. Leipzig, Germany: Abel.

Schultes, R., & Hofmann, A. (1979). *Plants of the gods: Origin of hallucinogenic use.* New York, NY: McGraw-Hill.

Scolnick, P., Popik, P., & Trullas, R. (2009). Glutamate-based antidepressants: 20 years on. *Trends in Pharmacological Science, 30*, 563-569. doi:10.1016/j.tips.2009.09.002

Seeman, P., Ko, F., & Tallerico, T. (2005). Dopamine receptor contribution to the action of PCP, LSD and ketamine psychotomimetics. *Molecular Psychiatry, 10*(9), 877-883. doi:10.1038/sj.mp.4001 682

Selby, N. M., Anderson, J., Bungay, P., Chesterton, L. J., & Kolhe, N. V. (2008). Obstructive nephropathy and kidney injury associated with ketamine abuse. *Clinical Kidney Journal, 1*(5), 310-312. doi:10.1093/ndtplus/sfn054

Shapira, Y., Artru, A. A., & Lam, A. M. (1992). Ketamine decreases cerebral infarct volume and improves neurological outcome following experimental head trauma in rats. *Journal of Neurosurgery and Anesthesiology, 4*, 231-240. doi:10.1097/00008506-199210000-00001

Shapira, Y., Lam, A., Eng, C., Laohaprasit, V., & Michel, M. (1994). Therapeutic time window and dose response of the beneficial effects of ketamine in experimental head injury. *Stroke, 25*, 1637-1643. doi:10.1161/01.STR.25.8.1637

Shapiro, M., Wyte, R., & Harris, B. (1972). Ketamine anaesthesia in patients with intracranial pathology. *British Journal of Anesthesiology, 44*(11), 1200-1204. doi:10.1093/bja/44.11.1200

Siegel, R. (1978). Phencyclidine and ketamine intoxification: A study of four populations of recreational users. *National Institute of Drug Abuse Research Monograph #21*, 119-147.

Siegel, R. (1980). The psychology of life after death. *American Psychologist, 35*, 911-931. doi:10.1037/0003-066X.35.10.911

Siegel, R. (1981). Accounting for after-life experiences. *Psychology Today, 15*, 67.

Sikich, N., & Lerman, J. (2004). Development and psychometric evaluation of the pediatric anesthesia emergence delirium scale. *Anesthesiology, 100*, 1138-1145. doi:10.1097/00000542-200405000-00 015

Simonov, P. (1987). *Motivated brain.* Moscow, Russia: Nauka.

Simson, P. E., Criswell, H. E., Johnson, D. B., Hicks, R. E., & Breese, G. R. (1991). Ethanol inhibits NMDA-evoked electrophysiological activity in vivo. *Journal of Pharmacology and Experimental Therapeutics, 257*(1), 225-231.

Slikker, W., Zou, X., Hotchkiss, C., Divine, R., Sadovova, N., Twaddle, N., ... Wang, C. (2007). Ketamine-induced neuronal cell death in the perinatal rhesus monkey. *Toxicological Sciences, 98*(1), 145-158. doi:10.1093/toxsci/kfm084

Smith, C. M. (1964). Exploratory and control studies of lisergide in the treatment of alcoholism. *Quarterly Journal of Studies in Alcohol, 25*(4), 742-747.

Smith, D. E., & Seymour, R. E. (1985). Dream becomes nightmare: Adverse reactions to LSD. *Journal of Psychoactive Drugs, 17*(4), 297-303. doi:10.1080/0 2791072.1985.10524334

Smith, D. J., Pekoe, G. M., Martin, L. L., & Coalgate, B. (1980). The interaction of ketamine with the opiate receptor. *Life Sciences, 26*, 789-795. doi:10.1016/0024-3205(80)90285-4

Smith, H. (2001). *Why religion matters.* San Francisco, CA: Harper-Collins.

Soyka, M., Krupitski, G., & Volki, G. (1993). Phenomenology of ketamine induced psychosis. *Sucht, 5*, 327-331.

Sputz, R. (1989, October). I never met a reality I didn't like: A report on Vitamin

K. *High Times,* 64-82.

Stafford, P., & Golightly, B. (1967). *LSD: The problem-solving psychedelic.* New York, NY: Award Books.

Stella, N., Schweitzer, P., & Piomelli, D. (1997). A second endogenous cannabinoid that modulates long-term potentiation. *Nature, 388*(6644), 773-778. doi:10.1038/42015

Stirling, J., Barkus, E., Nabosi, L., Irshad, S., Roemer, G., Schreudergoidheijt, B., & Lewis, S. (2008). Cannabis-induced psychotic-like experiences are predicted by high schizotypy: Confirmation of preliminary results in a large cohort. *Psychopathology, 41*(6), 371-378. doi:10.1159/000155215

Strassman, R. (1995). Hallucinogenic drugs in psychiatric research and treatment. Perspectives and prospects. *Journal of Nervous and Mental Disease, 183,* 127-138. doi:10.1097/00005053-199503000-00002

Strassman, R. (2000). *DMT: The spirit molecule: A doctor's revolutionary research into the biology of near-death and mystical experiences.* South Paris, ME: Park Street Press.

Strassman, R. (2014). *DMT and the soul of prophecy: A new science of spiritual revelation in the Hebrew Bible.* Rochester, VT: Inner Traditions.

Strayer, R. J., & Nelson, L. S. (2008). Adverse events associated with ketamine for procedural sedation in adults. *American Journal of Emergency Medicine, 26,* 985-1028. doi:10.1016/j.ajem.2007.12.005

Subramaniam, K., Subramaniam, B., Steinbrook, R. (2004). Ketamine as adjuvant analgesic to opioids: A quantitative and qualitative systematic review. *Anaesthesia and Analgesia, 99,* 482-495. doi:10.1213/01.ANE.0000118109.12855.07

Sun, L., Li, Q., Zhang, Y., Liu, D., Jiang, H., Pan, F., & Yew, D. (2014). Chronic ketamine exposure induces permanent impairment of brain functions in adolescent cynomolgus monkeys. *Addiction Biology, 19*(2), 185-194. doi:10.1111/adb.12004

Tam, Y. H., Ng, C. F., Pang, K. K., Yee, C. H., Chu, W. C., Leung, V. Y., ... Lai, P. B. (2014). One-stop clinic for ketamine-associated uropathy: Report on service delivery model, patients' characteristics and non-invasive investigations at baseline by a cross-sectional study in a prospective cohort of 318 teenagers and young adults. *BJU International, 114*(5), 754-760. doi:10.1111/bju.12675

Taylor, D., Paton, C., & Kapur, S. (2012). *The Maudsley prescribing guidelines.* London, UK: Informa.

Thomson, A. M., West, D. C., & Lodge, D. (1985). An N-methyl aspartate receptor mediated synapse in rat cerebral cortex: A site of action of ketamine? *Nature, 313*, 479-481. doi:10.1038/313479a0

Tobin, H. (1982). Low dose of ketamine and diazepam: Use as an adjunct to local anesthesia in an office operating room. *Archives of Otolaryngology, 108*(7), 439-442. doi:10.1001/archotol.1982.00790550043011

Toft, P., & Romer, U. (1987). Comparison of midazolam and diazepam to supplement total intravenous anaesthesia with ketamine for endoscopy. *Canadian Journal of Anaesthesia, 34*(5), 466-469. doi:10.1007/BF03014351

Tori, S. (1996). *Ketamine abuse: 'Special K.'* Newtown, PA: Middle Atlantic-Great Lakes Organized Crime Law Enforcement Network (MAGLOCLEN).

Toro-Matos, A., Rendon-Platas, A. M., Avila-Valdez, E., & Villarreal-Guzman, R. A. (1980). Physostigmine antagonizes ketamine. *Anesthesia and Analgesia, 59*(10), 764-767. doi:10.1213/00000539-198010000-00008

Travis, A. (2005, September 5). Special K, the horse pill taking over from ecstasy among clubbers. *The Guardian*, n.p. Retrieved from http://www.theguardian.com/society/2005/sep/06/drugsandalcohol.drugs

Trevisan, L., Fitzgerald, L. W., Brose, N., Gasic, G. P., Heinemann, S. F., Duman, R. S., & Nestler, E. J. (1994). Chronic ingestion of ethanol up-regulates NMDA R1 receptor subunit immunoreactivity in rat hippocampus. *Journal of Neurochemistry, 62*(4), 1635-1638. doi:10.1046/j.1471-4159.1994.62041635.x

Tsai, G., Gastfriend, D., & Coyle, J. (1995). The glutamatergic basis of human alcoholism. *American Journal of Psychiatry, 152*(3), 332-340.

Turner, D. M. (1994). *The essential guide to psychedelics*. San Francisco, CA: Panther Press.

United Nations Office on Drugs and Crime (2010). *Transnational drug market analysis*. New York, NY: United Nations.

U.S. Army Aeromedical Research Laboratory Warfighter Performance and Health Division Report (2010). *Comparison of the effects of ketamine and morphine on the performance of representative military tasks*. USAARL Report No. 2010-2017. Fort Rucker, AL: Author.

Valentine, G., Mason, G., Gomez, R., Fasula, M., Watzl, J., & Pittman, B. (2011). The antidepressant effect of ketamine is not associated with changes in occipital amino acid neurotransmitter content as measured by [(1)H]-MRS. *Psychiatry Research Neuroimaging, 191*, 122-127. doi:10.1016/j.pscychresns.2010.10.009

Vietnam Studies (1973). *Medical support of the U.S. Army in Vietnam 1965-1970* (Major General Surgeon Neel). Washington, DC: Department of the Army.

Visser, E., & Schug, S. (2006). The role of ketamine in pain management. *Biomedicine and Pharmacotherapy, 60*(7), 341-348. doi:10.1016/j.biopha.2006.06.021

Vollenweider, F., Scharfetter, C., Leenders, K., & Angst, J. (1994). Disturbances of serotonergic or glutamatergic neurotransmission results in hyperfrontality as measured by PET and FDG in acute human model psychoses. *European Neuropsychopharmacology, 4*(3), 367. doi:10.1016/0924-977X(94)90190-2

Walsh, R., & Grob, C. (2005). *Higher wisdom: Eminent elders explore the continuing impact of psychedelics.* Albany, NY: State University of New York Press.

Watts, G. (1973). Changing death's perspective. *World Medicine, 9*(2), 15-19.

Weil, A., & Rosen, W. (1983). *Chocolate to morphine: Understanding mind-active drugs.* Boston, MA: Houghton Miflin.

Weiss, J., Goldberg, M. P., & Choi, D. W. (1986). Ketamine protects cultured neocortical neurons from hypoxic injury. *Brain Research, 380*, 186-190. doi:10.1016/0006-8993(86)91447-2

White, P., Way, W., & Trevor, A. (1982). Ketamine: Its pharmacology and therapeutic uses. *Anesthesiology, 56*,119-136. doi:10.1097/00000542-198202000-000 07

White, P., Vasconez, L., Mathes, S., & Way, W. (1988). Comparison of midazolam and diazepam as adjuvants to ketamine for sedation during monitored ketamine anesthesia. *Anesthesia and Analgesia, 67*, S258. doi:10.1213/00000539-198802001-00258

Wijesinghe, R. (2014). Emerging therapies for treatment resistant depression. *The Mental Health Clinician, 4*(5), 226-230. doi:10.9740/mhc.n207179

Winters, W. D., Hance, A. J., Cadd, G. G., Quam, D. D., & Benthuysen, J. L. (1988). Ketamine- and morphine-induced analgesia and catalepsy. I. Tolerance, cross-tolerance, potentiation, residual morphine levels and naloxone action in the rat. *Journal of Pharmacology and Experimental Therapeutics, 244*, 51-57.

Wood, D. (2013). Ketamine and damage to the urinary tract. *Addiction, 108*(8), 1515-1516. doi:10.1111/add.12228.

World Health Organization (2013). *WHO Model List of Essential Medicines* (18th ed.). Geneva, Switzerland: Author.

Yensen, R. (1973). *Group psychotherapy with a variety of hallucinogens.* Joint presentation with Salvador Roquet at the Eleventh Annual Meeting of the Association for Humanistic Psychology. Montreal, Canada.

Yensen, R. (1985). From mysteries to paradigms: Humanity's journey from sacred plants to psychedelic drugs. *ReVision, 10*(4), 31-50.

Yensen, R., & Dryer, D. (1993/1994). Thirty years of psychedelic research: The

Spring Grove experiment and its sequels. *Yearbook of the European College for the Study of Consciousness, 1993/1994,* 73-102.

Zarate, C. A., Brutsche, N. E., Ibrahim, L., Franco-Chaves, J., Diaz-Granados, N., Cravchik, A., ... & Luckenbaugh, D. A. (2012). Replication of ketamine's antidepressants efficacy in bipolar depression: A randomized controlled add-on trial. *Biological Psychiatry, 71,* 939-946. doi:10.1016/j.biopsych.2011.12.010

Zarate, C. A., Mathews, D., Ibrahim, L., Chaves, J. F., Marquardt, C., Ukoh, I., ... Luckenbaugh, D. A. (2013). A randomized trial of a low-trapping nonselective n-methyl-d-aspartate channel blocker in major depression. *Biological Psychiatry, 74*(4), 257-264. doi:10.1016/j.biopsych.2012.10. 019

Zarate, C., Payne, J., Quiroz, J., Sporn, J., Denicoff, K., & Luckenbaugh, D. (2004). An open-label trial of riluzole in patient with treatment-resistant major depression. *American Journal of Psychiatry, 161,* 171-174. doi:10.1176/appi. ajp.161.1.171

Zarate, C., Quiroz, J., Singh, J., Denicoff, K., De Jesus, G., & Luckenbaugh, D. (2005). An open-label trial of the glutamate-modulating agent riluzole in combination with lithium for treatment of bipolar depression. *Biological Psychiatry, 57,* 430-432. doi:10.1016/j.biopsych.2004.11.023

Zarate, C., Singh, J., Carlson, P., Brutsche, N., Ameli, R., Luckenbaugh, D., ... Manji, H. (2006). A randomized trial of an N-methyl-D-aspartate antagonist in treatment-resistant major depression. *Archives of General Psychiatry, 63,* 856-864. doi:10.1001/archpsyc.63.8.856

Ketamine, Depression, and Current Research: A Review of the Literature

Wesley C. Ryan, M.D., Cole J. Marta, M.D., and Ralph J. Koek, M.D.

DESPITE SIGNIFICANT PROGRESS, DEPRESSION REMAINS A common and disabling condition that affects millions, leading to increased primary care visits and decreased productivity (Baune, Adrian, & Jacobi, 2007). Both psychotherapy and antidepressant pharmacotherapy are evidence-based treatments recommended by experts and treatment guidelines (Gelenberg, 2010). For those with more severe depression, pharmacotherapy is often required for recovery. However, inadequate response and lack of remission are common and characterize treatment-resistant depression (TRD; Keitner & Mansfield, 2012). The current pharmacopoeia available to clinicians is primarily based on modulation of serotonergic, noradrenergic, and dopaminergic transmission in the brain, with first line agents primarily consisting of selective serotonin reuptake inhibitors (SSRIs; Keitner & Mansfield, 2012).

As demonstrated by the STAR*D study, multiple trials of medications are frequently required to achieve remission, and despite this, about 35% of patients remain symptomatic after several successive interventions (Rush et al., 2006; Olin, Jayewardene, Bunker, & Moreno, 2012). When monoamine modulating antidepressant medications do work, there is a delay of typically weeks before response is achieved. In those first few weeks, antidepressant treatment may increase risk of suicidal behavior, and possibly including completed suicide (Björkenstam et al., 2013). With the lack of rapid response from existing medications, and indeed the apparent risk until such response, there is urgent need for development of rapid acting treatment alternatives for depression (Monteggia, Gideons, & Kavalali, 2013).

For severe depression, electroconvulsive therapy (ECT) is the only somatic intervention with the potential for more-rapid treatment effect; however, concern over adverse effects limit use. Alternative approaches utilizing direct electrical modulation, including repetitive transcranial magnetic stimulation (rTMS), trigeminal nerve stimulation, and deep brain stimulation (Cook, Espinoza, & Leuchter, 2014) as well as magnetic seizure therapy and vagal nerve stimulation (Wani, Trevino, Marnell, & Husain, 2013) are promising in terms of efficacy, but have not been shown consistently to have a more-rapid onset of effect than pharmacotherapy.

Studies suggest a role for the glutamate system in regulation of mood (Skolnick et al., 1996; Matthews, Henter, & Zarate, 2012; Machado-Vieira et al., 2009), and particular promise has been generated from studies looking at the N-methyl-D-aspartate (NMDA) receptor antagonist ketamine for this novel indication (Artigas, 2013; Zarate et al., 2013; Mathew, Manji, & Charney, 2008). Ketamine was developed in 1963, first tested on humans in 1964, and FDA approved for roles in anesthesia in 1970 (Reich & Silvay, 1989; JHP Pharmaceuticals, 2009). It was not until 2000 that ketamine was concretely demonstrated in the literature to have antidepressant properties (Berman et al., 2000). Ketamine has shown a large effect size, with onset on the order of hours, and duration of effect of approximately one week (Zarate et al., 2006). Reduction in suicidal thoughts is further described, similarly within hours of administration (Price, Nock, Charney, & Mathew, 2009, 2014).

A significant limitation exists in that ketamine is FDA-approved only for intravenous (IV) or intramuscular (IM) use in induction or maintenance of anesthesia, making administration in less controlled settings difficult. While most studies on ketamine thus far have looked at longer IV infusions, other routes have shown promise for increasing patient access to ketamine (Larkin & Beautrais, 2011; Harihar, Dasari, & Srinivas, 2013; Lara, Bisol, & Munari, 2013; Lapidus et al., 2014; Iglewicz et al. 2014; Loo et al., 2016).

This chapter reviews the extant literature regarding use of ketamine as an antidepressant, highlighting its role as a rapid acting agent for unipolar and bipolar depression. We report on and analyze efficacy, with additional attention to durability of response, improvement in suicidality, routes of administration, dosing protocols, and safety. Different stereoisomeric forms of ketamine are also reviewed, given the possibility that one form may be associated with fewer dissociative effects. We conclude with recommendations for future study design as well as potential off-label use in less structured settings. Detailed discussions on the history and neuropharmacology of ketamine, and the glutamate theory of depression are not included; the reader is referred to previous publications on these topics (Domino, 2010; Krystal, Sanatoria, & Duman, 2013; Caddy, Giaroli, White, Shergill, & Tracy, 2014; Naughton, Clarke, Olivia, Cryan, & Dinan, 2014). In this review, we build upon a less extensive article previously published elsewhere (Ryan, Marta, & Koek, 2014).

Materials and Methods

PubMed.gov was searched using the term "ketamine depression," with the filter of English language, through April 2016, yielding 1274 studies. Studies were excluded that did not investigate clinical use of ketamine in humans for treatment of depression, either unipolar or bipolar, or suicidality. Those utilizing ketamine as an anesthetic or augmenting agent for, or in combination with, ECT or rTMS were excluded, or in regards to ketamine misuse. The remaining articles were further reviewed for pertinent references. Data on depression response rates were combined and recalculated to include intent to treat (ITT) analysis, accounting for differences between rates reported in the studies and in this review. Data from randomized controlled trials were weighed more heavily over open label investigations, which in turn were weighed more heavily than individual cases or case series. At least three areas of research pertinent to ketamine treatment of depression were not reviewed in depth for this manuscript due to space limitations: biomarkers for response, neurocognitive effects, and neuroimaging correlates.

Results

Study population and methodology

Using the above search criteria, a total of 77 publications were included in this review. Of these, 56 utilized the IV route of administration, accounting for over 500 patients in total. A further 20 studies utilized IM, oral, intranasal, sublingual, or subcutaneous treatment in over 150 patients. Nearly all publications reported use of racemic ketamine, with only 13 patients in total receiving *S*-ketamine (Denk, Rewerts, Holsboer, Erhardt-Lehmann, & Turck, 2011; Paul, Schaaff, Padberg, Moller, & Frodl, 2009; Segmiller et al., 2013; Paslakis, Gilles, Meyer-Lindenberg, & Deuschle, 2010). Most studies utilized only one administration of ketamine, though six open label investigations (OLI), two randomized control trials (RCT), and 35 case studies/series assessed multiple doses, from one to three times per week, for up to four weeks. The majority of publications reported on patients with unipolar depression, though bipolar depression was also represented in 14 publications. Given the differences in presentation, etiology, and response between these two types of depression, these are considered separately. Save for a minority of case studies [table

5; suppl. table 1], articles utilized one or more validated depression rating scales, including the Montgomery-Åsberg Depression Rating Scale (MADRS; Montgomery & Åsberg, 1979), Hamilton Depression Rating Scale (HDRS; Hamilton, 1960), Beck Depression Inventory (BDI; Beck, Ward, Mendelson, Mock, & Erbaugh, 1961), or Clinical Global Impression scale (CGI; Guy et al. 1976). The only study to report on the pediatric population utilized rating scales more specific to that population (Papolos, Teicher, Faedda, Murphy, & Mattis, 2013). Studies of ketamine in hospice patients also utilized the Hospital Anxiety and Depression Scale (HADS; Zigmond & Snaith, 1983) [table 5; suppl. table 1].

We focused on the categorical outcome of response—defined as >50% reduction—within 24 hours because this was most commonly the primary outcome measure referred to in the studies reviewed. Remission was not consistently reported, and was also variably defined. Notably, too, the majority of these studies were performed in patients with treatment resistance, and while definitions varied between studies, this typically was qualified by at least two, if not more, failed trials of adequate dose and duration antidepressant treatment. Some also included failure of ECT and a few described failure of adequate psychotherapy. To objectively assess such trials, many studies utilized the Antidepressant Treatment History Form (Sackeim, 2001). Unless otherwise specified below, we accept the authors' descriptions of TRD. Of the studies employing ketamine IV infusions, most utilized racemic ketamine 0.5mg/kg over 40 minutes, with several more varying the duration from 30 to 60 minutes. For the sake of brevity, we abbreviate this protocol as KET in the rest of this document. In studies utilizing alternate routes of administration, the dose and protocol varied widely, and the majority utilized multiple ketamine administrations.

Efficacy from single doses (RCT and OLI data)

The nine RCTs reporting outcomes from single doses of ketamine included six crossover studies, all with saline placebo, and three parallel group designs, all with either lower ketamine doses or active controls [table 1]. Only one utilized a non-IV route of administration; the majority utilized a single ketamine infusion. Seven were done in patients with unipolar depression and the other two in patients with bipolar depression. The larger of the two active control and blinded RCTs utilized midazolam and included 72 patients in a 2:1 ratio of ketamine:midazolam, all with treatment-resistant unipolar depression, who were discontinued from any concomitant medications. In the ketamine group, 64% responded at 24 hour follow-up, compared to 28% in the midazolam group (Murrough et al., 2013). Response rate in the ketamine arm fell below 50% after day 3. The other active control blinded RCT utilized ECT as the comparison condition, demonstrating a more-rapid onset of action and greater response rates at 24 hours in the ketamine arm; KET elicited 78% response versus 11% with ECT (Ghasemi et al., 2013). Li et al. (2016) notably compared 0.2mg/kg to 0.5mg/kg of ketamine, though only reported response in the initial four hours: 44% and 38%, respectively. The other placebo controlled studies in unipolar depression generally recruited fewer patients, and found 24-hour outcomes of 45% with KET versus 2% with saline; and four-hour outcomes of 34% versus 13% [figure 1].

Both studies of patients with bipolar depression were performed by the same group and found more-rapid onset, but shorter duration, of benefit [table 1]. Response was 58% in the first four hours, but by day one, half of the cohort no longer met this criterion [figure 2]. While studies in unipolar depression generally discontinued psychotropic medications and provided a washout period, those in bipolar depression maintained patients on therapeutic levels of mood stabilizers, either lithium or valproic acid, which may have had an effect on outcome.

Limitations in blinding and control selection are prevalent in all but Murrough et al. (2013), who utilized midazolam as an active control. The trial with ECT as the active control (Ghasemi et al., 2013) did not appear to have had strict patient blinding, despite blinding of the treatment team. Valentine et al. (2011) was the opposite, with study personnel being aware of experimental conditions. Other studies utilized a saline placebo, but the apparent ease in recognition of dissociative effects likely sabotaged the blind.

Eighteen OLIs describe outcomes in unique depressed patients after KET, of which 17 were principally in unipolar depression [table 2]. Nearly half of the over 250 unipolar depression patients, 95% of whom were categorized as TRD, responded within four to six hours after KET [figure 3]. At 24 hours, the overall response rate increased to 59% and then gradually declined with time. While four-week outcomes were only available for 47 individuals, the 21% response rate after a single infusion is remarkable in light of the high degree of treatment resistance.

Each open-label trial was focused on some aspect of KET besides acute antidepressant efficacy *per se*, with several valuable findings. Thakurta et al. (2012) demonstrated robust, but short-lived (< 3 days) antidepressant effects of standard dose KET in an Indian population. Ibrahim et al. (2011) demonstrated that a history of nonresponse to ECT was not associated with a reduced likelihood of response to KET in TRD. Machado-Vieira et al. (2009) did not detect change in peripheral blood brain-derived neurotrophic factor (BDNF) levels or correlation between BDNF and MADRS scores, in 23 TRD subjects over the first four hours after KET. Salvadore et al. demonstrated correlations between short-term antidepressant response to KET and pretreatment signals in prefrontal cortex on magnetoenchephalography (2009, 2010) and proton magnetic resonance spectroscopy (2012). In support of this possibility, Cornwell et al. (2012) demonstrated that stimulus-evoked somatosensory cortical magnetoencephalographic responses were increased after ketamine infusion in responders, but not non-responders to KET.

Phelps et al. (2009) identified another link to a potential biomarker, demonstrating that non-alcohol-dependent MDD subjects with a family history of alcoholism had a substantially greater likelihood of response to KET than those without. Luckenbaugh et al. (2012) reported similar findings from a post-hoc analysis of RCT data (Diaz-Granados et al., 2010b; Zarate et al., 2012). Both Mathew et al. (2010) and Ibrahim et al. (2012) failed to demonstrate benefits from randomization to riluzole over placebo during planned monthlong follow-up treatment after response to open-label KET. Larkin and Beautrais (2011) found administration of a lower total ketamine dose (0.2 mg/kg), via IV bolus rather than slow infusion, permitted use in an emergency department setting by busy clinicians. While they reported cumulative remission of 71.4% in the first four hours, improved response in the subsequent two weeks must be interpreted in light of telephone follow-up and naturalistic treatment, including inpatient care (this data omitted from the table).

The one OLI solely in patients with treatment-resistant bipolar depression demonstrated progressive decreases in mean HDRS score and increases in response (Rybakowski, Permoda-Osip, Skibinska, Adamski, & Bartkowska-Sniatkowska, 2013) [table 2]. Response more than doubled from 24% at one day to 52% at one week, remaining stable for the duration of the two-week trial. Patients were maintained on a variety of mood stabilizing medications, although a limitation of the study is that subjects were tapered off of antidepressants as recently as two weeks prior to KET. This may potentially explain the large disparity in outcome data from the more rigorously designed RCTs.

Efficacy from multiple doses (RCT and OLI data)

Generally, the highest quality data describing the effects of multiple doses of ketamine draws from studies utilizing the IV route of administration. Two RCTs and six OLIs assessed multiple sequential doses of IV ketamine [table 3]. Of these, three utilized a regimen of thrice-weekly infusions for two weeks. Two others utilized twice-weekly infusions, one of which stopped infusions when patients achieved re-mission (Rasmussen et al., 2013), and the other of which increased the dose after the third infusion (Cusin et al., 2016). Two studies directly compared different dosing schedules of infusions, ranging from one to three times weekly over the course of three to four weeks (Diamond et al., 2014; Singh et al., 2016). All eight multidose studies noted either stable or increasing rates of response over subsequent infusions. The response rate for all subjects within 24 hours of their final infusion was 57%, though if the outliers are excluded (Diamond et al. 2014, Cusin et al., 2016), this increases to 74%. The majority of these studies also reported time to relapse after the final infusion, monitoring subjects over the subsequent four weeks or longer; however, criteria for relapse varied from liberal (aan het Rot et al., 2010) to conservative (Shiroma et al., 2014). Summing totals from these studies over each time point reveals 50% of patients no longer met response criteria seven to ten days following the final infusion, though this may potentially underestimate true benefit due to our conservative calculations [figure 4].

One RCT compared three ketamine infusions with three bilateral ECT treatments over one week, finding 89% response rate after three ketamine infusions versus 67% with ECT (Ghasemi et al., 2013). The other RCT compared two-times-a-week to three-times-a-week infusions, finding both conditions to be significantly better than saline placebo (Singh et al., 2016). They found no significant differ-ence in response between the two ketamine conditions, and in fact slightly better outcomes with the less frequent dosing condition, suggesting two times a week dosing may be just as efficacious as three time a week. Regarding the six OLIs, all unique patients are represented in Murrough et al. (2013), Rasmussen et al. (2013), Shiroma et al. (2014), Diamond et al. (2014), and Cusin et al. (2016). Response rates immediately after conclusion of the series of infusions were 71%, 60%, 79%, 29%, and 36%, respectively (ITT). Altogether, studies yielded a 20% response rate approximately a month after conclusion of the course. In Murrough et al. (2013), 17% remained responders over an additional three months' follow-up, with only one receiving other medication in the interim. These authors also observed that ini-tial nonresponders (at four hours after the first infusion) were four times less likely than initial responders to achieve response at the end of six infusions. Additionally, several studies noted that patients required up to two infusions before successfully achieving response (Rasmussen et al., 2013; Diamond et al., 2014), suggesting that one infusion may be insufficient. Rasmussen et al. (2013) added to the literature by extending 0.5mg/kg infusions over 100 minutes (0.3 mg/kg/hr), the slower rate permitting use without presence of anesthesia personnel. Interestingly enough, the study with the lowest response rate was conducted in an ECT recovery room and found that several patients complained the setting was too noisy, chaotic, or distressing (Diamond et al., 2014). Also notable is that this is the only study to use the BDI, a patient rated scale, as an outcome measure. The other study that was conducted in an ECT recovery room had the next lowest response rate (Rasmussen et al., 2013). Cusin et al. (2016) had poorer outcomes perhaps due to a highly treatment resistant population, despite escalating the dose to 0.75mg/kg mid way through the series of infusions. Diamond et al. (2014) also assessed memory at baseline and after the treatment course, finding improvements in autobiographical, episodic, and subjective memory. Both this study and Singh et al. (2016) were the only to directly compare different treatment frequencies, and found better results with the lower frequency arms.

Case reports, intravenous route

   We report data from case reports separately from RCTs and OLIs. The 22 published case studies (or judged equivalent) that utilized ketamine infusions (KET) comprised 40 patients and—save for one dose-finding study and another comparing racemic versus *S*-ketamine—mostly utilized multiple infusions [suppl. table 1]. These reports on one to three patients describe dramatic improvement in depressive symptoms and functioning in patients with TRD (Kollmar, Markovic, Thuerauf, Schmitt, & Kornhuber, 2008; Liebrenz, Borgeat, Leisinger, & Stohler; Liebrenz, Stohler, & Borgeat, 2009); geriatric TRD patients (Srivastava, Ganwar, & Kumar, 2015; Hassamal, Spivey, & Pandurangi, 2015); antidepressant effect of ketamine even when this was only arrived at serendipitously (Ostroff, Gonzales, & Sanacora, 2005); several descriptions of prolonged relief of depression with repeated dosing (Correll, 2006; Messer, Haller, Larson, Pattison-Crisostomo, & Gessert, 2010; Murrough, Perez, Mathew, & Charney, 2011; Hassamal et al., 2015); and safe use of ketamine in depressed patients with severe medical comorbidities or who were concomitantly treated with multiple other CNS-acting medications (Kollmar et al., 2008; Liebrenz et al., 2007, 2009; Stefanczyk-Sapieha, Oneschuk, & Demas, 2008). Hassamal et al. (2015) described a woman who was treated successfully with three separate series of infusions over the course of more than a year, each providing benefit for four to eight months. There was a notable case of rapid relief of intense dysphoria and crying in a terminally ill cancer patient on a palliative care unit (Stefanczyk-Sapieha et al., 2008). The cases of Yang, Zhou Gao, Shi, and Yang

(2013) demonstrated rapid relief of depression in young, drug-naïve men. Uniquely, da Frota Ribiero, Sanacora, Hoffman, and Ostroff (2016) described two cases of severe psychotic depression refractory to other treatments who were responsive to ketamine IV infusions with improvement in both psychosis and depression, suggesting psychosis may not necessarily be a contraindication to ketamine. Gowda et al. (2016) reported on a grieving man who experienced remission for three months after a single infusion, focusing on the phenomenological experience as integral to his improvement. Szymkowicz, Finnegan, and Dale (2013) administered between 16 and 34 repeated KET infusions to three TRD patients over a 12-month period, adjusting frequency depending on individual response. Their first patient remitted after the second infusion, and was maintained so with periodic treatments over the subsequent nine months. Their two other subjects suffered repeated relapses despite intermittent courses of repeat infusions. Lai et al. (2014) is a dose-finding study, which compared 0.1 to 0.4mg/kg of ketamine IV over five minutes with a saline control; however, due to low enrollment and poor retention, just four individuals received ketamine. Of those, only one displayed a clear dose response relationship for antidepressant response, though dissociative effects were clearly dose-related.

Efficacy from alternate routes of administration

In contrast to most studies of IV infusion, studies into intramuscular, subcutaneous, intranasal, oral, and sublingual dosing have mostly utilized multiple administrations attempting to extend response [table 5]. Bioavailability of these different formulations ranges from ~20% for oral, ~30% for sublingual, 45% for intranasal, to 93% for intramuscular (Clements, Nimmo, & Grant, 1982). Dose, frequency, follow-up interval, treatment setting, and response metrics varied greatly between publications. All patients had their existing medications continued, potentially biasing results. Onset of benefit was generally rapid with parenteral routes, and was successfully maintained with repeat dosing in several instances.

One unique dose- and route-finding study divided its 15-patient cohort into three arms and varied the route of administration: four patients via IV push, five patients via IM, and six patients via SC (Loo et al., 2016). Patients in each arm received 0.1–0.5mg/kg doses, in an ascending design, along with a midazolam control, finding that doses under 0.5mg/kg were effective in some patients, and no significant differences in outcome existed between the various routes of administration.

In regard to IM administration, one RCT, one OLI, and six case studies detailed effects in 31 patients. The one RCT by Loo et al. (2016) found a 60% response rate in the five subjects, versus 0% with the midazolam control. The OLI study (Chilukuri et al., 2014) was notable in that it directly compared outcomes from different routes of administration (0.5mg/kg IV over 40 minutes, 0.25mg/kg IM, and 0.5mg/kg IM) and found comparable response rates of 33–44% immediately and several days after administration. In contrast, in the case reports, doses ranged from 0.3mg/kg to 1.0mg/kg, from every two to eight days, and from two to 68 treatments. All but one patient with unipolar depression met formal criteria for response by 24 hours, and this outlier experienced an affective switch into mania (Banwari, Desai, & Patidar, 2015). Glue, Gulati, Le Nedelec, and Duffull (2011) also performed a dose-response assessment, finding greater improvements with higher doses; although 0.5mg/kg and 0.7mg/kg decreased MADRS scores, only 1.0mg/kg led to response. Zanicotti, Perez, and Glue (2012, 2013) described a woman with metastatic cancer and unipolar TRD who, after 1.0mg/kg, experienced remission of depression for five to six days, and pain for 24 hours. On a weekly outpatient regimen, response was largely maintained for eight months. Two patients with bipolar depression experienced qualitative improvement within days to a week after 0.5mg/kg or 0.9mg/kg IM that was maintained for nine to 12 months by dosing at three-to-four-day intervals, although one patient did require a dose increase after five months (Cusin, Hilton, Nierenberg, & Fava, 2012).

Three studies utilized intranasal administration, of which one was a double blind crossover RCT that compared ketamine 50mg with saline (Lapidus et al., 2014). This study found significant differences in MADRS through two days, and a response rate of 44% at 24 hours, comparable to other RCTs that utilized ketamine infusions [table 1, figure 1]. The second trial was a case series of 12 pediatric subjects (ages 6–19) with bipolar TRD that received a dose between 30-120mg. Onset of benefit was frequently within the hour, lasting for 3-4 days, and maintained for months with once- to twice-weekly dosing (Papolos et al., 2013). The final case describes successful long term maintenance of euthymia with twice weekly intranasal administration (Clark, 2014).

Two studies utilized sublingual administration, one in a mixed cohort of unipolar and bipolar depression (Lara et al., 2013). This study utilized a 10mg dose and found "rapid" improvements in 17 of the 26 patients, though the time frame was not defined. Using repeat dosing, from every two to seven days, ten patients were described as maintaining response over a period of months, based on a Likert scale. The other study with sublingual (transmucosal) ketamine is a chart review of 17 patients who were prescribed 0.5–1.0mg/kg every seven to 14 days, and found a

76% response rate, typically within 24 hours. This is likely an overestimate of true response, as responder classification was by chart review and refill history (Nguyen et al., 2015).

Subcutaneous (SC) administration has also been reported. The RCT by Loo et al. (2016) found 100% response in the six subjects treated by SC ketamine, versus 17% with the midazolam control. McNulty and Hahn (2012) describes a case of "dramatic relief" from depression in a hospice patient after initial subcutaneous administration of 0.5mg/kg, followed by the same amount by mouth daily, with maintenance for 11 weeks. Another case describes long-term maintenance of response with repeated doses, notably at only 0.2mg/kg (Gálvez et al., 2014).

We found four other case studies and a subsequent OLI that utilized oral administration. One case study (Irwin & Iglewicz, 2010) in two hospice patients with depression found response in both after a single dose of 0.5mg/kg, one within 120 minutes, the other at eight days. The follow-up OLI included 12 additional patients and utilized daily dosing of 0.5mg/kg (Irwin et al., 2013), finding 57% response rate, mean time to response of 14.4 days, and maintenance of response for at least 28 days. More recently the same authors published a retrospective chart review involving 31 patients finding 71% response at 24 hours after single oral doses of 0.5mg/kg (Iglewicz et al., 2014). It is unclear why this study displayed such rapid response, while the other did not. De Gioannis and Leo (2014) described use of oral ketamine outside the hospice setting, in two individuals with bipolar disorder and suicidality, demonstrating maintenance of response with escalating doses of oral ketamine every two to four weeks.

There have been relatively few investigations of doses other than the standard 0.5mg/kg; Loo et al. (2016) reported response to 0.1–0.5mg/kg via IV bolus, IM injection, and SC injection. A trial of 20 patients by Lenze et al. (2016), in contrast, tried a 96-hour ketamine infusion and found that, during eight weeks of follow-up, efficacy was no greater than for a 40-minute infusion.

S-Ketamine

Ketamine exists as a racemic mixture of the *S*- and *R*- stereoisomers, and while most studies have employed the racemate, a minority has solely used the more potent *S*- stereoisomer. There may be differences between the two, both in terms of antidepressant response and dissociative effects, though results are conflicting. Studies with *S*-ketamine describe treatment in just over 10 patients, all with unipolar depression [table 5, suppl. table 1]. No reports utilizing *R*-ketamine for treatment of depression exist. Only one publication, a case report, describes direct comparison between stereoisomeric forms of ketamine. Two patients were each given equian-algesic IV infusions of racemic ketamine 0.5mg/kg and *S*- ketamine 0.25mg/kg a week apart (Paul et al., 2009). Robust antidepressant response to both isoforms of ketamine was observed in one patient, while the other responded to neither. Further, both patients had mild dissociative/perceptual disturbances ("psychotomi-metic") with the racemate but not *S*-ketamine. Paslakis et al. (2010) treated four in-dividuals with *S*-ketamine using a total oral daily dose of 1.25mg/kg, bioequivalent to 0.25mg/kg IV, divided over three times daily, and similarly found no dissociative effects and a 50% response rate. Conversely, subsequent studies utilizing IV infu-sions of *S*-ketamine 0.25mg/kg, either one time or multiple, found comparable response rates soon after infusion, but did note strong dissociative effects (Denk et al., 2011; Segmiller et al., 2013).

Suicidality

Data regarding reduction of suicidality with ketamine is suggestive of benefit [table 4]. The majority of studies did not assess suicidality as a primary outcome measure, and also utilized group mean change in suicidality scales rather than more easily interpretable results such as percent of the cohort achieving lack of suicidality. In regards to unipolar depression, four RCTs and nine OLIs reported on suicidal-ity, typically utilizing either the HDRS or MADRS suicide items, or the scale for suicide ideation (SSI; Beck et al., 1979). Of these, only one OLI reported lack of benefit. The others showed benefit at disparate time points ranging from the first four hours post dose to three days out. Time course data is present in two studies, with one suggesting loss of significance after four hours. Murrough et al. (2015) found statistically significant differences between ketamine and midazolam, losing significance by three days. Four studies, however, reported categorical outcomes of percent of subjects attaining an SSI or MADRS-SI score below a certain threshold (resolution of suicidal thoughts). These "response rates" ranged from 81% to 90% within the first 24 hours. Another study found, at 4 hours, a 97% response rate in 33 previous ketamine responders, and a 100% response among the high suicidality sub-cohort (Diaz-Granados et al., 2010a). Price et al. (2014) reanalyzed data from the Murrough et al. (2013) RCT, finding decreases in both explicit suicidality as well as implicit associations ("Escape = Me"). Other case reports, utilizing IV infu-sions (Murrough et al., 2011; Zigman & Blier, 2013), and a case series with IM administration (Harihar et al., 2013), all showed benefit. Conversely, one OLI of oral ketamine in 14 hospice patients found no such benefit (Irwin et al., 2013).

In bipolar depression, three RCTs and two case series report on suicidality. Two of the RCTs by the same group conflict in finding significant benefit. Zarate et al. (2012) demonstrated significant differences in between-group MADRS-SI scores through three days. Diaz-Granados et al. (2010b), on the other hand, found no difference between IV ketamine and placebo, though these authors excluded patients with risk for suicide at baseline. Murrough et al. (2015) recruited both unipolar and bipolar subjects, and found benefit through two days follow-up. One case series utilized IM administration and showed qualitative improvement (Cusin et al., 2012), while the other did so with oral doses every two to four weeks (De Gioannis & Leo, 2014).

Adverse effects

During infusion, five different adverse events with ketamine led to discontinuation in RCTs [suppl. table 2]: hypotension and bradycardia, hypertension unresponsive to beta-blockers (Murrough et al., 2013), anxiety and paranoia in one patient, palpitations in another patient, and a combination of anxiety, dizziness, hypoesthesia, and feeling cold in a third (Singh et al., 2016). Following infusion, four adverse events led to discontinuation: worsening mood in three patients (one with suicidal ideation), and increased anxiety in another (Diaz-Granados et al., 2010b). Three placebo patients discontinued, for elevated blood pressure during infusion (Valentine et al., 2011), hypomania (Diaz-Granados et al., 2010b), and disc degeneration (Singh et al., 2016). In OLIs, only two adverse events led to treatment discontinuation out of nearly 300 individuals [suppl. table 3]: elevated blood pressure unresponsive to beta-blockers during infusion (Murrough et al., 2013), and a panic attack (Diamond et al., 2014). In case reports, one subject receiving *S*-ketamine at 0.25mg/kg discontinued during infusion due to dissociation (Segmiller et al., 2013).

Although clinically significant hemodynamic changes were rare, tachycardia and transient elevations in blood pressure were commonly reported across the various routes of administration in RCTs and OLIs [suppl. tables 2 and 3]. Two cases of hypotension (Murrough et al., 2013; aan het Rot et al., 2010), one case of bradycardia (aan het Rot et al., 2010), and one vasovagal episode were also reported. In regard to pulmonary effects, aan het Rot et al. (2010) reported one patient with bradypnea, with oxygen desaturation to 94%. To date, no RCTs or OLIs have reported these effects persisting beyond four hours, save for one patient with mild, asymptomatic hypotension lasting until discharge at 24 hours (aan het Rot et al., 2010).

Dissociation, psychotomimetic effects, manic symptoms, and other psychiatric effects were assessed in most investigations. In RCTs and OLIs adverse effects as measured by Clinician Administered Dissociative Symptom Scale (CADSS; Bremner et al., 1998), Brief Psychiatric Rating Scale (BPRS; Overall & Gorham, 1970) or Young Mania Rating Scale (YMRS; Young, Biggs, Ziegler, & Meyer, 1978) revealed significant increases compared with control/baseline, that generally resolved by 80 min to four hours, and was rarely reported as distressing.

We evaluated the adverse effects in multiple dose studies separately. Of the two RCTs utilizing repeat dosing, Singh et al. (2016) noted diminishing intensity of dissociative symptoms with repeat dosing. In the six OLIs utilizing repeat dosing, elevations in CADSS and BPRS were either similar or diminished across multiple infusions, with no progressive increase over multiple infusions. Cusin et al. (2016) administered three infusions at 0.5mg/kg followed by three more infusions at 0.75mg/kg, finding decreasing dissociative effects despite the dose increase. Similarly, hemodynamic and respiratory effects did not worsen with repeat administrations. Dose-dependent increases in dissociative symptoms were reported in two dose-finding studies, one with rapid IV infusions over two to five minutes (Lai et al., 2014) and the other with rapid administration via IV, IM, or SC routes (Loo et al., 2016). Transient tachycardia and asymptomatic premature ventricular contractions were described in one patient, and nausea and vomiting in another (aan het Rot et al., 2010; Shiroma et al., 2014). One suicide attempt occurred during the washout period before ketamine infusion (Murrough et al., 2013). One report of mania was found in a patient who received 34 doses of ketamine at variable intervals over a one-year period (Liebrenz et al., 2009), and another reported a "mild" hypomanic episode in a patient after his third infusion (Diamond et al., 2014). Niciu et al. (2013) analyzed data from three NIMH RCTs of IV ketamine infusion in bipolar depression, finding transient increases in YMRS scores lasting no more than a day after infusion, and no cases of full blown mania or hypomania. They also reported that within the YMRS elevations, none of the patients had specific elevations in the elevated mood item [suppl. table 2].

We evaluated the adverse effects in the non-IV alternate routes of administration separately. Intramuscular reports noted effects similar to those of IV, but with less intense dissociative effects and hemodynamic changes (Loo et al., 2016). In one case, decrease in dizziness and derealization occurred over repeat (41 total) injections (Zanicotti et al., 2013), whereas in another a dose of 1.0mg/kg resulted in intolerable dissociative effects necessitating a dose decrease to 0.5mg/kg (Cusin et al., 2012). In one intranasal study of 12 pediatric patients, transient (60 minutes) dissociative effects similar to IV were reported, as well as mild palpitations and moderate respiratory distress (Papolos et al., 2013), whereas in another intranasal case report the patient described feeling "high," but only during the first few of more than 30 administrations (Clark et al., 2014). The only RCT utilizing intranasal administration found a similar side effect profile (Lapidus et al., 2014). Sublingual dosing was evaluated in 43 patients across two studies, and resulted in no euphoria, psychotic, or dissociative symptoms (Lara et al., 2013; Nguyen et al., 2015). Light-headedness (mild, transient, and improving on repeat dosing) and one report of tachycardia (<30 minutes) occurred; mouth numbness was the only novel effect reported (Lara et al., 2013). In the 51 patients that received oral ketamine, essentially no adverse effects, including vital sign changes, were reported (Paslakis et al., 2010; Irwin and Iglewicz, 2010; Irwin et al., 2013), save for disorientation and hallucinations in a minority of a medically ill hospice population (Iglewicz et al., 2014). In fact, there were improvements in BPRS and adverse symptom checklists (Irwin and Iglewicz, 2010). Only diarrhea, trouble sleeping, and "trouble sitting still" occurred (one each) in a study of 14 patients (Irwin et al., 2013). The only study of oral *S*-ketamine, divided over three times daily, found essentially no side effects in all four patients. Loo et al. (2016) directly compared IV, IM, and SC administration and found the lowest side effect profile with SC dosing.

Lower urinary tract symptoms (LUTS) are common adverse effects in the ketamine abuse population. We looked systematically at the published data reviewed in previous sections of this chapter, and report the following: most RCTs (Berman et al., 2000; Zarate et al., 2006; Diaz-Granados et al., 2010b; Valentine et al., 2011; Sos et al., 2013; Ghasemi et al., 2013; Lenze et al., 2016; Loo et al., 2016; Singh et al., 2016) and OLIs (Machado-Viera et al., 2009; Phelps et al., 2009; aan het Rot et al., 2010; Mathew et al., 2010; Ibrahim et al., 2011; Cornwell et al., 2012; Salvadore et al., 2009, 2010, 2012; Larkin & Beautrais, 2011; Thakurta et al., 2012; Rasmussen et al., 2013; Rybakowski et al., 2013; Chilukurti et al., 2014; Niciu et al., 2014; Shiroma et al., 2014a, 2014b) involving intravenous ketamine for treatment-resistant unipolar or bipolar depression, did not specifically report on the presence or absence of LUTS, with follow-up periods varying from 1 to 14 days. In Murrough et al. (2013), some urinary symptoms were reported within the first day after infusion in two of the 26 patients, with such symptoms occurring in the subsequent week after serial infusions in one patient. In their large, two-site RCT comparing ketamine to midazolam, Murrough et al. (2013b) found during the one-to-seven-day period after infusion that four of the 47 ketamine patients (9%) reported frequent urination, three patients (6%) reported painful urination, and 1 patient (2%) reported difficulty urinating; in contrast, none of the 25 midazolam treated patients had urinary complaints. The study by Ibrahim et al. (2012) compared riluzole to placebo after a single open-label ketamine infusion. They found increased urinary frequency in three of 42 patients during the first several hours after infusion, and a combined five of 42 during the 28-day follow-up period (one of 20 in the riluzole group, and four of 22 in the placebo group). After six infusions, Diamond et al. (2014) described development of persistent cystitis in one of the 28 patients, which was attributed by the patient to sexual activity, and that resolved with antibiotics. No other patients reported cystitis or developed abnormalities on urine dipstick testing. Cusin et al. (2016) reported difficulty urinating in one of 14 subjects during treatment with thrice-weekly ketamine infusions at 0.5mg/kg, but none during subsequent treatment at 0.75 mg/kg. Lapidus et al. (2014) reported that there was no difference in the incidence of urinary urgency between subjects randomized to intranasal ketamine or placebo. Finally, in case studies involving repeated ketamine administrations and variable duration of follow-up, ranging from two to 36 infusions and 12 days to 18 months, "no adverse effects" was reported, but LUTS was not specifically addressed (Messer et al., 2010; Cusin et al., 2012; Segmiller et al., 2013; Szymkowitz et al., 2013; Hassamal et al., 2015; Srivastava et al., 2015).

Discussion
Antidepressant and antisuicidal effects

Ketamine appears to have remarkably robust efficacy in short-term relief of severe and treatment-resistant depression, with onset in hours, and duration of at least a few days. While this has been observed in both unipolar and bipolar depressed populations, in the latter, duration appears slightly shorter and there are fewer supporting studies. Similarly, in cases of non-TRD, this effect seems to hold, though relative efficacy is unclear. Ketamine's effectiveness in relief of acute suicidal ideation is also a highly valuable finding, though there are fewer studies on the matter. This benefit appears unique to ketamine, although comparisons with other active treatments are lacking. Furthermore, there are conflicting findings as to whether reductions in suicidality are specific, or rather related to overall reductions in depression (Price et al., 2009; Diaz-Granados et al, 2010a; Rasmussen et al., 2013; Murrough et al., 2013; Ballard et al., 2014; Murrough et al., 2015). Up until recently, most studies have excluded individuals with recent suicidality, and instead performed *post-hoc* re-analyses of suicidality subscales; Murrough et al. (2015) notably treated suicidal patients with ketamine, finding significant improvements. To date, however, there are still no data on suicide attempts, completed suicide, or other long-term effects, nor on parasuicidal behavior; this is fertile ground for further research given the great potential benefit for treating emergent suicidality or averting hospitalization. Ketamine deserves consideration for use in select patients who otherwise would continue to suffer severely, if only as a temporizing measure to give clinicians time to identify and implement alternative treatments.

The largest challenge with this promising agent remains the extension of benefit for the longer term, which is pertinent to the vast majority of depressed patients who have failed to benefit sufficiently from psychotherapy, psychosocial interventions, and the initial tiers of somatic intervention. Repeated ketamine infusions have shown promise, and there may be a cumulative dose effect similar to ECT, where a series of treatments are required to induce full response or remission (aan het Rot et al. 2010; Murrough et al., 2013b; Rasmussen et al., 2013; Singh et al., 2016). Indeed, several studies concluded patients require more than one infusion before being considered non-responders, and response rate appears to correlate with number of infusions [figure 3]. The comparison to ECT is tempting, and certainly makes for a good argument against those who would dismiss the potential for ketamine in depression because of the only short-term benefit of single infusions. It is far from clear what the optimum dose, frequency, duration, and number of infusions is, and how this might be individualized, though future studies will be revealing. The existing paradigm of the 0.5mg/kg dose is quite arbitrary, though several studies have assessed lower doses with success; it is not clear what the minimum effective dose is for antidepressant benefit, and if this could be a pathway to mitigate unwanted side effects. It also worth noting that some patients do not benefit from ketamine, despite multiple treatments (Symkowicz, Finnegan, & Dale, 2014), and tolerance has been reported (Bonnet, 2015). On the other hand, in loss of response after an initial series of infusions, repeat courses were shown to be effective and provide months more remission (Hassamal et al., 2015).

Alternatives to IV infusion, such as intramuscular (IM), intranasal (IN), oral, sublingual (SL), and subcutaneous (SC) routes, have been studied to a lesser extent, but do appear to work. The trade-off is potentially lower response rates with routes other than the IM, which results in ketamine bioavailability similar to, IV administration. These alternate routes offer a potentially greater benefit to risk ratio, given the more favorable side effect profile. Loo et al. (2016) did compare different routes of administration, finding non-IV routes were better tolerated. A significant limitation is lack of high-quality prospective studies: of these alternate routes, our review found only one robust RCT, which utilized IN administration (Lapidus et al., 2014). Compared with IV administration, IM, IN, and SL routes are similarly rapid acting, with conflicting and weaker data for SC and oral administrations. Duration of benefit is similar to IV infusions, on the order of days, but has been successfully prolonged with repeated dosing, which is notably easier given the relatively low resource requirements with such administrations (Cooper et al., 2016). Several cases describe treatment in an office-based setting, with patients returning to the office anywhere from multiple times a week to once a month, and maintaining response on the order of months. It is unclear if such response eventually fades, or rather if it could be continued indefinitely, though several cases describe maintenance for a year or more (Zanicotti et al., 2013; Cusin et al., 2012). Several series of infusions spaced out over the course of a year proved to be effective in one case, suggesting that a block of six infusions could be repeated after relapse (Hassamal et al., 2015). Oral dosing has thus far been used mostly in hospice populations, and of the various routes of administration likely produces the mildest dissociative side effect profile, but with a slower onset of antidepressant benefit. One case report mitigated this limitation through an initial single loading dose via a rapid acting route, followed by more convenient oral daily maintenance dosing (McNulty & Hahn, 2012). Oral ketamine administration, compared to parenteral, results in a higher blood nor-ketamine to ketamine ratio because of extensive first pass metabolism. Nor-ketamine is pharmacologically active as an NMDA antagonist and has analgesic and likely antidepressant effects, along with longer elimination half-life than ketamine itself. The clinical implications for treatment of depression, however, are unclear (Blonk, Koder, van den Bemt, & Huygen, 2010). Sos et al. (2013), however, found no correlation between blood levels of ketamine or nor-ketamine and antidepressant response.

Adverse effects

Ketamine appears to be well tolerated by the majority of individuals who receive it for short-term treatment of depression. The most commonly reported adverse effects are dissociative and psychotomimetic experiences, which are transient and typically resolve within an hour. Occasionally hemodynamic effects, also typically transient and mild, have led to treatment discontinuation, although in every case these have responded to conservative management. Even at doses as high as 4–6mg/ kg used for sedation in an emergency room setting, ketamine proved to be safe (Isbister, Calver, Downes, & Page, 2016). Assessment of hemodynamic effects and antidepressant response revealed no correlation (Luckenbaugh et al., 2014), though such a correlation may exist between dissociative symptoms and antidepressant response, as we later explore. Intramuscular, sublingual, subcutaneous, intranasal, and especially oral administration generally resulted in fewer adverse effects than seen after IV administration, possibly due to a slower increase in blood levels (Lara et al., 2013; Paslakis et al., 2010; Irwin & Iglewicz, 2010; Irwin et al., 2013; Iglewicz et al., 2014; Loo et al., 2016). Supporting this theory are data from Lai et al. (2014) that found extensive dissociative symptoms with IV administration over two minutes, and decreases in such symptoms with extension of administration over five minutes. Overall, the safety profile of short-term treatment with ketamine, particularly in closely monitored settings, is reassuring.

Conversely, there is a relative paucity of data on adverse effects from chronic repeated administrations of ketamine when used for treatment of depression. Long-term exposure in abuse populations, where dose and frequency far exceed those used in clinical protocols, does suggest potentially serious sequelae. In such populations, both short- and long-term neurocognitive adverse effects have been reported (Curran & Monaghan, 2001; Morgan, Monaghan, & Curran, 2004). Conversely, data from studies utilizing ketamine for treatment of depression indicate it may actually improve neurocognitive outcomes, most likely by reversing the "pseudo-dementia" seen in severe depression (Permoda-Osip, Kisielewski, Bartkowska-Sniatkowska, & Rybakowski, 2015; Shiroma et al., 2014). In further support of a benign cognitive safety profile, Murrough et al. (2015) found no neurocognitive impairments one week after ketamine when compared with midazolam. In chronic recreational use of ketamine, ulcerative cystitis has been identified as an important adverse effect (Shahani, Streutker, Dickson, & Stewart, 2007). Since initial discovery, the syndrome of lower urinary tract symptoms (LUTS) has been well characterized in this population and recognized by urologists as a new and serious medical condition (Chu et al., 2008; Tam et al., 2014; Middela and Pearce, 2011; Winstock, Mitcheson, Gillatt, & Cottrell, 2012; Yek et al., 2015; Wu et al., 2016). It occurs in 20–30% of chronic recreational ketamine users (Chu et al., 2008; Winstock et al., 2012), with incidence and severity proportional to cumulative dose and duration of use. Symptoms include increased frequency of urination (progressing to hourly or more frequent), painful urination, and ulceration of the bladder epithelium leading to bleeding. As the syndrome progresses, the bladder wall may thicken and stiffen, limiting drainage from the kidneys, eventually leading to hydronephrosis and renal failure. In the early stages, damage is reversible with abstinence from ketamine (Wein, 2013), though progresses to irreversible with continued use, eventually requiring urinary diversion or bladder replacement (Wu et al., 2016). Infection is not typical—there is sterile pyuria, with white blood cells reflecting inflammation—nor is malignancy, although this is still under study. Clinically, LUTS have been reported in monitored pain treatment programs utilizing high doses of daily oral ketamine: after months at >80mg in three palliative care patients (Storr & Ouibell, 2009), and after nine days of 8mg/kg/d in an adolescent with neuropathic pain (Grégoire, Maclellan, & Finley, 2008). Other reviewers, found, as we did, a lack of systematic data on the occurrence of LUTS in clinical use of ketamine for depression treatment, though this is certainly warranted (Katalinic et al., 2013; Bobo et al., 2015; Coyle & Laws, 2015). In regard to dissociative symptoms, several clinical studies have noted subjects develop tolerance to these effects with repeat dosing, but not to antidepressant benefit; that is, with serial infusions, tolerability appears to improve and antidepressant effect grows (Cusin et al., 2016; Singh et al., 2016).

Another setting in which ketamine's rapid onset of antidepressant—in addition to analgesic—effects has been used with success is the inpatient palliative care setting (Prommer, 2012; Iglewicz et al., 2014), though concern has been raised that in the cancer patients, ketamine's mTor upregulation could accelerate tumor growth (Yang et al., 2011). In treatment of bipolar depression, another important adverse effect to monitor for is induction of mania or cycle acceleration. As noted in the Niciu et al. (2015) review of three larger NIMH trials, this was not found to be a serious concern. Alternatively, Banwari et al. (2015) reported a case of mania induction in a unipolar patient.

Ketamine's stereoisomers

Ketamine exists as a racemic mixture of the *S*- and *R*- stereoisomers, yet these appear to have subtly different effects. *S*-ketamine has long been known to have approximately two to three times greater potency in terms of analgesia and anesthesia (Kohrs & Durieux, 1998), and three to four times greater affinity for the PCP binding site of the NMDA receptor, but only negligible binding to the sigma receptor. *R*-ketamine, on the other hand, has greater, although still weak, sigma receptor binding, but the significance of this is unclear (Vollenweider, Leenders, Oye, Hell, & Angst, 1997). Observations from the anesthesia literature initially noted that in equianalgesic doses, *S*-ketamine has a lower incidence of psychotomimetic side effects than either the racemate or *R*-stereoisomer (Raeder et al., 2000), leading some to investigate it for depression. In humans, both the racemate and *S*-ketamine appear to have antidepressant effects, but data regarding psychotomimetic effects of the component stereoisomers are more contradictory. A separate series of trials may perhaps explain this; one pilot study of healthy individuals found that the dose of *S*-ketamine required to induce psychosis is 60% of that of the racemate, suggesting the *S*-enantiomer is responsible for such effects (Vollenweider et al., 1997). These authors found psychotomimetic effects in *S*-ketamine versus "a state of relaxation" in *R*-ketamine (Vollenweider at al 1997). Similarly, a study in rodents reported minimal dissociative effects after *R*-ketamine (Yang et al., 2015). Animal studies assessing equimolar equivalents of each stereoisomer found both to provide a rapid and long lasting antidepressant effect, but ultimately a longer durability of effect with the *R*-enantiomer, leading them to speculate the *R*- form may be a good candidate for future study (Zhang, Li, & Hashimoto, 2014; Hashimoto, 2014; Yang et al., 2015). Further research directly comparing *S*-, *R*-, and racemic ketamine in humans is needed to clarify if one indeed exhibits fewer dissociative effects while still maintaining antidepressant efficacy.

Further clinical issues

There is no uniform definition of treatment resistance in the literature reviewed, although patients with or without treatment resistance, however defined, respond similarly. In assessing improvements in depression, the most commonly used measures—the MADRS and HDRS—may not adequately assess change over a time scale on the order of hours. Several questions, for example regarding sleep and appetite, cannot reflect change over the course of a 40-minute infusion; some studies have gotten around this by carrying forward prior subscores (Rasmussen et al., 2013). The issue of concomitant medications--or their discontinuation--is another confound which needs to be carefully managed in the design of future studies.

Several potential predictors of response have received attention. Our review suggests that patients with either unipolar or bipolar depression exhibit at least short term response to ketamine, likely more so in those with unipolar depression. Some authors have suggested that the melancholic subtype of major depression may augur a greater likelihood of response, but this not been studied prospectively (Paslakis et al., 2010; Atigari & Healy, 2013; Gálvez et al., 2014). At least two studies found a greater likelihood of antidepressant response in patients with a family history of alcoholism, compared to those without, although no relationship to personal history of alcoholism was seen (Phelps et al., 2009; Niciu et al., 2015). The presence of an anxiety component to depression predicted greater response in unipolar depression, but not bipolar depression (Ionescu et al., 2014a; Ionescu et al., 2014b). At least in bipolar depression, this is notable because those with the anxious subtype are frequently poorer responders to conventional treatment. To this end, in studies of conditions previously classified as anxiety disorders, such as post-traumatic stress disorder and obsessive-compulsive disorder, ketamine has also shown benefit (Feder et al., 2014; Rodriguez et al., 2013). Additionally, several other factors have been found to predictor antidepressant response to ketamine: slow processing speed (Murrough et al., 2015), reduced attention (Shiroma et al., 2014), small hippocampal volume (Adballah et al., 2015), pre-infusion standardized uptake values on PET imaging of the prefrontal cortex (Li et al., 2016), and MRI fractional anisotropy measurements of the cingulum and forceps (Vasavada et al., 2016).

To date, other agents directed at the neurochemical target most frequently held to account for ketamine's antidepressant effect—NMDA receptor antagonism—have been disappointing in terms of extending ketamine's short-term benefits (Ibrahim et al., 2012; Mathew et al., 2010; Zarate et al., 2006; Heresco-Levy et al., 2006; Mc-Cloud et al., 2015). Additional trials are underway to explore this strategy, although infusion of a specific NMDA antagonist, AZD6765, was not effective (Zarate et al., 2013). Another open label trial examined the combination of a single ketamine infusion followed by daily pyridoxine and D-cycloserine, the latter of which is an NMDA receptor antagonist at higher doses, and found remission in four of the eight subjects (Kantrowitz, Halberstam, & Gangwisch, 2015). Alternative mechanisms, such as ketamine's effects on seizure threshold, are also worth considering (Atigari & Healy, 2013).

An obvious question is how dissociative and antidepressant effects might be related. Our review found the time course of these effects differs substantially. Antidepressant effects can occur in patients who do not experience even transient dissociative effects, and vice-versa. One *post-hoc* analysis found that magnitude of acute dissociative symptoms partially correlated with later antidepressant response (Luckenbaugh et al., 2014). Thus, the dissociative effects are not necessarily part of the antidepressant effects *per se*. On the other hand, it is worth considering that dissociation is part of the unique effect of ketamine that is not shared by conventional antidepressants: an altered sense of self that can also lead to a new state of contentment. This could explain why recent trials with non-psychoactive NDMA antagonists have not demonstrated antidepressant efficacy, and may in fact represent an as yet unexplored aspect of mood regulation—what might be called the eudaimonic dimension (or "well-being," from Aristotle)—that ketamine has given the field an opening to better explore. In support of this, a review by McCloud et al. (2015) found no benefit from memantine and cytidine, both NMDA receptor antagonists without reported dissociative/psychotomimetic effects. In this context it is worth noting that nitrous oxide and classical hallucinogens, which share similar dissociative/psychotomimetic effects with ketamine, may have antidepressant properties (Nagele et al., 2015; Baumeister, Barnes, Giaroli, & Tracy, 2014; Carhart-Harris et al., 2016). When used in combination with quinidine, dextromethorphan, which can also have dissociative effects (Morris & Wallach, 2014), was found incidentally to have antidepressant effects (Pioro et al., 2010). Similarly, ketamine and the classic hallucinogens have each been employed in grief and end of life care, either for depression or anxiety, but perhaps with a similar mechanism (Gowda et al., 2016; Iglewicz et al., 2014; Gasser et al., 2014; Grob et al., 2011). It may be the case, as with classic hallucinogens, which were originally termed psychotomimetic, that these altered states are less "psychotic mimicking" and more psychedelic, or "mind manifesting." In the case of classic hallucinogens, concerns over these effects led their potential antidepressant benefit to be ignored for many years (Baumeister et al., 2014).

A corollary issue pertinent to ketamine's unique effects is what has been called "set and setting" (Johnson, Richards, & Griffiths, 2008); that is, the mind sets of the provider and the patient, and the environmental setting in which the treatment session occurs, may have particularly important impact on treatment outcome (Mithoefer, Grob, & Brewerton, 2016). Consistent with this, two studies conducted in noisy, crowded, high-intensity medical settings had the poorest outcomes among the studies of multiple ketamine infusions (Rasmussen et al., 2013; Diamond et al., 2014). Conversely, recent studies of MDMA-assisted psychotherapy for post-traumatic stress disorder (Mithoefer et al., 2013) and psilocybin for end of life anxiety (Grob et al., 2011) used carefully designed protocols to optimize these aspects of the interventions. It is possible that similar optimization of ketamine treatment would improve antidepressant outcomes.

Several other specific clinical issues deserve further exploration. One study found a single dose of ketamine to accelerate the onset of benefit with escitalopram from an average of 26.5 days to 6.4 days, suggesting a clinical application for ketamine to accelerate treatment response, another important limitation of current medications

(Hu et al., 2016). To date, studies in TRD have excluded psychotically depressed patients. However, da Frota Ribeiro et al. (2016) reported two cases of successful ketamine treatment in severe psychotic depression with remission from both depressive and psychotic symptoms, suggesting this contraindication for ketamine may not be necessary. Is the presence of an anesthesiologist required? By extending the duration of the ketamine infusion to 100 minutes, anesthesiology monitoring was determined to be unnecessary (Rasmussen et al., 2013). Another study reports infusions were performed by a psychiatrist with Basic Life Support training and code team backup (Zigman & Blier, 2013). A further question, as alluded to in discussion of alternate routes, is whether ketamine could be used in an office-based setting: the RCT using intranasal ketamine amended their protocol after demonstrated safety, and began discharging individuals four hours after receiving their doses (Lapidus et al., 2014). Furthermore, several case reports utilizing IM and other methods of administration describe successful long-term treatment in an office-based setting. Alternate routes of administration could benefit not only the cost and availability compared to IV administration, but have been shown to mitigate the side effects of ketamine (Cooper et al., 2016). Ultimately, more rigorous studies in such settings are needed.

Conclusion

Recommendations for future research

Based on this review, the following specific recommendations stand out:

1) Direct comparisons between various routes and durations of administration, both in acute and maintenance treatment, as well as to active placebo or standard agents. Less resource intensive routes of administration including intramuscular, intranasal, sublingual, subcutaneous, and oral routes should be studied as they offer potential advantages, including expansion of ketamine research to the outpatient setting.

2) Dose-response relationships for each route of administration, including monitoring of levels of both ketamine and nor-ketamine levels, in part to find the minimum effective dose for each route.

3) Examination of serial ketamine administrations and optimal dosing frequencies for each route of administration, or with augmenting agents, with the goal of extending the duration of response and long

term maintenance of benefit.

4) Trials that prospectively assess anti-suicidal effects as a primary study end point, in both acute and maintenance treatment, perhaps as a way to avert or shorter inpatient psychiatric admission.

5) Trials to further assess if benefit seen in treatment resistant depression extends to non-treatment resistant depression, and if ketamine is a viable treatment strategy in this population.

6) Systematic monitoring of psychotomimetic and dissociative effects with long-term treatment, and correlations with responses to treatment, including assessments of tachyphylaxis to these effects.

7) Systematic monitoring of neuropsychological functions, urinary tract related symptoms, suicidal behavior, and at least in bipolar subjects, mood switching, during long term treatment.

8) Careful analysis of ketamine's "eudaimonic" effects as they relate to antidepressant, dissociative, psychotomimetic, and antisuicidality effects.

9) Additional trials to follow-up on the suggested benefits of ketamine in other disorders such as PTSD and OCD; and as a transpersonal agent for those with life threatening illness or at the end-of life.

Recommendations for clinical use

A thorough review of the literature utilizing ketamine for treatment of refractory depression reveals rapid onset of action within hours, often lasting several days to a week, after a single infusion. We acknowledge a common criticism raised about the limited time frame of efficacy from a single dose of ketamine. However, this does not distinguish it from any other treatment of depression, including psychotherapy, medication, or ECT. Furthermore, multiple dosing studies and alternate routes of administration have safely and successfully extended the antidepressant benefit of ketamine, with select cases demonstrating maintenance for nearly a year. These findings are all the more impressive when viewed from the perspective of an already treatment-resistant population. We did not find evidence of serious neurocognitive adverse effects in clinical use, in contrast to what has been reported with ketamine abuse. This is an area in which ketamine may distinguish itself from ECT as an alternative for TRD. Similarly, we did not find evidence of LUTS, but this has not been systematically investigated. The frequency and seriousness of LUTS in the abuse population makes it an important adverse effect to monitor in clinical use. Dissociative effects are common, time-limited, generally well tolerated, and appear to subside in intensity with repeat dosing. At doses used for treatment of depression, significant hemodynamic effects requiring intervention are possible but uncommon, and do warrant monitoring. Other potential contraindications exist, such as abuse liability, but with care in patient selection unwanted outcomes can be minimized. Ketamine is clearly a very promising agent. While we currently urge caution in widespread clinical adoption for treatment of depression, our review of the risks and benefits supports its acute—and potentially repeated—use in carefully selected cases who have not benefited from other treatments. Our review provides strong suggestive support for the use of more "user friendly" non-IV alternate routes of administration, but the evidence base is not as robust. While the existing and somewhat arbitrary paradigm of 40-minute IV infusions has proven effective, much less-resource-intensive protocols such as intramuscular, intranasal, sublingual, sub-cutaneous, and oral methods of administration represent a potential revolution in the use of ketamine. These routes of administration have the advantage of expanding use of ketamine to the outpatient setting, along with corresponding cost reductions. Ketamine has not reached the status of being formally promoted for wider clinical use, although we acknowledge that it has seen growing use among psychiatrists in private practice and academic centers. Providers hoping to utilize ketamine for treatment of depression should take care to offer full informed consent as well as communicate that this use is off-label from FDA-approved indications.

Abbreviations Key

ADHD, attention deficit hyperactivity disorder

BDI, Beck Depression Inventory

BDI-SI, Beck Depression Inventory Suicide Item

BDNF, brain-derived neurotrophic factor

BPRS, Brief Psychiatric Rating Scale

CADSS, Clinician-Administered Dissociative States Scale

CBQ, Childhood Bipolar Questionnaire

COPD, chronic obstructive pulmonary disease

DS, Demoralization Scale

ECT, electroconvulsive therapy

HDRS, Hamilton Depression Rating Scale

HDRS-SI, Hamilton Depression Rating Scale Suicide Item

HTN, hypertension

ITT, intent to treat

LUTS, lower urinary tract symptoms

MADRS, Montgomery-Åsberg Depression Rating Scale

MADRS-SI, Montgomery-Åsberg Depression Rating Scale Suicide Item

MEP, motor evoked potentials

NMDA, *N*-methyl-D-aspartate

OAS, Overt Aggression Scale

QIDS, Quick Inventory of Depressive Symptoms

QIDS-SR Quick Inventory of Depressive Symptoms-Self Report

rTMS, repetitive transcranial magnetic stimulation

SEP, sensory evoked potentials

SI, suicidal ideation

SSF, Suicide Status Form

SSI, Scale for Suicide Ideation

SSRI, selective serotonin reuptake inhibitor

TRD, treatment-resistant depression

YBOCS, Yale Brown Obsessive-Compulsive Scale

YMRS, Young Mania Rating Scale

IV, intravenous

IM, intramuscular

IN, intranasal

SL, sublingual

SC, subcutaneous

t, time of first administration

mg, milligrams

kg, kilograms

mL, milliliters

hr, hours

min, minutes

mos, months

wk(s), weeks

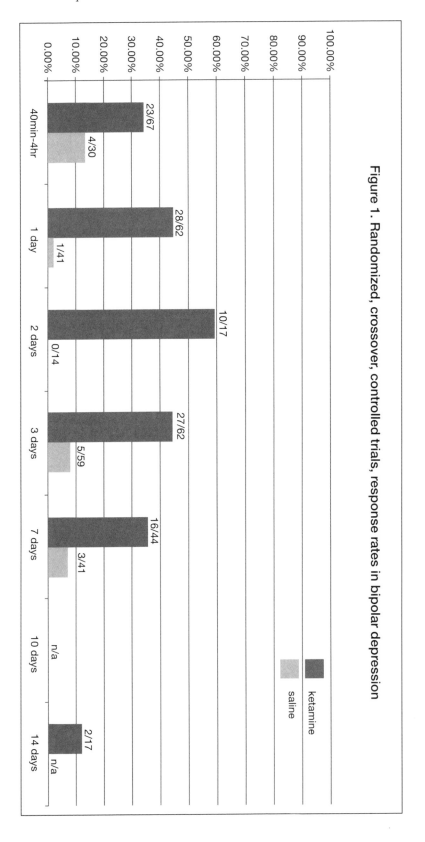

Figure 1. Randomized, crossover, controlled trials, response rates in bipolar depression

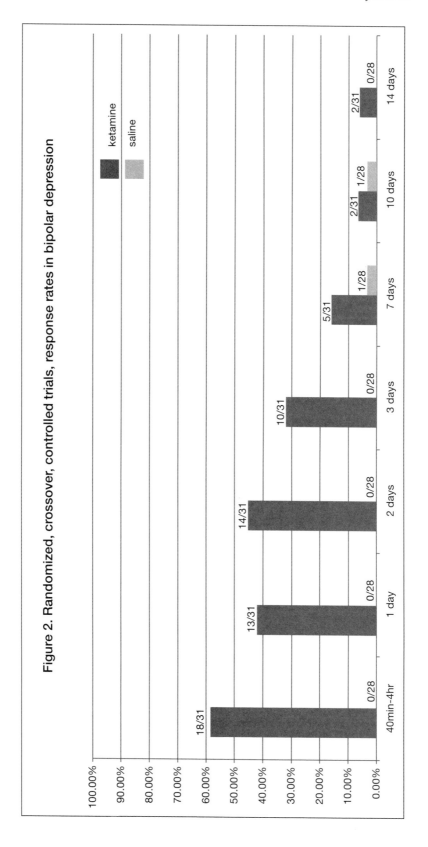

Figure 2. Randomized, crossover, controlled trials, response rates in bipolar depression

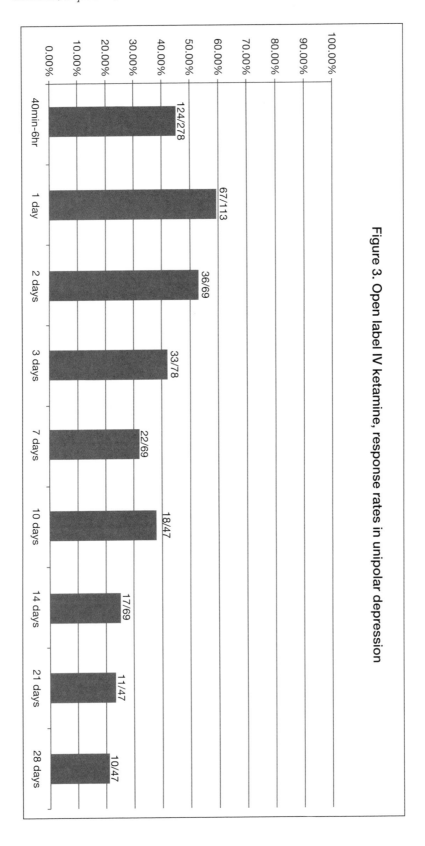

Figure 3. Open label IV ketamine, response rates in unipolar depression

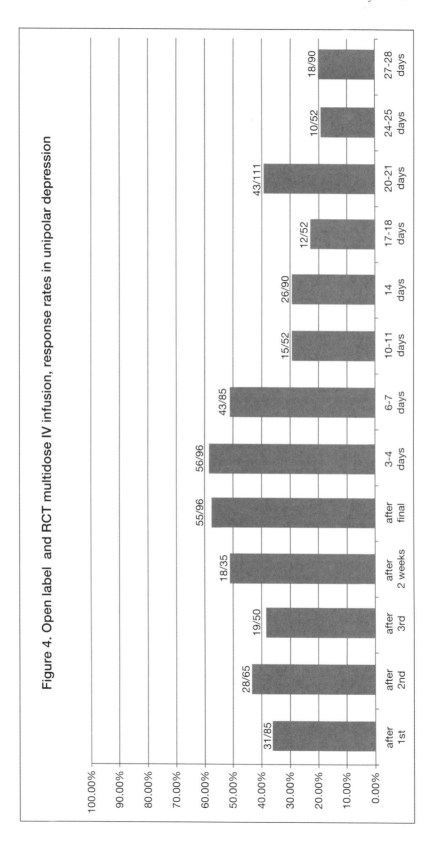

Figure 4. Open label and RCT multidose IV infusion, response rates in unipolar depression

Table 1. Efficacy in random controlled trials of ketamine for depression

	Study	Year	Design	Diagnosis	TRD	N	Gender	Age	Concomitant Medication	Interval	Response Measure:
Unipolar Depression	Berman et al. [1]	2000	double blind crossover	unipolar(8) bipolar(1)	no	9	4M/5F	37	no	72 hours	HDRS 25 decr 50%
	Zarate et al.	2006	double blind crossover	unipolar	yes	18	6M/12F	47	no	7 days	HDRS 21 decr 50%
	Valentine et al. [1]	2011	single blind crossover	unipolar	no	10	4M/6F	42	no	7 days	HDRS 25 decr 50%
	Sos et al. [2]	2013	double blind crossover	unipolar	no	27	15M/15F [3]	43	yes	7 days	MADRS decr 50%
	Li et al.	2016	parallel group	unipolar	yes	16/ 16/ 16	13M/35F	46	yes	4 hours	HDRS 17 decr 50%
										totals	KET
											saline
Bipolar Disorder	Diaz-Granados et al.	2010	double blind crossover	bipolar I and II	yes	22	7M/15F	48	yes	14 days	MADRS decr 50%
	Zarate et al.	2012	double blind crossover	bipolar I and II	yes	15	7M/8F	47	yes	14 days	MADRS decr 50%
										totals	KET +Li/VPA
											saline + Li/VPA
Active Controls	Murrough et al. [4]	2013	parallel group	unipolar	yes	47/ 25	35M/37F	47/43	no	7 days	MADRS decr 50%
	Ghasemi et al. [5]	2013	parallel group	unipolar	yes	9/9	8M/10F	38	yes	1 day	HDRS 25 decr 50%
Intranasal	Lapidus et al. [6]	2014	double blind crossover	unipolar	yes	20	10M/10F	48	yes	7 days	MADRS decr 50%

* Some studies did not report depression response at all time points.
The highest of available scores was utilized for the 40 min-4hr time point.
[1] Response data from Valentine et al. 2011 and Berman et al. 2000 were later published in aan het Rot et al. 2012.
All studies utilized single administration of racemic ketamine 0.5mg/kg IV infusion over 40 minutes, except [2] 0.54mg/kg over 30 minutes, [5] the first of three infusions, done over 45 minutes, [6] intranasal ketamine 50 mg.

Arm	40min -4hr	1 day	2 days	3–4 days	7 days	10 days	14 days	21 days	28 days
ketamine	1/8 (13%)	2/8 (25%)	*	4/8 (50%)					
saline	*	*	*	1/8 (13%)					
ketamine	9/17 (53%)	12/17 (71%)	10/17 (59%)	9/17 (53%)	6/17 (35%)		2/17 (12%)		
saline	1/14 (7%)	0/14 (0%)	0/14 (0%)	2/14 (14%)	0/14 (0%)				
ketamine	0/10 (0%)	4/10 (40%)	*	3/10 (30%)	*				
saline	*	*	*	1/10 (10%)	*				
ketamine	*	10/27 (37%)	*	11/27 (41%)	10/27 (37%)				
saline	*	1/27 (4%)	*	1/27 (4%)	3/27 (11%)				
0.5mg/kg ket	6/16 (38%)								
0.2mg/kg ket	7/16 (44%)								
saline	3/16 (19%)								
% responding	23/67 (34%)	28/62 (45%)	10/17 (59%)	27/62 (44%)	16/44 (36%)		2/17 (12%)		
% responding	4/30 (13%)	1/41 (2%)	0/14 (0%)	5/59 (8%)	3/41 (7%)				
KET +Li/VPA	9/17 (53%)	7/17 (41%)	9/17 (53%)	8/17 (47%)	2/17 (24%)	1/17 (6%)	1/17 (6%)		
saline + Li/VPA	0/16 (0%)	0/16 (0%)	0/16 (0%)	0/16 (0%)	1/16 (6%)	1/16 (6%)	0/16 (0%)		
KET +Li/VPA	9/14 (64%)	6/14 (43%)	5/14 (36%)	2/14 (14%)	1/14 (7%)	1/14 (7%)	1/14 (7%)		
saline + Li/VPA	0/12 (0%)	0/12 (0%)	0/12 (0%)	0/12 (0%)	0/12 (0%)	0/12 (0%)	0/12 (0%)		
% responding	18/31 (58%)	13/31 (42%)	14/31 (45%)	10/31 (32%)	5/31 (16%)	2/31 (6%)	2/31 (6%)		
% responding	0/28 (0%)	0/28 (0%)	0/28 (0%)	0/28 (0%)	1/28 (4%)	1/28 (4%)	0/28 (0%)		
ketamine	*	30/47 (64%)	28/47 (60%)	28/47 (60%)	21/47 (45%)	17/47 (36%)	13/47 (28%)	9/47 (19%)	9/47 (19%)
midazolam 0.045mg/kg	*	7/25 (28%)	6/25 (24%)	5/25 (20%)	4/25 (16%)	4/25 (16%)	2/25 (8%)	0/25 (0%)	0/25 (0%)
ketamine	*	7/9 (78%)							
ECT	*	1/9 (11%)							
ketamine 50 mg IN	6/18 (33%)	8/18 (44%)	4/18 (22%)	6/18 (33%)	1/18 (6%)				
saline	1/18 (6%)	1/18 (6%)	1/18 (6%)	2/18 (11%)	0/18 (0%)				

[3] Three subjects dropped out before receiving ketamine, so were excluded from modified intent to treat analysis.
[4] After 7 days measure was defined as loss of response, or MADRS>=20 maintained for two consecutive visits and meeting criteria for a major depressive episode for 1 week.

Table 2. Efficacy in open label investigations of ketamine for depression

	Study	Year	Diagnosis	TRD	N	Gender	Age	Concomitant Medication	Interval
Unipolar or Mixed	Machado-Vieira et al.	2009	unipolar	yes	23 [1]	14M/9F	44	no	240 minutes
	Phelps et al.	2009	unipolar	yes	26 [1]	14M/12F	44	no	230 minutes
	Ibrahim et al.	2011	unipolar	yes	42 [1]	24M/18F	47	no	230 minutes
	Cornwell et al.	2012	unipolar	yes	20, no unique [1]	15M/5F	46	no	230 minutes
	Ibrahim et al.	2012	unipolar	yes	42, 2 unique [1]	26M/16F	47	no [2]	28 days
	Salvadore et al.	2009	unipolar	yes	11 [3]	7M/4F	44	no	230 minutes
	Salvadore et al.	2010	unipolar	yes	15, 8 unique [3]	?	51	no	230 minutes
	Salvadore et al.	2012	unipolar	yes	14, 10 unique [3]	9M/5F	50	no	24 hours
	Mathew et al.	2010	unipolar	yes	26 [4]	16M/10F	48	no [2][5]	72hrs + 32 days
	Larkin and Beautrais [6]	2011	unipolar	no	14	7M/7F	31	yes	4hrs
	Thakurta et al.	2012	unipolar	yes	22 [7]	10M/12F	50	no	14 days
	Murrough et al. [8]	2013	unipolar	yes	24, 14 unique [4]	15M/9F	48	no	first infusion
	Rasmussen et al. [9]	2013	unipolar, bipolar II	yes	10	4M/6F	47	yes	first infusion
	Shiroma et al. [8]	2014	unipolar	yes	14	14M	54	yes	first infusion
	Diamond et al.	2014	unipolar (22), bipolar (6)	yes	28	16M/12F	47	yes	first infusion
	Chilukuri et al.	2014	unipolar	yes	9	3M/6F	36	yes	3 days
	Vasavada et al.	2015	unipolar	no	10	8M/2F	48	yes	24 hours
									totals
Bipolar	Rybakowski et al. [11]	2013	bipolar	yes	25	4M/21F	49	yes	14 days

* Some studies did not report depression response at all time points.

[1][3][4] Studies with overlapping patients.

[2] Responders were randomized to daily riluzole or placebo, but upon subsequent analysis differences determined to non-significant.

[5] Subjects randomized to pretreatment with one time dose of either lamotrigine 300 mg or placebo, to assay if this would attenuate dissociative effects and improve antidepressant benefit. No significant effect was found. Relapse criteria was defined as MADRS≥20 and MADRS increased by 10 from day 3 score, both for two consecutive visits.

Response measure	40min-6h	1 day	2 days	3 days	7 days	10 days	14 days	21 days	28 days
MADRS decr 50%	11/23 (48%)								
MADRS decr 50%	11/26 (42%)								
MADRS decr 50%	21/42 (50%)								
MADRS decr 50%	9/20 (45%)								
MADRS decr 50%, then returning above 25% decr	26/42 (62%)	10/21 (48%)	8/21 (38%)	8/21 (38%)	5/21 (24%)	4/21 (19%)	4/21 (19%)	3/21 (14%)	3/21 (14%)
MADRS decr 50%	5/11 (45%)								
MADRS decr 50%	6/15 (40%)								
MADRS decr 50%	2/14 (14%)	*							
MADRS decr 50% and MADRS-1/2<=2; then relapse [5]	16/26 (62%)	17/26 (65%)	14/26 (54%)	14/26 (54%)	14/26 (54%)	14/26 (54%)	12/26 (46%)	8/26 (31%)	7/26 (27%)
MADRS <=10	10/14 (71%)								
HDRS 17 decr 50%	15/22 (68%)	17/22 (77%)	14/22 (64%)	7/22 (32%)	3/22 (14%)	*	1/22 (5%)		
MADRS decr 50%	16/24 (67%)	15/24 (63%)							
MADRS decr 50%	2/10 (20%)	2/10 (20%)							
MADRS decr 50%	3/14 (21%)								
BDI decr 50%	3/28 (11%)								
HDRS 17 decr 50%	3/9 (33%)	*	*	4/9 (44%)					
MADRS decr 50%	*	6/10 (60%)							
% responding [10]	124/278 (45%)	67/113 (59%)	36/69 (52%)	33/78 (42%)	22/69 (32%)	18/47 (38%)	17/69 (25%)	11/47 (23%)	10/47 (21%)
HDRS 17 decr 50%	1/25 (4%)	6/25 (24%)			13/25 (52%)		13/25 (52%)		

[7] Subjects overlap with Thakurta et al. 2012.
All studies utilized a single 0.5mg/kg IV infusion over 40 minutes except [11] over 45 minutes, [6] 0.2mg/kg IV over 1-2 minutes, [9] 1-4 such IV infusions over 100 minutes; 2x/wk for 2wks or remission, [8] 6 infusions; 3x/wk for 2wks.
[10] Calculation excluded Cornwall et al. 2012 and Ibrahim et al. 2012 due to preponderance of non-unique subjects.

Table 3. Multidose ketamine efficacy for depression

	Study	Year	Diagnosis	TRD	N	Gender	Age	Concomitant Medication	Doses	Interval	Response Measure
Open Label	aan het Rot et al.	2010	unipolar	yes	10 [1]	5M/ 5F	51	no	6; 3x/wk	2wks of infusions + 4wks	MADRS decr 50%
	Murrough et al.	2013	unipolar	yes	24, 14 unique [1]	15M/ 9F	48	no [2]	6; 3x/wk	2wks of infusions + 12wks	MADRS decr 50%
	Rasmussen et al. [3]	2013	unipolar, bipolar II	yes	10	4M/ 6F	47	yes	1-4; 2x/wk for 2wks or remission	0-2wks of infusions + 4wks	MADRS decr 50%
	Shiroma et al.	2014	unipolar	yes	14	14M	52	yes	6; 3x/wk	2wks of infusions + 4wks	cumulative MADRS decr 50%
	Diamond et al.	2014	unipolar (22) bipolar (6)	yes	15	16M/ 12F	47	yes	3; 1x/wk	3wks of infusions + 6 months	BDI decr 50%
					13				6; 2x/wk		
	Cusin et al. [6]	2016	unipolar	yes	14	3M/ 11F	50	yes	6; 2x/wk	3wks of infusions + 3 months	HDRS28 decr 50%
RCT	Ghasemi et al. [4]	2013	unipolar	yes	9/9	8M/ 10F	38	yes	3; 3x/wk	1wk of infusions + 1 week	HDRS25 decr 50%
									3; 3x/wk	1wk of ECT	
	Singh et al.	2016	unipolar	yes	17/18/ 16/17	23M/ 45F	44	yes	8; 2x/wk saline	4wks of infusions + 3wks	MADRS decr 50%
									8; 2x/wk ketamine		
									12; 3x/wk saline		
									12; 3x/wk ketamine		
									totals		% responding to ketamine [5]

* Some studies did not report depression response at all time points.
Response data was recalculated conservatively, accounting for differences from published data. Data from first infusions are also reported on tables 1 and 2 where appropriate and available.
[1] Patients overlap between studies.
[2] Three responders were started on venlafaxine as part of another study.
All studies utilized 0.5mg/kg IV over 40 minutes except [3] over 100 minutes, [4] over 45 minutes, [6] 0.5mg/kg IV over 45 minutes for the first 3 infusions, then increased to 0.75mg/kg after.
[5] Calculation excluded aan het Rot et al. given these subjects are represented in Murrough et al. Calculations also exclude control results.

after 1st infusion	after 2nd infusion	after 3rd infusion	after 2 weeks	after final infusion	3-4 days	6-7 days	10-11 days	14 days	17-18 days	20-21 days	24-25 days	27-28 days
9/10 (90%)	*	*		9/10 (90%)	7/10 (70%)	5/10 (50%)	5/10 (50%)	4/10 (40%)	3/10 (30%)	2/10 (20%)	3/10 (30%)	2/10 (20%)
16/24 (67%)	*	*		17/24 (71%)	16/24 (67%)	15/24 (63%)	10/24 (42%)	10/24 (42%)	7/24 (29%)	6/24 (25%)	5/24 (21%)	4/24 (17%)
2/10 (20%)	6/10 (60%)	6/10 (60%)		6/10 (60%)	*	5/10 (50%)	*	3/10 (30%)	*	3/10 (30%)	*	3/10 (30%)
3/14 (21%)	*	*		11/14 (79%)	*	8/14 (57%)	*	7/14 (50%)	*	7/14 (50%)	*	5/14 (36%)
3/28 (11%)	5/15 (33%)	*		5/15 (33%)	5/15 (33%)	5/15 (33%)	4/15 (27%)	4/15 (27%)	4/15 (27%)	4/15 (27%)	4/15 (27%)	4/15 (27%)
3/28 (11%)	3/13 (23%)	*		3/13 (23%)	3/13 (23%)	1/13 (8%)	1/13 (8%)	1/13 (8%)	1/13 (8%)	1/13 (8%)	1/13 (8%)	1/13 (8%)
*	*	1/14 (7%)	*	5/14 (36%)	*	*	*	1/14 (7%)	*	*	*	1/14 (7%)
7/9 (78%)	7/9 (78%)	8/9 (89%)		8/9 (89%)	9/9 (100%)	9/9 (100%)						
1/9 (11%)	2/9 (22%)	6/9 (67%)		6/9 (67%)	8/9 (89%)	8/9 (89%)						
*	1/17 (6%)	*	2/17 (12%)	*	*	*	*	*	*	*		
*	7/18 (39%)	*	11/18 (61%)	*	13/18 (72%)	*	*	*	*	10/18 (56%)		
*	*	0/16 (0%)	1/16 (6%)	*	*	*	*	*	*	*		
*	*	4/17 (24%)	7/17 (41%)	*	10/17 (59%)	*	*	*	*	12/17 (71%)		
31/85 (36%)	28/65 (43%)	19/50 (38%)	18/35 (51%)	55/96 (57%)	56/96 (58%)	43/85 (51%)	15/52 (29%)	26/90 (29%)	12/52 (23%)	43/111 (39%)	10/52 (19%)	18/90 (20%)

Table 4. Suicidality

	Study	Year	Diagnosis	TRD	N	Gender	Age	Concomitant Medication	Number of infusions
Open Label Trials	Berman et al.	2000	unipolar (8), bipolar (1)	no	9	4M/5F	37	no	1
	Zarate et al.	2006	unipolar	yes	18	6M/12F	47	no	1
	Diaz-Granados et al.	2010	bipolar I and II	yes	18	6M/12F	48	yes	1
	Zarate et al.	2012	bipolar I and II	yes	15	7M/8F	47	yes	1
	Price et.al.	2014	unipolar	yes	36/21, no unique [1]	27M/30F	47	no	1
	Murrough et al.	2015b	unipolar (13), bipolar (7), PTSD (3), Borderline (1)	no	12/12	8M/16F	42	yes	1
RCTs	Price et.al.	2009	unipolar	yes	26, no unique [5]	16M/10F	48	no	1
	Aan Het Rot et al.	2010	unipolar	yes	10 [5]	5M/5F	51	no	6; 3x/wk for 2wks
	Diaz-Granados et al.	2010	unipolar	yes	33 [3]	20M/13F	46	no	1
	Larkin and Beautrais	2011	unipolar	no	14	7M/7F	31	yes	1
	Thakurta et al.	2012	unipolar	yes	27 [2]	13M/14F	49	no	1
	Ibrahim et al.	2012	unipolar	yes	42, 2 unique [3]	26M/16F	47	no [4]	1
	Murrough et al.	2013	unipolar	yes	24, 14 unique [5]	15M/9F	48	no	6; 3x/wk for 2wks
	Rasmussen et al.	2013	unipolar	yes	10	4M/6F	47	yes	1-4; 2x/wk for 2wks
	Diamond et al.	2014	unipolar (22) bipolar (6)	yes	28	16M/12F	47	yes	1-2x/wk for 3wks

* Some studies did not report data or depression response at all time points.
Suicidality was assessed as a secondary or post-hoc measure; trials were designed to assess response rates for depression as the primary outcome measure.
[1] Patients overlap with Murrough et al. (2013).
[2] Patients overlap with Thakurta et al. (2012).
[3] Patients overlap between these studies.

Interval	Outcome Measure	Baseline	40min-6h	1 day	2 days	3 days
72 hours	HDRS-SI group mean	*	*	*	*	"significantly decreased" (p=0.02)
7 days	HDRS-SI group mean	*	*	"significant effect" for ketamine	*	*
14 days	MADRS-SI group mean	*		not significant for any time point		
14 days	MADRS-SI group mean	2.3	0.25 (v.s. 2.2 with saline, p<0.001)	1.1 (v.s. 2.2 with saline, p<0.01)	1.1 (v.s. 2.1 with saline, p<0.01)	1.3 (v.s. 2.3 with saline, p<0.01)
7 days	SSI < 4	27/57 (47%)	*	86% (v.s. 62% with midazolam, p=0.04)	*	*
7 days	BSI / MADRS-SI	"Ketamine: 17.5 / 35.2 Midazolam: 17.9 / 34.3"	*	not significant / significant	significant / not significant	not significant / not significant
24 hours	MADRS-SI <=1	7/26 (27%)	*	21/26 (81%)		
2 wks of infusions + 4 wks [6]	MADRS-SI <=1	2/10 (20%)	*	9/10 (90%)	*	*
230 minutes	SSI < 4	23/33 (70%)	32/33 (97%)			
10 days	MADRS-SI group mean	3.9 (0.4)	0.6 (0.1) ("significantly lower than baseline")	*	*	*
2 days	SSI group mean	4.85 ± 5.37	0.78±1.48 (p=0.001)	~3.5 (p>0.05)	4.41±4.8; p=0.53	
28 days	SSI group mean	2.55		no significant changes throughout study		
2 wks of infusions + 12wks [6]	MADRS-SI group mean	*	1.9±0.66 (p<0.01)	*	*	*
0-2 wks infusions + 4wks [7]	SSI group mean	3.7±1.95	*	1.6±1.65 (p=0.007)	*	*
3 wks of infusions + 6 months	HAMD-SI group mean	2.0 (SD=0.9)	*	0.7 (SD=1.1)	*	*

[4] Responders were randomized to riluzole or placebo, but upon analysis differences found to non-significant.
[5] Patients overlap between studies.
[6] Data reported is for after completion of first infusion.
[7] Data reported is for after completion of all infusions.

Table 5. Alternate routes of ketamine administration

Route	Study	Type	Year	Diagnosis	TRD	N	Gender	Age	Comorbidities	Dose (racemic, unless noted)
Intramuscular	Glue et al.	case series	2011	unipolar	yes	2	2F	?	none reported	0.5, 0.7, and 1.0mg/kg
	Zanicotti et al. [1]	case	2012, 2013	unipolar	yes	1	F	36	metastatic ovarian cancer, pain	1.0mg/kg
	Harihar et al.	case series	2013	unipolar	unclear	2	M	23	obsessive-compulsive disorder	0.5mg/kg
							M	21	none reported	0.5mg/kg
	Cusin et al	case series	2012	bipolar II	yes	2	F	57	ADHD	50mg for 5mos, then 70mg for 4mos (55kg)
							F	48	ADHD, fibromyalgia, hypothyroid	50mg for 6mos (102kg)
	Chilukuri et al.	open label	2014	unipolar	yes	9	1M/8F	32	n/a	0.25mg/kg
						9	2M/7F	42	n/a	0.5mg/kg
	Banwari et al.	case	2015	unipolar to bipolar	yes	1	M	52	none reported	0.3mg/kg
Intranasal	Papolos et al.	case series	2013	bipolar I, Fear of Harm phenotype	yes	12	10M/2F	6 - 19	unclear	30-120mg [2]
	Clark	case	2014	unipolar	yes	1	1F	44	migraines	50mg
	Lapidus et al.	RCT, crossover	2014	unipolar	yes	20	10M/10F	48	none reported	50mg
										saline
Sublingual	Lara et al.	case series	2013	unipolar (12), bipolar (14)	yes	26	8M/18F	22-83	various	10 mg (100 mg/mL) for 5 minutes
	Nguyen et al.	chart review	2015	unipolar	yes	17	2M/15F	24-66	various	0.5-1.0mg/kg

Number of doses	Frequency	Duration of study	Outcome Measure	Depression response within 24 hours	Durability of benefit
3	unclear	unclear, at least 3 days	MADRS	yes, 3/3 (100%), but only at 1.0mg/kg	not reported
7, 34	every 7-8 days	2 months, 8 months	MADRS	yes, remission at 1hr	remission after each dose for 3-7 days, largely maintained for 8 months
2	every 3 days	1 month	HDRS	yes, remission at 2hr	remission through 1 month
2	every 3 days	unclear, at least 3 days	HDRS	yes, remission at 2hr	>3 days
68+	every 4 days	9 months	clinical assessment	unclear	remission "within a few days", maintained for 9 months
61+	every 3 days	12 months	clinical assessment	no	responded "after 1 week", maintained for 6 months
	once	3 days	HDRS	yes, 3/9 (33%)	increased to 44% at 3 days
	once	3 days	HDRS	yes, 4/9 (44%)	3 days
3	every 2 days	1 year	HDRS	unclear	n/a
many	every 3-7 days	several months	CBQ	yes, 12/12 (100%) within 24hr, and many within 1hr	"several months", 72-96hrs of benefit after each dose
32	twice weekly	4 months	clinical assessment	no	"euthymic" by day 3, maintained >4 months
	once	7 days	MADRS	yes, 8/18 (44%)	3 days
	once	7 days	MADRS	1/18 (6%)	low throughout study
1-90	every 2-7 days	up to 6 months	custom 0-10 mood scale	unclear, 17/26 (65%) with "rapid" response	20/26 (77%) had response to at least one dose; 10/26 (38%) maintained response for "months"
unclear	Every 7-14 days	up to 6 months	clinical assessment	unclear	76% responded, lasting from 1-2 weeks

continued next page

Table 5. Alternate routes of ketamine administration *continued*

Route	Study	Type	Year	Diagnosis	TRD	N	Gender	Age	Comorbidities	Dose (racemic, unless noted)
Subcutaneous	Galvez et al.	case	2014	unipolar, melancholic	yes	1	1F	62	HTN, hypothyroid, CVA	0.1mg/kg, then 0.2mg/kg 0.2mg/kg [5]
IV, intramuscular, and subcutaneous	Loo et al. [8]	RCT	2016	unipolar	yes	4 (IV) 5 (IM) 6 (SC) 15	2M/2F 4M/1F 5M/1F 11M/4F	53 46 48 49	none reported	IV 0.1-0.5mg/kg IM 0.1-0.5mg/kg SC 0.1-0.5mg/kg midazolam
Oral and subcutaneous	McNulty et al.	case	2012	unipolar	yes	1	M	44	hospice	0.5mg/kg SC, then daily [6]
Oral	Paslakis et al.	case series	2010	unipolar	no	4	?/1M/2F	36-57	melancholia; avoidant personality disorder, alcohol abuse	S-ketamine 1.25mg/kg
Oral	Irwin et al.	case series	2010	unipolar	no	2 [3]	1M/1F	64,70	hospice: COPD, neoplasia	0.5mg/kg
Oral	Irwin et al.	open label	2013	unipolar	no	14,12 unique [3]	?/1M/7F	?	hospice	0.5mg/kg
Oral	De Gioannis and Leo	case series	2014	bipolar, SI	yes	2	1F 1M	37 44	none chronic pain	0.5 - 1.5 mg/kg [4] 0.5 - 3.0 mg/kg [4]
Oral	Iglewicz et al.	case series	2014	unspecified depression	no	31 [3]	11M/20F	68	hospice	0.5mg/kg

All patients continued existing medications during treatment with ketamine.
[1] Includes follow-up publication on the same patient.
[2] Variable dose: 100 mg/mL solution via metered nasal spray pump bottle.
[3] Two patients overlap between these studies.
[4] Two patients received 0.5mg/kg orally, which was titrated up in 0.5mg/kg increments at follow-up sessions to final doses of 3.0mg/kg every 2-3 weeks and 1.5mg/kg monthly.

Number of doses	Frequency	Duration of study	Outcome Measure	Depression response within 24 hours	Durability of benefit
2	a month apart	9 months	MADRS	yes, only at higher dose	5 months
12	approx. weekly	9 months	MADRS	no, not until 3rd treatment	10 weeks
1-5	weekly	7 weeks	MADRS	unclear	75% response, 9 days (mean)
					60% response, 12 days (mean)
					100% response, 35 days (mean)
1					13% response
many	daily	11 weeks	clinical assessment	yes	11 weeks
12 to 14	split over three times daily	14 days	HDRS	no	2/4 (50%) responded at 7 days, maintained through 14 days
	once	several months	HDRS 17	yes, 1/2 (50%) patients responded by 120 min	1 month for initial responder; other responded at 8 days
28	nightly	28 days	HDRS 17	no	unclear; mean time to response 14.4±19.1 days for 8/14 (57%) responders
6 or more	monthly	>3 months	MADRS	yes	unclear
3 or more	every 2-3 weeks	>4 months	MADRS	yes	unclear
1 - 12 [7]	up to three times daily [7]	21 days	CGI	yes, 10/14 (71%)[7]	5/6 (83%) had response start to fade at day 2-3 [7]

[5] Patient received a second course of treatment after initial relapse.

[6] An initial one time 0.5mg/kg (40 mg) subcutaneous dose was followed by 0.5mg/kg (40 mg) daily oral maintenance.

[7] Of 31 subjects, 29 received ketamine orally, 1 received subcutaneous, and 1 received via both routes; 22 received 1 dose, 5 received 2 doses, and 4 received three times daily dosing for 3 days; time to first response and time to fading of response available for smaller sample.

[8] Utilized an ascending dose design in 0.1mg/kg increments, from 0.1 to 0.5mg/kg, with a midazolam control inserted randomly.

Supplemental Table 1. Cases with IV administration of ketamine

	Study	Year	Diagnosis	TRD	N	Gender	Age	Comorbidities	Medication Status	Formulation
Racemic	Ostroff et al.	2005	unipolar	yes	1	F	47	schizoaffective disorder	off for 1 day	racemic
	Correll and Futter	2006	unipolar	yes	2	F	39	none	continued	racemic
			unipolar	yes	2	M	33	none	continued	racemic
	Liebrenz et al [1]	2007, 2009	unipolar	yes	1	M	55	alcohol, benzodiazepine, and nicotine dependence	ativan continued, off antidepressants for 1 week	racemic
	Kollmar et al.	2008	unipolar	yes	1	F	47	none	unclear	racemic
	Stefanczyk-Sapieha et al.	2008	unipolar	yes	1	M	50	metastatic prostate cancer	methylphenidate held day of infusion	racemic
	Messer et al.	2010	unipolar	yes	2	M	50	obesity, sleep apnea	unclear	racemic
			unipolar	yes	2	M	45	history of alcohol abuse, hypertension	unclear	racemic
	Murrough et al.	2011	unipolar	yes	1	F	45	none	off	racemic
	Zigman and Blier	2013	unipolar	yes	1	F	37	prior pituitary adenoma resection, B12 deficiency, and hypothyroidism	continued	racemic
	Yang et al.	2013	unipolar	no	3	3M	19-31	none	off	racemic
	Szymkowicz et al.	2013	unipolar and bipolar II	yes	3	?	?	1) panic disorder, 2) none, 3) bulimia, bipolar II, cluster C	continued	racemic
	Szymkowicz et al.	2014	unipolar	yes	4	3M/1F	72	1) GAD, parkinsons, dementia 2) GAD, dementia, 3) GAD	continued	racemic
	Aligeti et al	2014	bipolar II	no	1	M	32	alcohol dependence	off	racemic
	Lai et al. [2]	2014	unipolar	yes	4	2M/2F	51	1) - 3) melancholic depression	continued	racemic

Dose	Number of Doses	Frequency	Duration of study	Measure	Depression Response within 24 hours	Durability of benefit
0.5mg/kg bolus (for ECT induction)	2	every 48 hours	5 days	custom scale	yes; mood rating improved from 2/10 to 7/10	5 days
0.27mg/kg/hr for 5 days	1	n/a	6 months	HDRS	no; remission via first HDRS time point at 5 days	12+ months
0.3mg/kg/hr for 5 days	3	2.5 and 7.5 months later	8 months	HDRS	no; remission via first HDRS time point at 5 days	"several weeks"
0.5mg/kg over 50min	2	35 days later	14 days, 7 days	HDRS	no; 1st infusion, response at 48hrs; 2nd infusion near response at 48hrs	1st infusion maintained for 14 days, 2nd infusion maintained 1 day
0.5mg/kg over 40 min	2	2 wks later	6 months	HDRS	yes, remission within 24 hours after each infusion	4 days
0.5mg/kg over 60min	2	10 days later	13 days	HDRS, BDI	no, near-response within first 6 hrs	6 hrs each time
0.5mg/kg over 40 min	6	every other day	12 days	BDI	no, only after 2nd infusion	relapse at 29 days
0.5mg/kg over 40 min	2	weekly	12 days	BDI	yes, after 1st infusion	relapse at 18 days
0.5mg/kg over 40min	6	three times a week	12 months	MADRS	yes, remission within 24 hrs	remission over 3 months via QIDS-SR
0.5mg/kg over 40 min	1	once	1 month	custom scale	yes, dysphoria from 10/10 to 3/10 at 40min	mood remained improved for 8 days
0.5mg/kg over 3 min	1	once	120 minutes	group mean MADRS	yes; halved at 120min	n/a
0.5mg/kg over 40 min	16 - 31	varied, from every other day to every 2 months	12 months	MADRS	yes; though after 2nd, 3rd, or 10th infusions	12 months in one patient
0.5mg/kg over 40 min	2 - 6	unclear	unclear	MADRS	no	n/a
0.5mg/kg IV push	1	once	6 months	HDRS7, MADRS	yes	through 5 days, unclear afterwards
saline	1	weekly	5 weeks	MADRS	no, 0/4 (0%)	n/a
0.1mg/kg over 2-5 min					yes, 2/4 (50%)	1 - 3 days
0.2mg/kg over 2-5 min					no, 0/4 (0%)	n/a
0.3mg/kg over 2-5 min					no, 0/4 (0%)	n/a
0.4mg/kg over 2-5 min					yes, 1/4 (25%)	1 day

continued next page

Supplemental Table 1. Cases with IV administration of ketamine *continued*

	Study	Year	Diagnosis	TRD	N	Gender	Age	Comorbidities	Medication Status	Formulation
Racemic	Srivastava et al.	2015	unclear	yes	1	F	65	none	yes	racemic
	Hassamal et al.	2015	unipolar	yes	1	F	65	none	yes	racemic
	da Frota Ribeiro et al.	2016	psychotic depression	yes	2	2F	54	delusions, auditory hallucinations	continued	racemic
	Gowda et al.	2016	unipolar, grief	no	1	M	28	none	continued	racemic
	Sampath et al.	2016	bipolar, rapid cycling	yes	1	F	19	hypoxic encephalopathy after suicide attempt	continued	racemic
S-ketamine	Paul et al. [3]	2009	unipolar	yes	2	1M/1F	51,58	1) nicotine dependence, HTN 2) none	continued	racemic
										S-ketamine
	Denk et al.	2011	unipolar	yes	1	F	56	none	unclear	S-ketamine
	Segmiller et al. [4]	2013	unipolar	yes	6	?	?	unclear	continued	S-ketamine

[1] Includes follow-up publication on the same patient.
[2] Subjects received ascending doses of ketamine, from 0.1 - 0.4mg/kg, interspersed with a saline treatment. Patients were blinded to the order.
[3] Two subjects received 0.5mg/kg racemic ketamine and 0.25mg/kg S-ketamine over 40 minutes in this open-label crossover study.
[4] Some data not available.

Dose	Number of Doses	Frequency	Duration of study	Measure	Depression Response within 24 hours	Durability of benefit
0.5mg/kg over 40 min	4	two times a week	1 year	HDRS	yes	1 year
0.5mg/kg over 35 min	12	two times a week, then three times a week	18 months	MADRS	yes	4, 8, and 6 months
0.5mg/kg over 40 min	3 – 5	unclear	unclear	HDRS	yes, 2/2 (100%)	unclear
0.5mg/kg over 40 min	1	once	3 months	clinical assessment	yes	3 months
0.5mg/kg over 40 min	2	5 days later	4 months	MADRS	no, near-response	4 months
0.5mg/kg over 40 min	1	weekly	2 weeks	HDRS	yes; 1/2 (50%)	3 days
0.25mg/kg over 40 min	1	weekly	2 weeks	HDRS	no; 0/2 (0%), though had near-response	n/a
0.25mg/kg over 40 min	1	n/a	100 minutes	MADRS	yes, remission immediately after infusion	n/a
0.25mg/kg over 40 min	6	1-2x/wk for 4 wks	4 weeks	HDRS	yes; though after 1st, 3/6 (50%), and 3rd, 4/6 (68%), infusions	not reported

Supplemental Table 2. Control trial adverse effects

	Study	Year	Design	Diagnosis	TRD	N	Gender	Age	CADSS ket vs. PBO	BPRS ket vs. PBO	YMRS ket vs. PBO
Unipolar Depression	Berman et al.	2000	double blind crossover	unipolar(8) bipolar(1)	no	9	4M/5F	37	not reported	Significantly greater BPRS scores. Non-significant by 80 min. Resolved at 110min	not reported
	Zarate et al.	2006	double blind crossover	unipolar	yes	18	6M/12F	47	not reported	Significantly greater BPRS positive symptoms subscale scores compared to placebo, only at +40 min	Higher at 40 min only
	Valentine et al.	2011	single blind crossover	unipolar	no	10	4M/6F	42	Significantly greater dissociation at +20 min; non-significant by +60 min	Non-significant greater BPRS positive symptom scores at +20 min to +80 min	not reported
	Sos et al.	2013	double blind crossover	unipolar	no	27	15M/15F	43	not reported	Non-significant BPRS increase (p=0.10)	not reported
	Murrough et al.	2013	parallel group	unipolar	yes	47/25	35M/37F	47/43	Significantly greater dissociation at 40min	No significant difference in BPRS or BPRS positive scale	Mean YMRS <1 for both groups at 40min
	Ghasemi et al.	2013	parallel group	unipolar	yes	9/9	8M/10F	38	not reported	not reported	not reported

Hemodynamic, Respiratory, EKG; more common with ketamine	Subjective adverse effects more common with ketamine	Subjective adverse effects more common in placebo	Adverse event leading to discontinuation	Miscellaneous
not reported	not reported	not reported	none reported	Changes in BPRS or VAS-high scores did not correlate with percent decreases observed in HDRS scores.
elevations in blood pressure	Perceptual disturbances, confusion, euphoria, dizziness, and increased libido. The majority of adverse effects ceased within 80 min after the infusion. Reports of derealization or depersonalization ceased by +110 min.	Gastrointestinal distress, increased thirst, headache, metallic taste, and constipation	none reported	A) Inverse relationship trend noted between the percentage change in HDRS score at day 1 and the peak percentage change in BPRS positive symptoms subscale score. B) No serious adverse events occurred during the study.
Significantly elevated SBP at 10-95 min mean, peak 40min of 14.1+/-13.4mmHG. Trend toward increased DBP. No effect on heart rate	not reported	not reported	Elevated blood pressure during placebo infusion	
"Mild" increases in BP	Dissociation/perceptual disturbances, confusion, emotional blunting, euphoria. All resolved at 60 min.	Worsening depression	Worsening depression in two receiving only KET	BPRS scores were significantly correlated with change in MADRS score at day 7 (P=0.04); trended toward significance at days 1 and 4 (p=0.06 and =<0.07).
Elevated blood pressure: mean 19 systolic, 9.1 diastolic, resolved at +240 min. Midazolam decreased mean blood pressure, hypotension in N=1.	Day of infusion: A) occurring in > 10% of patients: Nausea/vomiting, dry mouth, dizziness, palpitations, sweating, headache, poor coordination, tremor, blurred vision, poor concentration, restlessness, anxiety, decreased energy, and fatigue. B) Considered distressing in > 10%: Dizziness, blurred vision, and poor concentration. Day 1-7 after infusion: A) Nausea/vomiting, diarrhea, dizziness on standing, perspiration, dry skin, rash, dizziness, headache, blurred vision, poor concentration, restlessness, anxiety, fatigue, and malaise. B) Considered distressing in >10%: Poor concentration, restlessness, anxiety, decreased energy, and fatigue.	Day of Infusion: A) Occurring at > 10% incidence: General malaise B) Considered distressing in > 10%: Poor coordination. Day 1-7 after infusion: A) Palpitations and decreased energy. B) Considered distressing in >10%: General malaise and fatigue.	N=2 in ketamine condition (Hypertension unresponsive to beta blockers; hypotension, bradycardia)	N=2 SAE, considered unrelated (transient hypotension, bradycardia during venipuncture—vasovagal; Suicide attempt during washout period prior to administration of ketamine or midazolam)
Non-significant change in both groups. Non-significant and transient elevation in SBP, HR in N=3 ketamine on 2nd and 3rd administrations.	not reported	not reported	not reported	

continued next page

Supplemental Table 2. Control trial adverse effects *continued*

	Study	Year	Design	Diagnosis	TRD	N	Gender	Age	CADSS ket vs. PBO	BPRS ket vs. PBO	YMRS ket vs. PBO
Unipolar Depression	Lapidus et al.	2014	double blind crossover	unipolar	yes	20	10M/ 10F	48	"Small increases at 40 minutes" in ketamine group	"Small increases at 40 minutes" in ketamine group	not reported
	Lai et al.	2014	single blind crossover	unipolar	yes	4	2M/ 2F	51	unclear	unclear	unclear
	Murrough et al.	2015b	parallel group	unipolar (13), bipolar (7), PTSD (3), Borderline (1)	no	12/12	8M/ 16F	42	not reported	not reported	not reported
	Singh et al.	2016	parallel group	unipolar	yes	17/18/ 16/17	23M/ 45F	44	Significant only at +40 min, and diminished with repeated dosing (for both ketamine dose groups)	Increased significantly at +40 min only, no delusions or hallucinations reported	not reported
	Loo et al.	2016	parallel group	unipolar	yes	4/5/6	11M/ 4F	49	Dose-response relationship observed for all routes of ketamine, higher peak in IV group	Dose-response relationship observed for all routes of ketamine, higher peak in IV group	"No evidence of mania"
	Li et al.	2016	parallel group	unipolar	yes	16/16/ 16	13M/ 35F	46	not assessed	No significant difference in BPRS	not assessed
Bipolar Depression	Diaz-Granados et al.	2010	double blind crossover	bipolar I and II	yes	18	6M/ 12F	48	not reported	not reported	not reported
	Zarate et al.	2012	double blind crossover	bipolar I and II	yes	15	7M/ 8F	47	Significantly greater dissociation at +40 min	No significant difference in BPRS or BPRS positive subscale noted.	Non-significantly lower

Total N were reported for crossover studies, while N of each arm were reported for parallel group studies.

Hemodynamic, Respiratory, EKG; more common with ketamine	Subjective adverse effects more common with ketamine	Subjective adverse effects more common in placebo	Adverse event leading to discontinuation	Miscellaneous
Mean increase of 7.6 in SBP. 3 pts > 130 SBP. No pts >100 DBP. No pts over 110 BPM	In N>1: Feeling strange or unreal (8/18), poor memory, weakness/fatigue, dizziness, poor concentration, decreased sexual arousal/orgasm/interest, poor coordination, numbness/tingling; all resolved by +240 min.	Trouble sleeping at +240 min, and +240 min to +24 hrs. Sleep disturbance / nightmares and "overall" adverse effect at +240 min to +24hrs.	None; N=2 withdrew prior to treatment.	In ketamine responders versus nonresponders, higher increase in CADSS score at +40 min: 1.75 +/- 4.17 versus 1.09 +/- 1.76.
unclear	Dose dependent increase in psychotomimetic side effects.	n/a	none	Dose dependent increase in psychotomimetic side effects
N=1 died from cardiorespiratory disease, judged unrelated to study	Headache, poor concentration, poor coordination, restlessness, malaise.	Dizziness on standing, nausea/vomiting, diarrhea, xerostomia, chest pain	not reported	N=5 SAE, considered unrelated (N=4 hospitalization for worsening depression/ suicidality, N=1 death due to cardiorespiratory causes)
None outside of "normal limits"	3x/wk: headache, nausea, dizziness 2x/wk: anxiety, dissociation, nausea, dizziness	2x/wk: headache, intervertebral disc degeneration	N=2 in 2x/wk ketamine (anxiety; anxiety, paranoia), N=1 in 2x/wk placebo (disc degeneration), N=1 in 3x/wk ketamine (anxiety, hypoesthesia, dizziness, feeling cold).	N=2 SAE, all in 2x/wk ketamine group, considered unrelated (anxiety from unrelated life events; suicide attempt 4 weeks after last ketamine dose).
Increased MAP / SBP, DBP, HR to > 120% baseline in: N=2 IV and 2 IM / N=1 IV, 1 IM, and 1 SC.	Mild depersonalization, derealization, altered body perception, altered time perception; more so in IV group	not reported	none	All adverse effects resolved by 4 hours; all hemodynamic effects resolved by 30 minutes.
not reported	Cases of "floating sensation" significantly greater in higher dose 0.5mg/kg ketamine arm	none	none	Side effects were "mild and self-limiting and required no additional medical treatment."
Tachycardia and increased blood pressure; resolved in minutes.	Adverse events associated only with ketamine (≥10% of subjects) included dissociation; feeling strange, weird, or bizarre; dry mouth	unclear	Ketamine (4); anxiety, three with worsening mood (one worsening suicidal ideation). Placebo (1): Hypomania	A) No serious adverse events occurred during the study. B) No adverse event was significantly different from placebo at +80 min or thereafter.
Tachycardia in one patient	Dry mouth, headache, breast pain/ swelling, leg cramp, dizziness or faintness, difficulty falling asleep, decrease body temp, flatulence, concentration difficulty, drowsy/ sleepiness, woozy, loopy, early morning awkening, interrupted sleep, vivid dreams, difficulty speaking, skin irritation, sweating, noise sensitivity, fearfulness, cough, increased thirst, diarrhea, increaed appetite, stool discoloration, increased libido, tremor and menstrual irregularity.	Irritability, muscle, bone, or joint pain, increased body temp, "slowed", and decreased libido.	none reported	A) No serious adverse events occurred during the study. B) No adverse event was significantly different from placebo at +80 min or thereafter.

Supplemental Table 3. Open label trial adverse effects

Study	Year	Diagnosis	TRD	N	Gender	Age	CADSS Results	BPRS Results	YMRS Results
Machado-Vieira et al.	2009	unipolar	yes	23	14M/9F	44	not reported	not reported	not reported
Phelps et al.	2009	unipolar	yes	26	14M/12F	44	Those with positive family history of alcohol (FHP) had significantly higher scores at +40 min compared to family history negative (FHN).	Positive symptoms elevated in FHP and FHN groups at +40 min, back to baseline by +80 min. FHP had significantly fewer dysphoric symptoms at +120 and +230 min.	not reported
Price et.al.	2009	unipolar	yes	26, 0 unique	16M/10F	48	not reported	not reported	not reported
Salvadore et al.	2009	unipolar	yes	11	7M/4F	44	not reported	Significant decrease in psychotic symptoms after +230 min.	not reported
Diaz-Granados et al.	2010	unipolar	yes	33	20M/13F	46	Inadequate inter-rater reliability	Inadequate inter-rater reliability	not reported
Salvadore et al.	2010	unipolar	yes	15 (8 unique)	?	51	not reported	Significant decrease in positive subscale after +230 min	not reported
Mathew et al.	2010	unipolar	yes	26	16M/10F	48	not reported	Nonsignificant changes in positive symptoms at+240 min	Significant main effect of time on item 1. No effect of pretreatment.
aan het Rot et al. [1]	2010	unipolar	yes	10, 0 unique	5M/5F	51	Significantly increased at +40 min, normal by +2 hrs	Nonsigificant mean increase, baseline at +2 hrs	not reported
Larkin and Beautrais	2011	unipolar	no	14	7M/7F	31	not reported	No significant elevation at +40 min	No significant elevation at first time point of +40 min.
Ibrahim et al.	2011	unipolar	yes	42	24M/18F	47	Significantly increased at +40 min, normal by +80 min	not reported	not reported

Hemodynamic, Respiratory, and EKG effects	Subjective adverse effects	Adverse event leading to ending treatment	Miscellaneous
not reported	not reported	none reported	
not reported	not reported	none reported	
not reported	not reported	none reported	
not reported	not reported	none reported	
not reported	Mild perceptual disturbances observed in most patients only within +1 hr.	none reported	No serious adverse events occurred during the study.
not reported	not reported	none reported	
Elevated blood pressure during infusion (mean 19.8 +/- 10.9 systolic mmHg, 13.4 +/- 7.7 diastolic mmHg) and pulse (mean 10.9 +/- 11.9 bpm); back to baseline at +40-80 min.	Most common: blurry vision, diminished mental/sharpness, dizzy/faint, drowsy/sleepy, feeling strange/unreal, headache, numbness/tingling, ringing in ears/trouble hearing, and slurred speech.	none reported	There were no serious adverse events, and no treatment-emergent mania or suicidality.
A) Tachycardia and hypertension reported in two patients, resolved 5minutes after infusion. B) Bradycardia in one patient on initial and repeat infusions, resolved by 2hrs. C) Asymptomatic, mild hypotension (80/55) developed in one patient with baseline of 107/48, lasting until discharge at 24hours, and on two repeat infusions. D) Asymptomatic premature ventricular contractions reported in one patient on repeat infusions 4 and 5, resolved at 2hrs. E) Bradypnea noted in one patient on several infusions and one time desaturation 99% to 94%. No effect noted on respiratory rate after administration period.	No more than N=2 reported any of the following: abnormal sensations, blurred vision, diminished mental capacity, dizzy/faint, drowsy/sleepy, feeling strange/unreal, headache, hearing or seeing things, numbness/tingling, poor coordination/unsteadiness, poor memory, rapid or pounding heartbeat, weakness/fatigue. [4]	none	N=2 tachycardia and hypertension on repeat infusions; N=1 tachycardia on repeat infusions; N=1 hypertension on repeat infusions. All side effects were manageable. No significant change in peak BPRS+ scores or CADSS scores across the six infusions.
not reported	Mild positive psychotomimetic symptoms in N=2, resolving within 40 min; mild unpleasant dissociative symptoms in N=2, resolving within 30 min.	none	
not reported	not reported	none noted	

continued next page

Supplemental Table 3. Open label trial adverse effects *continued*

Study	Year	Diagnosis	TRD	N	Gender	Age	CADSS Results	BPRS Results	YMRS Results
Salvadore et al.	2012	unipolar	yes	14, 11 unique	9M/5F	50	not reported	not reported	not reported
Thakurta et al.	2012	unipolar	yes	27	13M/14F	49	not reported	Significant increase in positive subscale at +40 min only	not reported
Cornwell et al.	2012	unipolar	yes	20, 0 unique	15M/5F	46	Significantly increased at +40 min only	Significant decrease in positive subscale at +80 min, +120 min, and +230 min	not reported
Ibrahim et al. [2]	2012	unipolar	yes	42, 2 unique	26M/16F	47	Significantly increased at +230 min	Significantly increased at +230 min	Variably different through time course.
Thakurta et al.	2012	unipolar	yes	22	10M/12F	50	not reported	Significant increase in positive subscale at +40 min only	not reported
Rybakowski et al.	2013	bipolar, unspecified	yes	25	4M/21F	49	not reported	not reported	not reported
Rasmussen et al. [3]	2013	unipolar and bipolar II	yes	10	4M/6F	47	not reported	No significant change in positive subscale or total BPRS noted at +2 hrs or+1 day	Isolated symptoms. No mania.
Murrough et al. [1]	2013	unipolar	yes	24, 14 unique	15M/9F	48	Significant increase from pre-infusion mean of 0.3 ±0.5 to 7.8±12.0 at peak of infusion; baseline by +240 min.	Significant increase in positive symptoms subscale from pre-infusion mean of 4.0±0.1 to 4.5±0.9 at peak of infusion; baseline by +240 min.	Elevated mood measured by the YMRS-1, baseline by +240 min.
Shiroma et al. [1]	2014	unipolar	yes	14	14M	54	Significant increase from a pre-infusion mean of 0 to 8.60±6.49 at the end of infusion; returned to baseline by +120 min.	Significant increase in positive subscale from pre-infusion mean of 4.0±0 to 4.6±1.9 at end of infusion, returned to mean by +120 min.	not reported

Hemodynamic, Respiratory, and EKG effects	Subjective adverse effects	Adverse event leading to ending treatment	Miscellaneous
not reported	not reported	not reported	
Non-specific elevation of blood pressure	Generally reported: elevated blood pressure, euphoria, headache, increased thirst, and dizziness occurring with ketamine administration ceased within 60 min.	none reported	No serious adverse events occurred during the study.
not reported	not reported	none reported	Referred to Ibrahim et al. (2012)
Elevations in blood pressure and pulse, resolved within 80 min; no clinically meaningful EKG changes; no clinically meaningful changes in respiratory effects.	Generally reported: perceptual disturbances, drowsiness, confusion, and dizziness occurred during infusion, resolved within 80 min.	none reported	
Elevation in blood pressure with administration, resolved within 40 min.	Generally reported: euphoria, headache, increased thirst, and dizziness occurring with administration, resolved within 40 min.	none reported	No serious adverse events occurred during the study.
not reported	not reported	none reported	
No clinically significant elevation in blood pressure during the infusions. No arrhythmia. No patients required respiratory support.	N=1 vertigo, N=3 dizziness, N=1 visual hallucinations, N=3 drowsiness, N=1 dysmegalopsia/anxiety and diplopia, N=3 no adverse effects.	none reported	
Elevated blood pressure and/or heart rate (33%).	The most common effects were reported with prevalence: 58.3% of patients reported feeling unreal/strange. 54.2% reported abnormal sensations, 50% blurred vision, 45.8% reported feeling drowsy/sleepy; largely resolved prior to subsequent infusions.	Maximum blood pressure 180/115 during infusion. Unsatisfactory response to anti-hypertensives. Stabilized upon discontinuation.	No serious adverse events occurred during the study; 16.7% reported that any side effect impaired functioning at any time; no trend towards increasing dissociative or psychotomimetic effects over the course of the trial.
Elevation from normotensive to hypertensive blood pressure in N=1 (180/92) that rapidly responded to 10mg labetalol; no arrhythmia; no patients required respiratory support.	N=1 with gastroesophageal reflux disease had nausea and vomited after second infusion, responded to ondansetron.	none reported	A) Complete recovery in all patients after 2 hrs. B) Nausea and vomiting in N=1 on one infusion, responded to ondansetron IV 8 mg IV, and used as prophylaxis in subsequent infusions.

continued next page

Supplemental Table 3. Open label trial adverse effects *continued*

Study	Year	Diagnosis	TRD	N	Gender	Age	CADSS Results	BPRS Results	YMRS Results
Chilukuri et al.	2014	unipolar	yes	9/9/9		37	not reported	not reported	not reported
				9 (0.5mg/kg IV)	3M/6F	36	not reported	not reported	not reported
				9 (0.5mg/kg IM)	2M/7F	42	not reported	not reported	not reported
				9 (0.25mg/kg IM)	1M/8F	32	not reported	not reported	not reported
Diamond et al.	2014	unipolar and bipolar	yes	28	16M/12F	47	not reported	not reported	not reported
Vasavada	2015	unipolar	yes	10	8M/2F	48	not reported	not reported	not reported
Cusin et al.	2016	unipolar	yes	14	3M/11F	50	Increased in both 0.5mg/kg and 0.75mg/kg infusions, respectively: amnesia (36%, 31%), depersonalization (64%, 31%); derealization (71%, 62%).	not reported	not reported

[1] 6 infusions total, 3x/wk for 2wks; [3] up to 4 infusions total, 2x/wk for 2 wks or until remission
[2] Reported over 28 days and compared between post treatment with riluzole or placebo.
[4]From week 1 to week 2, prevalence of abnormal sensations increased from one patient to two patients, and additional patient reported weakness/fatigue at week two who had not the week prior.

Hemodynamic, Respiratory, and EKG effects	Subjective adverse effects	Adverse event leading to ending treatment	Miscellaneous
No change in mean SBP or DBP for all pts combined; max SBP was 160, max DBP was 90			
No change in mean SBP or DBP for all pts combined; max SBP was 160, max DBP was 90	Sedation/drowsy 22%, heavy head 11%	none	all well enough to return home at +4 hrs
No change in mean SBP or DBP for all pts combined; max SBP was 160, max DBP was 90	Sedation/drowsy 22%, lightness of body 22%, heavy head 11%	none	all well enough to return home at +4 hrs
No change in mean SBP or DBP for all pts combined; max SBP was 160, max DBP was 90	Sedation/drowsy 33%	none	all well enough to return home at +4 hrs
N=1 withdrew during their first treatment due to a panic attack nine minutes into the infusion, experiencing tachycardia and tachypnea. N=1 was withdrawn due to concurrent upper respiratory tract infection. N=1 had a 10 minute vasovagal episode (BP 77/47, HR 45, reduced level of consciousness) 11 minutes into his first infusion, resolved by +1 hr.	"Most patients" reported some transient effects, including perceptual distortions, detachment, anxiety, nausea, and confusion during infusion. "Most" experienced marked, but well tolerated dissociative symptoms. Specific data includes: anxiety 25%, mood 18% (see notes), nausea with vomiting 7%, Following infusions "the majority of patients experienced an increase in fatigue with a small number of patients also experiencing mild headaches", N=1 hypnagogic hallucination.	N=1, concurrent upper respiratory infection (unrelated); N=1 panic attack; N=1 vasovagal episode; N=4 anxiety; N=1 anxiety, mood, and worsening SI (reported as reaction to lack of effect).	All of the following completed the study: N=1 self-report of rapid cycling, clinically no change in behavior, resolved with increase in antipsychotic. N=3 worsening mood/SI, reported prone to fluctuation in mood/SI prior. N=1 mania, treating psychiatrist reported this as "consonant with pre-existing mood instability". N=1 symptomatic cystitis, self-reportedly secondary to sexual activity, resolved with single dose antibiotics. No other cystitis or abnormal urinary dipsticks reported.
not reported	not reported	none reported	not reported
Mild transient SBP and DBP increases during infusions; all had at least 10 mmHg SBP increase, and larger increase at the higher ketamine dose. No significant changes in pulse oxymetry or pulse.	Mild visual disturbances, moderate auditory disturbances ("buzzing sound"), headache, nausea, sedation, and "mild dissociative symptoms based on CADSS."	none reported	No serious adverse events reported; the majority of the minor effects dissipated by +120 min.

References

aan het Rot, M., Collins, K. A., Murrough, J. W., Perez, A. M., Reich, D. L., Charney, D. S., & Mathew, S. J. (2010). Safety and efficacy of repeated-dose intravenous ketamine for treatment-resistant depression. *Biological Psychiatry, 67*(2), 139-145. doi:10.1016/j.biopsych.2009.08.038

Abdallah, C. G., Salas, R, Jackowski, A., Baldwin, P., Sato, J. R., & Mathew, S. J. (2015). Hippocampal volume and the rapid antidepressant effect of ketamine. *Journal of Psychopharmacology* (Oxford), *29*(5): 591–595.

Aligeti, S., Quinones, M., Salazar, R. (2014). Rapid resolution of suicidal behavior and depression with single low-dose ketamine intravenous push even after 6 months of follow-up. *Journal of Clinical Psychopharmacology, 34*(4), 533-535. doi:10.1097/JCP.0000000000000146

Artigas, F. (2013). Developments in the field of antidepressants, Where do we go now? *European Neuropsychopharmacology*. Advance online publication. doi:10.1016/j.euroneuro.2013.04.013

Atigari, O. V., & Healy, D. (2013). Sustained antidepressant response to ketamine. *BMJ Case Reports, 2013*, bcr2013200370. doi:10.1136/bcr-2013-200370

Ballard, E. D., Ionescu D. F., Vande Voort, J. L., Niciu, M. J., Richards, E. M. Luckenbaugh, D. A., ¼ Zarate Jr., C. A. (2014). Improvement in suicidal ideation after ketamine infusion: Relationship to reductions in depression and anxiety. *Journal of Psychiatric Research, 58*, 161–166.

Banwari, G., Desai, P., & Patidar, P. (2015). Ketamine-induced affective switch in a patient with treatment-resistant depression. *Indian Journal of Pharmacology, 47*(4), 454–455.

Baumeister, D., Barnes, G., Giaroli, G., Tracy, D. (2014). Classical hallucinogens as antidepressants? A review of pharmacodynamics and putative clinical roles. *Therapeutic Advances in Psychopharmacology, 4*(4), 156-169. doi:10.1177/2045125314527985

Baune, B. T., Adrian, I., & Jacobi, F. (2007). Medical disorders affect health outcome and general functioning depending on comorbid major depression in the general population. *Journal of Psychosomatic Research, 62*(2), 109-118. doi:10.1016/j.jpsychores.2006.09.014

Beck, A. T., Kovacs, M., & Weissman, A. (1979). Assessment of suicidal intention: The scale for suicide ideation. *Journal of Consulting and Clinical Psychology, 47*(2), 343-352. doi:10.1037/0022-006X.47.2.343

Beck, A. T., Ward, C. H., Mendelson, M., Mock, J., & Erbaugh, J. (1961). An inventory for measuring depression. *Archives of General Psychiatry, 4*(6), 561-571. doi:10.1001/archpsyc.1961.01710120031 004

Berman, R. M., Cappiello, A., Oren, D. A., Anand, A.,Heninger, G. R., Charney, D. S., & Krystal, J. H.
(2000). Antidepressant effects of ketamine in depressed patients. *Biological Psychiatry, 47*(4), 351-354. doi:10.1016/S0006-3223(99)00

Björkenstam, C., Moller, J., Ringback, G., Salmi, P., Hallqvist, J., & Ljung, R. (2013). An association between initiation of selective serotonin reuptake inhibitors and suicide: A nationwide register-based case-crossover study. *PLoS ONE, 8*(9), 73973. doi:10.1371/journal.pone.0073973

Blonk, M. I., Koder, B. G., van den Bemt, P. M., & Huygen, F. J. (2010). Use of oral ketamine in chronic pain management: A review. *European Journal of Pain, 14*(5), 466-472. doi:10.1016/j.ejpain.2009.09.005

Bobo, W. V., Vande Voort, J. L., Croarkin, P. E., Leung, J. G., Tye, S. J., & Frye, M. A. (2016). Ketamine for treatment-resistant unipolar and bipolar major depression: Critical review and implications for clinical practice. *Depression and Anxiety,* epub ahead of print.

Boleslav Kosharskyy, M., Wilson Almonte, M., & Naum Shaparin, M. (2013). Intravenous infusions in chronic pain management. *Pain Physician, 16,* 231–249.

Bonnet, U. (2015). Long-term ketamine self-injections in major depressive disorder: Focus on tolerance in ketamine's antidepressant response and the development of ketamine addiction. *Journal of Psychoactive Drugs, 47*(4), 276–285.

Bremner, J. D., Krystal, J. H., Putnam, F. W., Southwick, S. M., Marmar, C., Charney, D. S., & Mazure, C. M. (1998). Measurement of dissociative states with the clinician-administered dissociative states scale (CADSS). *Journal of Traumatic Stress, 11*(1), 125-136. doi: 10.1023/A:1024465317902

Caddy, C., Giaroli, G., White, T. P., Shergill, S. S., Tracy, D. K. (2014). Ketamine as the prototype glutamatergic antidepressant: Pharmacodynamic actions, and a systematic review and meta-analysis of efficacy. *Therapeutic Advances in Psychopharmacology, 4*(2), 75-99.

Carlson, P. J., Diaz-Granados, N., Nugent, A. C., Ibrahim, L., Luckenbaugh, D. A., Brutsche, N., ¼ Drevets, W. C. (2013). Neural correlates of rapid antidepressant response to ketamine in treatment-resistant unipolar depression: A preliminary positron emission tomography study. *Biological Psychiatry, 73,* 1213–1221.

Carhart-Harris, R. L., Bolstridge, M., Rucker. J., Day, C. M. J., Erritzoe, D., Kaelen, M., ¼ Nutt, D. J. (2016). Psilocybin with psychological support for treatment-resistant depression: An open-label feasibility study. *Lancet Psychiatry.* Published Online: May 17, 2016. doi:10.1016/S2215-0366(16)30065-7

Chilukuri, H., Reddy, N. P., Pathapati, R. M., Manu, A. N., Jollu, S., & Shaik, A. B. (2014). Acute antidepressant effects of intramuscular versus intravenous ketamine. *Indian Journal Psychological Medicine, 36*(1), 71-76. doi:10.4103/0253-7176.127 258

Chu, P. S., Ma, W., Wong, S. C., Chu, R. W., Cheng, C., Wong, S., …. Man, C. (2008). The destruction of the lower urinary tract by ketamine abuse: A new syndrome? *BJU International, 102*(11), 1616-1622. doi:10.1111/j.1464-410X.2008.07920.x

Clark, P. (2014). Treatment-refractory depression: A case of successful treatment with intranasal ketamine 10%. *Annals of Clinical Psychiatry, 26*(1), E10.

Clements, J., Nimmo, W., & Grant, I. (1982). Bioavailability, pharmacokinetics, and analgesic activity of ketamine in humans. *Journal of Pharmaceutical Sciences, 71*(5), pp. 539-542. doi:10.10 02/jps.2600710516

Cook, I. A., Espinoza, R., & Leuchter, A. F. (2014). Neuromodulation for depression: Invasive and noninvasive (deep brain stimulation, transcranial magnetic stimulation, trigeminal nerve stimulation). *Neurosurgery Clinics of North America, 25*(1), 103-116. doi:10.1016/j.nec.2013.10.002

Cooper, M. D., Rosenblat, J. D., Cha, D. S., Lee, Y., Kakar, R., & McIntyre, R. S. (2016). Strategies to mitigate dissociative and psychotomimetic effects of ketamine in the treatment of major depressive episodes: A narrative review. *World Journal of Biological Psychiatry.* Advance online publication.

Cornwell, B. R., Salvadore, G., Furey, M., Marquardt, C. A., Brutsche, N. E., Grillon, C., & Zarate, C. A. (2012). Synaptic potentiation is critical for rapid antidepressant response to ketamine in treatment-resistant major depression. *Biological Psychiatry, 72*(7), 555-561. doi:10.1016/j.biopsych.2012.03. 029

Correll, G. E., & Futter, G. E. (2006). Two case studies of patients with major depressive disorder given low-dose (subanesthetic) ketamine infusions. *Pain Medicine, 7*(1), 92-95. doi:10.1111/j.1526-4637.2006.00101.x

Coyle C. M., & Laws, K. R. (2015). The use of ketamine as an antidepressant: A systematic review and meta-analysis. *Human Psychopharmacology, 30*(3), 152–163. doi:10.1002/hup.2475

Curran, H. V., & Monaghan, L. (2001). In and out of the K-hole: A comparison of the acute and residual effects of ketamine in frequent and infrequent ketamine users. *Addiction, 96*(5), 749-760. doi:10.1046/j.1360-0443.2001.96574910.x

Cusin, C., Hilton, G. Q., Nierenberg, A. A., & Fava, M. (2012). Long-term maintenance with intramuscular ketamine for treatment-resistant bipolar II depression. *American Journal of Psychiatry, 169*(8), 868-869. doi:10.1176/appi.ajp.2012.12020219

Cusin, C, Ionescu, D.F., Pavone, K. J., Akeju, O., Cassano, P., Taylor, N., ¼ Fava, M. (2016). Ketamine augmentation for outpatients with treatment-resistant depression: Preliminary evidence for two-step intravenous dose escalation. *Australian and New Zealand Journal of Psychiatry*. Advance online publication. doi:10.1177/0004867416631828

da Frota Ribeiro, C. M., Sanacora, G., Hoffman, R., & Ostroff R. (2016). The use of ketamine for the treatment of depression in the context of psychotic symptoms: To the editor. *Biological Psychiatry, 79*(9), e65–e66.

De Gioannis, A., & De Leo, D. (2014). Oral ketamine augmentation for chronic suicidality in treatment-resistant depression. *Australian and New Zealand Journal of Psychiatry, 48*(7), 686-686. doi:10.1177/0004867414520754

Denk, M. C., Rewerts, C., Holsboer, F., Erhardt-Lehmann, A., & Turck, C. W. (2011). Monitoring ketamine treatment response in a depressed patient via peripheral mammalian target of rapamycin activation. *American Journal of Psychiatry, 168*(7), 751-752. doi:10.1176/appi.ajp.2011.11010128

Diamond, P. R., Farmery, A. D., Atkinson, S., Haldar, J., Williams, N., Cowen, P. J., ... & McShane, R. (2014). Ketamine infusions for treatment resistant depression: A series of 28 patients treated weekly or twice weekly in an ECT clinic. *Journal of Psychopharmacology, 28*(6), 536-544. doi:10.1177/0269881114527361

Diaz-Granados, N., Ibrahim, L., Brutsche, N. E., Newberg, A., Kronstein, P., Khalife, S., ... Salvadore, G. (2010a). A randomized add-on trial of an *N*-methyl-D-aspartate antagonist in treatment-resistant bipolar depression. *Archives of General Psychiatry, 67*(8), 793-802. doi:10.1001/archgenpsychiatry.2010.90

Diaz-Granados, N., Ibrahim, L., Brutsche, N., Ameli, R., Henter, I. D., Luckenbaugh, D. A., ... Zarate, C. A. (2010b). Rapid resolution of suicidal ideation after a single infusion of an NMDA antagonist in patients with treatment-resistant major depressive disorder. *The Journal of Clinical Psychiatry, 71*(12), 1605.

doi:10.4088/JCP.09m05327blu

Domino, D. (2010). Taming the ketamine tiger. *Anesthesiology, 113*(3), 678-684. doi:10.1097/ALN.0b013e3181ed09a2.

Feder, A., Parides, M. K., Murrough, J. W., Perez, A. M., Morgan, J. E., Saxena, S., ... & Charney, D. S. (2014). Efficacy of intravenous ketamine for treatment of chronic posttraumatic stress disorder: a randomized clinical trial. *JAMA Psychiatry, 71*(6), 681-688. doi:10.1001/jamapsychiatry.2014.62

Gálvez, V., O'Keefe, E., Cotiga, L., Leyden, J., Harper, S., Glue, P., ... & Loo, C. K. (2014). Long-lasting effects of a single subcutaneous dose of ketamine for treating melancholic depression: A case report. *Biological Psychiatry, 76*(3), e1-e2. doi:10.1016/j.biopsych.2013.12.010

Gasser, P., Holstein, D., Michel, Y., Doblin, R., Yazar-Klosinski, B., Passie, T., & Brenneisen, R. (2014). Safety and efficacy of lysergic acid diethylamide-assisted psychotherapy for anxiety associated with life-threatening diseases. *The Journal of Nervous and Mental Disease, 202*(7), 513. doi:10.1097/NMD.0000000000000113

Gelenberg, A. J. (2010). A review of the current guidelines for depression treatment. *The Journal of Clinical Psychiatry, 71*(7), e15. doi:10.4088/JCP.9078tx1c

Ghasemi, M., Kazemi, M. H., Yoosefi, A., Ghasemi, A., Paragomi, P., Amini, H., & Afzali, M. H. (2013). Rapid antidepressant effects of repeated doses of ketamine compared with electroconvulsive therapy in hospitalized patients with major depressive disorder. *Psychiatry Research, 215*(2), 355-361. doi:10.1016/j.psychres.2013.12.008.

Glue, P., Gulati, A., Le Nedelec, M., & Duffull, S. (2011). Dose- and exposure-response to ketamine in depression. *Biological Psychiatry, 70*(4), 9-12. doi:10.1016/j.biopsych.2010.11.031

Gowda, M. R., Srinivasa, P., Kumbar, P. S., Ramalingaiah, V. H., Muthyalappa, C., & Durgoji, S. (2016). Rapid resolution of grief with IV infusion of ketamine: A unique phenomenological experience. *Indian Journal of Psychological Medicine, 38*(1), 62–64.

Grégoire, M., Maclellan, D., & Finley, G. (2008). A pediatric case of ketamine-associated cystitis (Letter-to-the-Editor RE: Shahani R, Streutker C, Dickson B, et al: Ketamine-associated ulcerative cystitis: a new clinical entity. Urology 69: 810-812, 2007). *Urology, 71*(6), 1232-1233. doi:10.1016/j.urology.2007.11.141.

Grob, C. S., Danforth, A. L., Chopra, G. S., Hagerty, M., McKay, C. R., Halberstadt, A. L., & Greer, G. R. (2011). Pilot study of psilocybin treatment for anxiety in patients with advanced-stage cancer. *Archives of General Psychiatry, 68*(1), 71-78. doi:10.1001/archgenpsychiatry.2010.116

Guy, W. (1976). *ECDEU Assessment Manual for Psychopharmacology, Revised.* Bethesda, MD: US Department of Health, Education, and Welfare; 1976.

Hamilton, M. (1960). A rating scale for depression. *Journal of Neurology, Neurosurgery& Psychiatry, 23*(1), 56. doi:10.1136/jnnp.23.1.56

Hashimoto, K. (2014). The *R*-Stereoisomer of ketamine as an alternative for ketamine for treatment-resistant major depression. *Clinical Psychopharmacology and Neuroscience, 12*(1), 72-73. doi:10.9758/cpn.2014.12.1.72

Hassamal, S., Spivey, M., Pandurangi, A. K. (2015). Augmentation therapy with serial intravenous ketamine over 18 months in a patient with treatment resistant depression. *Clinical Neuropharmacolo*gy, *38*(5), 212–216.

Harihar, C., Dasari, P., & Srinivas, J. S. (2013). Intramuscular ketamine in acute depression: A report on two cases. *Indian Journal of Psychiatry, 55*(2), 186. doi:10.4103/0019-5545.111461

Heresco-Levy, U., Javitt, D. C., Gelfin, Y., Gorelik, E., Bar, M., Blanaru, M., & Kremer, I. (2006). Controlled trial of d-cycloserine adjuvant therapy for treatment-resistant major depressive disorder. *Journal of Affective Disorders, 93*(1), 239-243. doi:10.1016/j.jad.2006.03.004

Hu, Y. D., Xiang, Y. T., Fang, J. X., Zu, S., Sha, S., Shi, H. … Wang, G. (2016). Single IV ketamine augmentation of newly initiated escitalopram for major depression: Results from a randomized, placebo-controlled 4-week study. *Psychological Medicine, 46*(3), 623–635.

Ibrahim, L., Diaz-Granados, N., Franco-Chaves, J., Brutsche, N., Henter, I. D., Kronstein, P., ... Zarate, C. A., (2012). Course of improvement in depressive symptoms to a single intravenous infusion of ketamine vs add-on riluzole: Results from a 4-week, double-blind, placebo-controlled study. *Neuropsychopharmacology, 37*(6), 1526-1533. doi:10.1038011.338

Ibrahim, L., Diaz-Granados, N., Luckenbaugh, D. A., Machado-Vieira, R., Baumann, J., Mallinger, A. G., & Zarate, C. A. (2011). Rapid decrease in depressive symptoms with an *N*-methyl-D-aspartate antagonist in ECT-resistant major depression. *Progress in Neuro-Psychopharmacology & Biological Psychiatry, 35*(4), 1155-1159. doi:10.1016/j.pnpbp.2011.03.019

Iglewicz, A., Morrison, K., Nelesen, R. A., Zhan, T., Iglewicz, B., Fairman, N., ... & Irwin, S. A. (2014). Ketamine for the treatment of depression in patients receiving hospice care: A retrospective medical record review of thirty-one cases. *Psychosomatics*, Advance online publication. doi: 10.1016/j.psym.2014.05.005.

Ionescu, D. F., Luckenbaugh, D. A., Niciu, M. J., Richards, E. M., Slonena, E. E., Vande, V. J., ... & Zarate, C. A. (2014a). Effect of baseline anxious depression on initial and sustained antidepressant response to ketamine. *The Journal of Clinical Psychiatry, 75*(9), e932-e938. doi:10.4088/JCP.14m09049

Ionescu, D. F., Luckenbaugh, D. A., Niciu, M. J., Richards, E. M., & Zarate, C. A. (2014b). A single infusion of ketamine improves depression scores in patients with anxious bipolar depression. *Bipolar Disorders*, Advance online publication. doi:10.1111/bdi.12277

Irwin, S. A., & Iglewicz, A. (2010). Oral ketamine for the rapid treatment of depression and anxiety in patients receiving hospice care. *Journal of Palliative Medicine, 13*(7), 903-908. doi:10.1089/jpm.2010.9808

Irwin, S. A., Iglewicz, A., Nelesen, R. A., Lo, J. Y., Carr, C. H., Romero, S. D., & Lloyd, L. S. (2013). Daily oral ketamine for the treatment of depression and anxiety in patients receiving hospice care: A 28-day open-label proof-of-concept trial. *Journal of Palliative Medicine, 16*(8), 958-965. doi:10.1089/jpm.2012.0617

Isbister, G. K., Calver. L. A., Downes, M. A., & Page, C. B. (2016). Ketamine as rescue treatment for difficult-to-sedate severe acute behavioral disturbance in the emergency department. *Annals of Emergency Medicine, 67*(5), 581–587. Advance online publication. doi:10.1016/j.annemergmed.2015.11.028

JHP Pharmaceuticals, LLC. (2009). *Ketalar® ketamine hydrochloride injection [package insert]*. Rochester, MI: JHP Pharmaceuticals, LLC.

Johnson, M. W., Richards, W. A., & Griffiths, R. R. (2008). Human hallucinogen research: guidelines for safety. *Journal of Psychopharmacology, 22*(6), 603-620. doi:10.1177/0269881108093587

Kantrowitz, J. T., Halberstam, B., & Gangwisch, J. (2015). Single-dose ketamine followed by daily D-Cycloserine in treatment-resistant bipolar depression. *Journal of Clinical Psychiatry, 76*(6), 737–738.

Katalinic, N., Lai, R., Somogyi, A., Mitchell, P. B., Glue, P., & Loo, C. K. (2013). Ketamine as a new treatment for depression: A review of its efficacy and adverse effects. *Australia and New Zealand Journal of Psychiatry, 47*(8), 710–727. doi:10.1177/0004867413486842

Keitner, G., & Mansfield, A. (2012). Management of treatment-resistant depression. *Psychiatric Clinics of North America, 35*(1), 249-265. doi:10.1016/j.

psc.2011.11.004

Kohrs, R., & Durieux, M. E. (1998). Ketamine: Teaching an old drug new tricks. *Anesthesia & Analgesia, 87*(5), 1186-1193.

Kollmar, R., Markovic, K., Thuerauf, N., Schmitt, H., & Kornhuber, J. (2008). Ketamine followed by memantine for the treatment of major depression. *The Australian and New Zealand Journal of Psychiatry, 42*(2), 170-175-4. doi: 10.1080/00048670701787628

Krystal, J. H., Sanacora, G., & Duman, R. S. (2013). Rapid-acting glutamatergic antidepressants: The path to ketamine and beyond. *Biological Psychiatry, 73*(12), 1133-1141. doi:10.1016/j.biopsych.2013.03. 026

Lai, R., Katalinic, N., Glue, P., Somogyi, A. A., Mitchell, P. B., Leyden, J., ... & Loo, C. K. (2014). Pilot dose-response trial of IV ketamine in treatment-resistant depression. *World Journal of Biological Psychiatry, 15*(7), 579-584. doi:10.31 09/15622975.2014.922697

Lapidus, K. A., Levitch, C. F., Perez, A. M., Brallier, J. W., Parides, M. K., Soleimani, L., ... & Murrough, J. W. (2014). A randomized controlled trial of intranasal ketamine in major depressive disorder. *Biological Psychiatry, 76*(12), 970-976. doi:10.1016/j.biopsych.2014.03.026

Lara, D. R., Bisol, L. W., & Munari, L. R. (2013). Antidepressant, mood stabilizing and procognitive effects of very low dose sublingual ketamine in refractory unipolar and bipolar depression. *The International Journal of Neuropsychopharmacology, 16*(09), 2111-2117. doi:10.1017/S1461145713000485

Larkin, G. L., & Beautrais, A. L. (2011). A preliminary naturalistic study of low-dose ketamine for depression and suicide ideation in the emergency department. *The International Journal of Neuropsychopharmacology, 14*(08), 1127-1131. doi:10.1017/S1461145711000629

Lenze, E. J., Farber, N. B., Kharasch, E., Schweiger, J., Yingling, M., Olney, J., and Newcomer, J. W. (2016). Ninety-six hour ketamine infusion with co-administered clonidine for treatment-resistant depression: A pilot randomised controlled trial. *World Journal of Biological Psychiatry, 17*(3), 230–238. doi:10.3 109/15622975.2016.1142607

Li, C. T., Chen, M. H., Lin, W. C., Hong, C. J., Yang, B. H., Liu, R. S., ... Su, T. P. (2016). The effects of low-dose ketamine on the prefrontal cortex and amygdala in treatment-resistant depression: A randomized controlled study. *Human Brain Mapping, 37*(3), 1080–1090. doi:10.1002/hbm.23085

Liebrenz, M., Borgeat, A., Leisinger, R., & Stohler, R. (2007). Intravenous ketamine therapy in a patient with a treatment-resistant major depression. *Swiss Medical Weekly, 137*(15/16), 234.

Liebrenz, M., Stohler, R., & Borgeat, A. (2009). Repeated intravenous ketamine therapy in a patient with treatment-resistant major depression. *World Journal of Biological Psychiatry, 10*(4:2), 640-643. doi:10.1080/15622970701420481

Loo, C. K., Gálvez, V., O'Keefe, E, Mitchell, P. B., Hadzi-Pavlovic, D., Leyden, J., ... Glub, P. (2016). Placebo-controlled pilot trial testing dose titration and intravenous, intramuscular and subcutaneous routes for ketamine in depression. *Acta Psychiatrica Scandinavica, 134*(1), 48–56. doi:10.1111/acps.12572

Luckenbaugh, D. A., Ibrahim L., Brutsche, N., Franco-Chaves, J., Mathews, D., Marquardt, C. A., ... Zarate, C. A . (2012). Family history of alcohol dependence and antidepressant response to an *N*-methyl-D-aspartate antagonist in bipolar depression. *Bipolar Disorders, 14*(8), 880-887. doi:10.1111/bdi.12003

Luckenbaugh, D. A., Niciu, M. J., Ionescu, D. F., Nolan, N. M., Richards, E. M., Brutsche, N. E., ... & Zarate, C. A. (2014). Do the dissociative side effects of ketamine mediate its antidepressant effects? *Journal of Affective Disorders, 159*, 56-61. doi:10.1016/j.jad.2014.02.017

Machado-Vieira, R., Salvadore, G., Diaz-Granados, N., & Zarate, C. A. (2009). Ketamine and the next generation of antidepressants with a rapid onset of action. *Pharmacology & Therapeutics, 123*(2), 143-150. doi:10.1016/j.pharmthera.2009.02.010

Machado-Vieira, R., Yuan, P., Brutsche, N., Diaz-Granados, N., Luckenbaugh, D., Manji, H. K., & Zarate, C. A. (2009). Brain-derived neurotrophic factor and initial antidepressant response to an *N*-methyl-D-aspartate antagonist. *The Journal of Clinical Psychiatry, 70*(12), 1662. doi:10.4088/JCP.08m04659

Mathew, S. J., Manji, H. K., & Charney, D. S. (2008). Novel drugs and therapeutic targets for severe mood disorders. *Neuropsychopharmacology, 33*(9), 2080-2092. doi:10.1038/sj.npp.1301652

Mathew, S. J., Murrough, J. W., aan het Rot, M., Collins, K. A., Reich, D. L., & Charney, D. S. (2010). Riluzole for relapse prevention following intravenous ketamine in treatment-resistant depression: A pilot randomized, placebo-controlled continuation trial. *The International Journal of Neuropsychopharmacology, 13*(01), 71-82. doi:10.1017/S1461145709000169

Matthews, D., Henter, I., & Zarate, C. (2012). Targeting the glutamatergic system to treat major depressive disorder: Rationale and progress to date. *Drugs, 72*(10), 1313-1333. doi:10.2165/11633130-000000000-00000

McCloud, T.L., Caddy, C., Jochim, J., Rendell, J. M., Diamond, P. R., Shuttleworth, C., … Cipriani, A. (2015). Ketamine and other glutamate receptor modulators for depression in bipolar disorder in adults. Cochrane Database Syst Rev. 29 September 2015: CD011611.

McNulty, J. P., & Hahn, K.(2012). Compounded oral ketamine for severe depression, anxiety, and pain in a hospice patient with end-stage chronic obstructive pulmonary disease, cardiopulmonary failure, and severe renal insufficiency: A case report. *International Journal of Pharmaceutical Compounding*, 16(5), 364-368.

Messer, M., Haller, I., Larson, P., Pattison-Crisostomo, J., & Gessert, C. (2010). The use of a series of ketamine infusions in two patients with treatment-resistant depression. *The Journal of Neuropsychiatry and Clinical Neurosciences*, 22(4), 442-444. doi:10.1176/jnp.2010.22.4.442

Middela, S., & Pearce, I. (2011). Ketamine-induced vesicopathy: A literature review. *International Journal of Clinical Practice*, 65(1), 27–30.

Mithoefer, M. C., Wagner, M. T., Mithoefer, A. T., Jerome, L., Martin, S. F., Yazar-Klosinski, B., ... & Doblin, R. (2013). Durability of improvement in posttraumatic stress disorder symptoms and absence of harmful effects or drug dependency after 3, 4-methylenedioxymethamphetamine-assisted psychotherapy: A prospective long-term follow-up study. *Journal of Psychopharmacology*, 27(1), 28-39. doi:10.1177/0269881112456611

Mithoefer, M. C., Grob, C. S., & Brewerton, T. D. (2016). Novel psychopharmacological therapies for psychiatric disorders: Psilocybin and MDMA. *Lancet Psychiatry*, 3(5), 481–488.

Monteggia, L. M., Gideons, E., & Kavalali, E. T. (2013). The role of eukaryotic elongation factor 2 kinase in rapid antidepressant action of ketamine. *Biological Psychiatry*, 73(12), 1199-1203. doi:10.1016/j.biopsych.2012.09.006

Montgomery, S. A., & Åsberg, M. (1979). A new depression scale designed to be sensitive to change. *The British Journal of Psychiatry*, 134(4), 382-389. doi:10.1192/bjp.134.4.382

Morgan, C. J., Monaghan, L., & Curran, H. V. (2004). Beyond the K-hole: A 3-year longitudinal investigation of the cognitive and subjective effects of ketamine in recreational users who have substantially reduced their use of the drug. *Addiction*, 99(11), 1450-1461. doi:10.1111/j.1360-0443.2004.00879.x

Morris, H., & Wallach, J. (2014). From PCP to MXE: A comprehensive review of the non-medical use of dissociative drugs. *Drug Testing and Analysis*, 6(7–8),

614–632.

Murrough, J. W., Iosifescu, D. V., Chang, L. C., Al Jurdi, R. K., Green, C. M., Perez, A. M., ... Mathew, S. J. (2013a). Antidepressant efficacy of ketamine in treatment-resistant major depression: A two-site randomized controlled trial. *American Journal of Psychiatry, 170*(10), 1134-1142. doi:10.1176/appi.ajp.2013.13030392

Murrough, J. W., Perez, A. M., Mathew, S. J., & Charney, D. S. (2011). A case of sustained remission following an acute course of ketamine in treatment-resistant depression. *The Journal of Clinical Psychiatry, 72*(3), 414-415. doi:10.4088/JCP.10l06447blu

Murrough, J. W., Perez, A. M., Pillemer, S., Stern, J., Parides, M. K., aan het Rot, M., ... Iosifescu, D. V. (2013b). Rapid and longer-term antidepressant effects of repeated ketamine infusions in treatment-resistant major depression. *Biological Psychiatry, 74*(4), 250-256. doi:10.1016/j.biopsych.2012.06.022

Murrough, J. W., Burdick, K. E., Levitch, C. F., Perez, A. M., Brallier, J. W., Chang, L. C., … Iosifescu, D. V. (2015). Neurocognitive effects of ketamine and association with antidepressant response in individuals with treatment-resistant depression: A randomized controlled trial. *Neuropsychopharmacology, 40*(5), 1084–1090. doi:10.1038/npp.2014.298

Nagele, P., Duma, A., Kopec, M., Gebara, M. A., Parsoei, A., Walker, M., ... & Conway, C. R. (2014). Nitrous oxide for treatment-resistant major depression: A proof-of-concept trial. *Biological Psychiatry*, Advance online publication. doi:10.1016/j.biopsych.2014.11.016

Naughton, M., Clarke, G., Olivia, F. O., Cryan, J. F., & Dinan, T. G. (2014). A review of ketamine in affective disorders: Current evidence of clinical efficacy, limitations of use and pre-clinical evidence on proposed mechanisms of action. *Journal of Affective Disorders, 156*, 24-35. doi:10.1016/j.jad.2013.11.014

Nguyen, L, Marshalek, P. J., Weaver, C. B., Cramer, K. J., Pollard, S. E., & Matsumoto, R. R. (2015). Off-label use of transmucosal ketamine as a rapid-acting antidepressant: a retrospective chart review. *Neuropsychiatric Disease and Treatment, 11*, 2667–2673.

Niciu, M. J., Luckenbaugh, D. A., Ionescu, D. F., Richards, E. M., Voort, J. L. V., Ballard, E. D., ... & Zarate, C. A. (2014). Ketamine's Antidepressant efficacy is extended for at least four weeks in subjects with a family history of an alcohol use disorder. *International Journal of Neuropsychopharmacology, 18*(1), 1-7.

Niciu, M. J., Luckenbaugh, D. A., Ionescu, D. F., Mathews, D. C., Richards, E.

M., & Zarate Jr., C. A. (2013). Subanesthetic dose ketamine does not induce an affective switch in three independent samples of treatment-resistant major depression. *Biological Psychiatry, 74*(10), e23-e24.   doi:10.1016/j.biopsych.2013.01.038

Olin, B., Jayewardene, A. K., Bunker, M., & Moreno, F. (2012). Mortality and suicide risk in treatment-resistant depression: An observational study of the long-term impact of intervention. *PLOS ONE, 7*(10), e48002. doi:10.1371/journal.pone.0048002

Ostroff, R., Gonzales, M., & Sanacora, G. (2005). Antidepressant effect of ketamine during ECT. *American Journal of Psychiatry, 162*(7), 1385-1386. doi:10.1176/appi.ajp.162.7.1385

Overall, J. E., & Gorham, D. R. (1962). The brief psychiatric rating scale. *Psychological Reports, 10*(3), 799-812. doi:10.2466/pr0.1962.10.3.799

Papolos, D. F., Teicher, M. H., Faedda, G. L., Murphy, P., & Mattis, S. (2013). Clinical experience using intranasal ketamine in the treatment of pediatric bipolar disorder/fear of harm phenotype. *Journal of Affective Disorders, 147*(1), 431-436. doi:10.1016/j.jad.2012.08.040

Paslakis, G., Gilles, M., Meyer-Lindenberg, A., & Deuschle, M. (2010). Oral administration of the NMDA receptor antagonist *S*-ketamine as add-on therapy of depression: A case series. *Pharmacopsychiatry, 43*(01), 33-35. doi:10.1055/s-0029-1237375

Paul, R., Schaaff, N., Padberg, F., Moller, H., & Frodl, T. (2009). Comparison of racemic ketamine and *S*-ketamine in treatment-resistant major depression: Report of two cases. *World Journal of Biological Psychiatry, 10*(3), 241-244. doi:10.1080/15622970701714370

Permoda-Osip, A., Kisielewski, J., Bartkowska-Sniatkowska, A., & Rybakowski, J. K. (2015). Single ketamine infusion and neurocognitive performance in bipolar depression. *Pharmacopsychiatry, 48*(2), 78-79. doi:10.1055/s-0034-1394399

Phelps, L. E., Brutsche, N., Moral, J. R., Luckenbaugh, D. A., Manji, H. K., & Zarate, C. A. (2009). Family history of alcohol dependence and initial antidepressant response to an *N*-methyl-D-aspartate antagonist. *Biological Psychiatry, 65*(2), 181-184. doi:10.1016/j.biopsych.2008.09.029

Pioro, E. P., Brooks, B. R., Cummings, J., Schiffer, R., Thisted, R. A., Wynn, D., ... Kaye, R. (2010). Dextromethorphan plus ultra low-dose quinidine reduces pseudobulbar affect. *Annals of Neurology, 68*(5), 693–702.

Price, R. B., Iosifescu, D. V., Murrough, J. W., Chang, L. C., Al Jurdi, R. K.,

Iqbal, S. Z., ... & Mathew, S. J. (2014). Effects of ketamine on explicit and implicit suicidal cognition: A randomized controlled trial in treatment-resistant depression. *Depression and Anxiety, 31*(4), 335-343. doi:10.1002/da.22253

Price, R. B., Nock, M. K., Charney, D. S., & Mathew, S. J. (2009). Effects of intravenous ketamine on explicit and implicit measures of suicidality in treatment-resistant depression. *Biological Psychiatry, 66*(5), 522-526. doi:10.1016/j.biopsych.2009.04.029

Prommer, E. E. (2012) Ketamine for pain: An update of uses in palliative care. *Journal of Palliative Medicine, 15*(4), 474-483. doi:10.1089/jpm.2011.0244

Raeder, J. C., & Stenseth, L. B. (2000). Ketamine: A new look at an old drug. *Current Opinion in Anesthesiology, 13*(4), 463-468. doi:10.1097/00001503-200008000-00011

Rasmussen, K. G., Lineberry, T. W., Galardy, C. W., Kung, S., Lapid, M. I., Palmer, B. A., ... Frye, M. A. (2013). Serial infusions of low-dose ketamine for major depression. *Journal of Psychopharmacology, 27*(5), 444-450. doi:10.1177/0269881113478283

Reich, D. L., & Silvay, G. (1989). Ketamine: An update on the first twenty-five years of clinical experience. *Canadian Journal of Anaesthesia, 36*(2), 186-197. doi:10.1007/BF03011442

Rodriguez, C. I., Kegeles, L. S., Levinson, A., Feng, T., Marcus, S. M., Vermes, D., ... & Simpson, H. B. (2013). Randomized controlled crossover trial of ketamine in obsessive-compulsive disorder: Proof-of-concept. *Neuropsychopharmacology, 38*(12), 2475-2483. doi:10.1038/npp.2013.150

Rush, A. J., Trivedi, M. H., Wisniewski, S. R., Nierenberg, A. A., Stewart, J. W., Warden, D., … Fava, M. (2006). Acute and longer-term outcomes in depressed outpatients requiring one or several treatment steps: A STAR*D report. *American Journal of Psychiatry, 163*(11), 1905-1917. doi:10.1176/ajp.2006.163.11.1905

Ryan, W. C., Marta, C. J., & Koek, R. J. (2014). Ketamine and depression: A review. *International Journal of Transpersonal Studies, 33*(2), 40–74.

Rybakowski, J. K., Permoda-Osip, A., Skibinska, M., Adamski, R., & Bartkowska-Sniatkowska, A. (2013). Single ketamine infusion in bipolar depression resistant to antidepressants: Are neurotrophins involved? *Human Psychopharmacology: Clinical and Experimental, 28*(1), 87-90. doi:10.1002/hup.2271

Sackeim, H. A. (2001). The definition and meaning of treatment-resistant depression. *Journal of Clinical Psychiatry, 62*(Suppl. 16), 10-17.

Salvadore, G., Cornwell, B. R., Colon-Rosario, V., Coppola, R., Grillon, C., Zarate, C. A., & Manji, H. K. (2009). Increased anterior cingulate cortical activity in response to fearful faces: A neurophysiological biomarker that predicts rapid antidepressant response to ketamine. *Biological Psychiatry, 65*(4), 289-295. doi:10.1016/j.biopsych.2008.08.014

Salvadore, G., Cornwell, B. R., Sambataro, F., Latov, D., Colon-Rosario, V., Carver, F., … Zarate, C. A. (2010). Anterior cingulate desynchronization and functional connectivity with the amygdala during a working memory task predict rapid antidepressant response to ketamine. *Neuropsychopharmacology, 35*(7), 1415-1422. doi:10.1038/npp.2010.24

Salvadore, G., Van Der Veen, J. W., Zhang, Y., Marenco, S., Machado-Vieira, R., Baumann, J., … Zarate, C. A. (2012). An investigation of amino-acid neurotransmitters as potential predictors of clinical improvement to ketamine in depression. *International Journal of Neuro-Psychopharmacology, 15*(8), 1063. doi:10.1017/S1461145711001593

Sampath, H., Sharma, I., & Dutta, S. (2016). Treatment of suicidal depression with ketamine in rapid cycling bipolar disorder. *Asia-Pacific Psychiatry, 8*(1), 98–101.

Schak, K. M., Vande Voort, J. L., Johnson, E. K, Kung, S., Leung, J. G., Rasmussen, K. G., … Frye, M. A. (2016). Potential risks of poorly monitored ketamine use in depression treatment. *American Journal of Psychiatry, 173*(3), 215–218.

Segmiller, F., Ruther, T., Linhardt, A., Padberg, F., Berger, M., Pogarell, … Schule, C. (2013). Repeated *S*-ketamine infusions in therapy resistant depression: A case series. *The Journal of Clinical Pharmacology, 53*(9), 996-998. doi:10.1002/jcph.122

Shahani, R., Streutker, C., Dickson, B., & Stewart, R. J. (2007). Ketamine-associated ulcerative cystitis: A new clinical entity. *Urology, 69*(5), 810-812. doi:10.1016/j.urology.2007.01.038

Shiroma, P. R., Albott, C. S., Johns, B., Thuras, P., Wels, J., & Lim, K. O. (2014a). Neurocognitive performance and serial intravenous subanesthetic ketamine in treatment-resistant depression. *International Journal of Neuropsychopharmacology, 17*(11), 1805–1813.

Shiroma, P. R., Johns, B., Kuskowski, M., Wels, J., Thuras, P., Albott, C., & Lim, K. O. (2014b). Augmentation of response and remission to serial intravenous subanesthetic ketamine in treatment resistant depression. *Journal of Affective*

Disorders, 155, 123-129. doi:10.1016/j.jad.2013.10.036

Singh, J. B., Fedgchin, M., Daly, E. J., De Boer, P., Cooper, K., Lim, P., ... Van Nueten, L. A. (2016). Double-blind, randomized, placebo-controlled, dose-frequency study of intravenous ketamine in patients with treatment-resistant depression. *American Journal of Psychiatry, 173*(8), 816–826. doi:10.1176/appi.ajp.2016.16010037

Skolnick, P., Layer, R., Popik, P., Nowak, G., Paul, I., & Trullas, R. (1996). Adaptation of *N*-methyl-D-aspartate (NMDA) receptors following antidepressant treatment: Implications for the pharmacotherapy of depression. *Pharmacopsychiatry, 29*(1), 23-26. doi:10.1055/s-2007-979537

Sos, P., Klirova, M., Novak, T., Kohutova, B., Horacek, J., & Palenicek, T. (2013). Relationship of ketamine's antidepressant and psychotomimetic effects in unipolar depression. *Neuroendocrinology Letters, 34*(4), 101-107.

Srivastava, S., Gangwar, R. S., & Kumar, A. (2015). Safety and efficacy of ketamine infusion in late onset depression, and conversion to treatment response. *Indian Journal of Psychiatry, 57*(3), 328–329.

Stefanczyk-Sapieha, L., Oneschuk, D., & Demas, M. (2008). Intravenous ketamine "burst" for refractory depression in a patient with advanced cancer. *Journal of Palliative Medicine, 11*(9), 1268-1271. doi:10.1089/jpm.2008.9828

Storr, T., & Quibell, R. (2009). Can ketamine prescribed for pain cause damage to the urinary tract? *Journal of Palliative Medicine, 23*(7), 670-672. doi:10.1177/0269216309106828

Szymkowicz, S. M., Finnegan, N., & Dale, R. M. (2013). A 12-month naturalistic observation of three patients receiving repeat intravenous ketamine infusions for their treatment-resistant depression. *Journal of Affective Disorders, 147*(1), 416-420. doi:10.1016/j.jad.2012.10.015

Szymkowicz, S. M., Finnegan, N., & Dale, R. M. (2014). Failed response to repeat intravenous ketamine infusions in geriatric patients with major depressive disorder. *Journal of Clinical Psychopharmacology, 34*(2), 285-286. doi:10.1097/JCP.0000000000000090

Tam, Y. H., Ng, C. F., Pang, K. K., Yee, C. H., Chu, W. C., Leung, V. Y., ... Lai, P. B. (2014). One-stop clinic for ketamine-associated uropathy: Report on service delivery model, patients' characteristics and non-invasive investigations at baseline by a cross-sectional study in a prospective cohort of 318 teenagers and young adults. *BJU International, 114*(5), 754–760.

Thakurta, R. G., Das, R., Bhattacharya, A. K., Saha, D., Sen, S., Singh, O. P.,

& Bisui, B. (2012). Rapid response with ketamine on suicidal cognition in resistant depression. *Indian Journal of Psychological Medicine, 34*(2), 170. doi:10.4103/0253-7176.101793

Thakurta, R. G., Ray, P., Kanji, D., Das, R., Bisui, B., & Singh, O. P. (2012). Rapid antidepressant response with ketamine: Is it the solution to resistant depression? *Indian Journal of Psychological Medicine, 34*(1), 56. doi:10.4103/0253-7176.96161

Valentine, G. W., Mason, G. F., Gomez, R., Fasula, M., Watzl, J., Pittman, B., ... Sanacora, G. (2011). The antidepressant effect of ketamine is not associated with changes in occipital amino acid neurotransmitter content as measured by [1H]-MRS. *Psychiatry Research: Neuroimaging, 191*(2), 122-127. doi:10.1016/j.pscychresns.2010.10.009

Vasavada, M. M., Leaver, A. M., Espinoza, R. T., Joshi, S. H., Njau, S. N., Woods, R. P., & Narr, K. L. (2016). Structural connectivity and response to ketamine therapy in major depression: A preliminary study. *Journal of Affective Disorders, 190,* 836–841. doi: 10.1016/j.jad.2015.11.018

Vollenweider, F., Leenders, K., Oye, I., Hell, D., & Angst, J. (1997). Differential psychopathology and patterns of cerebral glucose utilisation produced by (*S*)- and (*R*)-ketamine in healthy volunteers using positron emission tomography (PET). *European Neuropsychopharmacology, 7*(1), 25-38. doi:10.1016/S0924-977X(96)00042-9

Vollenweider, F., Leenders, K., Scharfetter, C., Antonini, A., Maguire, P., Missimer, J., & Angst, J. (1997). Metabolic hyperfrontality and psychopathology in the ketamine model of psychosis using positron emission tomography (PET) and [18F] fluorodeoxyglucose (FDG). *European Neuropsychopharmacology, 7*(1), 9-24. doi:10.1016/S0924-977X(96)00039-9

Wani, A., Trevino, K., Marnell, P., & Husain, M. M. (2013). Advances in brain stimulation for depression. *Annals of Clinical Psychiatry: Official Journal of the American Academy of Clinical Psychiatrists, 25*(3), 217-224.

Wan, L. B., Levitch, C. F., Perez, A. M., Brallier, J. W., Iosifescu, D. V., Chang, L. C., ... Murrough, J. W. (2015). Ketamine safety and tolerability in clinical trials for treatment-resistant depression. *Journal of Clinical Psychiatry, 76*(3), 247–252.

Wein, A. J. (2013). Re: The prevalence and natural history of urinary symptoms among recreational ketamine users. *The Journal of Urology, 190*(5), 1816-1818. doi:10.1016/j.juro.2013.07.091

Winstock, A. R., Mitcheson, L., Gillatt, D. A., & Cottrell, A. M. (2012). The prevalence and natural history of urinary symptoms among recreational ketamine users. *BJU International, 110,* 1762–1766.

Wu, P., Wang, Q., Huang, Z., Wang, J., Wu, Q., & Lin, T. (2016). Clinical staging of ketamine-associated urinary dysfunction: A strategy for assessment and treatment. *World Journal of Urology, 34,* 1329-1336. doi:10.1007/s00345-016-1759-9

Yang, C., Shirayama Y., Zhang J. C., Ren, Q., Yao, W., Ma, M. … Hashimoto, K. (2015). *R*-ketamine: A rapid-onset and sustained antidepressant without psychotomimetic side effects. *Translational Psychiatry, 5,* e632. doi:10.1038/tp.2015.136

Yang, C., Zhou, Z., Gao, Z., Shi, J., & Yang, J. (2013). Acute increases in plasma mammalian target of rapamycin, glycogen synthase kinase-3beta, and eukaryotic elongation factor 2 phosphorylation after ketamine treatment in three depressed patients. *Biological Psychiatry, 73*(12), 35-36. doi:10.1016/j.biopsych.2012.07.022

Yang, C., Zhou, Z., & Yang, J. (2011). Be prudent of ketamine in treating resistant depression in patients with cancer. *Journal of Palliative Medicine, 14*(5), 537. doi:10.1089/jpm.2010.0525

Young, R., Biggs, J., Ziegler, V., & Meyer, D. (1978). A rating scale for mania: Reliability, validity and sensitivity. *The British Journal of Psychiatry, 133*(5), 429-435. doi:10.1192/bjp.133.5.429

Yek, J., Sundaram, P., Aydin, H., Kuo, T., Ng, L. G. (2015). The clinical presentation and diagnosis of ketamine-associated urinary tract dysfunction in Singapore. *Singapore Medical Journal, 56*(12), 660–664.

Zanicotti, C. G., Perez, D., & Glue, P. (2012). Mood and pain responses to repeat dose intramuscular ketamine in a depressed patient with advanced cancer. *Journal of Palliative Medicine,* 15(4), 400-403. doi:10.1089/jpm.2011.0314

Zanicotti, C. G., Perez, D., & Glue, P. (2013). Case report: Long-term mood response to repeat dose intramuscular ketamine in a depressed patient with advanced cancer. *Journal of Palliative Medicine, 16*(7), 719-720. doi:10.1089/jpm.2013.0057

Zarate, C. A., Brutsche, N. E., Ibrahim, L., Franco-Chaves, J., Diaz-Granados, N., Cravchik, A., … Luckenbaugh, D. A. (2012). Replication of ketamine's antidepressant efficacy in bipolar depression: A randomized controlled add-on trial. *Biological Psychiatry, 71*(11), 939-946. doi;10.1016/j.biopsych.2011.12.010

Zarate, C. A., Mathews, D., Ibrahim, L., Chaves, J. F., Marquardt, C., Ukoh, I.,

... & Luckenbaugh, D. A. (2013). A randomized trial of a low-trapping non-selective *N*-methyl-D-aspartate channel blocker in major depression. *Biological Psychiatry*, *74*(4), 257-264. doi:10.1016/j.biopsych.2012.10.019

Zarate, C. A., Singh, J. B., Carlson, P. J., Brutsche, N. E., Ameli, R., Luckenbaugh, D. A., ... Manji, H. K. (2006). A randomized trial of an *N*-methyl-D-aspartate antagonist in treatment-resistant major depression. *Archives of General Psychiatry*, *63*(8), 856-864. doi:10.1001/archpsyc.63.8.856

Zarate, C., Duman, R. S., Liu, G., Sartori, S., Quiroz, J., & Murck, H. (2013). New paradigms for treatment-resistant depression. *Annals of The New York Academy of Sciences*, *1292*(1), 21-31. doi:10.1111/nyas.12223

Zhang, J., Li, S., & Hashimoto, K. (2014). *R* (-)-ketamine shows greater potency and longer lasting antidepressant effects than *S* (+)-ketamine. *Pharmacology Biochemistry & Behavior*, *116*,137-141. doi:10.1016/j.pbb.2013.11.033

Zigman, D., & Blier, P. (2013). Urgent ketamine infusion rapidly eliminated suicidal ideation for a patient with major depressive disorder: A case report. *Journal of Clinical Psychopharmacology*, *33*(2), 270-272. doi:10.1097/JCP.0b013e3182856865

Zigmond, A. S., & Snaith, R. P. (1983). The hospital anxiety and depression scale. *Acta Psychiatrica Scandinavica*, *67*(6), 361-370. doi:10.1111/j.1600-0447.1983.tb09716.x

Sustainable Ketamine Therapy: An Overview of Where We are and Where We May Go

Stephen J. Hyde, M.D.

THE FIRST TANTALIZING GLIMPSE OF EVIDENCE that ketamine could help patients with treatment-resistant major depression emerged 15 years ago with the publication of the Berman et al. study (2000), which used sub-anesthetic doses of ketamine (0.5mg/kg bodyweight) slowly infused intravenously over 40 minutes. The positive outcomes from this double-blind, placebo-controlled trial have since been replicated by different research groups in the United States, and more recently there have been papers describing similar improvement in patients suffering from bipolar depression and acute suicidality. There have also been preliminary studies indicating that low-dose intravenous ketamine can help patients with OCD, PTSD, and eating disorders. In recent years research into the use of ketamine for psychiatric disorders has moved slowly from the domain of the so-called "lunatic fringe" to relative respectability.

So where are we now? There is now firm evidence presented in a number of recent meta-analyses (Fond et al., 2014; McGirr et al., 2014; Caddy, Giaroli, White, Shergill, & Tracy, 2014) that a single dose of intravenous ketamine can induce a rapid improvement in mood lasting for a week or longer. There have also been studies showing a more lasting benefit following the administration of multiple doses of ketamine (aan het Rot et al., 2015).

Although the large, multicenter, randomized, double-blind, placebo-controlled trials are yet to be done (thankfully the Australian government is funding such a study beginning mid-2016), many doctors and patients have decided that the best currently available evidence indicates a favorable risk/benefit ratio for treatment-resistant psychiatric conditions and have proceeded to use ketamine on an off-label basis. This approach has been supported in Australia by the Royal Australian and New Zealand College of Psychiatrists, who have described the use of ketamine to be a "novel" and "innovative" (not "experimental") therapy suitable, with appropriate safeguards, for patients suffering from treatment-resistant depression (RANZCP, 2015).

In the United States the majority of doctors prescribing ketamine have continued the original Berman approach of using the intravenous route of administration, giving courses of injections in clinic settings with appropriate monitoring. Some of these clinics are run primarily by anesthetists. Although this has been an understandable development, elsewhere a much wider range of administration methods has been, and continues to be, explored. This is very important, as the use of the intravenous route requires regular clinic attendance over two to three weeks for a course of therapy. The whole process can be inconvenient, is beyond most psychiatrists' skill-sets to administer, and, most importantly, is financially out of reach for many patients, particularly when repeated courses are required. I have summarized the published literature on the use of these alternative approaches below, and more detailed information can be found in my recently published book, *Ketamine for Depression* (Hyde, 2015).

Oral administration

G. Paslakis from the Department of Psychiatry, Mannheim, Germany, in 2009 (Paslakis, Gilles, Meyer-Lindenberg, & Deuschle, 2010) described the use of oral S-ketamine at a dose of 1.25mg/kg in four patients. The ketamine was started simultaneously with venlafaxine, continued in doses up to 150mg daily over two weeks and then stopped, with the venlafaxine being continued thereafter. Two of the patients improved rapidly within a week and sustained this improvement when taking venlafaxine alone. There were no problems with side effects.

Scott Irwin working at the San Diego Hospice in 2010 (Irwin & Iglewicz, 2010) reported the use of 27mg of oral ketamine added to regular medications for two patients with terminal illnesses and depression. Both patients had a rapid and sustained response to a single dose. In 2013, Irwin published the results of a further study in which 14 patients in palliative care were given oral ketamine for 28 days at a dose of 0.5mg/kg body weight. Eight patients who completed the course had positive results with improvements evident by day 3 for anxiety symptoms and day

14 for depression. Side effects were mild and included diarrhea and restlessness.

In 2015 (Iglewicz et al., 2015), Irwin described a retrospective study of 31 hospice patients with depression given oral ketamine; in this study response was usually apparent in the first three days. There were no serious side effects.

Angelo de Gioannis and colleagues working in Brisbane, Australia, have treated more than six hundred patients in the past three years using oral ketamine with around 66% responding and 50% remitting. Typically patients have been given ketamine twice weekly in a monitored clinic setting with concurrent psychotherapy. Average doses of ketamine given were 100–200mg with neither serious side effects nor problems with abuse or dependence experienced. A study is currently being prepared for publication.

Professor R. Schoevers from the Department of Psychiatry, Gröningen, Germany, has a review article on the use of oral ketamine due for publication shortly in the *British Journal of Psychiatry* and, with colleagues, he has embarked on a pilot study using the oral approach.

Sublingual administration

Diogo Lara and colleagues from Porte Alegre, Brazil, in 2013 (Lara, Bisol, & Munari, 2013) published the results of a trial of giving ultra-low-dose sublingual ketamine to 26 patients with treatment-resistant unipolar and bipolar depression. Following an initial test dose of 10mg patients took further doses at home according to response, typically at intervals between two and seven days. They achieved a 77% response rate with very few side effects. There was no reported abuse or dependence.

After reading about this trial, I began treating my long-term, treatment-resistant patients in a similar fashion. After a year of using this approach, around 70% (of 18) have responded and 40% have remitted. These patients had previously endured multiple trials of medication and psychotherapy, many had received ECT, and one had undergone psychosurgery. Side effects from the ketamine have been mild and easily managed and there have been no indications of abuse or dependence. Effective doses have ranged between 10mg and 100mg and using further courses of ketamine after relapses has been successful. The process is explained further in *Ketamine for Depression*. (Hyde, 2015)

"Cathy," a contributor to the Medchat online forum in 2014, described her successful use of sublingual ketamine using a dose of 1.6mg/kg every three to five days for three months with benefit for both anxiety and depressive symptoms.

L. Nguyen and colleagues (2015), from West Virginia, published a retrospective case note review of 17 patients with treatment-resistant depression using a transmucosal strategy (liquid was placed on the tongue and held until absorbed). The dose of ketamine prescribed varied between 0.5mg/kg and 1mg/kg given in addition to regular medications. The dosage interval was seven to fourteen days, side effects were mild and transient, and they described a 76% response rate.

Varun Jaitly, a British anesthetist who treated 249 patients with treatment-resistant pain conditions between 2000 and 2012, has explored the safety and efficacy of the prolonged use of sublingual ketamine. He published on his management of 32 of these patients who had been taking ketamine daily for more than two years as part of their therapy for chronic severe pain conditions (Jaitly, 2013). After an initial monitored sublingual dose of 20mg, patients took daily doses, usually three times a day, at home. Patients did not experience problems with either urinary or hepatic symptoms and there was no evidence to suggest abuse or dependence. Most of his patients do not take more than 120mg of ketamine daily

Intranasal administration

Demitri Papolos, in the *Journal of Affective Disorders*, outlined their use of intranasal ketamine for the treatment of pediatric bipolar disorder (Papolos, Teicher, Faedda, Murphy & Mattis, 2013). This was a retrospective study of the chart records of 12 youths aged 6 to 19 out of a total of 40 patients who had been treated. The initial dose given was 10mg of intranasal ketamine, building to between 30 and 120mg a day, taken at intervals of three to seven days. Positive effects were reported on depressive, anxiety, and manic symptoms; concurrent medications were gradually withdrawn and some patients were then managed on ketamine alone. Side effects were dose-dependent and tolerable; there was no reported abuse or dependence.

Patricia Clark (2014) described treating a patient with a 10-year history of recurrent major depression and migraine with 50mg of intranasal ketamine given twice weekly for four months. Complete remission was attained after two weeks, and her mood remained stable over the four-month period, with some mild mood shifts the day prior to a few of the treatments. Side effects were mild and transient.

K. A. Lapidus from the Mt. Sinai group (Lapidus et al., 2014) presented the results of a randomized, double-blind, placebo-controlled, crossover trial of intranasal ketamine 50mg for treatment-resistant depression. This was a single-dose study with a saline placebo and the ketamine recipients showed a 44% response after 24 hours compared to a 6% response for the placebo. There were no problematical side effects.

"Esketamine" development

The pharmaceutical company Johnson & Johnson commenced Phase 3 trials of an intranasal preparation of S-ketamine in October 2015. This preparation has been designated a "breakthrough therapy" by the FDA. All being well, final approval is anticipated in 2018.

Subcutaneous administration

McNulty in 2012 (19) reported a single case study of a patient with a terminal illness experiencing pain, anxiety, and depression. He was treated with one 0.5mg/kg dose of subcutaneous ketamine, which gave him substantial relief for 80 hours. He was then maintained on daily oral ketamine with continuing benefit and minimal side effects.

In 2014 Associate Professor Graham Barrett from the University of Melbourne, Australia, became the consulting doctor for the Aura medical group, which opened clinics in Melbourne, Sydney, and Brisbane. This group reported treating more than five hundred patients with subcutaneous injections of ketamine, typically 40–60 mg twice a week for six weeks and then weekly for six weeks thereafter. They described a 65% success rate in treating "severe depression." Dr. Barrett personally treated fifty patients over a period of eight months and achieved a 70% response rate—he plans to report his findings shortly.

Gálvez, et al. (2014) from Australia described in a case report the use of subcutaneous ketamine at doses 0.1–0.2 mg/kg in the treatment of a 62-year-old woman with recurrent major depression. After treatment with the higher dose she remitted for five months and her subsequent relapse was successfully treated with a longer course of ketamine.

Intramuscular administration

From New Zealand, Claudia Zanicotti, with Perez and Glue (2012), described a single case study of a woman with terminal cancer who was treated with 1mg/kg of ketamine intramuscularly weekly for seven months with full remission of her depression and no untoward side effects.

Paul Glue with Gulati, Le Nedelec, and Duffull (2011) from Dunedin, New Zealand, investigated the effects of varying doses of intramuscular ketamine in two patients with treatment-refractory depression. They used doses of 0.5mg/kg, 0.7mg/kg and 1.0mg/kg and found that the higher the dose, the better the scores, with 15%, 44% and 70% improvements respectively.

Cusin with Hilton, Nierenberg, and Fava (2012) described the use of repeated doses of intramuscular ketamine in two patients with treatment-refractory bipolar 2 disorders. They gave doses of 32–100mg every three to four days for several months. Both patients improved, with one experiencing brief dissociative side effects and headaches at the time of the infusions. This patient interestingly had a positive response to an initial course of intravenous ketamine infusions, but when she relapsed 19 days later she was not helped by subsequent courses of oral and then intranasal ketamine. However, she then remitted after two intramuscular injections.

From India, Harihar Chilukuri with Dasari and Srinivas (2013) reported on their management of two patients with treatment-resistant depression given intramuscular ketamine as an alternative to ECT. They used 0.5mg/kg doses with the positive response to the first treatment lasting a week and ongoing benefit being obtained from follow-up injections.

In 2014, Chilukuri with another group compared the use of intravenous ketamine (0.5mg/kg) with two doses of intramuscular ketamine (0.25mg/kg and 0.5mg/kg) in three groups of treatment-resistant depressive patients. There were nine patients in each group and outcomes were similar in all three, with a 60% response rate and rapid mood improvements lasting for three days on average.

"Foreigner" posted on the Bluelight online ketamine forum (2013) on his use of repeated hourly intramuscular injections of ketamine over seven days to treat his depression. He began with 10mg and aimed for a dose causing a feeling of mild inebriation. He maintained this dose to a "saturation point" (usually by the third day), where this effect disappeared, then gradually lengthened the time between injections. He and others reported positive effects from this regime.

Terrence Early (2014) in a paper in the *International Journal of Transpersonal Studies* described having treated 120 patients with more than one thousand doses of intramuscular ketamine over the preceding eight years in association with his colleague Jeffrey Becker. Their usual dose was 0.5mg/kg and the ketamine was given as part of a comprehensive psychotherapeutic program. Side effects were mild, with nausea being the most common; there were no reported instances of abuse or dependence.

Continuous ketamine infusions

Intravenous ketamine in psychiatry is usually given slowly over 40 minutes but there have been two interesting overseas studies using more prolonged infusions.

In 1998, Professor I. H. Mills and colleagues from the University of Cambridge,

England (Mills, Park, Manara & Merriman, 1998), outlined their use of 10-hour continuous intravenous ketamine infusions to treat 15 patients with severe chronic eating disorders using a dose of 20mg/hour. Nine of the fifteen responded, with prolonged remissions after receiving between two and nine infusions given at intervals between five and twenty-one days according to clinical response. Side effects were tolerable and there were no issues with abuse or dependence reported.

From Australia in 2006, Graeme Correll and Graham Futter described giving five-day continuous ketamine infusions to two patients with treatment-resistant depression. They began with a dose of 15mg hourly and titrated to a point where patients felt "heady" but were not dissociated. Both patients remitted and one had a positive response to a further infusion when he relapsed several months later.

Pain physicians are increasingly using continuous subcutaneous infusions of ketamine as a more practical alternative to the intravenous route and I have recently treated a patient with treatment-refractory depression for five days using this method.

Summary
Overall the clinical data for these different modes of administration suggest that 70% response rates and 30–40% remission rates are attainable for patients who have not responded well to a range of current treatments including psychotherapy and, for some, ECT.

Safety
Over the past 50 years ketamine has been one of the most widely studied agents in our medical armamentarium—there are more than 200 trials currently planned or underway in the United States alone, approximately 50 being focused on psychiatric conditions. In 2008 Reuben Strayer published a review of more than 70,000 anesthetic cases, finding only one ketamine-related death in a medically compromised patient (Strayer & Nelson, 2008). Allergic responses are very rare (four reported by 2012) and non–life threatening. Repeated intravenous infusions for the treatment of pain have been associated with rare instances of elevated liver enzymes and urinary symptoms, all of which have resolved with cessation of the therapy.

There have been no published reports of abuse, dependence, or addiction arising from properly supervised medical prescription of ketamine, as opposed to the evidence that 5–10% of those who use ketamine "recreationally" can go on to develop dependence and addiction with serious physical and psychological consequences. This does not suggest we should be cavalier in our prescribing, but it does give lie to the oft-repeated claims by some researchers that ketamine is unsafe and unsuitable for more widespread clinical use.

Where to from here? For ketamine practitioners and their patients, the most important question is not "does it work?" but rather, "how can it be most safely, effectively, affordably, and practically administered?" And crucially, "how can initial benefits be sustained?"

Whereas the current evidence base for routes other than intravenous can be characterized as "a mile wide and a foot deep," there are now clear indications that the non-injection approaches are effective, give rise to low levels of side effects, do not carry a high risk for abuse or dependence, and can be prescribed and monitored by all psychiatrists as part of a comprehensive treatment plan. Apart from the acutely suicidal and the severely ill patients where speed of response is critical, the clinical approach of starting with low doses and titrating both the dose and dosage intervals according to response ensures that side effects and costs are minimized. We need studies comparing the effects of different doses, different routes of administration, and varying dosage intervals.

Strategies currently being trialed to manage partial responses to ketamine include dose-escalation, using alternative routes, adding lithium, nuedexta (a combination of dextromethorphan and quinidine), D-cycloserine, and incorporating a variety of electrostimulation methods. In addition, using concurrent psychotherapy and intensive management of residual symptoms with particular attention to sleep, diet, and exercise are also recommended.

A variety of maintenance strategies to sustain remissions are being explored, including giving preemptive doses of ketamine if there is a clear periodicity of relapse (Messer & Haller, 2013) and treating relapses rapidly (Szymkowicz, Finnegan, & Daleb, 2012). For every patient, before giving ketamine, it is important to discuss the options in the event that the outcome is not positive: e.g., trialing the combination of sleep deprivation, chronotherapy, and lithium; exploring electrostimulation; and investigating the use of low-dose buprenorphine.

There is mounting evidence that for both the acutely suicidal and those suffering from chronic depression, time lost is brain lost is lives lost. Finding more rapidly acting and more effective therapies is essential. And so to ketamine. On one hand we have people suffering from debilitating, life-shortening illnesses, and on the other a new treatment with all its residual doubts and uncertainties. In my experience, patients when presented with the available facts have overwhelmingly elected to try ketamine and have welcomed the opportunity to do so.

Ketamine does not exist in nature—it is purely a product of the human imagination and its uses are only limited by our lack of imagination. From stress inoculation to infusions for the severely ill, from augmenting psychotherapy to helping the acutely suicidal, there are opportunities for all to explore its benefits.

Most importantly at an individual and societal level we need to avoid premature closure; the ketamine mansion has many rooms, there are many different brains, different types of depression, different approaches that can work and there is "no one way, just the way that gets you there."

For ketamine therapy to be sustainable, we must make the best use of available resources; continue to look for biomarkers that can predict response; employ strategies that maximize the benefits and minimize the risks; and never cease from exploring ways of making this exciting new treatment accessible and affordable for all.

In the end, ketamine is many things to many people, but most of all it is hope.

References

aan het Rot, M., Collins, K. A., Murrough, J. W., Perez, A. M., Reich, D. L., Charney, D. S., & Mathew, S. J. (2015). Safety and efficacy of repeated-dose intravenous ketamine for treatment-resistant depression. *Biological Psychiatry*, *67*(2), 139-145. doi:10.1016/j.biopsych.2009.08.038

Berman, R. M., Cappiello, A., Anand, A, Oren, D. A., Heninger, G. R., Charney, D. S., & Krystal, J. H. (2000). Antidepressant effects of ketamine in depressed patients. *Biological Psychiatry, 47*(4), 351–354.

Caddy, C., Giaroli, G., White, T. P., Shergill, S. S., & Tracy, D. K. (2014). Ketamine as the prototype glutamatergic antidepressant: Pharmacodynamic actions, and a systematic review and meta-analysis of efficacy. *Therapeutic Advances in Psychopharmacology*, *4*(2), 75–99. doi:10.1177/2045125313507739

Cathy. (2014, May 21). MedsChat.com. Retrieved from www.medschat.com

Chilukuri, H., Dasari, P., & Srinivas, J. S. (2013). Intramuscular ketamine in acute depression: A report on two cases. *Indian Journal of Psychiatry*, *55*, 186–188.

Chilukuri, H., Reddy, N. P., Pathapati, R. M., Manu, A. N., Jollu, S., & Shaik, A. B. (2014). Acute antidepressant effects of intramuscular versus intravenous ketamine. *Indian Journal of Psychological Medicine, 36*(1), 71–76. doi: 10.4103/0253-7176.127258

Clark, P. (2014). Treatment-refractory depression: A case of successful treatment with intranasal ketamine 10%. *Annals of Clinical Psychiatry, 26*(2), 145.

Correll, G. E. & Futter, G. E. (2006). Two case studies of patients with major depressive disorder given low-dose (subanesthetic) ketamine infusions. *Pain Medicine, 7*(1), 92–95.

Cusin, C., Hilton, G. Q., Nierenberg, A. A., & Fava, M. (2012). Long-term maintenance with intramuscular ketamine for treatment-resistant bipolar II depression. *American Journal of Psychiatry, 169*, 868–869.

Early, T. S. (2014). Making ketamine work in the long run. *International Journal of Transpersonal Studies, 33*(2), 141–150.

Fond, G., Loundou, A., Rabu, C., MacGregor, A., Lançon, C., Brittner, M., … Boyer, L. (2014). Ketamine administration in depressive disorders: A systematic review and meta-analysis. *Psychopharmacology, 231*(18), 3663-3676. doi:10.1007/s00213-014-3664-5

Foreigner. (2013). Bluelight ketamine forum. Retrieved from http://www.bluelight.org/vb/forum

Gálvez, V., O'Keefe, E., Cotiga, L., Leyden, J., Harper, S., Glue, P., … Loo, C. K. (2014). Long-lasting effects of a single subcutaneous dose of ketamine for treating melancholic depression: A case report. *Biological Psychiatry, 76*(3), e1–e2.

Glue, P., Gulati, A., Le Nedelec, M., & Duffull, S. (2011). Dose- and exposure-response to ketamine in depression biological psychiatry. *Biological Psychiatry, 70*(4), e9–e10. doi:10.1016/j.biopsych.2010.11

Hyde, S. J. (2015). *Ketamine for depression.* Bloomington, IN: Xlibris.

Iglewicz, A., Morrison, K., Nelesen, R. A., Zhan, T., Iglewicz, B., Fairman, N., … Irwin, S.A. (2015). Ketamine for the treatment of depression in patients receiving hospice care: A retrospective medical record review of thirty-one cases. *Psychosomatics, 56*(4), 329–337. doi:10.1016/j.psym.2014.05.005

Irwin, S. A., & Iglewicz, A. (2010). Oral ketamine for the rapid treatment of depression and anxiety in patients receiving hospice care. *Journal of Palliative Medicine, 13*(7), 903–908. doi:10.1089/jpm.2010.9808

Irwin, S. A., Iglewicz, A., Nelesen, R. A., Lo, J. Y., Carr, C. H., Romero, S. D.,

& Lloyd, L. S. (2013). Daily oral ketamine for the treatment of depression and anxiety in patients receiving hospice care: A 28-day open-label proof-of-concept trial. *Journal of Palliative Medicine, 16*(8), 958–965. doi:10.1089/jpm.2012.0617

Jaitly, V. K. (2013). Sublingual ketamine in chronic pain: Service evaluation by examining more than 200 patient years of data. *Journal of Observational Pain Medicine, 1*(2).

Lapidus, K. A., Levitch, C. F., Perez, A. M., Brallier, J. W., Parides, M. K., Soleimani, L., ... Murrough, J. W. (2014). A randomized controlled trial of intranasal ketamine in major depressive disorder. *Biological Psychiatry, 76*(12), 970–976. doi:10.1016/jbiopsych.2014.03.026

Lara, D. R., Bisol, L. W., & Munari, L. R. (2013). Antidepressant, mood stabilizing and procognitive effects of very low dose sublingual ketamine in refractory unipolar and bipolar depression. *International Journal of Neuropsychopharmacology, 16*, 2111–2117. doi:10.1017/S1461145713000485

McGirr, A., Berlim, M. T., Bond, D. J., Fleck, M. P., Yatham, L. M., & Lam, R. W. (2014). A systematic review and meta-analysis of randomized, double-blind, placebo-controlled trials of ketamine in the rapid treatment of major depressive episodes. *Psychological Medicine, 45*(4), 693-704. doi:10.1017/S0033291714001603

McNulty, J. P., & Hahn, K. (2012). Compounded oral ketamine for severe depression, anxiety, and pain in a hospice patient with end-stage chronic obstructive pulmonary disease, cardiopulmonary failure, and severe renal insufficiency: A case report. *International Journal of Pharmaceutical Compounding, 16*(5), 364–368.

Messer, M. & Haller, I. (2013). Maintenance ketamine treatment produces long-term recovery from depression. *Primary Psychiatry, 17*(4), 48-50.

Mills, I. H., Park, G. R., Manara, A. R., & Merriman, R. J. (1998). Treatment of compulsive behaviour in eating disorders with intermittent ketamine infusions. *QJM: An International Journal of Medicine, 91*(7), 493–503.

Nguyen, L., Marshalek, P. J., Weaver, C. B., Cramer, K. J., Pollard, S. E., & Matsumoto, R. R. (2015). Off-label use of transmucosal ketamine as a rapid acting antidepressant: A retrospective chart review. *Journal of Neuropsychiatric Disease and Treatment, 11*, 2667–2673. doi:10.2147/NDT.S88569

Papolos, D. F., Teicher, M. H., Faedda, G. L., Murphy, P., & Mattis, S. (2013). Clinical experience using intranasal ketamine in the treatment of pediatric bipolar disorder/fear of harm phenotype. *Journal of Affective Disorders*, *147*(1), 431–436.

Paslakis, G., Gilles, M., Meyer-Lindenberg, A., & Deuschle, M. (2009). Oral administration of the NMDA receptor antagonist S-ketamine as add-on therapy of depression: A case series. *Pharmacopsychiatry*, *43*(1), 33–35. doi:10.1055/s-0029-1237375

RANZCP. (2015). Use of ketamine for treating depression [Clinical memorandum]. Retrieved from https://www.ranzcp.org/Files/Resources/College_Statements/Clinical_Memoranda/CLM-PPP-Ketamine-to-treat-depression-(November-201.aspx

Strayer, R. S., & Nelson, L. S. (2008). Adverse events associated with ketamine for procedural sedation in adults. *American Journal of Emergency Medicine*, *26*, 985–1028.

Szymkowicz, S. M., Finnegan, N., & Daleb, R. M. (2012). A 12-month naturalistic observation of three patients receiving repeat intravenous ketamine infusions for their treatment-resistant depression. *Journal of Affective Disorders*, *147*(1), 416-420.

Zanicotti, C. G., Perez, D., & Glue, P. (2012). Mood and pain responses to repeat dose intramuscular ketamine in a depressed patient with advanced cancer. *Journal of Palliative Medicine*, *15*(4), 400–403. doi:10.1089/jpm.2011.0314

Ketamine in Current Clinical Practice

Intravenous Ketamine

Steven P. Levine, M.D.

ONE OF THE CHALLENGES OF INTRODUCING a new medical therapy outside the usual progression of large-scale clinical trials is the lack of consistency in its application. How do we know which protocol is correct? Typically, a new drug is introduced with narrowly defined manufacturer-suggested parameters for dose, route of administration (ROA), frequency, and duration. Following the accumulation of real-world data, we often find that adjustments to those recommendations are required. However, there is a consistent starting point, relatively minor deviation from the "standard dose," and limited opportunity to vary ROA given restricted, proprietary preparations.

In the case of ketamine, we have an available, cheap, generic drug that can be easily compounded into a variety of formulations. Its psychiatric applications for mood and anxiety disorders are based on relatively small-scale studies for which the investigators somewhat arbitrarily chose one ROA and one pattern of treatment that may or may not be superior to others. In the first published study of ketamine for depression (Berman et al., 2000), the choices of an intravenous (IV) ROA dose of 0.5 mg/kg and administration over 40 minutes were both somewhat arbitrary. Nonetheless, this quickly became the standard followed by subsequent studies, and ultimately, the choice of some other early-adopter clinicians.

There are numerous ROAs of ketamine. "Off-the-shelf," it is available only as a liquid for either IV or intramuscular (IM), injection. It may also be compounded into intranasal inhalers and powder, oral tablets or capsules, and sublingual lozenges. Each of these routes has its relative advantages and disadvantages clinically, partly depending upon its application. All have widely varying bioavailabilities and effects relative to each other, among individuals, and within a given individual over time.

In figure 1, we see the relative bioavailabilities of the five most common routes of administration (Clements, Nimmo, & Grant, 1982; Yanagihara et al., 2003; Chong, Schug, Page-Sharp, Jenkins, & Ilett, 2009). Of particular interest given the anticipated arrival of a new commercial, patented ketamine product is the intranasal route. There is wide variability in the bioavailability of nasal ketamine. This may be due to differences among individuals in thickness of nasal mucosa, congestion due to allergic or infectious rhinitis, saturation of the mucosa following repeated administration (due to the small amount of medicine delivered per spray and higher doses relative to IV required to achieve therapeutic response, multiple sprays are required in a given session), and structural accommodation (septal damage) over time secondary to exposure to ketamine. To further complicate matters, because of the importance of instructing the patient in proper technique (and the possibility of error in this technique), the already-mentioned mucosal saturation, and gravity, inevitably some amount of ketamine will be swallowed. Therefore, one would be unlikely to get pure intranasal administration, and instead a nasal-oral hybrid in uncertain proportions.

Figure 1

Route	Bioavailability (%)
IV	100
IM	93
Nasal	25–50
Oral	17–24
Sublingual	24–30

This uncertainty in absorption further compounds the complexity of the way ketamine is delivered. We now have a Tower of Babel where numerous clinicians are providing treatment in inconsistent and difficult-to-compare fashions, many claiming superiority based on shaky grounds. This is akin, in some ways, to the nosological crisis psychiatry faced in the last century that prompted the publication of the third edition of the *Diagnostic and Statistical Manual of Mental Disorders* in 1980 (DSM III; American Psychiatric Association; Kawa & Giordano, 2012). This standardization of description required many compromises and even some suspension of disbelief, but overall restored some credibility to a faltering field.

As one of the first psychiatrists to make IV ketamine available for the treatment of mood and anxiety disorders in the United States in 2010, I decided to hedge uncertainty with consistency. I believed I could deliver a consistent treatment that would be highly effective: through standardization of dose and ROA, supplies, physical environment, methods, training of staff, and measurement of outcomes. We now have multiple locations across the country, but in every one, patients complete the same screening scales, receive the same preparation for treatment in consultation, receive their treatment in a similarly decorated room in an office of a similar size and layout, delivered by clinical and administrative staff following a procedure manual, and have their response measured by the same self-reporting post-treatment scale.

We now recognize that there are many factors that account for variable metabolism of medications, particularly by the oral route. On the other hand, as an example of predictability and consistency, IV ketamine metabolism is so regular that merely by observing the meniscus of the ketamine/saline level in the IV bag, one can accurately estimate the progress of a patient through their infusion. There are many ways to deliver ketamine, just as there are many ways to make a hamburger, but using the IV ROA with 100% bioavailability, under standardized conditions, you know what you are going to get every time.

Our Process

Upon first contact by email or phone, patients receive general information from the clinical coordinator and are instructed to complete screening scales: the Quick Inventory of Depression Symptoms (16-item Self Report [QIDS-SR 16], Rush et al., 2003); the Zung Anxiety Scale (Zung, Richards, & Short, 1965); the Psychosis Screener (Hall, Korten, & Jablensky, 2005); the Altman Self-Rating Mania Scale (Altman, Hedeker, Peterson, & Davis, 1997); and a combined Michigan Alcohol Screening Test (MAST; Selzer, 1971) and Drug Abuse Screening Test (DAST; Skinner, 1982). Patients are also screened for relevant medical contraindications.

Those who meet appropriate inclusion criteria of moderate to severe unipolar major depression, bipolar depression, post-traumatic stress disorder (PTSD), or obsessive compulsive disorder (OCD) and do not meet exclusion criteria of having a primary psychotic disorder, current manic episode or mixed state, current clinically significant substance abuse, unstable cardiac illness, or untreated thyroid illness are asked to obtain a referral from their primary psychiatrist or psychotherapist and are scheduled for consultation. Consultations are conducted in-office and serve to gather appropriate history and confirm the diagnosis and indication for ketamine treatment, as well as to educate patients about ketamine and prepare them for the experience of an infusion. We find that adequate preparation has a significant bearing upon the tolerability of the experience. To accomplish this, all patients hear the following presentation:

> *Unlike many other medications that were discovered "by accident," ketamine was developed very much on purpose. It was first synthesized in 1962 at Parke-Davis, where they sought to develop a new dissociative anesthetic. This is a very valued class of medication because of its safety. Unlike typical anesthetics like propofol, where an anesthesiologist is holding you on the thin line between life and death (lowering your breathing rate, blood pressure, heart rate—all of your vital signs), ketamine is actually a stimulant, especially at the dose we use here.*

> *It cut its teeth during the Vietnam War, where it was known as the "buddy drug." It was called that because it was considered so safe that your relatively untrained buddy could administer it to you under uncontrolled conditions on the battlefield. You didn't need a controlled airway, an anesthesiologist or a controlled setting; it could be given to you right on the battlefield to treat physical trauma, even if there was a lot of blood loss.*

> *It then moved into the operating room for surgery, but pretty quickly, it was relegated to children and animals. What happened was adults who still were under the influence of ketamine when they woke up from surgery had what the anesthesiologists call "the emergence reaction," which is what someone can experience when they are not prepared for what ketamine feels like. Why kids? Because kids think magically already—they think their stuffed animals are alive and they have imaginary friends, so it doesn't bother them.*

> *However, more recently, many surgeons and anesthesiologists are going back to ketamine because of its safety. Especially orthopedic surgeons. They love it because they do big painful surgeries like joint replacements—knees, hips—and these days they want you up and participating in physical therapy as soon as possible, the same day or next day at the latest. If you are on high-dose opiate pain medications, you can't do PT. What they have found is that if they use ketamine during the surgery, people have lower pain med requirements post-op, so they can get up and around more quickly.*

The antidepressant potential of ketamine has been considered since the 1970s, but it wasn't until the 1990s that formal studies were started. The first paper was published in 2000, and the results were very dramatic. After more studies replicated the results, Dr. Levine started the process of treating patients in 2010. He has treated over 700 patients with thousands of infusions at this point.

To give you a sense of scale, if a small child were to fall down outside this building right now and be brought over to the ER at the local hospital, and they wanted to give him a short-acting anesthetic so they could stitch him up, they would give him ketamine. They would give him something in the neighborhood of 2–4 mg/kg as a shot, all at once, and they wouldn't think twice about it. The dose we use here for depression is 0.5 mg/kg and we give it slowly over 40 minutes.

On top of that, ketamine is very short-acting. The half-life is only 2.5 hours, and the first stage of its metabolism, which is responsible for the side effects you can have during an infusion, is only 10–15 minutes. That means that if for any reason we want the effects of the medicine to stop, we can shut it off, and within minutes it will have cleared. Now, we've given thousands of infusions here, and we won't need to stop it, but if we wanted to, we could.

One of the interesting things about IV ketamine is that, as different as people are in all the ways that people are different—including reactions to medications—the timing of a ketamine infusion is always the same. You can set your watch by it. We know that it will take about 20 minutes to start feeling the effects, and then 45–50 minutes later, they will clear. It has never been different than that, it can't be, and it won't be today. That is a very reassuring thing. It's also one of the things that differentiates a ketamine infusion from a psychedelic experience, with something like LSD. One of the opportunities to get anxious on LSD and have a "bad trip" is that it is long-lasting and unpredictable. That gives people an opportunity to wonder, "Oh, no, am I losing my mind, will I ever go back to normal, when will this end?" With ketamine, you maintain an awareness the whole time that what you are experiencing is the effects of a medicine, that you are safe in a medical setting, and that no matter what you are feeling, it will clear in a matter of minutes. I'm going to go through with you what it's like to have a ketamine infusion before we wrap up here, so you know what to expect. When people are well-prepared for what it feels like, it is typically a pleasant experience.

We go on to present a distillation of the descriptions of our first 700 plus patients:

The number one thing that people say to me after the first infusion—fortunately, it's almost always with a smile on their faces—is something like, "I know you said that was gonna be weird, but that was really weird." The top five words that people use are weird, odd, strange, different, and intense. However, if we think about the nature of this medicine, and the way in which it's weird, it actually makes a lot of sense.

This is a dissociative anesthetic, so it induces a feeling of dissociation or disconnection. There's a feeling of separation of mind from body. Now, that falls along a spectrum. On the mild end it feels light, bubbly, floaty. More typically, it's a bit more intense than that and people feel more frankly disconnected. People described the sense that their body is in the chair while their mind is floating above them: their mind is floating above them looking down on them observing them, a feeling of traveling or motion like their mind is traveling around the room, or even, "My mind is way out there. It feels like I'm off in another dimension." However even if you feel like you're in another dimension, there's a tether back to reality. You maintain the awareness the entire time that you're in a medical office, having a medical procedure, and that what you're feeling is the result of a medication. You maintain the awareness that that medicine is going to wear off within a matter of minutes, and then you go back to feeling normal.

What's also important to note is that if you read the popular press articles on ketamine, or even some of the studies, they use words like "schizophrenia-like," "psychotic," or "hallucination." Those words are all technically incorrect, because they refer to false, fixed perceptions: for example, hearing a voice that's not in the room or seeing a vision of something that's not in the room. It would be like someone walking into this room right now and asking you, "Who are you talking to? There's no one there!" That would probably be very frightening to you, because you plainly see me and hear me, and no one would be able to talk you out of that. What happens during ketamine is more accurately a dreamlike or illusory experience. It is an alteration of perception, during which you maintain a connection to reality.

I mentioned before that what you experience during this actually makes a lot of sense. What I mean is that everything follows from the feeling of disconnection. Our bodies are constantly gathering information from the environment, whether we're directly focused on it or not. We only have so much attention to pay at any one moment, and our bodies take up a portion of that—the temperature of the room, our clothes against our skin, physical pain, the chair under us, etc. If you feel disconnected from your body, you don't have to pay attention to all of that, and you have more attention to pay to your others senses. So, in general, there is an amplification of your other senses: The volume knob is turned up.

You become more sensitive to stimuli in the environment. Everything feels like "more." Because of that, we try to minimize stimuli around you. We have private rooms, we put white-noise machines in the rooms to block out background noise, we try not to bang pots and pans around you, and we try to leave you alone as much as possible. We've learned this the hard way. When Dr. Levine first started treating people, he was pretty nervous, because this was new and no one else was using this medicine clinically. So he was right in people's faces asking them, "Are you OK? What are you feeling now? Are you alright?" People don't want to be asked a lot of questions during this. They want to be left alone. It is a very internal, introspective experience, and outside interference tends to be unwelcome. People tend to be most comfortable in a darkened room, with minimal noise, reclining, listening to music, with their eyes closed.

The nurse will check your vital signs, then start the IV line and the medicine. The nurse will be back every 15–20 minutes to recheck your vital signs. We expect your blood pressure and heart rate to go up a bit, and that will be fine. I'll be peeking in on you too, but if you're doing OK and feeling comfortable, we hang back and let you be. We're listening carefully for any sign that you need us, and if you do, we'll spend as much time with you as you need, but you will most likely be fine, so we'll let you be.

People often find music helpful. It grounds them and gives them something familiar to hold onto. You're also welcome to have someone in the room with you, but I recommend that you not talk during the time you feel the medicine. It can be hard to find the words or keep track of where your thoughts were going, which can then feel frustrating or confusing. Now, if you are feeling uncomfortable at all, and it's reassuring to talk, then by all means. But barring that, I recommend just sitting back and going with it.

Visually, it depends if your eyes are open or closed. If they're open, you can have some blurring or doubling of your vision, and there can be a sense of motion or travelling. Once the medicine starts to clear, that sometimes can give people of feeling of motion sickness and nausea. Therefore, if you feel comfortable with it, I recommend keeping your eyes closed. If your eyes are closed, then it's a different visual experience. If you close your eyes even right now and actually look at what you're seeing, it's not just darkness or nothing—you see lights, and shapes, and colors. Most of us tend not to sit around on a daily basis with our eyes closed just watching the show, but during a ketamine infusion, you may watch the show, and it will likely be more colorful, brighter, it can have a texture to it, and you can feel like you're travelling around in it. You're not hallucinating—it's really there, and it just takes on a different meaning. But this is why people sometimes describe it as psychedelic or "trippy."

There's a paradox with ketamine. In a couple of ways, it can feel like you're out of control. However, you are fully in control the whole time. You can feel out of control of your body, because you feel separated from it. You can also have some physical numbness—usually just toes, fingers, and the area around your mouth/lips/teeth. That combination might lead an unprepared person to believe they can't move. However, you can easily move, and I encourage you to test it out. In fact, even if you needed to get up and walk to the restroom in the middle of the infusion, you could do that. So, it feels like you can't control your body, but you actually can.

The other way people can feel out of control, is that there is a natural assumption that the weirdness you feel internally is apparent to an outside observer. This can make some people feel self-conscious. People have said, "I wouldn't want to see a video tape of this later. I'd be really embarrassed."

Now, we don't videotape this—that would be weird—but I always tell people that if they saw a videotape of this later, they'd be bored, because all they would see is themselves sitting in a chair. You may feel out of control, but you have full control over what you say, full control over what you do, and you'll have full memory of the events later on.

Most people who go into this accepting the idea that they will feel a little weird for a little while, but then it will clear, and in the meantime they'll be completely safe, and hopefully a little later they'll be feeling better, actually find this to be a pretty pleasant experience—either calming and relaxing, euphoric, or very interesting and introspective. People often feel like they are doing important psychological work during this, and that may actually be a part of how this medicine works.

Our Protocol

In consideration of the fact that many of our patients travel a distance for treatment, as well as to most closely pair the timing of preparation for treatment with the treatment itself, we typically schedule the consultation and first infusion for the same day. We ask that patients withhold benzodiazepines and amphetamine-based stimulants the day of treatment. Prior to initiating treatment, we obtain informed medical consent and for our treatment policies, which clarify our role as consultants in our patients' overall treatment plan.

The dose for the initial infusion is 0.5 mg/kg, based on actual body weight, diluted in 50 ml of normal saline, infused slowly by gravity-based drip over 40 minutes. We follow this with a flush of another 50 ml of normal saline. No other medications are administered before or during the infusion. For subsequent treatments, if the patient has demonstrated significant nausea, we may offer ondansetron orally disintegrating tablets 30 minutes prior to the infusion. Vital signs (blood pressure, heart rate, pulse oximetry) are checked manually every 15–20 minutes during the procedure. The psychiatrist checks on the patient periodically, aiming to be as unobtrusive as possible, and then sits with the patient in the treatment room after recovery to listen in an open-ended way to the patient's discussion of the experience.

Upon discharge, patients are instructed not to drive until the next day, avoid alcohol for 48 hours, continue prescribed medications as usual (except for benzodiazepines, which should be avoided for at least two hours post-treatment), and complete the post-treatment scale (see below) after 24 hours. In the past, we asked patients to re-take the QIDS-SR 16 and Zung Anxiety scales post-treatment. Invariably, they complained that they had difficulty selecting answers that accurately reflected their current state, and that many of their answers could not have changed after 24 hours despite the fact that they did feel different. These complaints highlighted the fact that these scales were not designed or intended for measuring response to a rapid-acting treatment. Of course, there has been no need for a patient self-rated scale to measure change after 24 hours until now, because we have not had a treatment that can work within that time frame.

I created the Levine Rapid Treatment Depression Scale to meet this need, though I acknowledge that it is not yet a validated scale. We ask patients to complete this scale following their first two to three treatments to help determine response and decide whether to continue treatment. Those who have no response after three treatments will not continue.

If there has been no discernible response after a first treatment, we will titrate the dose upwards by 20%. If there has been mild or plateauing response following the first or subsequent treatments, we will typically increase the dose 10% at a time. The typical course in the acute phase of treatment is six total infusions over the first two weeks, patterned after the first study of repeated dose IV ketamine that has been replicated numerous times since then (aan het Rot et al., 2010) Following that, we ask patients to schedule a first, single maintenance infusion three weeks later, based on an average time to symptom relapse. However, during that time, we ask patients to fill out QIDS-SR 16 and Zung Anxiety scales on a weekly basis. We check in with them, and we coordinate with their primary treatment team. In this way, the timing of maintenance treatment can be adjusted to be clinically appropriate. Over time, most of our patients require a maintenance infusion once every four to 12 weeks.

Those who have the most durable responses tend to be the ones who take to heart the message that ketamine is not "the thing." It is not a magic bullet that will make everything better. Rather, it can be a rapid jump-start on a path to healing and wellness. We strongly advocate for continuing with or starting psychotherapy. In particular, we emphasize short-term skill and learning-based modalities such as Cognitive Behavioral Therapy (CBT) and Dialectical Behavior Therapy (DBT) as well as trauma-specific therapies for those with PTSD, and Exposure and Response (ERPP) as well as systemic desensitization for those with OCD. We believe that ketamine helps to facilitate new learning, and we seek to capitalize upon that through psychotherapy.

Following the above protocol, we have been able to achieve remarkable outcomes,

Figure 2: Levine Rapid Treatment Depression Scale

	No change	NA	Mild improvement (25%)	Moderate improvement (50%)	Significant improvement (75%)	Complete improvement (100%)	Mild worsening (25%)	Moderate worsening (50%)	Severe worsening (75%)	Extreme worsening (100%)
Feelings of sadness	No change	NA	Mild improvement (25%)	Moderate improvement (50%)	Significant improvement (75%)	Complete improvement (100%)	Mild worsening (25%)	Moderate worsening (50%)	Severe worsening (75%)	Extreme worsening (100%)
Crying	No change	NA	Mild improvement (25%)	Moderate improvement (50%)	Significant improvement (75%)	Complete improvement (100%)	Mild worsening (25%)	Moderate worsening (50%)	Severe worsening (75%)	Extreme worsening (100%)
Feelings of guilt	No change	NA	Mild improvement (25%)	Moderate improvement (50%)	Significant improvement (75%)	Complete improvement (100%)	Mild worsening (25%)	Moderate worsening (50%)	Severe worsening (75%)	Extreme worsening (100%)
Feelings of hopelessness	No change	NA	Mild improvement (25%)	Moderate improvement (50%)	Significant improvement (75%)	Complete improvement (100%)	Mild worsening (25%)	Moderate worsening (50%)	Severe worsening (75%)	Extreme worsening (100%)
Ability to experience pleasure/joy	No change	NA	Mild improvement (25%)	Moderate improvement (50%)	Significant improvement (75%)	Complete improvement (100%)	Mild worsening (25%)	Moderate worsening (50%)	Severe worsening (75%)	Extreme worsening (100%)
Suicidal thoughts	No change	NA	Mild improvement (25%)	Moderate improvement (50%)	Significant improvement (75%)	Complete improvement (100%)	Mild worsening (25%)	Moderate worsening (50%)	Severe worsening (75%)	Extreme worsening (100%)
Energy level	No change	NA	Mild improvement (25%)	Moderate improvement (50%)	Significant improvement (75%)	Complete improvement (100%)	Mild worsening (25%)	Moderate worsening (50%)	Severe worsening (75%)	Extreme worsening (100%)
Interest in people or activities	No change	NA	Mild improvement (25%)	Moderate improvement (50%)	Significant improvement (75%)	Complete improvement (100%)	Mild worsening (25%)	Moderate worsening (50%)	Severe worsening (75%)	Extreme worsening (100%)
Level of irritability	No change	NA	Mild improvement (25%)	Moderate improvement (50%)	Significant improvement (75%)	Complete improvement (100%)	Mild worsening (25%)	Moderate worsening (50%)	Severe worsening (75%)	Extreme worsening (100%)
Time spent worrying	No change	NA	Mild improvement (25%)	Moderate improvement (50%)	Significant improvement (75%)	Complete improvement (100%)	Mild worsening (25%)	Moderate worsening (50%)	Severe worsening (75%)	Extreme worsening (100%)
Ability to concentrate	No change	NA	Mild improvement (25%)	Moderate improvement (50%)	Significant improvement (75%)	Complete improvement (100%)	Mild worsening (25%)	Moderate worsening (50%)	Severe worsening (75%)	Extreme worsening (100%)
Level of calmness	No change	NA	Mild improvement (25%)	Moderate improvement (50%)	Significant improvement (75%)	Complete improvement (100%)	Mild worsening (25%)	Moderate worsening (50%)	Severe worsening (75%)	Extreme worsening (100%)
Presence of physical anxiety (shakiness, restlessness, rapid heart beat)	No change	NA	Mild improvement (25%)	Moderate improvement (50%)	Significant improvement (75%)	Complete improvement (100%)	Mild worsening (25%)	Moderate worsening (50%)	Severe worsening (75%)	Extreme worsening (100%)

both in terms of percentage of patients achieving response and remission, as well as quality of life improvement. However, we also recognize the limitations of the IV ROA and the evidence guiding our treatment parameters. IV is a relatively expensive and time-intensive ROA. However, regardless of the ROA, ketamine should be administered in a supervised medical setting. The potential for addiction, particularly in a cultural and political climate that has always been mistrustful of medicine that "doesn't taste bad," as well as the influence of setting and a rarified learning state post-treatment, all argue for in-office administration. While we are open to changes in our protocol as further evidence comes to light, our current practices represent an evidence-based manualized treatment that can be consistently replicated on a large scale.

References

aan het Rot, M., Collins, K. A., Murrough, J. W., Perez, A. M., Reich, D. L., Charney, D. S., & Mathew, S. J. (2010). Safety and efficacy of repeated-dose intravenous ketamine for treatment-resistant depression. *Biological Psychiatry, 67*(2), 139–145. doi:10.1016/j.biopsych.2009.08.038

Altman, E. G., Hedeker, D., Peterson, J. L., & Davis, J. M. (1997). The Altman self-rating mania scale. *Biological Psychiatry, 42*(10), 948–955. doi:10.1016/S0006-3223(96)00548-3

American Psychiatric Association. (1980). *DSM-III-R: Diagnostic and statistical manual of mental disorders.* Author.

Berman, R. M., Cappiello, A., Anand, A., Oren, D. A., Heninger, G. R., Charney, D. S., & Krystal, J. H. (2000). Antidepressant effects of ketamine in depressed patients. *Biological Psychiatry, 47*(4), 351–354. doi:10.1016/S0006-3223(99)00230-9

Chong, C., Schug, S. A., Page-Sharp, M., Jenkins, B., & Ilett, K. F. (2009). Development of a sublingual/oral formulation of ketamine for use in neuropathic pain. *Clinical Drug Investigation, 29*(5), 317–324. doi:10.2165/00044011-200929050-00004

Clements, J. A., Nimmo, W. S., & Grant, I. S. (1982), Bioavailability, pharmacokinetics, and analgesic activity of ketamine in humans. *Journal of Pharmaceutical Sciences, 71,* 539–542. doi:10.1002/jps.2600710516

Hall, W., Korten, A., & Jablensky, A. (2005). *Use of a brief screening instrument for psychosis: Results of an ROC analysis.* Sydney, Australia: National Drug and Alcohol Research Centre.

Kawa, S., & Giordano, J. (2012). A brief historicity of the *Diagnostic and Statistical Manual of Mental Disorders*: Issues and implications for the future of psychiatric canon and practice. *Philosophy, Ethics, and Humanities in Medicine, 7*(2), 9 pp. doi:10.1186/1747-5341-7-2

Rush, A. J., Trivedi, M. H., Ibrahim, H. M., Carmody, T. J., Arnow, B., Klein, D. N., ... & Thase, M. E. (2003). The 16-Item Quick Inventory of Depressive Symptomatology (QIDS), clinician rating (QIDS-C), and self-report (QIDS-SR): A psychometric evaluation in patients with chronic major depression. *Biological psychiatry, 54*(5), 573–583. doi:10.1016/S0006-3223(02)01866-8

Selzer, M. L. (1971). The Michigan Alcoholism Screening Test: The quest for a new diagnostic instrument. *American Journal of Psychiatry, 127*(12), 1653–1658. doi:10.1176/ajp.127.12.1653

Skinner, H. A. (1982). The drug abuse screening test. *Addictive Behaviors, 7*(4), 363–371. doi:10.1016/0306-4603(82)90005-3

Yanagihara, Y., Ohtani, M., Kariya, S., Uchino, K., Hiraishi, T., Ashizawa, N., ... Iga, T. (2003), Plasma concentration profiles of ketamine and nor-ketamine after administration of various ketamine preparations to healthy Japanese volunteers. *Biopharmaceutics & Drug Disposition, 24*, 37–43. doi:10.1002/bdd.336

Zung, W. W., Richards, C. B., & Short, M. J. (1965). Self-rating depression scale in an outpatient clinic: Further validation of the SDS. *Archives of General Psychiatry, 13*(6), 508–515. doi:10.1001/archpsyc.1965.01730060026004

Making Ketamine Work in the Long Run

Terrence S. Early, M.D.

TREATMENTS SUCH AS KETAMINE PSYCHOTHERAPY FACE substantial financial and regulatory obstacles to dissemination into widespread use. Newly patented medications are able to generate enough capital to pay for studies required for FDA approval, personnel to apply for coverage on insurance plans, and marketing to establish a successful launch. Ketamine is an older drug with considerable evidence of efficacy for treatment-resistant depression, and almost 50 years of data concerning safety as an anesthetic agent. However, it can no longer be patented, so there is no incentive for pharmaceutical companies to help get it into widespread use. In this paper we discuss some of the complex issues surrounding use of ketamine in the outpatient setting and share information and practice pearls that have been gathered through communication with other practitioners and through direct experience with over 1,000 treatments involving 120 patients in the last eight years. The safety and appropriateness of intramuscular, ketamine treatment in the outpatient psychiatric office is discussed. We hope to help proponents of effective mental health interventions navigate the actual and potential challenges involved in safe application of this treatment option outside of hospital-based programs.

This report is based on the experience of the author and a colleague (Jeffrey Becker), who have had direct experience with over 1,000 ketamine treatments conducted with 120 patients over the past eight years; in addition, the author is in communication with other practitioners involved in ketamine treatment. Based on this clinical experience, the current paper reports on the actual and potential challenges involved in safe application of intramuscular, ketamine treatment for psychological conditions such as depression in outpatient settings.

Early's interest in ketamine for depression began after studying another anesthetic treatment approach that never became mainstream—halothane isoelectric therapy, using sevoflurane. Langer, Neumark, Koinig, Graf, and Schoenbeck (1985) originally reported that a related anesthetic agent, isoflurane, had a robust antidepressant effect comparable to electroconvulsive therapy (ECT) in an open-label trial. These results were later replicated in a double-blinded trial (Langer et al., 1995). Early found similar results with an open-label trial of sevoflurane therapy and a blinded comparison to ECT (Early et al., unpublished results). Langer's isoflurane results were recently replicated by Weeks et al. (2013). Halothane isoelectric therapy produces a period of isoelectric electroencephalography (EEG) similar to the state that follows an ECT-induced seizure, but without seizure-related cognitive side effects. Early found it impossible to disseminate the technique, since there was no mechanism to pay for anesthesiology and hospital time to provide the treatment and no way to obtain insurance coverage. Ketamine offered a less expensive and less invasive alternative, and Early began using it in 2007.

Becker examined the potential of ketamine on depression in medical students and psychiatric residents at UCLA. While looking at the N-methyl-D-aspartate (NMDA) receptor related neurological substrates of transcendent experience, it became clear that ketamine might provide relief from depression. Multiple clinical studies now confirm this (Mathews & Zarate, 2013).

A Mandate for New Treatment Options

Ketamine represents the first new receptor-based treatment for depression in decades and has the potential to provide profound relief from great suffering. In contrast with monoamine oxidase inhibitors and tricyclic antidepressants that typically take weeks or months to reach full effectiveness—and too often are not effective at all—ketamine appears to provide rapid relief from symptoms of depression, even in treatment-resistant cases (Zarate et al., 2006; Diaz-Granados et al., 2010). Ketamine may represent a breakthrough in the broader treatment of depression by offering a novel pharmacological strategy focused on the glutamatergic system, which may be more central to the neurobiological mechanisms of mood disorders than the serotonergic, noradrenergic, and dopaminergic systems typically targeted in conventional pharmacological treatments for mood disorder (Sanacora, Zarate, Krystal, & Manji, 2008). There is evidence that ketamine impacts the NMDA receptor complex, which may itself mediate the delayed relief in conventional treatment strategies; targeting this system directly may represent a significantly more efficient approach to the treatment of depression, and of mood disorders more broadly, with a potentially large impact on public health (Zarate et al., 2010).

The use of medications as psychotherapeutic adjuncts has a long history in psychiatry (Kolb, 1985). Barbiturate-facilitated psychotherapy, introduced by Blackwenn (1930), was practiced for over 80 years to treat conversion symptoms and *traumatic war neurosis* or PTSD. The amytal and pentothal interviews were developed later, along with other forms of drug-facilitated psychotherapy (Grinker & Spiegel, 1945; Horsely, 1943; Lindemann, 1932). Sometimes called abreactive psychotherapy, this approach was reported to produce rapid relief of classic symptoms such as flashbacks, nightmares, hypervigilance, and autonomic hyper-reactivity (Hoch, 1946). Shovrin and Sargant (1947) introduced an excitatory abreactive therapy using ether and a variety of other agents, which later were used to facilitate learning during psychotherapy (Sargant & Slater, 1972).

Clearly the psychological effects that occur with ketamine use as an antidepressant treatment touch similar themes. While these older treatment techniques were in danger of becoming a simple footnote in psychiatric history, the improved safety and efficacy of ketamine may eventually provide PTSD patients with a viable treatment model in this mode. Indeed, Feder et al. (2014) recently reported a robust effect on core symptoms of PTSD with ketamine treatment.

However, perception of safety is likely to be one of the largest challenges to broader acceptance of ketamine's role in psychiatry and the adoption of this treatment within outpatient psychiatric offices. Despite the fact that the outpatient psychiatric office is likely to be the most efficient and effective in delivering treatment to those in need, currently the majority of participating practitioners are anesthesiologists or are at hospital-based programs. The author hopes to clarify issues that will allow broader adoption of this effective treatment option in outpatient psychiatric clinics. Fear regarding safety, both founded and often unfounded, should be balanced by clinical evidence and an awareness of the immense need for effective treatment delivery.

Safety of Low-Dose Ketamine Therapy

Intramuscular ketamine, is generally considered safe at subanesthetic doses, even in non-medical settings. When used to induce general anesthesia, ketamine is generally administered at a dose range of 3–8 mg/kg IM or 1–4.5 mg/kg IV. The usual maintenance dose for ketamine is an IV bolus of 0.1–0.5 mg/kg/minute. Ketamine is often combined with other anesthetic agents (such as propofol), and the dose is typically less in this situation. Even at doses used for general anesthesia, ketamine is associated with normal pharyngeal-laryngeal reflexes, and usually cardiovascular and respiratory stimulation, though there may occasionally be a transient and minimal respiratory depression. In the low-dose range 0.5–1 mg/kg, patients experience conscious sedation, which means they remember the experience and respond to stimuli during the session. The physiologic effects of subanesthetic ketamine provide a large margin of safety in the treatment of depression through preservation of responsivity to the practitioner, cardiac stimulation, and maintenance of respiratory function and the gag reflex (Hass & Harper, 1992).

Early and Becker have found use in the outpatient setting to be remarkably free of adverse effects. Nausea and occasional vomiting are the most common negative effects, which are minimized by fasting four to six hours prior to treatment or through the use of ondansetron. Anxiety upon arrival at a session is common and is managed through pretreatment discussion, clonidine and/or, if needed, oral lorazepam. Blood pressure increases of 5–10 mm/hg diastolic and 5–15 mm/hg systolic are routine while heart rate increases of 10–20 bpm are seen less commonly. We have not seen laryngospasm, severe hypertension, respiratory distress, or severe agitation in any of our cases. Our experience is consistent with the experience of other clinicians with whom we consult and with existing research.

Ketamine's large safety margin provides reassurance in settings where anesthesiologists and monitoring are not available, such as the battlefield, veterinary medicine, dentistry, and pediatric anesthesia. O'Hara, Ganeshalingam, Gerrish, and Richardson (2014) reported no adverse cardiac or respiratory events after 131 sedation procedures by nursing with oral ketamine, which is known to be more unpredictable than IM or IV routes. In this study, an anesthesiology consult was only required to further deepen sedation or deal with excessive sedation. The National Clinical Guideline Centre recommends that anesthesiology be present only when ketamine is administered with opiates (National Institute for Health and Care Excellence [NICE], 2010). Even in full anesthesia, reflecting doses up to 10 times those used for depression (e.g., 2 mg/kg IV to 5 mg/kg IM), ketamine is remarkably safe. A review of over 70,000 published anesthesia cases reported only one ketamine-related fatality occurring in a seriously medically compromised individual (Strayer & Nelson, 2008).

Given the confusion between full anesthesia and conscious sedation, a few issues do deserve further clarification.

Respiratory Drive

Bourke, Malit, and Smith (1987) reported minimal changes in respiratory drive with low-dose IV ketamine and a 5% drop in minute ventilation (l/min) at 1.08 mg/kg. Mankikian, Cantineou, Sortene, Clergue, and Viars (1986) reported no significant change in respiratory functional residual capacity and minute ventilation or tidal volume after full anesthetic induction with 3 mg/kg. Morel, Forster, and Gemperle (1986) reported increased respiratory drive, stable arterial oxygen saturation, and end-tidal carbon dioxide concentration with 1 mg/kg delivered IV. In addition, bronchodilatory effects of ketamine, likely second to circulating catecholamines, have been observed in canine models. Ketamine has been used successfully in pediatric status asthmaticus to facilitate intubation (Reich & Silvay, 1989). While salivary secretions increase with ketamine-induced full anesthesia, this does not appear to be a problem in conscious sedation due to intact swallow reflexes and the vastly lower doses involved. In short, respiratory drive remains intact with low dose (and even high dose) ketamine (Hass & Harper, 1992).

Blood Pressure and Intercranial Pressure

It is understood that ketamine can increase heart rate and arterial pressure (Hass & Harper, 1992) at least partially through increases in free norepinephrine (Zsigmond, Kelsch, & Kothary, 1973). Hypertension should therefore be well controlled prior to treatment. Mild increases in intracranial pressure have been noted with ketamine, and Haas and Harper (1992) saw this as a contraindication for use in vulnerable individuals.

Emergence Reaction

Ketamine's psychological effects are often reported in anesthesia and surgery research as an adverse effect. While these effects may actually be inherent to antidepressant effects, ketamine and other dissociative drugs have been reported to exacerbate psychotic symptoms in schizophrenia. While Carpenter (1999) reported a lack of significant negative effects after administration to 12 subjects with stable schizophrenia, ketamine is not likely to be indicated for treatment in cases involving primary psychosis.

Screening and Contraindications

Given physical safety considerations and the unique psychological effects of ketamine, treatment with minimal monitoring is relatively contraindicated in the following physical and psychiatric conditions:

- Uncontrolled hypertension
- Congestive heart failure
- Other impaired cardiac status
- Severe chronic obstructive pulmonary disease (COPD)
- Severe obesity
- Increased intracranial or cerebrospinal (CSF) pressure
- Schizophrenia and schizoaffective disorder
- Severe or primitive personality disorders

Patient Selection and Evaluation

During an initial evaluation, psychiatric and medical history is reviewed along with lab work, past treatment history, and history of substance abuse. Issues relating to cardiac and pulmonary history, prior adverse response to anesthesia, evidence of sleep apnea, and history of primary psychosis are assessed. The patient is considered a candidate for a ketamine session if they have already failed multiple antidepressant trials and specific contraindications do not exist. If the patient is severely ill or suicidal, ketamine may be the treatment option most likely to produce rapid, if temporary, remission.

Consent for Treatment

A thorough informed consent process educates patients to the psychological effects of treatment and addresses the expectations and questions of the patient and their family. Topics for discussion include acute and residual side effects, potential risks and benefits, the off-label nature of the treatment, and the research supporting ketamine's use in the treatment of depression. The scope and duration of potential positive effects should be discussed with every patient. Discussion regarding the frequency and number of treatments required can be informed by the naturalistic outcomes seen in ECT, in that some patients respond after relatively few treatments while others require a longer course of treatment.

The consent process helps to set realistic but positive expectations, which may be an essential element to success. With proper control of the physical environment (e.g., dim light, music, reclining position), the treatment experience is usually described by patients as meaningful and positive. Psychotherapy is an essential part of the process of recovery and is recommended to every patient receiving ketamine treatment. Our considerations regarding therapy are beyond the scope of this paper, however, and will be provided in another forum (see "Regarding the Transpersonal Nature of Ketamine Therapy" by Jeffrey Becker, page 323).

The Ketamine Treatment

Patients are advised to take morning medications, particularly antihypertensive medication, given ketamine's tendency to increase arterial pressure. Our list of medications that are held off from use for at least 24 hours prior to a ketamine session include these:

> lamotrigine—for its ability to block the psychological effects of ketamine
>
> bupropion—for observed anxiety and mild agitation during treatment
>
> stimulants—for similar reasons as bupropion and blood pressure elevation

These medications may be resumed later in the day after the treatment session concludes.

When patients arrive, there is discussion as to their current psychiatric status, and any appropriate psychological assessments are completed (e.g., Beck Depression Inventory), though particularly anxiety-provoking discussions are avoided. Patients are asked to recline and spend time deep breathing as the treatment is made ready and blood pressure is taken. Lights are dimmed and soft music is provided if the patient has not opted to bring their own. We remain with the patient monitoring status, blood pressure, and safety considerations for 60 to 90 minutes during the active period of the treatment, and patients will spend additional time as needed to fully recover.

The setting is designed to facilitate a sense of safety, comfort, and warmth. This is a lesson well learned during early studies of psychedelic psychotherapy that found the setting to contribute much to the effect of treatment. There is stark contrast between ketamine experienced in a fluorescent hospital setting surrounded by detached strangers with a clinical stance versus a warm and comfortable setting accompanied by loved ones. This may be in part why we rarely see anxiety or dysphoria to any significant degree. Patients usually lie quietly during the session as we sit nearby to offer assistance as needed.

Monitoring and Safety During Therapy

Ketamine produces conscious sedation within three to five minutes at 0.5 mg/kg IM, which means that patients are responsive to verbal and physical prompts. Intravenous infusions over 45 minutes are associated with a more gradual alteration in consciousness, with altered awareness usually reported within 10 minutes. In every patient, vital signs and mental status should be monitored with an auto-inflatable pressure cuff before treatment, at least once during the session, and after the treatment concludes. To reduce the incidence of nausea and vomiting, we recommend fasting for eight hours before the initial treatment, reducing to four hours for subsequent treatments in individuals without evidence of delayed gastric emptying and who establish tolerance to treatment side effects. Patients are advised to arrange for transportation home and agree not to drive after treatment until they have slept a full night.

Some patients with controlled hypertension will present with elevations due to anticipatory anxiety. In these cases treatment is rescheduled and a prescription is given for clonidine 0.1 or 0.2 mg PO one to two hours before arrival. Clonidine is generally sufficient to reduce blood pressure within protocol range, consistent with Tanaka and Nishikawa (1994), who reported that administration of clonidine 5 mcg/kg with ketamine in full anesthesia abolished increases in arterial pressure seen in controls. While it is also possible to use propranolol in these situations, this may diminish the bronchodilatory effect of ketamine (Reich & Silvay, 1989) and thus is an inferior option and should not be used in patients with asthma.

Although we have not witnessed severe anxiety or agitation in our clinic, lorazepam or alprazolam for oral or IM administration is always available. Ondansetron 4–8 mg ODT or 2 mg liquid for IM injection is also available for patients who experience nausea despite fasting. Patients are advised to use acetaminophen or ibuprofen for any headaches that may occur after treatment. We also recommend that patients take 500 mg of n-acetyl cysteine (NAC) prior to arrival to support glutathione production.

Dosing and Duration of Effect

A target dose of 0.5 mg/kg IM may be initiated in the first session at the clinician's discretion, or the initial dose may be reduced by 25–50% in potentially sensitive individuals. The total dose may also be divided and separated by 10–15 minutes to reduce the speed of onset and peak blood levels. Some patients have required increased doses to improve efficacy.

Peak effects are felt within the first 10–20 minutes and patients are usually mostly recovered 90 minutes after injection. Some cognitive fog and fatigue may linger for some hours, or until sleep resets brain function.

Beneficial Effects

The medical literature now provides extensive reports of clinical efficacy. The following are clinical impressions based upon a broad range of patients and treatment outcomes. Beneficial psychiatric effects on depression, anxiety, and pain are usually seen during and immediately following treatment, though some patients begin to notice effects up to 48 hours later. Patients who ultimately respond will almost always have a robust antidepressant effect with the first treatment.

In our experience, the duration of the effect on depression is generally from one to four weeks. For unclear reasons, in some cases the effect fades after only a few days, while in others it may last for months. As such, frequency of treatment must be adjusted to effect—some patients require only a single session to resolve a depressive episode while others may require a series of treatments over a few weeks or months, similar to the frequency of acute and maintenance ECT. We generally treat patients once every two to four weeks to maintain remission if depression recurs, concurrently adjusting medications and psychotherapy to achieve a lasting remission.

Patients with both unipolar (typical and atypical) and bipolar depression often respond to ketamine offered in our clinic. We have seen patients with psychotic depression improve with resolution of psychosis. But we have also observed a tendency for mania to become more pronounced with ketamine. On two occasions, we have had patients who failed to respond to low-dose treatment go on to respond to a higher dose (3–8 mg/kg) received during an unrelated surgical procedure. We have repeatedly seen rapid and robust remission of severe suicidal ideation, consistent with reports from preliminary research on ketamine treatment (Price, Nock, Charney, & Mathew, 2009).

It is notable that even when the strong acute effect on depression fades, there tends to be residual improvement in mood that persists. In addition, we suspect that it is helpful for patients to experience an interval of recovery, however brief, after prolonged periods of depression. They are generally encouraged to know that recovery is possible. Our patients routinely report that ketamine provides them hope, reminding them what it feels like to be free of depression.

Storage and Documentation

Ketamine and syringes for IM delivery may be ordered for office use through a pharmacy or a medical supply company. Ketamine should be stored under double lock-and-key as per Drug Enforcement Administration (DEA) regulations for in-office storage of scheduled medications. A log should be kept recording receipt and use of medication, including date, amount received, amount used, amount wasted, expired medication that is destroyed, vial number, patient name, indication, and any other relevant comments.

Towards a Mechanism of Action-Facilitated Emotional Learning

Enduring psychological change often requires facing emotionally painful topics, and exposure can be a powerful treatment technique. We have found that ketamine therapy facilitates this process in the days following treatment, when patients encounter anxiety cues during exposure therapy with reduced anxiety and defensive responses. They discuss difficult areas in psychotherapy with notably improved comfort and insight.

It seems likely that ketamine may intervene specifically at the crossroads of extinction and reconsolidation, two processes capable of altering the response to fearful memory (Centonze, Siracusano, Calabresi, & Bernardi, 2005; Schiller, Raio, & Phelps, 2012; Soeter & Kindt, 2010).

Extinction of the response to fearful memory can occur through prolonged exposure within a safe environment. This allows a competing extinction memory associated with safety rather than fear to become associated with the trauma cues. However, short exposure to fearful memory can instead initiate reinforcement of a pathologic response through reconsolidation (Schiller et al., 2012). With severe PTSD, recall of the fearful memory during therapy often produces freezing and dissociation, and the resulting brief recall may reconsolidate and reinforce the memory, rather than produce extinction (Centonze et al., 2005; Myers, Carlezon, & Davis, 2011; Schiller et al., 2012).

In the days following ketamine therapy, patients typically find it easier to discuss and encounter reminders of previous trauma. They do not generally experience the extreme anxiety and freezing produced by previous recall of the traumatic memory. Ketamine attenuates the anxiety response produced by recalling the traumatic memory, and thus patients engage in more extended discussions of the traumatic memory, potentially allowing for the development of extinction memory.

A Second Mechanism of Action-Accelerated Self-Reliance

Treatment-resistant patients often show complex medical and psychiatric comorbidity, social isolation, and avoidant behaviors that point toward attachment difficulties. Attachment trauma, a common feature of PTSD (Courtois, Ford, Herman, & Van der Kolk, 2009), and perhaps of treatment-resistant patients in general, inhibits recovery through its detrimental effects upon interpersonal intimacy and trust, self-conception, and life-perspective. It has become clear in the last few decades that the neurobiological substrate of change through psychotherapy includes improvements in attachment patterns (Cozolino, 2010).

An important aspect of psychotherapy is the provision of a mature psychological model as an attachment structure that permits the development of new and secure attachment patterns within and, eventually, outside of the therapeutic relationship. The therapeutic bond acts as proxy for the patient's relation to the Self (the personal and transpersonal subconscious—capitalized from here on, in the tradition of Jung, to distinguish as the counter to ego) until authentic restitution can develop, bringing this process inward to allow a new orientation toward the outside world. Unfortunately, this process often advances so slowly as to be inconsistent with the resources of the patient. We have come to see ketamine treatment as an accelerant to this mysterious process. Perhaps through its capacity to engender self-acceptance, intuition, and awareness, patients more rapidly begin the process of relying upon themselves, in a deep sense, rather than the therapeutic bond.

Group Therapy

We provide a didactic component in a group therapy setting, discussing topics such as the neurobiology of depression, pain, and anxiety, as well as an introduction to effective psychotherapy and pharmacotherapy techniques for addressing psychological symptoms. As an organizing principle, ketamine patients participating in group therapy are asked to focus their efforts in four areas.

1. *Automatic Scripts*
The depth of each patient's experience with ketamine therapy usually exposes some of the cognitive distortions they experience on a daily level. Patients often have the nature of their limited and disengaging programmatic scripts revealed to them by the experience. They may appreciate a new venue to consider and practice new scripts. Patients complete a script/schema inventory and the group may be educated about cognitive-behavioral links as leverage points for growth.

2. *Mindfulness*
Mindfulness meditation has been shown to improve attention and emotional self-regulation, as well as enhancing white matter integrity around the anterior cingulate gyrus, a cortical component of the voluntary attention system (Tang, Lu, Fan, Yang, & Posner, 2012; Tang & Posner, 2009). Mindfulness skills are an important part of effective psychotherapy for a broad variety of psychiatric conditions (Omidi,

Mohammadi, Zargar, & Akbari, 2013; Teasdale, Segal, & Williams, 1995), and we find them helpful in this setting as well. We commonly use the book, *Mindfulness: A Practical Guide to Finding Peace in a Frantic World* (Williams & Penman, 2011) to educate about daily practice techniques. In addition, we practice 10-minute mindfulness meditation techniques during the group session.

3. *Attachment / Compassion*

We find that education regarding attachment theory can help patients identify their specific attachment patterns and facilitate insight-oriented change. After years of observing treatments with ketamine therapy, we believe that identifying the effect of attachment issues on symptoms such as depression and social detachment is particularly valuable. Here, we find discussions on compassion and the use of loving-kindness or Metta Bhavana Meditation helpful (Hofmann, Grossman, & Hinton, 2011). We also discuss self-compassion, using exercises detailed by Paul Gilbert (2009) in *The Compassionate Mind: A New Approach to Life's Challenges.*

4. *Life Narrative / Mythic Reframing*

Patients often experience substantial changes in areas such as self-concept, life goals, and personal understanding of life-meaning. We encourage discussion of authentic truth and meaning and support efforts to reframe major themes and archetypal forces within their lives. Some patients experience this process as occurring within a particular religious tradition, but others do not. We do not think it is the role of the therapist to indoctrinate patients into any particular religious tradition, but it is important to acknowledge the spiritual nature of their efforts to gain a deeper understanding of who they are. Ketamine permits a "panoramic" view of life, not only one's own life but the life of others.

Treatment Beyond Depression

Major depression is a significantly heterogeneous disorder that is often comorbid with other psychiatric conditions. As such we have been able to observe the positive effect of ketamine upon a number of other disorders.

Use in Pain

Chronic pain frequently becomes associated with depression and anxiety. Fortunately, ketamine has numerous beneficial effects on pain, and many of our patients report that ketamine is the most effective treatment they have used for chronic pain. Complex regional pain disorder (CRPS), also known as reflex sympathetic dystrophy, is notoriously difficult to treat but sometimes responds to high-dose ketamine protocols offered in the United States and Germany (Schwartzmann et al., 2009). In five CRPS patients we have also observed low-dose ketamine providing noticeable acute pain relief. Three of these patients gradually experienced a permanent overall reduction in pain intensity over several months. We have seen ketamine improve chronic daily headaches, new daily persisting headache, neuropathic pain, and chronic pelvic pain.

Use in PTSD and Anxiety Disorders

Following ketamine sessions, our patients with PTSD often report reduced reaction to trauma cues, with effects usually lasting from one to four weeks. During this "grace period" patients seem to be more capable of tolerating graded exposure. One patient, who was abused and tormented with rodents as a child, could not be near a rodent without experiencing dissociative anxiety and flashbacks. Following ketamine, she was able to enter a pet store and touch pet rats without severe anxiety. We have seen patients tolerate discussion of emotionally distressing events without feeling overwhelmed, and therapists often report making considerable headway in sessions scheduled a few days after ketamine treatment. Patients with social phobia and generalized anxiety disorder have generally reported benefits distinct from the antidepressant effect as well. While we have not treated enough patients with obsessive-compulsive disorder (OCD) to have an opinion, two patients with body dysmorphic disorders did not show any appreciable effect with over six sessions.

Eating Disorders

We have observed one patient with severe mixed anorexia and bulimia of 12 years' duration recover over the course of 12 months with treatments occurring once per week for a total of 48 treatments. Purging and restriction patterns resolved completely. Psychological growth was demonstrated through increasingly meaningful and rewarding inter-personal relationships and an ability to tolerate a healthy romantic dyad for the first time. Mills, Park, Manara, and Merriman (1998) reported a 70% response rate with multiple 10-hour extended infu-sions of a low-dose of ketamine in a group of patients hospitalized with anorexia and bulimia.

Conclusion

Ketamine treatment shows great potential as a new pharmacological strategy in the treatment of depression in that it produces relief of symptoms rapidly, even in treat-ment-resistant cases. Ketamine appears to target the glutamatergic system that may be central to the neurobiology of mood disorders, and may represent a more direct treatment strategy than that offered by more conventional approaches. Its excel-lent safety record has been demonstrated over decades. Despite potential regulatory hurdles given that the drug cannot be patented, and thus poses little opportunity for pharmacological industry profit, the clinical observations presented here are offered with the hope that ketamine treatment for depression may find its way into more widespread use in outpatient settings.

Note

1. This work was supported in part by grants from NARSAD and the Stanley Foun-dation.

References

Blackwenn, W. J. (1930). Narcosis as therapy in neuropsychiatric conditions. *Journal of the American Medical Association, 95,* 1168–1171. doi:10.1001/jama.1930.02720160028009

Bourke, D. L., Malit, L. A., & Smith, T. C. (1987). Respiratory interactions of ketamine and morphine. *Anesthesiology, 66*(2), 153–156. doi:10.1097/00000542-198702000-00008

Carpenter, W. T. (1999). The schizophrenia ketamine challenge study debate. *Biological Psychiatry, 46*(8), 1081–1091. doi:10.1016/S0006-3223(99)00194-8

Centonze, D., Siracusano, A., Calabresi, P., & Bernardi, G. (2005). Removing pathogenic memories: A neurobiology of psychotherapy. *Molecular Neurobiology, 32*(2), 123–132. doi:10.1385/MN:32:2:123

Courtois, C. A., & Ford, J. D. (2009). *Treating Complex Stress Disorders: An Evidence-based Guide.* New York, NY: Guilford Press.

Cozolino, L. (2010). *The Neuroscience of Psychotherapy: Healing the Social Brain.* New York, NY: W. W. Norton.

Diaz-Granados, N., Ibrahim, L., Brutsche, N., Ameli, R., Henter, I. D., Luckenbaugh, D. A., ... Zarate, C. A. (2010). Rapid resolution of suicidal ideation after a single infusion of an NMDA antagonist in patients with treatment-resistant major depressive disorder. *Journal of Clinical Psychiatry, 71*(12), 1605–1611. doi:10.4088/JCP.09m05327blu

Feder, A., Parides, M. K., Murrough, J. W., Perez, A. M., Morgan, J. E., Saxena, S., ... Charney, D. S. (2014). Efficacy of intravenous ketamine for treatment of chronic posttraumatic stress disorder: A randomized clinical trial. *JAMA Psychiatry, 71*(6), 681–688. doi:10.1001/jamapsychiatry.2014.62

Gilbert, P., & Choden. (2014). *Mindful compassion: How the Science of Compassion Can Help You Understand Your Emotions, Live in the Present, and Connect Deeply with Others.* New York, NY: New Harbinger.

Grinker, R., & Spiegel, J. P. (1945). *Men under stress.* Philadelphia, PA: Blakiston. doi:10.1037/10784-000

Haas, D. A, & Harper, D. G. (1992). Ketamine: A review of its pharmacologic properties and use in ambulatory anesthesia. *Anesthesia Progress, 39,* 61–68.

Hoch, P. H. (1946). The present status of narco-diagnosis and therapy. *The Journal of Nervous and Mental Disease, 103*(3), 248–259. doi:10.1097/00005053-194603000-00005

Hofmann, S. G., Grossman, P., & Hinton, D. E. (2011). Loving-kindness and compassion meditation: Potential for psychological interventions. *Clinical Psychology Review, 31*(7), 1126–1132. doi:10.1016/j.cpr.2011.07.004

Horsley, J. S. (1943). *Narco-analysis.* London, UK: Oxford University Press.

Kolb, L. C. (1985). The place of narcosynthesis in the treatment of chronic and delayed stress reactions of war. In S. M. Sonnenberg, A. S. Blank, & J. A. Talbott (Eds.), *The Trauma of War: Stress and Recovery in Vietnam Veterans* (pp. 211–226). Washington, DC: American Psychiatric.

Langer, G., Karazman, R., Neumark, J., Saletur, B., Schoenbeck, G., Grunberber, J., ... Linzmaer, L. (1995). Isoflurane narcotherapy in depressive patients refractory to conventional antidepressant drug treatment. A double-blind comparison with electro-convulsive therapy. *Neuropsychobiology, 31*(4), 182–194. doi:10.1159/000119190

Langer, G., Neumark, J., Koinig, G., Graf, M., & Schoenbeck, G. (1985). Rapid psychotherapeutic effects of anesthesia with isoflurane (ES narcotherapy) in treatment-refractory depressed patients. *Neuropsychobiology, 14*(3), 118–120. doi:10.1159/000118216

Lindemann, E. (1932, May). Psychological changes in normal and abnormal individuals under the influence of sodium amytal. *American Journal of Psychiatry, 11*, 1083–1091. doi:10.1176/ajp.88.6.1083

Mankikian, B., Cantineau, J. P., Sartene, R., Clergue, F., & Viars, P. (1986). Ventilatory pattern and chest wall mechanics during ketamine anesthesia in humans. *Anesthesiology, 65*(5), 492–499. doi:10.1097/00000542-198611000-00007

Mathews, D. C., & Zarate, C. A. (2013). Current status of ketamine and related compounds for depression. *The Journal of Clinical Psychiatry, 74*(5), 516–517. doi:10.4088/JCP.13ac08382

Mills, I. H., Park, G. R., Manara, A. R., & Merriman, R. J. (1998). Treatment of compulsive behaviour in eating disorders with intermittent ketamine infusions. *QJM, 91*(7), 493–503. doi:10.1093/qjmed/91.7.493

Morel, D. R., Forster, A., & Gemperle, M. (1986). Noninvasive evaluation of breathing pattern and thoracoabdominal motion following the infusion of ketamine or droperidol in humans. *Anesthesiology, 65*, 392–398. doi:10.1097/00000542-198610000-00008

Myers, K. M., Carlezon, W. A., & Davis, M. (2011). Glutamate receptors in extinction and extinction-based therapies for psychiatric illness. *Neuropsychopharmacology, 36*(1), 274–293. doi: 10.1038/npp.2010.88

National Institute for Health and Care Excellence [NICE]. (2010). *Sedation in children and young people: Sedation for diagnostic and therapeutic procedures in children and young people.* Retrieved from http://www.nice.org.uk/nicemedia/live/1329 6/52124/52124.pdf

O'Hara, D., Ganeshalingam, K., Gerrish, H., & Richardson, P. (2014). A 2 year experience of nurse led conscious sedation in paediatric burns. *Burns, 40*(1), 48–53. doi:10.1016/j.burns.2013.08.021

Omidi, A., Mohammedi, A., Zargar, F., & Akbari, H. (2013) Efficacy of mindfulness-based stress reduction on mood states of veterans with post-traumatic stress disorder. *Archives of Trauma Research, 1*(4), 151-154 doi:10.10.5812?atr.8226

Price, R. B., Nock, M. K., Charney, D. S., & Mathew, S. J. (2009). Effects of intravenous ketamine on explicit and implicit measures of suicidality in treatment-resistant depression. *Biological Psychiatry, 66*(5), 522–526. doi:10.1016/j.biopsych.2009.04.029

Reich, D. L., & Silvay, G. (1989). Ketamine: An update on the first twenty-five years of clinical experience. *Canadian Journal of Anesthesia, 36*(2), 186–197. doi:10.1007/BF03011442

Sanacora, G., Zarate, C. A., Krystal, J., & Manji, H. K. (2008). Targeting the glutamatergic system to develop novel, improved therapeutics for mood disorders. *Nature Reviews: Drug Discovery, 7*(5), 426–437. doi:10.1038/nrd2462

Sargant, W. W., & Slater, E. (1972). *An Introduction to Physical Methods of Treatment in Psychiatry.* Edinburgh, Scotland: Churchill Livingstone.

Schiller, D., Raio, C. M., & Phelps, E. A. (2012). Extinction training during the reconsolidation window prevents recovery of fear. *Journal of Visualized Experiments: JoVE, 66*, e3893. doi: 10.3791/3893

Schwartzman, R. J., Alexander, G. M., Grothusen, J. R., Paylor, T., Reichenberger, E., & Perreault, M. (2009). Outpatient intravenous ketamine for the treatment of complex regional pain syndrome: A double-blind placebo controlled study. *PAIN, 147*(1), 107–115. doi:10.1016/j.pain.2009.08.015

Shorvon, H. J., & Sargant, W. (1947). Excitatory abreaction: With special reference to its mechanism and the use of ether. *The British Journal of Psychiatry, 93*(393), 709–732. doi:10.1192/bjp.93.393.709

Soeter, M., & Kindt, M. (2010). Dissociating response systems: Erasing fear from memory. *Neurobiology of Learning and Memory, 94*(1), 30–41. doi:10.1016/j.nlm.2010.03.004

Strayer, R. J., & Nelson, L. S. (2008). Adverse events associated with ketamine for procedural sedation in adults. *The American Journal of Emergency Medicine,*

26(9), 985–1028. doi:10.1016/j.ajem.2007.12.005

Tanaka, M., & Nishikawa, T. (1994). Oral clonidine premedication attenuates the hypertensive response to ketamine. *British Journal of Anaesthesia, 73*(6), 758–762. doi:10.1093/bja/73.6.758

Tang, Y.-Y., Lu, Q., Fan, M., Yang, Y., & Posner, M. I. (2012). Mechanisms of white matter changes induced by meditation. *Proceedings of the National Academy of Sciences, 109*(26), 10570–10574. doi:10.1073/pnas.1207817109

Tang, Y. Y., & Posner, M. I. (2009). Attention training and attention state training. *Trends in Cognitive Sciences, 13*(5), 222–227. doi:10.1016/j.tics.2009.01.009

Teasdale, J. D., Segal, Z., & Williams, J. M. G. (1995). How does cognitive therapy prevent depressive relapse and why should attentional control (mindfulness) training help? *Behaviour Research and Therapy, 33*(1), 25–39. doi:10.1016/0005-7967(94)E0011-7

Weeks, H. R., Tadler, S. C., Smith, K. W., Iacob, E., Saccoman, M., White, A. T., … Light, K. C. (2013). Antidepressant and neurocognitive effects of isoflurane anesthesia versus electroconvulsive therapy in refractory depression. *PLoS ONE, 8*(7), e69809. doi:10.1371/journal.pone.0069809

Williams, M., & Penman, D. (2011). *Mindfulness: A Practical Guide to Finding Peace in a Frantic World.* London, UK: Piatkus.

Zarate, C., Machado-Vieira, R., Henter, I., Ibrahim, L., Diaz-Granados, N., & Salvadore, G. (2010). Glutamatergic modulators: The future of treating mood disorders? *Harvard Review of Psychiatry, 18*(5), 293–303. doi:10.3109/1067322 9.2010.511059

Zarate, C. A., Singh, J. B., Carlson, P. J., Brutsche, N. E., Ameli, R., Luckenbaugh, D. A., … Manji, H. K. (2006). A randomized trial of an *N*-methyl-D-aspartate antagonist in treatment-resistant major depression. *Archives of General Psychiatry, 63*(8), 856–864. doi:10.1001/archpsyc.63.8.856

Zsigmond, E. K., Kelsch, R. C., & Kothary, S. P. (1973). Rise in plasma free-norepinephrine during anesthetic induction with ketamine. *Behavioral Neuropsychiatry, 6*(1–12), 81–84.

Regarding the Transpersonal Nature of Ketamine Therapy: An Approach to the Work

Jeffrey Becker, M.D.

KETAMINE THERAPY HAS POWERFUL AND IMMEDIATE psychological effects that may enhance psychotherapy. Chronic stress and depression are likely associated with increased glutamatergic neurotransmission and changes in neuronal plasticity, including dendritic remodeling and atrophy (Sanacora, Treccani, & Popoli, 2012). While these changes may be adaptive in the short term, there is little doubt that, unmitigated, they contribute to depressive patterning and reduce awareness through fear, shame, and dread.

Ketamine powerfully reduces glutamatergic tone through NMDA-receptor antagonism and produces a complex range of biochemical effects that ultimately enhance neural plasticity and synaptogenesis. This may partially explain the neurological changes that resolve depression (Kavalali & Monteggia, 2012), but it is clear that ketamine's effects as an antidepressant are unlike traditional medications. On a molecular level, ketamine might be considered a "plastistogen," producing alterations through effects on glutamate receptors involved in emotional learning (Myers, Carlzon & Davis, 2011). On a conscious level however, ketamine can produce a phenomenological experience that is emotionally arousing and profoundly meaningful, often reflective of the archetypal nature of the patient's emotional turmoil. There is even evidence that these effects are directly correlated to the degree of achieved antidepressant effect (Luckenbaugh et al., 2014). From this perspective, it is desirable to amalgamate psychotherapy with ketamine therapy to effect change on many levels.

Depression is an exemplary condition to illustrate the layered therapeutic potential of ketamine. With depression every facet of the person is affected—what I refer to as body, mind, and spirit. In my experience, ketamine treatment effects change in any or all of these aspects, often simultaneously. It is common after treatment to observe reductions in physical vigilance and agitation, improved productivity and thought patterns, and a spiritual expansion toward the qualities of authenticity, inner peace, and hope.

Preparation for Treatment

The decision to engage in ketamine therapy for depression or other psychiatric problems and diagnoses must occur in the context of a thorough informed consent process that educates patients as to the psychological effects of treatment and addresses the concerns or expectations of the patient and family. The consent process helps set realistic expectations for treatment outcomes, and helps patients prepare for the specific psychological effects of treatment. This is usually where the introduction of transpersonal psychological ideas can begin if they have not already. In this way the potential transpersonal experience may be interpreted as an opportunity for growth rather than a negative side effect to be managed or suffered through, as some proponents of a reduced dose ketamine approach have argued.

Patients receive individual psychotherapy either from the psychiatrist directly or in collaboration with their current psychotherapist. The therapist's belief in the potential universal meaning in each patient's journey can provide some of the security needed to accept new intuitive truths or a heroic call for action. Regarding the nuts-and-bolts of sessions, psychotherapeutic techniques and tools can be tailored to the patient's capacities and condition. These may include exposure, cognitive behavioral teaching, and supportive techniques or other strategies. Supportive therapy can provide the structure for positive regard, interpersonal warmth, trust, and a natural belief in healing. These qualities are essential to supporting the patient's recovery, especially in such a potentially vulnerable mode of treatment. Nevertheless, supportive therapy it is not nuanced enough to cover the deeper themes that often emerge, and, because it is not the primary focus of this paper, the interested reader is referred to an excellent review on this subject by Donald Misch (2000).

The Ketamine Session

The primary goal of the structuring of a ketamine session is to ensure the patient feels safe and secure. Monitoring for physical or psychological discomfort with proper control over the physical environment is essential. This may include the provision of appropriate music during therapy, dim lighting, and minimal outside noise. With these considerations, the subjective experience of ketamine therapy is usually described as meaningful and positive. Indeed, this issue is critical. In one anesthesia clinic the simple suggestion that a patient would find the emergence dreams after ketamine "pleasant" versus no suggestion increased the number of patients who rated emergence as "quite pleasant or very pleasant" from 22% to 54% (Cheong et al., 2011). The importance of this process—one that addresses the "set and setting" of the patient and treatment—has been established in the medical literature related to psychedelic therapy both past and present. Readers unfamiliar with these ideas are directed to resources for further reading in this regard (Eisner, 1997; Goldsmith, 2007; Greer & Tolbert, 1998; McElrath & McEvoy, 2002).

The clinician sits near the patient in order to monitor vital signs and to provide reassurance as needed. Patients experience psychological changes within minutes of an intramuscular, injection, and the peak experience generally occurs at about 10–25 minutes. While most patients lie quietly, occasionally patients communicate the need for reassurance or may need the therapist's encouragement to fully re-enter the ketamine space. Extreme agitation is very rare. As patients recover they may or may not feel like talking, though later that day and on subsequent days improved mood and decreased anxiety can augment the insight and benefits from the ketamine session. Facilitation of the recovery of the memory of the experience can also be encouraged in the immediate aftermath.

The Transpersonal Nature of the Ketamine Experience

Most patients marvel at the depth and power of their experience, but the attendant intense themes can be confusing to patients and clinicians alike. Both may understand that "something profound happened here," yet find clarity elusive without a consonant therapeutic orientation and methodology. The clinician has the potential to add or subtract therapeutic value depending upon their knowledge and comfort with transpersonal or "peak" experiences and, what I propose to be of fundamental value for working in these experiences, the *ego-Self axis restitution* as an accepted psychotherapeutic mode of healing (Edinger, 1972; James, 1993; Kasprow & Scotton, 1999; Majić, Schmidt, & Gallinat, 2015; Miovic, 2004). I have found that the themes that often emerge through ketamine therapy at least warrant a working familiarity with the concept of the "encounter with the Self," and "ego-Self axis restitution" described within Jungian psychology. Clinicians may be certain that they will observe their patients struggling with archetypal concepts surrounding estrangement and reconciliation of the ego-Self axis through their transpersonal experience.

In this treatment model, the rich archetypal experience that ketamine treatment brings is an opportunity for growth rather than a negative side effect to be managed or suffered through. The clinician who misunderstands or dismisses the value of a patient's emergent insight with ketamine treatment will be out of synch with the healing processes at work. Even worse, fear within the clinician may easily transfer to the patient, potentially reducing the breadth and depth of recovery.

Given the tendency of researchers to label the spiritually themed experiences of ketamine as "psychotomimetic" (e.g., Mason, Morgan, Stefanovic, & Curran, 2008), I hope to help a generation of clinicians avoid this linguistic reductionism by identifying more effective interpretive models. Because supportive modes of therapy are simply insufficient to constellate these themes, transpersonal and Jungian psychology can be helpful to the clinician offering ketamine to their patients.

One of the hallmarks of transpersonal approaches is the directness with which spiritual experience is addressed as part of the therapeutic process. Ultimately the goal is not merely to remove psychopathology, but to foster higher human development ... involving a deepening and integration of one's sense of connectedness, whether it be with self, community, nature, or the entire cosmos. (Kasprow & Scotton, 1999, p. 13)

It is clear that deep transpersonal themes are an essential aspect of the experience. To illustrate, Krupitsky and Klop (2007) reported that patients often experience:

- Feeling that one has left one's body (i.e., out-of-body experience);

- Awareness of becoming a nonphysical being;

- Emotionally intense visions;

- Feelings of ego dissolution and loss of identity;

- Visits to mythological realms of consciousness;

- Re-experiencing the birth process;

- Feelings of cosmic unity with humanity, nature, the universe, and God.

The Psychic Life Cycle and the Ego-Self Axis:
A Presentation of this Theory and its Application
to Ketamine Assisted Psychotherapy for Depression

Transpersonal psychology has a long history that predates its modern description and formal inception in the 1960s. William James (1993) and Carl Jung (1966), along with some of the world's mystics, have described experiential states that reveal depths of consciousness that go beyond or "transcend" the personal nature of the ego. While many have contributed to this field, it is my view that foundational theories flow easily from Jung. The context and structure of transpersonal experience with ketamine can often be effectively constellated through the symbolic paradigms dealing with the interrelation of ego and Self.

Within this paradigm, two dysfunctional relational patterns commonly exist between ego and Self within the depressed or dysthymic individual. Each represents a constriction or stasis at a specific point in the individuation of ego from Self. This individuation process requires repeated navigation of a three-stage cycle represented as the psychic life cycle from Edinger (1972, p. 41). One must understand this cycle as it occurs in health to understand the forms of psychic distress that occur when it goes awry.

The first stage involves ego inflation as the ego naturally attempts to transcend "the physical, social, or interpersonal limits it experiences. The ego in this state is identified primarily with the powers of the Self, which can feel expansive and profoundly less limited than natural existential boundaries. In negative form this inflation can be characterized behaviorally as selfishness, grandiosity, arrogance, lust, and rage, and is commonly associated with obsessions centering on power and omnipotence. While behaviors originating within this stage can be narcissistic and destructive, overreaching is a fundamental aspect of maturation and growth. Ego inflation prepares for the next stage in this growth cycle, and without attempts to transcend" perceived physical, emotional, or social limits, we do not grow into our full potential.

Inevitably, the world intervenes to teach the ego where proper boundaries lie, especially when excessive inflation occurs. When a deflation occurs for various reasons (e.g., parental discipline, public exposure, failed plans, disappointment) the second stage in the cycle characterized by alienation begins. Shame, regret, embarrassment, and even despair are common characteristics of alienation. While these emotions can be unpleasant, they are quite necessary to catalyze the final step in the process, one that brings restitution of the ego-Self axis.

In this final stage the humbled ego both requests and accepts forgiveness for the inflated transgression across appropriate boundaries into territory ruled by the Self. Through this penance (and an intact ability to accept forgiveness), communication across the ego-Self axis is restored. The alienated wanderer ceases to be "lost in the forest," and a new state of psychic integration invigorates the individual toward investment in authentic potentials. In this model, wisdom, intuition, discipline, and potency grow with repeated successful navigation of this process of ego-Self restitution throughout child and early adult development. Rather than engaging in inner fantasy, the individual who successfully navigates these cycles applies the vast resources of the Self toward authentic goals in the real world, this with the mature collaboration of an individuated ego capable of exercising judgment, discipline, and patience when inevitable frustrations occur.

However, the Psychic Life Cycle may easily stagnate within the stage of alienation. Deflation is accompanied by shame and wounded alienation, emotions that provides the raw material for depression if they are unremitting. In many depressed and dysthymic individuals the path through repentance and humility to self-acceptance and forgiveness is too difficult to achieve.

Within this model, gross imbalance between parental permissiveness and discipline in early stages of development may set the stage for future depression and dysthymia. Too permissive an environment may form personalities characterized by excessive inflation, while excessive discipline without forgiveness may lead to a chronic state of alienation and shame. While these principles are more guidelines than rules, individuals in the former scenario may primarily display narcissism while the latter exhibit depression. The parent's efforts at discipline or guiding their child through inflationary stages must be balanced by forgiveness and loving acceptance of the individual as a whole.

This is no small task, yet this balancing act may be essential. A relative balance between these two forces permits integration of dual psychic aspects within the child and provides the safety needed to repeat this essential cycle throughout maturation. An overly punishing or humiliating parental style may lead to stagnation within the alienated position as shaming patterns become codified in the individual's sense of self and internal dialog. In this situation even everyday examples of inevitable deflation after a period of appropriate inflation can be accompanied by crippling shame and embarrassment (e.g., overcommitment at work only to eventually need help, a failed relationship despite having tried, a business failure, confronting one's own limits regarding perfect parenting). Self-forgiveness and reconciliation to the Self in cases of such perceived transgression can be hard to achieve.

It is my belief that the psychological effects of ketamine constitute a release of psychic obstruction in the chronically alienated, depressed individual. In essence a rapid shift toward self-acceptance and forgiveness allows a reconnection with the Self and a return to wholeness.

The themes that emerge with treatment usually center on acceptance, reconciliation, forgiveness, and freedom. These themes are so ubiquitous that they should be accounted for in any theory regarding the antidepressant mechanism of action of ketamine treatment. Understanding the nature of these experiences can help the clinician support the patient because the reconnection of the ego with the healing power of the Self has great capacity for healing. As Edward Edinger (1972) stated:

> *The connection between ego and Self is vitally important to psychic health. It gives foundation, structure, and security to the ego and also provides energy, interest, meaning, and purpose. When the connection is broken, the result is emptiness, despair, meaninglessness, and, in extreme cases, psychosis or suicide.* (p. 43)

Incorporating the Transpersonal in Therapy

Following are four transpersonal themes or concepts that may help anchor psychotherapeutic treatment associated with ketamine therapy.

The Psychic Life Cycle and Restitution of the Ego-Self Axis.

Within this process, the therapist acts as both teacher and student, especially given the complex mix of personal and transpersonal themes present in each patient's experience. The therapist is tasked with collaborative interpretation of the emergent archetypal and transpersonal themes to facilitate an upward arc of growth within body-mind-spirit axis. While this is not an easy task, it is rewarding and can help catalyze rapid shifts in the patient's understanding and investment in their authentic self.

Clinicians offering ketamine to their patients may feel overwhelmed by the vastness of Jungian psychology, but they should consider making efforts to understand at least these specific themes. Specifically the writer points clinicians and patients alike to the concepts that are discussed within Part I of *Ego and Archetype* by Edinger (1972). Any who struggle with this material will likely be rewarded by increased capacity for understanding and integrating the truths they experience.

Therapy provided during ketamine treatment may include direct candid discussion regarding the nature of a chronically alienated ego-Self axis and the enriching potential of axis restitution. In my experience, these discussions are usually met with gratitude, interest, and invigoration. Deconstructing these themes can help provide a translational key to the patient's experience, and repeated exposure to these themes can catalyze a patient's deepening awareness of the vast resources located within the Self. What hopefully follows is a reorganization of operational premises, beliefs, and scripts, allowing an integration of the intuitive and healing powers of the Self.

The Encounter with the Self

The themes that patients present in discussions after treatment will often involve symbolic experience of the deep Self. Patients may describe an experience of inner richness and power (e.g., an invitation to a rich banquet with foods containing power), a vision of themselves in pure archetypal form (e.g., becoming an experience of pure love), an interaction with a powerful and pure animal (e.g., circled three times by a commanding white horse), or a return to a previously pure state (e.g., a return to protected childhood or infancy). It is common for patients to feel that they have been invited in to experience secret knowledge provided by benevolent inner forces.

All of these experiences can be interpreted as examples of an encounter with Self. History and religion are rife with examples of the powerful transformative nature of this particular psychological experience. Discussing these ideas directly in therapy is both warranted and effective, and this concept alone may be the single most important anchoring principle that occurs in therapy surrounding the interpretation of ketamine treatment. Acceptance of this principle can help a patient resist more diminutive interpretations that drastically reduce the potential of powerful symbols to catalyze healing (e.g., it was just a silly dream, it wasn't real, it was psychosis).

Depression can be interpreted through many lenses, but the universal and ever-present theme is one of "alienation." Patients feel small, cut off from previously available sources of strength both within themselves and within in the social milieu they belong to. Whatever the formulation, there is always a sense that a core source of inner strength, creativity, intuition, and clarity has somehow been cut off, leaving the individual hopeless and drained of vital life force. What exactly is the depressed person alienated from? What is this missing inner core of consciousness that ketamine allows patients to access so quickly and clearly? It seems quite likely that patients gain access to an aspect of their core being that can only be described as the Self.

The Hero's Call to Action

Restitution of the ego-Self axis is likely an important aspect of ketamine's acute antidepressant effect. This realignment may help provide rapid relief of the suffering that is characterized by the alienated state (e.g., hopelessness, boredom, fatigue, self-loathing). However, ego-Self axis restitution may bring much greater reward through allowing the Psychic Life Cycle to begin again.

It is commonplace when working with depressed individuals to witness repeated, pervasive refusals to take action even when the personal stakes become enormous. The curiosity in this circumstance is that inaction is often born of impotence rather than fear. After ketamine treatment, it is common to find patients invigorated with a sense of purpose, taking appropriate action where needed and problem-solving aspects of their life that had suffered from severe inattention.

Through the lens provided by Joseph Campbell's (1949) description of the Hero's Journey (also known as the Monomyth), it is possible to interpret the depressed individual as stuck in a pattern of chronic refusal of the "Call to Action" whenever and wherever it arises. One of the most delightful and satisfying aspects of working with ketamine therapy is to witness a rapid infusion of vitality and purpose with which patients begin to effectively tackle their problems. For example, after only a few ketamine treatments, a 50-year-old individual went back to finish their undergraduate education, a woman in her 30s resolved difficult lingering aspects of an old relationship that were inhibiting new love, and a middle-aged man accepted previously unaccepted aspects of his sexuality. It is not hard to imagine that the resolution of primary psychic conflicts and an acceptance of a mandate for effective action may aid in long-term recovery from depression.

Active Imagination and the Philosopher's Stone

In many ways, the therapeutic engagement of the psychological aspects of ketamine therapy can be conceptualized as a modern version of the Jungian technique know as "Active Imagination." In this case however, the process is powerfully facilitated by the molecular effects of ketamine on consciousness . This technique was designed to strengthen the "feeling relationship" with the contents of the unconscious, a stage of psychological growth Jung felt was necessary before broader psychological integration and growth of the intuitive function occur.

Jung felt that by deepening beyond intellectualization the stage would be set for this function—*intuition*. This stage is the authentic goal of human growth and psychic development; it is only through this deep integration and the availability of this function that the individual accesses their true potential. Perhaps by activating the imaginative capacities, ketamine treatment can accelerate or unlock this process in depressed individuals. It clearly allows patients to strengthen their relationship to the unconscious, a capacity that Jung (1966) felt was necessary for further psychic evolution. He stated:

> *Nor is realization through feeling the final stage .... The fourth stage is the anticipation of the lapis. The imaginative activity of the fourth function—intuition, without which no realization is complete—is plainly evident in this anticipation of a possibility whose fulfillment could never be the object of empirical experience at all .... Intuition gives outlook and insight; it revels in the garden of magical possibilities as if they were real. Nothing is more charged with intuitions than the lapis philosophorum. This keystone rounds off the work into an experience of the totality of the individual. Such an experience is completely foreign to our age, although no previous age has ever needed wholeness so much. It is abundantly clear that this is the prime problem confronting the art of psychic healing in our day.*

As further clarification, the *lapis philosophorum*—or Philosopher's Stone—is a rich symbol from the tradition of alchemy frequently referred to by Jung. According to alchemical legend, the stone was a powerful material formed by trapping the spirit of Mercurius in matter. Alchemical procedures were performed to free the pure substance, which was believed to have broad powers to transmute base materials in the physical and spiritual planes to their finest forms. Given the power within the Philosopher's Stone—power that can transform lead into gold—it is easy to understand why Jung saw the stone as a symbol for Self *per se*, and the process of alchemy as a symbol for the transformational process of individuation and ego-Self restitution.

It is quite possible that Jung would have viewed the application of ketamine in the treatment of depression as a modern psychospiritual alchemical procedure with the capacity to unlock the latent power of the deep Self locked away by the leaden properties of depression. I imagine he would have been very excited about this amazing treatment option.

Case Reports

Following are two case reports illustrating some of the transpersonal themes that occurred during successful treatment with ketamine and psychotherapy.

32-Year-Old, Female Physician
112 lb., Ketamine HCl 25 mg, Two Sessions
(This dose reflects research-based dosing at 0.5mg/kg, but was given intramuscularly, rather than through IV drip infusion.)
Diagnoses: 1) Major Depression—recurrent, severe; 2) Eating Disorder Not Otherwise Specified

Patient is a physician who presented with acute depression in the context of long-standing obsessional perfectionism fueled by layers of doubt and shame that would flare with the slightest personal mistakes. Her deep-seated doubt and self-destructive feelings manifested behaviorally as caloric restriction, skin picking and self-harm gestures. She presented with a career at risk, a deeply troubled marriage, and severe depressive symptoms with suicidal ideation despite standard psychiatric medication treatments.

During ketamine treatment she directly experienced an aspect of her being she had not felt before—a pure and powerful aspect of her inner being in primary form with deeply apparent inherent goodness and broad potential powers. This core perception was surrounded by a cloud of stinging and irritating pests that would try to destroy and steal the power of the pure force. Discussing her experience after treatment, the patient came to feel these entities represented the false beliefs and destructive premises she struggled with each day. Regarding the powerful inner core, she found herself able to hold on to that sense of herself. She knew for the first time that she was supported by an authentic Self that could confront these draining sources of shame.

After two sessions of ketamine therapy there were noticeable changes in her behavior that were consistent with her interpretation of the experience wherein that "pure being" was now helping to inform her choices in day-to-day issues. She became more capable of caring for herself in meaningful ways. She engaged in her therapy and medication management more seriously (while actually needing less medication) and became more participatory and compliant with treatment planning. She started to eat regular meals rather than withholding nutrition and calories. She found it easier to leave her work at work, making room for interpersonal growth and her marriage. She stopped flirting with harming herself and began to set more effective boundaries with her intrusive and deeply critical parents. The quality of intimacy in her marriage improved and she began to experience pleasure through practicing medicine for the first time in years.

48-Year-Old Female Psychologist
132 lb., Ketamine HCl 25 mg, One Session
(This dose reflects a slight reduction from the research-based dose of 0.5mg/kg due to the patient's request. It was given intramuscularly, rather than through IV drip infusion.)
Diagnosis: 1) Bipolar Affective Disorder—Type I, Depressed

The patient is a highly intelligent mental health professional with a convincing history of bipolar affective disorder. She had fallen into a depressive episode in the context of two concurrent stressors—ending a seven-year relationship and experiencing professional career difficulties that included a feeling of betrayal by a previous mentor. The patient usually performed effectively and efficiently at her work despite her deep vulnerability to questions of self-worth. Through previous therapeutic work she had developed the tools and strength needed to deal with a strongly critical sense of self, but these acute losses were proving to be too much this time.

After six weeks her mood continued to deteriorate despite increasing her dose of valproic acid and other minor changes in her medication regimen. Ketamine therapy was initiated and her Beck Depression Index dropped from 19 at treatment to 3 the next day. Two weeks later it had only risen to a score of seven, and two months later it was six. Her powerful response may be partially be due to previously cultivated introspective skills and her capacity to make effective use of psychological insight. Her description of a rapid realignment and connection to deep internal resources characterized by love and forgiveness speaks for itself. Following are her words in a voice message (permission given):

> I have been feeling amazing all week honestly. The depression is completely lifted. So, I'm on day 7 and I still have zero depression. It really was a kind of truth serum for me. I've realized that those insights we discussed after the session are really all of the things that I already know about myself ... but without all of the inhibitory thoughts in the way. It was about embracing myself and the love that I feel, which is at the core of my sense of meaning. It's just been an unbelievable week since that experience.

Conclusions

Ketamine can be a rapid and effective treatment for depression and other adverse mental states, though the mechanisms that underlie its efficacy are still debated and much work needs to be done to identify the factors that best facilitate recovery. During treatment, many participants experience a rich tapestry of universal symbols and archetypes woven through connections to core values, internal relational objects and transpersonal resources. Because the themes regarding the universal tensions across the ego-Self axis (i.e., inherently repeating cycles of alienation and restitution) are so common, clinicians providing therapeutic support to these patients are encouraged to familiarize themselves with these themes.

Indeed, the recurrent nature of this symbolism and emergent meaning that patients draw from their experience likely reveal that some form of ego-Self axis restitution is occurring, and that this is possibly at the heart of the therapeutic response. In fact, this powerful realignment may be the source of the efficacy of the treatment. The controversy within psychiatry as to the negative or positive benefits of a transformative psychedelic experience remains heated. In my practice with ketamine psychotherapy, I have come to regard that it is unlikely that patients heal in spite of the acute psychological effects, but rather, they heal because of them.

Given the tendency of modern psychiatry to be suspicious of peak experiences, it is important to note that the great religious scholar Huston Smith once stated that he believed psychedelic experiences may be capable of acting as "helpful adjuncts to faith." He felt that transcendental experience, however it may occur, can allow some of us to accept a deeper spirituality. He believed that, for many, faith alone is simply not enough (Smith, 1964).Ketamine therapy may provide this service, allowing individuals suffering from depressive alienation to briefly experience the complex richness and inherent depths of their own Self, never again needing to accept on faith alone their right to exist.

Given that the primary character of ketamine experience is undeniably transpersonal, it is not surprising that it may facilitate recovery from depression when viewed from this altitude. Yet, evidence that ketamine may quickly realign the ego-Self axis relationship implies that these obscure layers of psyche are more biologically maintained than anyone would likely have previously proposed. Thus, ketamine treatment presents a unique opportunity to integrate two aspects of the psychiatric community mindset, one of which is arguably in its own form of ego-Self alienation. It offers us a chance to integrate the biological theories regarding depression that have failed us in so many ways (i.e., the alienated ego after an initial state of inflation) with the deeper but less scientifically tethered transpersonal theories that emerge from psychodynamic theory (the vastness of the Self).

It seems clear now that the period of ego inflation that occurred as biological psychiatry gained power has shifted to deflation and alienation as myriad examples of overreaching have amassed (e.g., inflated claims of efficacy, drug company influence on medical literature, excessive polypharmacy, poor diagnostics, loss of therapy skills). Many clinicians today express dismay and distress at the limitations of their biologically oriented tools, and the research supports at least certain aspects of their despair. Ketamine's psychological effects and unique efficacy in depression provide psychiatry as a whole with a unique and potentially healing opportunity as it integrates biological and psychological explanations of recovery.

A coherent unification of theories across competing fields is indeed a special event and the fact that a biologically active molecule can cause such a powerful depth of awareness and transpersonal insight clearly unites modern biological psychiatry with aspects of Jungian and transpersonal psychology. The growing acceptance of this mode of treatment will hopefully be inspiring to practitioners and patients alike.

References

Campbell, J. (1949). *The hero with a thousand faces*. New York, NY: Pantheon.

Cheong, S. H., Lee, K. M., Lim, S. H., Cho, K. R., Kim, M.H., Ko, M. J., … Lee, S. E. (2011). Brief report: The effect of suggestion on unpleasant dreams induced by ketamine administration. *Anesthesia & Analgesia, 112*(5), 1082–1085. doi:10.1213/ANE.0b013e31820eeb0e

Edinger, E. (1972). *Ego and archetype*. Boston, MA: Shambhala.

Eisner, B. (1997). Set, setting, and matrix. *Journal of Psychoactive Drugs, 29*(2), 213–216. doi:10.1080/02791072.1997.10400190

Goldsmith, N. (2007). Ten lessons of psychedelic psychotherapy, rediscovered. In M. J. Winkelman & T. B. Roberts (Eds.), *Psychedelic medicine: New evidence for hallucinogenic substances as treatments* (Vol. 2, pp. 107–141).Westport, CT: Praeger/Greenwood.

Greer, G. R., & Tolbert, R. (1998). A method of conducting therapeutic sessions with MDMA. *Journal of Psychoactive Drugs, 30*(4), 371–379. doi:10.1080/02791072.1998.10399713

James, W. (1993). The varieties of consciousness: Observations of nitrous oxide. In R. N. Walsh & F. E. Vaughan (Eds.), *Paths beyond ego: The transpersonal vision* (pp. 94–95). Los Angeles, CA: Putnam.

Jung, C. G. (1966). The practice of psychotherapy (G. Adler & R. F. C. Hull, Trans.). In H. Read, et al. (Eds.), *The collected works of C. G. Jung* (Vol. 16, 2nd ed.). Princeton, NJ: Princeton University Press.

Kasprow, M. C., & Scotton, B. W. (1999). A review of transpersonal theory and its application to the practice of psychotherapy. *Journal of Psychotherapy Practice Research, 8*(1), 12–23.

Kavalali, E. T., & Monteggia, L. M. (2012).Synaptic mechanisms underlying rapid antidepressant action of ketamine. *American Journal of Psychiatry, 169*(11), 1150–1156. doi:10.1176/appi.ajp.2012.12040531

Krupitsky, E., & Kolp, E. (2007). Ketamine psychedelic psychotherapy. In M. J. Winkelman & T. B. Roberts (Eds.), *Psychedelic medicine: New evidence for hallucinogenic substances as treatments* (Vol. 2, pp. 67–85). Westport, CT: Praeger/Greenwood.

Luckenbaugh, D. A., Niciu, M. J., Ionescu, D. F., Nolan, N. M., Richards, E. M., Brutsche, N. E., … Zarate, C. A. (2014). Do the dissociative side effects of ketamine mediate its antidepressant effects? *Journal of Affective Disorders, 159*, 56–61. doi:10.1016/j.jad.2014.02.017

Majić, T., Schmidt, T. T., & Gallinat, J. (2015). Peak experiences and the afterglow phenomenon: When and how do therapeutic effects of hallucinogens depend on psychedelic experiences? *Journal of Psychopharmacology, 29*(3), 241–253. doi:10.1177/0269881114568040

Mason, O. J., Morgan, C. J. M., Stefanovic, A., & Curran, H. V. (2008). The Psychotomimetic States Inventory (PSI): Measuring psychotic-type experiences from ketamine and cannabis. *Schizophrenia Research, 103*, 138–142. doi:10.1016/j.schres.2008.02.020

McElrath, K., & McEvoy, K. (2002). Negative experiences on ecstasy: The role of drug, set and setting. *Journal of Psychoactive Drugs, 34*(2), 199–208. doi:10.1080/02791072.2002.10399954

Myers, K. M., Carlezon, W. A., & Davis, M. (2011). Glutamate receptors in extinction and extinction-based therapies for psychiatric illness. *Neuropsychopharmacology, 36*, 274–293. doi:10.1038/npp.2010.88

Miovic, M. (2004). An introduction to spiritual psychology: Overview of the literature, East and West. *Harvard Review of Psychiatry, 12*(2), 105–115. doi:10.1080/10673220490447209

Misch, D. A. (2000). Basic strategies of dynamic supportive therapy. *Journal of Psychotherapy Practice Research, 9*(4), 173–189.

Sanacora, G., Treccani, G., & Popoli, M. (2012). Towards a glutamate hypothesis of depression: An emerging frontier of neuropsychopharmacology for mood disorders. *Neuropharmacology, 62*(1), 63–77. doi:10.1016/j.neuropharm.2011.07.036

Smith, H. (1964). Do drugs have religious import? *Journal of Philosophy, 41*, 517–530. doi:10.2307/2023494

Opportunities and Strategies for a Ketamine Psychotherapeutics (KAP)

Phil Wolfson, M.D.

KETAMINE, IN ITS TWO-FOLD POTENTIALITY in *sub-anesthetic* formats offers the possibility for a unique and beneficial approach toward developing and amalgamating psychotherapeutic methodologies. With low doses, ketamine produces a mild mood/mind altering trance-state and in moderately higher doses ketamine will create a transformative mood and mind-shifting psychedelic experience. In combination, the two formats and their attendant psychotherapies may complement and potentiate each other, increasing beneficial outcomes for a variety of psychological problems and disorders.

Ketamine is a drug, a medicine, a psychedelic, a psychotherapeutic tool, an experience. Its effects depend entirely on route of administration, dosage, set and setting (Collins et al., 2010; Duman & Aghajanian, 2012; Jansen, 2004; Katalinic et al., 2013; Khorramzadeh & Lofty, 1973; Kolp et al., 2014; Krupitsky & Grinenko, 1997; Ryan, Marta, & Koek, 2014; Wolfson, 1986). It can be abused and addictive, but this has not been reported in relationship to clinical usage, whether in psychiatric, emergency room (ER), or anesthesiologist practices. Its proven safety record and lack of impact on respiratory drive, unlike that of many anesthetics, makes for its safe and reliable application in office-based psychiatric/psychotherapeutic practices.

The Ketamine Trance Psychotherapeutic Experience

Within the past year there has been a shift in the understanding and use of low-dose oral and sublingual ketamine, calling into question the need for intravenous (IV) administration. This emerging view surfaced at a November 2015 KRIYA Ketamine

Conference organized by Raquel Bennett, PsyD, that created linkages with Stephen Hyde of Tasmania, author of *Ketamine for Depression*, and the Queensland, Australia, psychiatric group (Hyde, 2015; Katalinic, 2013; Wolfson, 2014). Their use of sublingual and oral administration of ketamine at dosages generally between 50 and 400 mg has called into question the need for IV administration with its cumbersome medical format, and the general lack of provision of a therapeutic relationship.

Ketamine as a medicine that induces a light trance-state has the capacity to ameliorate depression and other disorders, whatever the route of administration (Krystal et al., 1994; Luckenbaugh et al., 2014). In addition, the uniqueness of this trance-state provides an extraordinary opportunity to facilitate psychotherapy and has led to our development of therapeutic procedures that appear to be having an additional positive effect with patients. This is an evolving practice and we offer here our view and practice at this juncture.

We pursue two vectors with low-dose ketamine within the ketamine-assisted psychotherapy (KAP) format: 1) Abreaction and working-through of past developmental and specific trauma embedded formats as a more emotionally accessible state is obtained given the reduction in defensiveness (Golechha, Rao, & Ruggu, 1985); and 2) New mind—free of the past and its obsessional burdens, creative and open— a new and immediate experience of the self and connection. This also relies on ketamine's ability to improve mood, or more correctly to leave behind depressive and obsessional consciousness at least partially, for the period of its administration and frequently, in the aftermath of the session as well. Patients often experience less anxiety and an emergent optimism within the new freer state of mind that is engendered by the experience. We take measures to anchor this more liberated consciousness, emphasizing the retention and repetition of insights and essence statements that may serve as reminders to remain awakened to change. And because we are working with "states of mind" as such, with this new openness and emotional flexibility, we can highlight and emphasize those triggered states of mind that we often take for granted as our inevitable, fixed self.

Treatment-resistant depression (TRD), defined as depression continuing despite two appropriately applied antidepressants, is not a diagnostic entity in itself (Souery et al., 1999). This has been the rubric that has paved the way for the off-label proliferation of ketamine use and, indeed, has enabled the amassing of powerful data for the success of stand-alone multiple sessions of ketamine treatment. In truth, it is a category that exists because of the frequent failures of the existing antidepressants, with their limitations that leave 40% or more of people with significant depression still depressed. But both TRD and depression itself are conceptual containers in which myriad aspects of the complexities of mind and connection are subsumed without adequate consideration, or are entirely left out as causative and potentially ameliorable factors. Buried within—and this is not meant to be exhaustive—are the developmental trauma, complex trauma, attachment and PTSD disorders (these are also conceptual frameworks and may be overlapping and complementary), past and present trauma being a frequent basis for depression. Add to this our inherent but mutable personalities, the existential struggles for meaning and spirit, our failures, obsessional nature, shame and humiliations, oppressions and injustices. Above all lie our motivations for being and belonging, connecting, our core morality and compassion, our sense of justice and fairness, and our motivation to be healthy and loving (Greenberg, 2010; Wolfson, 2013).

Addressing ourselves to the actual situations of humans is a complex and difficult process, one which has generally come to be spoken of in its myriad forms as "psychotherapy," and which is differentiated from just applying medicines, or substances to the diagnostic entities of the DSM catalogues. This is where the opportunity for the development of an encompassing ketamine psychotherapeutics begins.

We are excited by this new potentiality as we have come to participate in remarkable transformations of consciousness, behavior, and connection, sometimes immediately, and more often as a crescendo of positive emotional energy over time, with baby steps, leaps, and faltering that make our work challenging, interesting, and rewarding. We are also aware of its limitations and the sadness of not being able to affect everyone who comes our way—this for many reasons, including the lack of response to ketamine itself.

During the early 1980s a loose network of therapists formed who recognized the therapeutic revolution that MDMA work offered (Wolfson, 1986). This was before the DEA arbitrarily consigned MDMA—against the findings of their own administrative law judge—to the therefore illicit-use-promoting Schedule I (hundreds of millions of experiences have since ensued). Later, labeled functionally as an "empathogen," its use over many hours brought therapists, patients, couples, and even families into closer understanding of each other and fostered alignment. The rapidity of MDMA therapy's effects on life were astounding. Today, in small Phase 2 studies, that potency of effect is again being demonstrated within the framework of FDA-approved protocols (Mithoefer, Grob, & Brewerton, 2016; Mithoefer et al., 2013), including the MAPS-sponsored study of MDMA Assisted Psychotherapy of Subjects with Anxiety Due to Life Threatening Illnesses in which I serve as principal investigator. This study fits within the concluded and ongoing studies of MDMA Assisted Psychotherapy for PTSD.

Our work with ketamine has been deeply influenced by our MDMA experience. There, we came to recognize the value of having a team therapist approach (male and female) on transferential and counter-transferential aspects; on making the work easier—it is stressful and two is better than one; and on the re-parenting effect of having a couple with whom to interact. In our ketamine work, we have applied the co-therapist model. Within the world of psychotherapy, having two therapists collaborating is both rare and unusually impactful.

Ketamine is not the same as MDMA, and I would hesitate to label it an empathogen. Rather, perhaps, a "euphorogen," as its effects in our context to foster a diminution or cessation of dysphoria and despair are often remarkable and generally significant. While the timeframe for ketamine work is shorter—sessions generally last for two to three hours, the full, intense ketamine experience with lozenges and/ or intramuscular (IM) administration, lasts anywhere from half an hour to over an hour, followed by continued ketamine influence for a much longer duration. This is a significantly amplified time for interaction and psychotherapy, especially with a patient with a receptive altered state of mind. Much as with MDMA-assisted psychotherapy, the ketamine approach can and often does have remarkably fast results in patients who have suffered for many years, even much of their lives, including those with treatment-resistant depression.

Also, as in MDMA work, KAP softens defenses, enabling PTSD memory awakenings to occur more easily. Verbalization and processing fosters a reduction in the severity of response to triggers that arouse operative, traumatized states of mind that cause suffering, negatively influence relationships and narrow here-and-now life and situational responsivity. Regression and the arousal of greater compassion for self allows for clarity about developmental trauma and attachment states (van der Kolk, 2014).

Ketamine is hallucinogenic, often at sublingual and IV drip dosages. Depending on patient sensitivity, which in general does not conform to milligrams per kilogram at the subanesthetic doses we use, patients may experience sensory highlighting in a spectrum that extends to what has been termed the K-hole, or a full dissociative, psychedelic experience. This is not predictable. The experience tells the tale. With the IM format, at 50 mg or greater, patients reliably have expansive experiences that open them to the breadth of their creative minds and the possibility for larger, less confined experience of self and the world. MDMA is not a hallucinogen, and in this sense the IM ketamine experience has greater similarity to the more extended in time psilocybin work that the Heffter Research Institute has conducted in its Phase 2 trials with that substance (Griffiths, 2015; Griffiths et al., 2011).

This more powerful and disembodied experience serves to loosen tight controls and engender flexibility of mind and behavior in its aftermath. It may well have a spiritual aspect of awe and engender a reduction of negative or inflated ego. As dysphoria is left behind, new energies for life are experienced and can be brought into play in ordinary life. The dissolution of body sensation as the drug takes effect, varying in depth with dosage and sensitivity, opens the patient to a unique realm. Disruption of form and the experience of becoming "as if energy itself" engenders a new view of essence and essentials. Ego dissolution and the rectification of narcissism—positive and negative—to a balanced sense of our personal and universal proportions is generally a welcome therapeutic and transformative aspect of the experience.

Reliving the experience in the aftermath, as the patient returns, solidifies memory and the cognitive hold on the experience. Explicitly discussing the experience of difference from ordinary consciousness and what is extracted and valued in potential new and enlivened consciousness assists the process of change. The experience itself is retained as intuition and modification of affect and executive function, this in varying degree—whether or not it is fully remembered, given that observing consciousness is present throughout the IM experience.

As a result of the preparation going into the session and our constant presence, preparing for the experience with guidance for navigation and reassurance, providing physical presence in the form of noninvasive body contact, initial anxiety (that can be strong) is quickly left behind as the internal experience unfolds—within two or three minutes from the injection. Often we smooth the way with an initial lozenge experience that, while adding to the overall dose of ketamine in a modest way, enables an easier transition from trance to transformation.

Ketamine-Assisted Psychotherapy Methodologies

We begin with a thorough history, using an intake questionnaire as a scaffold, and then the exploration of psychodynamic themes, including developmental, traumatic, relationship, and medical/psychiatric aspects. Based on this data, we create a story-telling psychodynamic hypnotic induction, which we call an invocation. This is aided by administration of the Resilience Scale and, in our presence, the Adverse Childhood Experiences (ACE) trauma questionnaire—which can be emotionally difficult and generally more revealing than historical questioning. We follow with the BDI (Beck, Steer, & Carbin, 1988), the MADRS (Montgomery & Åsberg, 1979), the HAM-A (Hamilton, 1959) and our own State of Change questionnaire. This detailed interest in the patient adds to a sense of the nest being prepared, a sense that we are truly interested in the person who comes before us for aid.

This protocol has been created to facilitate our own data collection as well as for the exchange of information between multiple practitioners. As ketamine is an orphan drug and will not receive research support from the pharmaceutical industry, it is necessary to create a multisite open-label collaborative effort as the basis for knowledge of treatment practices and effectiveness.

Sessions are supported by attention to sound—bells, rattles, and/or meditative music as a means for moving our subjects toward a release from what Buddhists call "ordinary mind." With the IM sessions, we provide specialized music that moves the patient through the extraordinary experiences they encounter. Synesthesia—the mingling of senses that distorts each sensory channel by combination—is reliably encountered in this state, and music that is oriented toward this facilitates the quality of experience and the movement through altered time and space.

Hypnosis has long been known as a successful method for treating PTSD. Our Ericksonian approach utilizes the actual trance-state that ketamine produces to introduce the difficult material that makes for the depressive and negative states our patients are experiencing that have not been sufficiently relieved and have been left behind by preceding treatment (Bandler & Grinder, 1975; Gilligan, 2012; Haley, 1967). Coupled with mindfulness meditative guidance and breathwork, the reduction in dysphoria in a session tends to be rapid and reliable. As patients feel less defensive and experience our understanding of them framed in a verisimilitude story that fits them, relaxation and the experience of relative trust is engendered. This is often coupled with access to difficult historical and emotional material, manifesting as heightened self-awareness. By objectifying states of mind against a background of emerging awareness of personal flexibility and the desire for relief from suffering, difficult states of mind are highlighted as just that—transient states and therefore nonessential. This engenders an awareness of the "stuckness" of mind, repetition compulsion, and defensive structuring that keeps these states operational—as if they were in fact the core person.

As the session continues, the freedom to be different emerges—to be in the present—and liberated from the oppressive weight of the dysphoria, sadness, fear, and obsession. Having that bit of a break is often experienced as light and lightness, as a relief, and we anchor that as knowledge that the suffering and being the same can lift and new mind and life emerge.

Following the pattern of what Peter Levine has dubbed "pendulation," the KAP trance allows for moving into difficult terrain and then out again, leaving affliction gracefully for the zone of the present moment (P. A. Levine, 2015; S. Levine, 2005). Moving back and forth creates balance and reference for the alive safety of the here and now in which trauma can be evaluated and reliably moved back to the time of its occurrence in the past. In our language, we ask to "send a probe" back in time to find the source of persistent states of mind that reflect trauma as defensive, protective structures that were adaptations or "decisions" that no longer serve and actually cause pain and disruption in present mind and behavior. If this work becomes overwhelming, we swing the pendulum back to the liberated spaciousness of the trance-state, in which dysphoria is reduced or absent, allowing for recovery and reflection. The trance-state creates a new sense of time and relative relationship to the present, as well as a greater mental flexibility and fear reduction. Generally, there is a slowing of mentation and this allows for expanded reflection and a new ability to know how to go back and forth, isolating states of mind as such, rather than feeling them as intrinsic aspects of the self.

To be sure, repetition of this experience, as well as the cumulative effect of ketamine experiences themselves, are responsible for growth and relief. We typically return to our usual modes easily, what I call the "rubber band effect." Repetition of the ketamine state is an ongoing resource for whatever time is necessary to consolidate effects and experience a new approach to life. While we have had multiple experiences of single-session miracles, rising off the ketamine couch, as a phoenix from the ashes, after years of chronic depression, support for the new state of mind is essential. We have no fixed formula and adapt to each person's presentation and needs. We rely on the input and often the presence of partners and relatives, who need to support the at-home work that continues with multiple lozenge sessions.

In general, we suggest that patients arrange for six lozenge sessions over two weeks, reproducing as much as possible our office experience at home—quiet instrumental music, no food for three to four hours prior, no alcohol the night before or after the session, meditative awareness—allowing what will arise to flow and move through them. Sessions at home may not have the same power as in our office given our absence. Yet they are essential for the sustained attention to respite and for the success of the cumulative effects of ketamine. These sessions are also empowering to patients as they validate their capacity to change mind and inner experience on their own. We ask patients to focus particularly on the period after the sessions as sessions themselves vary in effect—depth, highlights, reduction in dysphoria, euphoria, relief. We are looking for the effects of treatment over a longer time period, especially after the six at home sessions that continue what we have begun.

The duration and depth of ketamine sessions are unpredictable vectors and can only be assayed by direct experience. We have no means available to do so otherwise. Weight tends to provide an upper limit for dosing and we do not exceed 1.5 mg/kg, which generally is a very significant experience. Beyond this, there is a greater risk of nausea and vomiting, and memory for the experience is reduced as one moves toward greater analgesia and anesthesia. Virtually everyone has a significant psychedelic experience in the 50mg to 100mg IM range of our work. We begin naïve patients at the lower dose and move higher after assessing the depth and duration of the IM experience. Most often we are working at mid-range, even with experienced patients.

With our initial session—which tends to be a lozenge introduction to be followed by six at-home sessions over two weeks—we do a dosage ranging assessment for depth of trance-, beginning with a 50 or 100 mg lozenge and if necessary working up to 200 mg total for the session. In the interest of providing reliable lozenge dosages, we have the lozenges assayed by an outside independent laboratory. This eliminates the quantitative issue of reliability, but the absorption through the oral mucosa and losses due to lack of absorption and premature swallowing do affect this method of administration. To maximize the effect, we coach our patients in the retention of lozenges and saliva without swallowing through the lozenge's complete dissolution.

A great advantage of lozenges is the lack of ability to abuse them—it is unpleasant and difficult to jam many lozenges into one's mouth and hold them for sufficient minutes until dissolved. Safety is also facilitated by prescribing specific amounts tailored to the number of sessions at home performed within an individualized treatment plan.

Duration tends to be similar between the lower-dose sublingual 50–200 mg trance- experience and the IM method. Generally, the deep, effective portion of both experiences lasts 25 minutes to one hour. We have had patients emerge in as little as 12 minutes and spend as long as 90 minutes under significant influence. If an experience has been particularly short lived, we will begin an IM session preloading with lozenges and waiting for their effect and then proceeding to the injection. This has successfully prolonged and deepened sessions productively.

Depending on the person, we will schedule an integrative session one to three weeks after our initial session. We then may make a decision to incorporate the IM procedure, for which we ask for a three-session commitment, usually at intervals of two to four weeks, in the office, interspersed with the lozenge sessions at home, and/ or in the office. Or, we may make a decision to continue with lozenges only, as their effect is sufficient. After a remission is obtained, we structure a program for follow-up and maintenance of effect. This includes lozenge sessions if a relapse is felt to be impending. We follow the model for this set by Hyde and the Queensland group. Our initial expectations of rapid and sustained change from a small number of sessions has morphed through experience into a recognition that KAP work may be longer term, supported by somatic and meditative experiences and perhaps medication—for anxiety in particular. We collaborate with existing therapists to form a full program for recovery.

In our experience to date, the most difficult conditions to treat have been rigid personalities, somatization disorders, obsessive-compulsive disorder (OCD), and personality disorders compounding depression and other diagnoses. Ketamine sessions tend to give a brief view of the possible, but the rubber band effect is strong and may make for prolonged treatment or treatment failure.

We do not enroll psychotic persons or those with significant dissociative disorders. We are very careful with bipolar I patients and insist on mood stabilizers being prescribed. We are not treating addictions because patients with addiction would be best served by KAP while involved in a substance abuse program.

It has turned out that ketamine's effects are remarkably unaffected by the presence of other psychiatric medicines. We ask for a hiatus of 24 hours from stimulants, but rarely any other drug.

Couples Therapy With KAP

Working with couples in the KAP format is rewarding and interesting. Depression and obsessional foci are often shared, and individuals will react to each other with behavior that may reinforce staying in patient roles, a sharing that can reach folie à deux levels. Another complex we work with is frozen roles of caretaker and recipient as identified patient. And there are the couples that have become estranged and stay together because of children or other enwrapping concerns—money, fear, lack of self-esteem, being worn down, and so forth—where love and concern may remain as threads to potentially be made into a fabric that warms.

We have used KAP

- To reverse the roles of caretaker–recipient of care, in which a couple will change the person receiving ketamine, this with the prior identified patient (IP) recipient now as caretaker. This may restore a sense of balance and competency—from passive to active—and needs to be reinforced over time.

- To experience together KAP sublingual and/or IM as a shared letting go and an opportunity to cohere and find connection; as a fulcrum around which to restore and create intimacy.

- As a continuation at home for sexual and emotional intimacy with the lozenges abetting a relaxation and a recognition of the potential for loving connection and cooperation.

Invocations

Offered as examples of ketamine induction and bonding with the patient, their complex and their opportunity for liberation.

These are always specific to the person.

First Invocation: For a 46-year-old woman with severe PTSD and a chronic bipolar I diagnosis. Lozenge session: 100 mg to start and amplified to 200 mg total at 25 minutes after the initial lozenge and our assessment for effect.

With bells—turning mind to sound—and following a breath induction.

Welcome _____ to our sweet space
Letting sound penetrate mind for spaciousness and clarity
Letting go to allow whatever arises to arise
Whatever ceases to stop
Watching mind, knowing your body by feel,
Aware of pain and pleasure, of where it hurts and when you feel free,
Breathing deeply the great good air that is free and yours,
Relaxing vigilance by knowing it
And feeling that you are safe and home in your own true self
Allowing breath and sound to move you into this ketamine space

You who have been so hurt by life,
By your mother's brutality and craziness
Her spoken wish for you to die
Whose struggle with madness and hatred allowed her
To repeatedly hurt her own child
Creating fear and confusion
A lack of trust in yourself and others
That permeates your experience still
That is such unnerving suffering
Making your here and now life so difficult

Yet you have cared about her
And want to care as any child wants
To love and be loved
By her mother.

Left to fend for yourself
Without a father's protection
Left to fend for yourself as early as you can remember
No place or person for safety
Left with the inability to trust those
Who must be trustworthy
To enable your life, a child's life
That is not threatened
And left with great doubt about
Your own ability to love.

Or to whom you can give your love
Who will treat it well
All the poor choices for love
Created by this great confusion of trust

With your own emotional lability and
This trauma-given uncertainty of where you are
Moment to moment
Of not knowing your center as reliable

Being able to put your feet down and find
Terra firma for heart and soul

Yet, here we are
And all of that pain can go
And you may change
And your heart opens to yourself
To feel a relief
A great boundless relief
From this past
And its torment
So that kindness can enter you
A kindness that is deep and based
On knowing how a little girl suffered
Undeservedly
By an accident of birth

Not knowing
Nor being responsible
In any way
For the hatred and neglect, she received
Removing that hatred
Like pulling a dagger out of your heart
Removing that hatred
Knowing in its fullness
It was not about you whatsoever.

Knowing your essential own goodness
And that you are a truly lovable being
This without doubt

Knowing of your own invariable commitment
To be
And to give
The myriad ways you have stood tall
Caring for others

Devoted
Knowing that this is your insistence
On the truth of who you really are
Letting go of that hatred and neglect
That has made this so much more difficult than it has to be

Bringing light and optimism
And delight in being alive
Knowing this is your precious life
And it belongs to no other

Kindness, relaxation and relief
From this awful past and its burdens
All you carry of it
Removed from you
To make this your life now.

Relaxing. Letting go. Just being here. Here.

Later in the same session, working with her desire to be compassionate to her mother, drawn in as she has been, despite the continuing emotional violence and threats, we help her to come to a new view which she adopts, makes her own, to use as needed as she lapses into her state of mind: *Underneath the insanity and hatred, your mother as a mother could want only for your happiness and well being, much like all beings have an essential compassionate nature that can be obscured—a basic spaciousness and compassion—so too a mother's unobscured essence is to love and hold that child she nurtured inside her and brought forth into the world.*

And you and we know that to be true.
And can draw comfort from holding that mother essence without creating an expectation that you can give up your self-protection from the other mother who seeks to harm and cannot express love.

She responded: *Yes, I can feel and see that mother and hold that for myself.*

Moral: Always seek traumatic origins for difficult states of mind. Feel the potency of the life built despite, in spite of .... There are always two directions to the work—reworking the past; taking joy in the freedom of the present.

Second Invocation: For a 32-year-old woman whose father was killed in a bicycle accident at age 12, after which her mother took to herself and her family disintegrated. She suffers with chronic depression, OCD focused on failed, hopeless relationships, yet is functional as an attorney.

Blessings to you
Our precious being
Who comes knowingly to change
To free yourself
From depression and haunting trauma
That mars and distorts present consciousness
And also operates underneath consciousness
Shaping the moment's experience
In ways that hurt and constrict
This opportunity for just being.

We feel your deep sorrow and despair
Your desperation to be loved
And your hopelessness to ever have that happen
That creates this troubled holding on to tidbits of connection
Which goes on and on inside you
So long after you have been left
The image of 'him' calling you
And telling you
That which you so desperately wish to feel
In the core of you.

Much like holding onto your father's return
Long after he had been killed
When you were just 12
Waiting and hoping
That he would come home
And time would revert

And the destitution of your family
Would be mended
Wishing
Imagining the miraculous
As a young girl would.

And, indeed, he never came
He could not come
Or he would have
To be with you
And share your lives
And you had to care for yourself
And support yourself
Resenting for good reasons
Your mother's retreat into herself
Her selfish, wounded abandonment of you
When all you needed was her holding and reassurance
And you had to rock yourself
Tears turning to numbness and resignation.

This continues in you
And makes your path so difficult
With men and love and making a choice for relationship
Not trusting your beauty, intelligence and heartfulness to be enough
Your essence being enough.

And in this moment as ordinary mind fades
And obsessional mind relaxes
In this moment of spaciousness
You may allow your wisdom
And discriminating awareness
To reign
Creating a path in the present
Away from the repetition
And holding on
Free of these men phantoms

And open to finding love that is genuine
That lasts in truth and reciprocity
As your potential is
Realized in staying open
To what is real
What you truly know is real
Because it is given freely
By the other
In recognition of you.

Relaxing. Letting go. Just being here. Here.

Treatment of this patient is ongoing and movement has been bit by bit. Rigid patterns of being are more difficult to unwind and move toward here-and-now consciousness. The therapist with KAP work has the advantage of implementing time-outs from the obsessional pressure in which awareness of the complex and its repetitive arising can occur and healthy mind wend its way toward a healing.

Moral: Patience and reliability, steadfastness and confidence in the process making for benefit.

Knowing the traumatic origin and the density of the pattern laid down and weaving the demonstration of its effect into the nature of the affected, distorted process that is damaging present life.

Ketamine Sitting—Being the Therapist—Our Role and Stance

With you
As you fly
Keeping you safe
Wishing the best
—a breakthrough
—a relief
—a bit of new you
—a change of character
—levitation
—energetic formlessness

—an observer's egolessness
So that reformation
—when it comes
Is vivacious
Breath giving
Expansive
Open-hearted
Kind

Sitting with you
—in the great trance
I am expecting
Without expectation
Awake
For your awakening
Breathing
For your breathfulness.
Sitting with you
Knowing your suffering
As my own
Knowing the path
For suffering's cessation
Helping you to open that door
At least a crack
For your entry

Sitting with you
You will come back
And relate your journey
And we shall
Know together
Of where you have gone
And how you have returned
Taking this journey.

Congratulations!

Ketamine sitting
Teaches patience
And quiet
The mutuality of meditation
Doing my part
Listening to my mind
Listening to your breath
Alert to your groans and sounds
Yet meditating nonetheless
Meditating on your arisings
And offerings
In this sacred mostly stillness
It is like sky watching
Birds and clouds cross my open vision
Like your gifts of breath and sound
Your energy is like the sky
Vast and spacious
Potential
Life affirming
A consciousness that is novel
Precious
And to be cultivated
For your benefit
And so it is my benefit as well.

KAP Evolving

To conclude, KAP is an evolving, developing practice with its own set of limitations and possibilities. As practitioners enter the field and recognize the possibility with ketamine for rapid, intensive, and often effective psychotherapy, new and exciting treatment modalities will be added to what we have presented as our evolving practice. We hope that our work contributes to this process.

References

Bandler, R., & Grinder, J. (1975). *Patters of the hypnotic techniques of Milton H. Erickson (Vol. 1).* Cupertino, CA: Meta.

Beck, A. T., Steer, R. A., & Carbin, M. G. (1988). Psychometric properties of the Beck Depression Inventory: Twenty-five years of evaluation. *Clinical Psychology Review, 8*(1), 77–100. doi:10.1016/0272-7358(88)90050-5

Collins, K. A., Murrough, J. W., Perez, A. M., Reich, D. L., Charney, D. S., & Mathew, S. J. (2010). Safety and efficacy of repeated-dose intravenous ketamine for treatment-resistant depression. *Biological Psychiatry, 67*(2), 139–145. doi:10.1016/j.biopsych.2009.08.038

Duman, R. S., & Aghajanian, G. K. (2012). Synaptic dysfunction in depression: Potential therapeutic targets. *Science, 338* (6103), 68–72. doi:10.1126/science.1222939

Gilligan, S. (2012). *Generative trance.* Bancyfelin, Carmarthen, UK: Crown House.

Golechha, G. R., Rao, A. V., & Ruggu, R. K. (1985). Ketamine abreaction—Two case reports. *Indian Journal of Psychiatry, 27*(4), 341–342.

Greenberg, G. (2010). *Manufacturing depression: The secret history of a modern disease.* New York, NY: Simon & Schuster.

Griffiths, R. (2015). *Phase I study characterizing effects of hallucinogens and other drugs on mood and performance.* Retrieved from http://www.clinicalconnection.com/exp/EPVS.aspx?studyID=355992&slID=13163552

Griffiths, R. R., Johnson, M. W., Richards, W. A., Richards, B. D., McCann, U., & Jesse, R. (2011). Psilocybin occasioned mystical-type experiences: Immediate and persisting dose-related effects. *Psychopharmacology (Berlin), 218*(4): 649–665.

Haley, J. (Ed.). (1967). *Advanced techniques of hypnosis and therapy: Selected papers of Milton H. Erickson.* New York, NY: Grune & Stratton.

Hamilton, M. (1959). The assessment of anxiety states by rating. *British Journal of Medical Psychology, 32,* 50–55.

Hyde, S. J., (2015) *Ketamine and depression.* Bloomington, IN: Xlibris.

Jansen, K. (2004). *Ketamine: Dreams and Realities* (2nd ed.). Sarasota, FL: Multidisciplinary Association for Psychedelic Studies (MAPS).

Katalinic, N., Lai, R., Somogyi, A., Mitchell, P. B., Glue, P., & Loo, C. K. (2013). Ketamine as a new treatment for depression: A review of its efficacy and adverse effects. *Australian and New Zealand Journal of Psychiatry, 47*(8), 710–727. doi:10.1177/0004867413486842

Khorramzadeh, E., & Lofty, A. (1973). The use of ketamine in psychiatry. *Psychosomatics*, *14*, 344–346. doi:10.1016/S0033-3182(73)71306-2

Kiloh, L. G., Andrews, G., & Neilson, M. (1988). The long-term outcome of depressive illness. *The British Journal of Psychiatry*, *153*(6), 752–757. doi:10.1192/bjp.153.6.752

Kolp, E., Friedman, H., Krupitsky, E., Jansen, K., Sylvester, M., Young, M. S., & Kolp, A. (2014). *International Journal of Transpersonal Studies*, *33*(2), 84–140.

Krupitsky, E. M., & Grinenko, A. Y. (1997). Ketamine psychedelic therapy (KPT)—A review of the results of ten years of research. *Journal of Psychoactive Drugs, 29*(2), 165–183. doi:10.1080/02791072.1997.10400185

Krystal, J. H., Karper, L. P., Seibyl, J. P., Freeman, G. K., Delaney, R., Bremner, J. D., ... Charney, D. S. (1994). Subanesthetic effects of the noncompetitive NMDA antagonist, ketamine, in humans: Psychotomimetic, perceptual, cognitive, and neuroendocrine responses. *Archives of General Psychiatry, 51*(3), 199–214. doi:10.1001/archpsyc.1994.03950030035004

Levine, P. A. (2015). *Trauma and memory.* Berkeley, CA: North Atlantic Books.

Levine, S. (2005). *Unattended sorrow.* Emmaus, PA: Rodale.

Luckenbaugh, D. A., Niciu, M. J., Ionescu, D. F., Nolan, N. M., Richards, E. M., Brutsche, N. E., ... Zarate, C. A. (2014). Do the dissociative side effects of ketamine mediate antidepressant effects? *Journal of Affective Disorders, 159*, 56–61. doi:10.1016/j.jad.2014.02.017

Mithoefer, M. C., Grob, C. S., & Brewerton, T. D. (2016). Novel psychopharmacological therapies for psychiatric disorders: psilocybin and MDMA. *The Lancet Psychiatry 3*(5), 481–488, May 2016.

Mithoefer, M. C., Wagner M. T., Mithoefer, A. T., Jerome, L., Martin, S. F., Yazar-Klosinski, B. ... Doblin, R. (2013). Durability of improvement in post-traumatic stress disorder symptoms and absence of harmful effects or drug dependency after 3,4-methylenedioxymethamphetamine-assisted psychotherapy: a prospective long-term follow-up study. *Journal of Psychopharmacology, 27* (1): 28–39.

Montgomery, S. A. & Åsberg, N. (1979). A new depression scale designed to be sensitive to change. *British Journal of Psychiatry, 134,* 382–389.

Ryan, W. C., Marta, C. J., & Koek, R. J. (2014). Ketamine and depression: A review. *International Journal of Transpersonal Studies*, *33*(2), 40–74. Updated version in this book.

Souery, D., Amsterdam, J., De Montigny, C., Lecrubier, Y., Montgomery, S., Lipp, O., ... Mendlewicz, J. (1999). Treatment resistant depression: Methodological overview and operational criteria. *European Neuropsychopharmacology, 9*(1), 83–91. doi:10.1016/S0924-977X(98)00004-2

van der Kolk, B., (2014). *The body keeps the score.* New York, NY: Penguin.

Wolfson, P., (1986). Meetings at the edge with Adam: A man for all seasons? *Journal of Psychoactive Drugs, 18*(4), Oct–Dec 1986, 319–328.

Wolfson, P. (2013). Hark! The psychiatrists sing, hoping glory for that revised DSM thing! *Tikkun Magazine.* July 2013.

Wolfson, P. (2014). Ketamine for depression: A mixed methods study. *International Journal of Transpersonal Studies, 33*(2), 75–83.

Zarate, C., Duman, R. S., Liu, G., Sartori, S., Quiroz, J., & Murck, H. (2013). New paradigms for treatment-resistant depression. *Annals of the New York Academy of Sciences, 1292*(1), 21–31. doi:10.1111/nyas.12223

Ketamine-Assisted Psychotherapy (KAP), Sublingual and IM: A Potential Model for Informed Consent

Phil Wolfson, M.D.

Introduction

Ketamine is increasingly a clinically applied "off-label" treatment for various chronic treatment-resistant mental conditions. Ketamine is a Schedule III medication that has long been used safely as an anesthetic and analgesic agent and now, often effectively for treatment of depression, alcoholism, substance dependencies, post-traumatic stress syndrome (PTSD), and other psychiatric diagnoses.

How Does It Work?

The current, most probable, understanding of ketamine's mode of action is as an NMDA antagonist working through the glutamate neurotransmitter system. This is a very different pathway than that of other psychiatric drugs such as the SS-RIs, SNRIs, lamotrigine, antipsychotics, and benzodiazepines. However, there is no consensus on mode of action. Other mechanisms may well be found central to ketamine's effects.

Ketamine is classified as a dissociative anesthetic, dissociation meaning a sense of disconnection from one's ordinary reality and usual self. At the dosage level administered to you, you will most likely experience mild anesthetic, anxiolytic, antidepressant and, potentially, psychedelic effects. More recent work has demonstrated the possibility of an antidepressant response to low dosages of ketamine—administered intravenously, intranasally and sublingually (orally)—which produce minimal psychedelic effects; this anti-depressant effect tends to be more sustained with repeated use—a cumulative effect. It is our view that psychedelic, "dissociative" experiences may well be instrumental in providing a more robust effect. This may well include a positive change in outlook and character that we term a "transformative" response. We may employ both methods together, as will be described herein.

Essential to both methods is a time-out of usual experience, this period being of varying duration, usually 30 minutes to two hours, which tends to be dose and method of administration related. Relaxation from ordinary concerns and usual mind, while maintaining conscious awareness of the flow of mind under the influence of ketamine, is characteristic. This tends to lead to a disruption of negative feelings and obsessional preoccupations. It is our view that this relief and the exploration and experience of other possible states of consciousness are singularly impactful. As therapists we act as guides to the experience and process the experience and its impacts with our patients before and after the sessions.

Monitoring

It is essential that you be followed very closely during and after your treatment. This will include blood pressure and pulse measurements, as appropriate, and psychological assessment tools administered before your first and subsequent sessions to measure effects. Follow-up will be by telephone and/or email and in-person contact as needed.

You will be entering a psychotherapy program that will prepare you for your ketamine session(s) and assist you in integrating your experience(s) afterwards. This program emphasizes the possibilities for change and the seriousness of your effort and our effort to assist you. For most people entering ketamine-assisted psychotherapy (KAP), there will be a sustained period for therapy to continue to benefit emotional healing and growth. Support from family, partners, and close friends is desirable, and they will be included in sessions or parts of sessions as deemed appropriate by you and us as your therapists.

How Long Will It Take Before I Might See Beneficial Effects?

You may experience important changes in personality, mood, and cognition during treatment, in the aftermath, and in the days and weeks that follow. Some experiences may be temporarily disturbing to you. The ketamine experience itself is designed to enable your own healing wisdom to be accessed and beneficial to you. The psychotherapy support you will receive will aid you in making your experience(s) valuable and understandable to you. We will endeavor to assist you in changing patterns of mind and behavior that are of concern and cause you difficulty.

Why Ketamine Assisted-Psychotherapy?

The purpose of the intramuscular (IM) ketamine experience is to create a non-ordinary ("altered") state of consciousness in order to facilitate profound transpersonal ("transcendental," "mystical," "spiritual," "religious") peak experiences.

These may prove to be auspicious in resolving your existential problems, accelerating your psychospiritual growth and leading to a deep personal transformation and optimization of your lifestyle. Such change is best facilitated within a structured supportive psychotherapeutic milieu in connection with therapists who have a view of your issues, hopes, desires, and struggles. As a byproduct of your experience you may well feel improvement in your emotional state and reduction in symptoms that bother you, such as depression, anxiety, and post-traumatic manifestations. You may well notice that you are a bit different after a ketamine experience, and that difference may well be liberating and allow for new mindfulness and new behavior.

With respect to intramuscular ketamine, we are asking that new patients make a commitment for three IM sessions as a minimum exposure to ketamine. Additional sessions may occur if deemed appropriate and beneficial. We understand that you are able to withdraw from our treatment at any time.

Your experience will be unique to you. And if you and we decide to have additional sessions using ketamine, each of your sessions will be different. All such journeys are adventures that cannot be programmed. They evolve from your own being in relation to this substance. While it is best to form an intention for your journey, you may or may not be able to hold on to that. Indeed, no holding on is best, and the journey will flow whether you hold on and resist or follow the path that unfolds and relax into it. Holding on is the main source of anxiety in this and other related journeys. A ketamine session can be light, dark, or both. There will be concepts, visions, encounters, and you may well deal with your own death, mortality, and immortality. Not everyone enjoys the journey, but everyone comes through it.

The purpose of the sublingual ketamine lozenge sessions is to generate a robust antidepressant or other (PTSD, etc.) benefit that often occurs over time with repetition of administration of the lozenges. For some people, the lozenges may be used in concert with the IM sessions, but for many others, the lozenge experience may well be sufficient and healing. The sublingual method is equivalent in effect to the intravenous (IV) method and much less expensive and cumbersome.

We generally begin with assessing responsiveness to the lozenge. This enables us to make a decision about the effectiveness of the lozenge and to adjust the dose. You will be given lozenges to take at home for designated evening ketamine sessions, in between IM sessions or on their own. Such sessions will be supported with periodic psychotherapy sessions in which you will meet with us. Please understand that if you prove to be responsive to the ketamine experience, treatment may well continue for a period of time based on your continued response and benefit, as well as prevention of relapses. In concert with you, we will work out a schedule appropriate to your needs, history and responsivity.

The literature indicates a 70% response rate to ketamine, as well as a remission rate for treatment-resistant depression of 40–50% using multiple sessions of either the low-dose IV drip method or the sublingual method. Relapses do occur and may require periodic additional sessions. Over time, a certain number of patients may become unresponsive to further ketamine sessions. Based on our growing experience, we believe the sublingual method, either on its own or with the IM sessions—within a framework of intensive psychotherapy designed explicitly for the ketamine experience—will exceed this rate of response.

Eligibility for KAP

This consent form contains information about the use of subanesthetic dosages of ketamine for psychiatric purposes including depression. Ketamine was approved by the FDA for use as an anesthetic agent several decades ago. The administration of ketamine in lower, subanesthetic doses to treat pain and depression or other psychiatric diagnoses is a newer, off-label use of ketamine. Psychiatric use of ketamine has become relatively widespread in recent years, has been studied and promoted by researchers at the National Institute of Mental Health, and has had front-page publicity as the newest antidepressant with its own novel pharmacological mechanism of action. Ketamine has been administered by intravenous, intramuscular, sublingual, oralsublingual, and intranasal routes. Often, it has been used after other treatment approaches have been unsuccessful.

Once you indicate that you have understood the benefits and risks of this treatment, you will be asked to sign this form at your first visit in order to participate in this treatment. This process is known as giving *informed consent*.

By signing this document, you indicate that you understand the information provided and that you give your consent to the medical procedure to be performed during your participation in ketamine treatment.

Please read this consent form carefully, and feel free to ask questions about any of the information in it.

Eligibility for Ketamine Treatment

Before participating in ketamine treatment, you will be carefully interviewed to determine if you are eligible for ketamine therapy, including a medical/psychiatric history, review of your medical/psychiatric records if necessary, and administration of brief psychological tests to assess your state of mind.

Pregnant women and nursing mothers are not eligible because of potential effects on the fetus or nursing child. The effects of ketamine on pregnancy and the fetus are undetermined, and therefore, it is our policy that you protect yourself against pregnancy while exposing yourself to ketamine or in the immediate aftermath of its use.

Untreated hypertension is a contraindication to ketamine use because the substance causes a rise in blood pressure (BP). Similarly, a history of heart disease may make you ineligible to participate.

Information on ketamine's interaction with other medicines is only partially available and it will be assessed as to your eligibility for KAP.

Ketamine should not be taken if you have untreated hyperthyroidism. There have also been reports of some decrease in immune function in patients receiving surgical doses of ketamine.

Ketamine has an extensive record of safety and has been used at much higher doses for surgical anesthesia, without respiratory depression.

Overview of Ketamine-Assisted Therapy

During the ketamine administration session, you will be asked to make two agreements with the therapist(s) to ensure your safety and well-being:

1. You agree to follow any direct instructions given to you by the therapist(s) until it is determined that the session is over, and:

2. You agree to remain at the location of the session until the therapist(s) decides you are ready to leave.

The length of ketamine sessions varies from person to person and from experience to experience. You will be mostly internally focused for the first 30 minutes to one hour or more. With the sublingual lozenges, we refer to this state as a light trance. Following IM administration of ketamine, the experience is much deeper and yet you remain conscious of your experience. With either method or in combination, you will continue to remain under ketamine's influence at a lesser level for at least one hour. Under my care, ketamine will be given as an intramuscular injection into the shoulder or buttocks at doses of 50 mg to 100 mg (130 mg maximally). The choice of dose will depend on prior exposure to ketamine and other psychedelics, body weight, and sensitivity. Naïve subjects will receive a lower dose at their initial session. It is always better to start with a lower dose to reduce anxiety and become familiar with what a substance may produce in you. There is always an opportunity to make a choice for a larger dose at a future date. Individuals experienced with psychedelics may receive a higher initial dose. Ketamine IM creates an unusual experience of formlessness and a dissolving of boundaries and has novel effects on the mind. Therefore, it is much better to have an initial learning experience.

The initial IM injection may be preceded by administration of a sublingual lozenge containing 50 or 100 mg of ketamine. Or we will elect to do lozenges only to begin your ketamine treatment. Lozenges dissolve slowly and we ask you not to swallow your saliva until after the lozenge has dissolved, typically about five minutes. Ketamine will penetrate the oral mucosa—lining of your mouth—and will be absorbed rapidly in that manner. This will give us a measure of your responsivity to ketamine. Additional lozenges may be given to you during the session to enable optimal effect for you. At the end of the session you will be given lozenges, a prescription will be called in to our formulating pharmacy for additional lozenges, and a plan created with you for their use at home. We suggest you use the lozenge in the evening at least two hours before your usual bedtime; that you lie in a quiet, comfortable space, assuming a meditative attitude; that you listen to gentle instrumental music of your choice; that you not watch television or use the computer; and that you not drive afterward or operate potentially hazardous machinery. We advocate that you do not use alcohol before and after ketamine sessions because its use may have negative emotional and physiological consequences. If you are unable to do evening sessions, daytime sessions are fine with the same provisos. Do not eat anything for at least three hours prior to a lozenge session to prevent nausea and enable absorption from ketamine that reaches the alimentary tract. Please refrain from using stimulants the same day. If ketamine causes you to experience an increase in your energy that affects sleep, change your timing to earlier in the day.

Preparation for a ketamine session requires assessment by your therapist of your readiness and a sense of connection between you and your therapist. We are engaging in a therapeutic endeavor to benefit you and those who are affected by you. Together, we are creating a state of mind (set) in a safe and conducive setting. After ketamine IM and sublingual use, you will have follow-up sessions that focus on integration of your experience and may lead to further sessions, if you so wish, and if that is in accord with your therapist's view of your treatment.

You may ask the therapist(s) any questions you may have concerning the procedure or effects of ketamine at any time. Your consent to receive ketamine may be withdrawn by you, and you may discontinue your participation at any time up until the actual injection or lozenge has been given.

Potential Risks of KAP

You will be asked to lie still during the ketamine administration because your sense of balance and coordination will be adversely affected until the drug's effect has worn off—generally two and up to four hours after the injection. It is possible you may fall asleep, though this is a rare event. Other possibilities for adverse effects include blurred and uncomfortable vision (you are advised to keep your eyes closed until the main effects have worn off), slurred speech, mental confusion, excitability, diminished ability to see things that are actually present, diminished ability to hear or to feel objects accurately including one's own body, anxiety, nausea and vomiting. Visual, tactile and auditory processing are affected by the drug. Music that may be familiar may not be recognizable. Synesthesia—a mingling of the senses—may occur. Ordinary sense of time will morph into time dilation.

Because of the risk of nausea and vomiting, please refrain from eating and drinking for three or four hours preceding the session and eat lightly when you do. Hydrate well in that same time frame.

If you are unduly nauseated, you may be offered an antinausea medication—ondansetron—as an oral dissolving tablet.

Ketamine generally causes a significant but not dangerous increase in blood pressure (BP), but usually not in pulse rate. If blood pressure monitoring reveals that your blood pressure is too high, you may be offered clonidine to remedy this. There is also a very small risk of lowering BP and pulse rate.

Agitation may occur during the course of a ketamine session. If your agitation is severe, you may be offered lorazepam orally or by injection to help you relax. This too is a rare event in our experience.

The administration of ketamine may also cause the following adverse reactions: tachycardia (elevation of pulse), diplopia (double vision), nystagmus (rapid eye movements), elevation of intraocular pressure (feeling of pressure in the eyes) and anorexia (loss of appetite). The above reactions occurred after rapid intravenous administration of ketamine or intramuscular administration of high doses of ketamine (in a range of greater than 5 mg/kg used for surgical anesthesia. The dose to be used in this subanesthetic ketamine therapy is much lower (2 mg/kg or less).

Driving an automobile or engaging in hazardous activities should not be undertaken until all effects have stopped. If for any reason the effects continue, a driver may be necessary. You will be assessed for safety prior to leaving the office premises.

In terms of psychological risk, ketamine has been shown to worsen certain psychotic symptoms in people who suffer from schizophrenia or other serious mental disorders. It may also worsen underlying psychological problems in people with severe personality disorders and dissociative disorders.

During the experience itself, some people have reported frightening and unusual experiences. These frightening experiences, however, may be of paramount value to your transition to recovery from the suffering that brought you to your KAP work. They will stop! You will receive psychotherapeutic help and ongoing guidance from your therapist.

Potential for Ketamine Abuse and Physical Dependence

Ketamine belongs to the same group of chemicals as phencyclidine (Sernyl, PCP, "angel dust"). This group of chemical compounds is known chemically as arylcyclohexylamines and is classified with hallucinogens ("psychedelics"). Ketamine is a controlled substance and is subject to Schedule III rules under the Controlled Substances Act of 1970. Medical evidence regarding the issue of drug abuse and dependence suggests that ketamine's abuse potential is equivalent to that of phencyclidine and other hallucinogenic substances.

Phencyclidine and other hallucinogenic compounds do not meet criteria for chemical dependence, since they do not cause tolerance and withdrawal symptoms. However, "cravings" have been reported by individuals with the history of heavy use of "psychedelic" drugs. In addition, ketamine can have effects on mood (feelings), cognition (thinking), and perception (imagery) that may make some people want to use it repeatedly. Therefore, ketamine should never be used except under the direct supervision of a licensed physician.

Repeated high-dose, chronic use of ketamine has caused urinary tract symptoms and even permanent bladder dysfunction in individuals abusing the drug. This does not occur within the framework of our study.

You will be provided or prescribed just the amount of lozenges necessary for your treatment between sessions with us. They have no street value.

We and our colleagues doing clinical ketamine work have not had patients become dependent on ketamine.

Alternative Procedures and Possibilities

No other procedure is available in medicine that produces ketamine's effects. Major depressive disorder (MDD), PTSD and bipolar disorders are usually treated with antidepressant medications, tranquilizers, mood stabilizers and psychotherapy. Electroconvulsive therapy (ECT) and the recently introduced transcranial magnetic stimulation (TMS) are also in use for treatment-resistant-depression. Ketamine has also been used in the treatment of addictions and alcoholism as part of comprehensive and usually residential treatment programs, primarily abroad.

Confidentiality

Your privacy and all therapy records will be kept confidential. They will be maintained with the same precautions as ordinary medical records. To allow others access to your records, you will have to provide a signed release form. The results of this ketamine therapy may be published in clinical literature. Published reports will not include your name or any other information that would identify you.

Voluntary Nature of Participation

Please be aware that the Food and Drug Administration (FDA) has not yet established the appropriateness of ketamine-assisted psychotherapy and its use is considered off-label, the only official 'indication' for use of ketamine being anesthesia. Your awareness of this situation is key to understanding any liability associated with your use of ketamine. Your informed consent indicates you are aware of this situation.

Ketamine is a new psychiatric treatment—the primary studies have been with depression, bipolar disorders and alcoholism. It is not yet a mainstream treatment, though there are now many studies that demonstrate that it may be an effective treatment. That effect generally occurs with more than one treatment and is most robust when part of an overall treatment program. It may not permanently relieve depression. If your depressive symptoms respond to ketamine-assisted psychotherapy, you may still elect to be treated with medications and ongoing psychotherapy to try to reduce the possibility of relapse and anxiety. Over time, you may also need additional ketamine treatments or other therapies to maintain your remission.

I practice psychiatry/psychotherapy and may offer to assist you with other medications, to consult with your therapists and MDs, and to make recommendations to you about your treatment in addition to our ketamine work. You may, if you wish, consult with me about these treatment issues.

Your decision to undertake ketamine-assisted psychotherapy is completely voluntary. Before you make your decision about participating in KAP, you may ask—and will be encouraged to ask—any questions you may have about the process.

Withdrawal from KAP is always your option. Even after agreeing to undertake ketamine-assisted psychotherapy, you may decide to withdraw from treatment at any time.

I understand that I am to have no food or drink at least three and preferably four hours prior to my ketamine session

I understand that I may need to have someone drive me home from the sessions, and that I must not engage in any driving or hazardous activity for at least six hours or more, depending on the continued presence of effects after my session has concluded.

Informed Consent Attestation

By signing this form, I agree to the following:

1. I have fully read this informed consent form describing ketamine-assisted psychotherapy.

2. I have had the opportunity to raise questions and have received satisfactory answers.

3. I fully understand that the ketamine session(s) can result in a profound change in mental state and may result in unusual psychological and physiological effects.

4. I give my consent to the use of lorazepam if deemed necessary for agitation, to ondansetron for nausea, and for clonidine for high blood pressure.

5. I have been given a signed copy of this informed consent form, which is mine to keep.

6. I understand the risks and benefits, and I freely give my consent to participate in KAP as outlined in this form, and under the conditions indicated in it.

7. I understand that I may withdraw from KAP at any time up until the actual injection or lozenge has been given.

Signature:

Date:

Printed Name:

Physician/Therapist Statement

I have carefully explained the nature of ketamine-assisted psychotherapy to _____. I hereby certify that to the best of my knowledge the individual signing this consent form understands the nature, conditions, risks and potential benefits involved in participating in KAP.

A medical problem or language or educational barrier has not precluded a clear understanding of the subject's involvement in KAP.

Signature of Physician: _____

Date: _____

Ketamine:
Consciousness and Transformation

The Transformative Power of Ketamine: Psychedelic States and a Personal History of Self-Transformation

A Guide to Ketamine Experiences

Phil Wolfson, M.D.

TRANSFORMATION CAN BE UNDERSTOOD IN TERMS of the alternative: staying the same. Staying the same—it is perhaps the greatest problem for the human species. Staying the same means that people repeat their mistakes, keep their biases and prejudices, and maintain their difficult behaviors. It means that obedience—to religions, national formations, groups, tribes, and cults—too often trumps personal beliefs, self-awareness, and self-interest. Staying the same is the great purveyor of psychotherapy, the source for authoritarianism's success, the frustrator of communitarianism and empathy. It is what makes us inflexible, repetitive, and argumentative. Change is difficult!

In psychotherapy, one refers variously to character, to self and Self, to ego and Ego, personality and personality disorders, obsessions, obsessive-compulsive disorder (OCD), muscular armoring, defensiveness and defenses, rigidity, the repetition compulsion, and so forth. All of these are descriptors in one form or another for staying the same. In truth, individuals are trained to underplay the corresponding social expressions of staying the same since their understanding and the potential breakage from control becomes too close to political revelation and liberation—compliance, passivity, soldiering-on, authoritarian, conformist, conservative, diehard, reactionary, pessimistic, alien and alienated, fundamentalist, the "isms," and so on. Each of us has some of these elements going on at some level of control—within each of us, within others, within the ebbs and flows of relationship.

Buddhists have wrestled with this one for their 2,500 years. Buddhism comes down to the presentation of deep formulas for liberation from this suffering, such as, "there is no intrinsic self," or to the great medicine of the Buddha's Fourth Noble Truth, "the letting go of attachments"; or in Vajrayana (Tibetan)—Dzogchen or primordial awareness; or Rigpa—both referring to the endlessly generative spaciousness we each contain. Change is life's constant, yet annoyingly, staying the same also seems to be very with us. Somehow as we develop, grow, age, confront endless scenarios for learning and adaptation, as our molecules are exchanged for new ones, as the air we breathe is renewed with each respiration, as we have the opportunity to change our views and approaches, our attitudes and beliefs—somehow structures of mind are retained, even if maladaptive and afflictive.

Of course, there are essential structures such as memory, learned responses to contacts with the world and self, our language and its formats and so much more that are essential to function and quality of life, that give us a continuity, a sense of self, without which we would be lost much as if we were immersed in a formless ocean. That is the great dialectic—between rigid limiting conceptual structures and those that are necessary for us to be social, survivable, functional, creative, and nurturing beings. That is the ridge on which transformation rides. On one side is staying the same with its attendant suffering and difficulties that in this continuum ranges towards paranoid structuring; and on the other, the bliss of openness, new mental maps, and re-constitution—ranging in this continuum to formless confusion. Transformation is not unidirectional or certain. Bumps in the road of life shove us all over the mental places we may inhabit. New partly formed characters arise within us with their own—our own—personalities arranged around cores of belief and reaction—often to our surprise as to who we suddenly have become—this in relation to new challenges, trauma, and aging. Our response repertoire narrows and expands continuously. At the biological level, this corresponds to our remarkable neuroplastic capacity and functional neuronal rearrangement constancy, also known as learning and adaptation.

Here is my working definition of transformation: A change in one's core conceptual and even physical structure that interrupts the prior sense of self and world view and induces an altered, at least partially different, sense of self and world view immediately and/or over time with some degree of persistence. Transformation is a reboot of our operating system with at least some new programming and sometimes even a change from system 1.0 to 2.0. It is analogous to neuroplasticity but occurs at a much faster rate—generally with an immediacy—and may well lead to an eventual corresponding revamping of dendritic relations—and who truly knows what that looks like in humans.

Psychedelics and Transformation: A Personal Overview

One set of the transformative experiences I have sought over a major portion of my personal history has been with the non-compulsive and deliberate use of psychedelic substances. As with most people who repeat, an initial powerful experience oriented me to the possibility for inner work and alternative experiences—that I would be different as a result of use and these differences would be sufficiently beneficial to explore additional trips and different mind-altering substances. I will present a schema for looking at the allure of these substances and their transformative powers. In this presentation, the mental ambience in which I write is particularly oriented towards ketamine experiences, which I view as singularly and rapidly productive of transformational experiences.

First, a bit of background to situate the presentation of subjective states. Psycho-active substance induced alteration of consciousness is age old, the specific history dependent on humans' particular geographic location and corresponding native plant habitats. It is important to differentiate between our equally ancient propensity to "get high" with those particular substances that induce intoxicated states and, in contrast, the often difficult deliberate journey of the psychonautical pioneer and the culturally embedded shaman. This is an imperative for clarity about psychedelic use—although there is certainly a mid-region of experience where recreational use meets transformation. For in fact, the inadvertent, non-deliberate, spontaneous and profound psychedelic arising is ever a potentiality of any use, and a significant aspect of the allure—and the risk of casual use. The remarkable discovery, perpetuation, refinement of use, and sacralization of psychoactive substances, even with stone age cultures, testifies to the timeless power of human interest in transcending "ordinary" historical and cultural realities and the enduring strength of human mind exploration.

Remains of marijuana plants in human contexts have been found as early as 4,000 years BCE—the earliest plant remains known having been carbon dated to that time. Humans and marijuana have co-evolved, influencing each other recipro-cally in terms of cultivation and culture. Mushroom and other psychoactive plant use in Mesoamerica is likely thousands of years old and was ineradicable despite the deliberate murder of practitioners by the Inquisition and genocidal suppression of indigenous cultures by the colonizing Europeans. In fact, Europe was desperately poor in psychedelics, these being limited to the toxic tropane alkaloids contained in such plants as mandrake and henbane with their datura-like effects. European consciousness developed its particular distortions in concert with the addictive and easily manufactured toxin known as ethanol—of limited value for mental and spiritual transformation.

Most remarkable is the Amazonian creation of ayahuasca, or yage, the admixture of two separate plants that had to be bundled to create the remarkable oral DMT-based experience that was practiced as divination and personal transformation by native shamans. Ayahuasca use has recently spread to North America, culminating in the U.S. Supreme Court's recognition of the União do Vegetal (UDV) with hoasca as an acceptable sacrament and indispensable part of the UDV Church's ceremonial life, much as peyote is for the Native American Church—deliberate uses of mind altering substances for the purpose of transformation within bounded social and religious frameworks.

As to the allure of psychedelics, the most potent explanation is that they offer the possibility of a transformation of consciousness. That may occur as an intimate acute experience or a form-shaking permanent alteration—it is a spectrum of effect that ranges to incalculable personal and social consequences. The introduction of psychedelic substance use to masses of people in the 1960s was part and parcel of the immense cultural change that occurred. Liberation from the suppressive, repressive yoke of McCarthyism that had penetrated darkly into the family culture of the late '40s and '50s was in part due to the mind expansion of psychedelic use that blew up restrictive mental fetters and fear of the personal imagination. Huddled in social phobia and conformism after the great cultural and political awakening of the post–World War II epoch by the repressive political reaction and domination of the late '40s and '50s, there lay latent in the populace a great desire for a spring blooming of equality, justice and freedom of mind and life. This latent corrective can be envisioned as an inherent sense of justice, and nurturance—of the pleasurable nature of the freedom to think and to be in open connection.

This psychedelic transformation of sectors of Western societies and of the overall cultural stream was transmitted reciprocally to and from new cultural and political formations. Politically for example, if the entire New Left did not succumb to rigid and dogmatic Leninism, it was to a great extent protected from that by personal mind-expanded experiences that escaped control by all ideologies and consciousness. But it is not a perfect record, and psychedelics were also used to corrupt and control humans. For example, from opposite perspectives, this applies both to the final catastrophic period of the Weather Underground, and to the CIA—which has had a compulsive interest in using psychedelics coercively to extract information or to create group and personal confusion, even madness (Lee, 1994; Stevens, 1998).

As the vector of transformational change with psychedelics is uncertain in a general sense and deterministic in an individual sense by personal experience and values, psychedelic experiences that are dissociative in nature are potentially transformative. This is caused by the rupture of conceptual structures and the induction to some extent or more of a confusional state—a scramble of categories and of the process of categorization—in the Brunerian (Bruner, 1991) sense. It is this potentiality that makes us anxious about beginning a profound trip, and it is the letting go of control within a trip that facilitates our resilience and restructuring with the fullness of the experience. Integration during and after a psychedelic experience therefore is an essential component of consolidating and perpetuating change. It is an essential component of any thoughtful and potentially helpful psychedelic psychotherapy.

There are basically three schools in this regard, with many practitioners doing combinations. The Grof approach (referring to Stanislav Grof) asserts the value of the healing potential in the experience of the journey itself that requires support but not guidance and little in the way of interpretation. Inner wisdom knows what needs to be transformed. The Metzner approach (indicating Ralph Metzner) asserts the benefit of guided interventions that are felt to increase the depth, diversity, and the psychotherapeutic aspect of psychedelic experiences. Preparation and clear intentionality are considered essential. However, for both, creation of a pluripotential setting—rich in ritual and suggestion—that is safe but provocative is essential. The third and again overlapping approach that I am labelling as the Roquet tendency (after Salvador Roquet; Krippner, 2016; Wolfson, 2016) is challenging in both the provision of the setting and the provocation of intensity. Egolysis, or ego dissolution, is deliberate and amplified with reconstruction in the integration phase a necessity. This has been well described in the pages of this issue by Richard Yensen and others. With recent neurocognitive research this can be described functionally as the disintegration of the Default Mode Network by psychedelic influences (Lebedev et al., 2015).

Some aficionados of the pure psychedelic experience argue that the unmitigated experience itself is sufficient to deliver transformation. Sasha Shulgin (Shulgin & Shulgin, 1991) often took this position, and as his experience was of the greatest depth and diversity, it certainly deserves credence. Empathogenic and dissociative experiences may very well lead to incredible changes in our consciousness and behavior. Then, there are others such as I who find that the transformative influence of the psychedelic experience makes a quantum leap when integrated with spiritual practice, such as Buddhist contemplation and with a liberating psychotherapy. Unsupported psychedelic experience tends to be unpredictably transformative, and integrations from the spirit side with ordinary lived reality are more difficult without recognizing that psychedelic transformation is but one prong of conscious intent to transform ourselves from the capture of the corporate materialist culture and its introjects. That is not a simple or straightforward task. The value vectors of personal ethics and social morality that have been developed, or not, over our personal/social histories truly guide us in the path of our psychedelic experiences. Psychedelics can be tools for deliberate exploration of our lives and tendencies, for examination, contemplation, and for transcending ordinary reality and our adherence to its format.

The Varieties of Psychedelic Experience

To convey the varieties of psychedelic experience is to have the experience of words faltering as descriptive. Hopefully, without intending to reify, or circumscribe, I will present a taxonomy of experience that reflects my personal history and observations over 52 years' time, since I and a small group of new friends, just commencing medical school in New York City, dropped acid—LSD. With this rubric, I am attempting to convey the psychedelic allure as well as a schema for recognizing and understanding transformation. I am using the term *states* rather than some hierarchical notion based on "levels"—all such states having value for transformation.

The Mundane State

Conventional allure to trip flows from curiosity, a desire to change oneself, temptation for forbidden fruit, getting high, and the emulation of others. This is "tripping" with little or no intention regarding what will come, or what will change—experience without intentionality. There is no pejorative here, no judgment. Many of us have and will do this and find extraordinary experiences. Our minds are endlessly entertaining to ourselves and we try either to increase the entertainment value, to leave boredom, to find relief from sameness and negative states, to explore inwardly our potentialities, and break out of our molds and moulds.

The Personal/Psychotherapeutic State

In 1964, I was a young, awkward, and self-conscious male, repressed, having just finished a psychoanalytically oriented psychotherapeutic experience that had helped me to alleviate some of the pain of my hypercritical feuding parents that I had introjected. I was beginning to find my own voice and guidance. In the flash dance of a few hours, my inner structure rocked and shifted. LSD and I met and I passed through great fear to feel alleviated of self-hate and my imagination freed to inform a creative new consciousness. Art came alive, as did everyday experience. After I came down from the LSD trip, integration included a deliberate determination to hold onto that freedom informed by a structural psychological awareness that had been obtained in the intensity of my earlier psychotherapy experience. Pockets of repressive structure opened for awareness work. Subsequent introduction to marijuana freed me of physical and sexual awkwardness, turned me on to intimate discourse, a heightened closeness in friendship, and furthered my sense of being a creative person. This was not completely linear—there were ups and downs—and it took place with absorption in the growing Movement—a sense of being in a community of progressive people worldwide. Psychedelic use in that formative period increased my self-confidence and sensuality. It did not prevent me from making all manner of errors in personal and political life, but I was much better at discernment, moving on, kindness, and forgiveness.

Psychedelic use invariably affects the personal/psychological matrix. Starting a journey forces an encounter with fear—of the unknown, of the lurking dangers believed hidden in one's own mind, of coming back altered. In the encounter the first period is generally absorbed with the personal—relationships, guilt, love, longing, grief, attachments, self-concepts. This encounter opens the possibility of examination, release, and change, of reframing and heightened awareness of self and the other(s). A bad trip—usually in an uncomfortable setting under stressful circumstances—can result in fear, paranoia, and recoil from the opened space that is perceived as threatening. Some folks never use psychedelics again. Occasional young people and some others—I know personally of several 12- and 13-year-olds—suffer with mental effects that damage and may last far too long. Set—the mind's orientation—and setting—the circumstances of use—always affect the quality of significant psychedelic experiences. Conscious preparation, good location, presence of support and friends benefit experiences and outcomes.

The Empathic State

Generally, any psychedelic experience may heighten empathy and empathic awareness—as love and affection, as the ability to see another's point of view and put oneself in the other person's shoes, as deep respect and regard, as elimination of barriers that separate, as communion with nature, and as a transcendent feeling of warmth for all things. In the 1980s, the potency of MDMA was recognized as a means—a tool—for heightening the quality of communication between people and for fairly reliably producing a state of warmth, affection, and nonsexual sensuality. Many therapists, including myself, introduced MDMA psychotherapy within couple, family, and group contexts. Because the experience was fairly replicable, generally positive, and without much in the way of distortion and hallucination, a new name was coined for a cluster of substances for which MDMA—ecstasy—was the exemplar: empathogens.

Before the DEA's own administrative law judge, those of us who saw MDMA's potential for positive impact were able to demonstrate its medical utility. Despite the judge's ruling, which would have placed MDMA in an accessible Schedule II classification, the DEA went against its own judge's finding and placed it in the highly criminalized and inaccessible Schedule I group of substances that included heroin, and other banned psychedelics. In the years that followed the 1986 ruling, MDMA use soared, and the "rave" phenomena began—again a testimony to the power of the substance to facilitate loving, intimate, sensual experience—even with huge numbers of people. MDMA's appeal continues to be based on the facilitation of a state of communion and community larger than the personal self's usual strictures allow. MDMA consciousness can be learned and generated without the drug on board as part of an expansive, loving daily life. Much of the concern about brain damage due to serotonin depletion was based on phony research that was retracted from the literature when it was exposed. After almost 40 years of use, 31 of it in this continuing prohibition era, with an unimagined scale of use—hundreds of millions of doses consumed—my informal census of other therapists and friends who were there from the start fails to reveal names and numbers of MDMA brain-damaged individuals.

All psychedelics can generate a sense of deep compassion for self and others, both within the experiences themselves—and as part of the aftermath with a re-opening of heart and accessibility to humility and warmth. Some seem more explicit in that capacity and we have come to call these empathogens, in addition to MDMA, 2CB and MDA, to name a few that tend to be more psychedelic than MDMA. All are fostered in this capacity by the creation of a situational ambience that facilitates heart openings.

The Egolytic State

For the most part the psychedelic experience exerts a damper on egotism and ego centrality. A sense of smallness and particulate being in the universe may be a fundamental part—that is, "I am truly insignificant and yet I have a limited significance in this time and space I occupy." A reduced sense of attachment to material goods, awestruckness with life and the psychic ground, spaciousness of mind, a situating of the self as but a speck in the cosmos, a sense of ease at being free of self-inflated importance may compose much of the trip. For some, this can be difficult and disorienting as a loss of the centrality of self and confusion as to how to manifest and re-integrate. For most, this state provides a welcome relief from the tension of being a particular totalization in the personal world and the competitive, demanding outer life.

The Transcendent Transpersonal State

Stripped of ego, of personal psychology and investments, the psychedelic traveler enters the ground state from which thought, feeling, form, and formlessness emanate. It is as if the source of mind becomes the mind experience itself. This is certainly not restricted to psychedelic states. In the unadorned meditative experience, this too is highlighted for periods of time. An apocryphal story from those who travel in both the spiritual and psychedelic realms is that the great guru drops a bazillion micrograms of LSD and stays beaming and untouched the entire trip time and is in his nature so spiritually elevated that the drug is not altering or transformative—he is the ground state itself. Ram Dass among others is fond of this tale. I have my doubts. In the psychedelic state it is the flux, the movement, of stimulated consciousness—that is there to be experienced at a heightened level of manifestation. Some psychedelic experiences are difficult to recall and difficult in which to maintain an observational awareness. However, most experiences include intense observational awareness. Dose is a factor—generally, the more you take the more observational awareness tends to diminish. By amplifying the phenomena coming into being, placing our attention on the background generative source of mind, psychedelics tend to make more available for experience and scrutiny what Tibetans refer to as *Dzogchen*, or *primordial awareness* as it is commonly translated, the *sunyata* state in Sanskrit, and in the less developed Western explication the state of awe. By learning to reside in a non-dualistic state of mind, by choosing to enter that state and by having experiences which create faith in the goodness of that state, spaciousness, creativity, and compassion arise from non-attachment, from living in the flow, from not grasping at every object that comes to mind and attracts our attention.

Within a transcendent transpersonal State, a multiplicity of experiences and views will arise and are generally not pre-programmable, but have some degree of specificity depending on the substance ingested—different substances tend to produce a quality of experience specific to those substances—and state of mind. I will mention a few by description that I class as "vistas"—this is certainly not meant to be exhaustive. I am referencing primarily ketamine and ayahuasca experiences as well.

The Sensual Universe Vista. Traveling through space as on a rocket ship, or being that rocket ship, I encounter extraordinary forms and shapes. Neon colored blazing fractal worlds open. Forms emerge—animals, beings from other galaxies, lovers and forgotten friends. I morph to meet them and my morphing morphs. I am eaten and eat, am absorbed and absorb. Sexual encounters may occur. Love spills everywhere. Or fear brings on its own forms and monsters. Psychological themes come from my everyday life and are given forms, often allowing for a working through of trapped emotional energies. There is a sense of great exploration and great bliss, and at other times of the terror of being alive and vulnerable.

The Entheogenic Vista. A personal experience of being of god, or a relationship to the personally held notion of god that deepens may occur. A sense of traveling in the starry cosmos freed from all constraint may occur, of being part of a perceived universe. Buddhists are told that they have, as do all sentient beings, Buddha Nature. In the psychedelic realm, I became the Buddha and felt that meaning and that responsibility. I moved about as the Buddha. I have tried to maintain that sense of awesome responsibility in my usual unenhanced state, to varying depth and effect—it is difficult. But at other times, there can be the sense of the devil within, of the play of evil and the hunter/murderer, which we also contain and constrain. In mind travelling, there is no risk in exploring this aspect of us, knowing and accepting of what we are capable and explicitly reject as actual behavior.

The Connection Vista. The experience of connection and interdependency gives rise to feelings of gratitude, love, humility, and desire to benefit others. Our personal lifeline extends backwards through a near infinite unbroken number of progenitors to the unformed stuff of the great earthly soup from which first life forms emerge—this may be experienced—and forward to the future as well. I have felt myself to be much as a mushroom sprouts from the great mycelial mass, its myriad threads stretching underground in all directions, sprouting beings who as their time ends return to the rich mulch while new sprouts—humans—emerge—a sense of vibrant biological immortality. Or in contrast, the direct experience of the human mass as itself a cancer, having all of those characteristics—unrestrained expansionism, proliferation in all directions, lack of concern for others' needs and requirements—eating everything in its path, out of control. Or as group mind, the experience of sensation outside the confines of the personal body/mind, in resonance with the others with whom one is travelling as a new assemblage in which the mind is of its nature intrapersonal.

The Cartesian Vista. I am the source of all that I experience. I create it. The outside realm—all of it—is a manifestation of my mind. This passes before me as I scan all of my creations from scientific texts to great vistas and friends and my partner. I am the author of life and death. Moving about within this perspective, I am able to revise what exists and what will be—for a time—until I am drawn back to the usual perspective of subject and object. That experience, while a false consciousness, increases the sensitivity to the difficulty of being an interpretive, removed from direct experience, consciousness with only mediated awareness of the external and personal awareness of the interior. While in this inflated state, I am god and master of the universe, prophet, seer, enlightened being. Then there is the crash, and, hopefully, great humility—redemption from being too central.

Integration

In the post-psychedelic condition, integration is the key to maintaining transformation. Integration is a function of intentionality—conscious and unconsciously maintained, or incorporated. Integration occurs both without effort—as a re-design of the central processor of our minds—and voluntarily as a deliberate effort to understand, find meaning, and as rectification—of our behavior towards others and towards ourselves. The psychedelic experience in and of itself may be transformative of our consciousness, but support for change by deliberate and disciplined absorption in the myriad spiritual/emotional/psychological/activist opportunities for increasing clarity and breadth most probably results in a more long-term and positive transformation of self. The human mind, while extraordinarily plastic, adaptable, and mutable, is also built with a great rubber band that returns us to our dominant character. This serves both as preserver of the integrity of the self and as a block to transformation—holding onto our deluded self, or neurologically our Default Mode—which I am sure, absolutely certain, can be modified and upgraded.

Grounding in the world of the interior and the external world—finding balance—is a prerequisite for successful psychonautical voyaging and for a mind expansion that is in essence kind, creative, and loosens the spell of the propaganda-filled social world we inhabit that tells us what to think and feel and especially what to desire and purchase.

To conclude, psychedelic exploration has been part and parcel of this culture for several decades. Both inadvertent change from recreational use of mind-altering substances and the deliberate pursuit of a transformative path have occurred for many millions of people, yet as a result of the illegal status of psychedelics, there has been a restricted discussion and sharing of experience, despite the extraordinary numbers involved. I have presented one schema among many possibilities for sharing and conveying transformations that occur with psychedelics and hope this inspires both research and sharing by others of the qualities of mind and behavior that result from psychedelic use as transformations of self.

A Longitudinal View of Personal Transformation
(presented as a humble exemplar and an encouragement to view your own path)

I am 72 years old, rapidly approaching 73. Aging is transforming my physical capacities; my desires—fewer of them; my interests—perhaps more of them; my sense of time—moving faster and less of it; and the immediacy of death itself—close by, inevitable. My mental abilities have yet to atrophy—so I am told—for how would I know if I lacked them? I have spent my life transforming. I am certainly not with the consciousness I can remember from my start in life. Nor from my teenage years. Nor even from my 30s and 40s. Yet I have a sense of continuity and that commences with my first memories at about age 3 and includes a sense, a feeling, of me-ness. I seem still to be enough of the "me" that arose that I recognize a strand. Life is truly a dream and my experience seems more and more a mediation between me and my past, and me and the world outside. It is this sense from which more profound psychological states of dissociation arise. I am fortunate in that I have dreamt the entire night, every night, so long as I can remember.

If sleep architecture with its discontinuities and non-dreaming states is to be believed, it does not correspond to my own uninterrupted experience of constant nightly movies. The usual marking of day and night is more of a slippery transition for me, and while I have no trouble discerning the two consciousnesses from each other, I have virtually no experience of being fully unconscious. My five surgeries with general anesthesia gave me the most pertinent information on ceasing to be—from complete darkness with re-entry as the sensation from whence arising consciousness emanated. Before that sense of darkness, I had no prior sensation of existence whatsoever. All of this convinces me and highlights my sensation of a stream of consciousness that begins for me at about 3 years of age, also emanating from darkness, and continues unbroken, like a moving river, a dream state, during each 24 hours, part of the time in contact—more or less—with a mediated reality outside of me, and part of the time just with me, an interiority, that also has an awake interiority that is more cognitive, less imaginal than night dreaming, but with many of the same elements, sensations and removal from direct sensory contact.

If personal life is a stream dream, how then to view transformation? There is that classical argument in Zen schools between gradual and saltatory transformations—getting to Kensho and Satori. The same dualism occurs in Vajrayana Buddhism with schools making differing claims on the means for transformation, the prerequisites, the rapidity and the immanency. If I have learned anything it is that there are as many schools as there are humans. Even my dogs have their views, which they espouse as well in their own ways, according to their capabilities of reaching my awareness and my capabilities of understanding their communication—some of that an empathic mutual understanding—making me aware of their needs and views. What many do agree upon is that they experience transformation of consciousness and life behavior both gradually and also in sudden spurts of fierce energy and realization. The direction is not always pleasant. Transformation can go either way, through unpleasant experience and chosen unpleasant means, and through pleasant, even ecstatic states. Transformation can be courted, seduced, planned, practiced for over time, induced, and can be involuntary, unplanned, damaging, life-threatening, grievous and disabling. Since conscious life is an experience related to a seamless existential dreaming, transformation is a constant moving thing. Peak experiences, as per Abraham Maslow, may entail transformation—or not, whereas transformation may contain or entail peak experiences—or not. Historically, discussion of transformation has focused on mystical, and sudden transformations that are often only partially integrated and are experienced as "stand alone" experiences, unclassifiable and ineffable. While such significant events are unforgettable and momentous, they tend to be overemphasized and to obscure other more prolonged experiences of fundamental change and the effects of deliberate practices aimed at transformation.

So, my experience of me over time is that I have changed and that this has been reflected in my contexts, connections and behavior. I am unable to isolate a single experience as The Transformational Transcendent Singular Event (TTSE)—sounds like the Higgs Boson. I am unlike Saint Augustine for example. Rather, as I look back over time, there have been numerous transformational moments and processes, a catalog of which would be voluminous and necessarily incomplete because of faulty memory and inadequate retrieval—too much time and too many events. If this seems too mundane, not sufficiently spectacular, one factor is that of time, which blunts immediacy and tall peaks. Nonetheless, it appears to me to be a truthful representation of my experience that goes back as far as I am able to remember.

If transformation is not restricted to peak experiences, but rather to an awareness of change over some time scale, it is clear that transformation is not discrete, has long slow waves, and sudden lurches, and things in between.

Some transformation is clearly developmental but still contingent. For example, I recall falling in love (FIL) at 3 to 5 years of age. Though I never again saw any of the three girls with whom I played in my early Manhattan apartment house culture, I was permanently altered by an awareness of attraction at that age that made me seek them out, made me miss them after I moved—never to see them again—and dreams of them that occur even now—their names affixed to imagined representations of them as adult women who come in and out of my dream life on occasion. The integration was my experience of love and arousal for girl strangers with whom I bonded at a high level—nonsexual but aroused intimacy. In that same early period, I made close friendships (FNDS) with boys and had a very different, but complex and loving set of feelings for them—friendship as a mode arose in me—clearly both of these transformational and not inevitable. Thereafter, I sought out both experiences throughout my life. When we left for Queens and a small, isolating private house, I grieved and was depressed for quite some time. That too was poignantly transformational as I learned of loneliness and the inability to rectify my heartbreak, and the arbitrariness of adult authority—out of touch with my love and need for my companions. Transformational indeed. In childhood, transformations are a frequent part of life as part and parcel of development, but from the adult vantage point we forget that we were incredibly mutable and affected—by love, trauma, and the vectors of growth and mastery. Nevertheless, the notice internally—the awareness at the meta-level—of the occurrence of a transformational experience is set up during childhood.

A taxonomy can be developed for transformational experiences and is offered for your potential use [table 1].

Clearly these are continuums and capable of being placed in a matrix: The Transformation Codex. I use Codex deliberately to represent the book of changes, which can be compiled for any of us, at virtually any stage of life.

Examining my chart indicates the variety of powerful transformational events spread over a lifetime, their different experiential time frames, my tendency to focus on events that resulted in what I regard as long-term and integrated changes, and the mix of inadvertent and deliberately sought for experiences. The list is suggestive and not meant to be exhaustive by any means. I hope it provides an encouragement for others to look at their history.

Table 1. The Transformation Codex

Life Event	Age	Time Scale	Volition	Integration	Quality	Validated	Self-Validated	Duration	Awareness
Early Love FIL	3 on	P	IA	I	AH	V+/-	SV+	ALC+	SCs, UCs
Friendship FNDS	3 on	P	IA, then D+/-	I	3AH	V+	SV+	ALC+	SCs, UCs
Leaving Home LHC	16	S	D+	I	2AH	V+	SV+	ALC+	Cs
First Psychoth FPE	17–18	ST	D+	I	3AH	V+	SV+	ALC+	Cs, SCs, UCs
Mature Love FMLS	17–18	ST	D+/-	I	3AH	V+	SV+	ALC+	CS
College CIGA	17–20	P	D+/-	I	AH	V+	SV+	ALC+	Cs, UCs
Trip LSDT	21	S	D-	I	3AH	V-	SV+	ALC+	Cs, UCs
Sixties SM	20 on	S, P	D+/-	I	3AH	V+	SV+	ALC+	Cs, UCs
Family FB	27 on	P	D+/-	I	3AH	V+	SV+	ALC+	Cs, SCs, UCs
Loss LOAC	44	S, P	IA	PI	2OV-	V+	SV+	ALC+	Cs, SCs, UCs
Buddha BP	52 on	P	D+/-	PI	2AH	V+	SV+	ALC+	Cs, SCs, UCs
Psychedelic PP	40 on	S, P	D+/-	PI	2AH	V+	SV+	ALC+	Cs, UCs

Key:

Time Scale of Transformation Event: sudden, short-term, prolonged: S, ST, P
Volition: deliberate-just as planned, somewhat, not at all as planned: D+, D+/-, D-; or inadvertent: IA
Integration: integrated, partially integrated, stands alone: I, PI, SA
Quality: positive, ah ah, aah haa, aaah haaa: AH, 2AH, 3AH; negative, oy, oy vey, ouuy, veey: O, OV, OV-
Validated: others concur or give evidence of my change: V+, V-
Self-Validated: I am different and my consciousness, choices, and actions are different-totally, somewhat, not at all: SV+, SV+/-, SV-
Duration: a lasting change-fully, partially, overridden, deleted: ALC+, ALC+/-, ALC-
Awareness of the occurrence and nature of Transformation: immediately conscious, semi-conscious, unconscious: Cs, SCs, UCs

To play with this classification schema, I will share with you a partial temporal review of some of my transformational experiences, with the classification as above—to tweak your own sense of history and its partial correspondences:
Leaving home for college (LHC): transformation, partial independence and autonomy.
First psychotherapy experience (FPE): at college, transformation, reduction of tyrannous super-ego influences, finding my own mind and speaking it.
First mature love and sexuality (FMLS): transformation, being loved by another fully (or as much as possible under those circumstances), less self-conscious and negative.
College intellectual growth and assurance (CIGA): transformation, independent thinking possibility enhanced social capacity.
LSD trip (LSDT): transformation, loss of fear of incipient madness, access to another realm of mind, enhanced imagination and creativity, unique experience.
Sixties Movement (SM): transformation, citizen of the world, brotherhood/sisterhood, loss of fear of confronting authority, physical trauma, enhanced creativity and empowering sensation of freedom.
Family building (FB): transformation, experience of the absolute love of children, new sense of wider responsibilities and larger sense of self, enhancement of the child consciousness within.
Loss of a child after prolonged illness (LOAC): transformation, loss of orientation and meaning, permanent grief, dissolution of marriage, extraordinary anxiety, greater coping skills, awareness of my own imperative to stay alive.
Buddhist practice (BP): transformation, explicit meditative states and the freedom occasionally from grasping and attachment, valuing that experience and seeking it.
Psychedelic practice (PP): transformation, sudden dissolution of my self and reconstitution, deliberately sought for its transformative power, experience of group mind and being out of my own particular body experience, improvisation and intuitive mindfulness and creativity.

Some limiting factors: To reach significance, a transformative experience has to be at the level of an Ah or an Oy. The duration of an experience can be prolonged and over years of time. Aging tends to diminish former peaks and there is an undoubtedly "besotted with change" factor that alters the drama of change to some incalculable effect. Finally, this is an almost entirely subjective method, save for the subjective awareness of others' views of our sense of transformation, which has some verifiability attached. I am—and hope you are—a fan of qualitative research.

My hope is that you will play with this schema, fill in your own experiences and have a better grasp on how you have changed over time and space. It may serve to guide future practice and the deliberate courting of experiences including the psychedelic. Bon voyage!

Conclusion

A ketamine psychedelic experience tends to offer up the possibility for transformation of the self by isolating the mind to some extent from external sensations, altering body consciousness toward an experience of being energy without form, and by amplifying and scrambling the contents of mind in unpredictable ways—all of this generating the potentiality for changes in consciousness that may be beneficial and persistent. Coming back from a ketamine journey as a somewhat different being is quite predictable. The supportive nature of setting, facilitation, and integration are indispensable for reducing confusional aftermaths and having a positive sense of the experience and its outcome. As described, the nature of experiences will be quite variable and unpredictable for each individual's repetition of a ketamine experience. Relaxing of control and resorting to observation of the flow of the experience are important means for having an experience that is beneficial.

In conducive settings, ketamine experiences that are transformative may well result in a qualitative improvement in affect and consciousness that can result in a lessening of depression, of the hold on us of traumas and obsessions, of negativity and pessimism, and an improvement of our self-regard. There are various ways to conceptualize this reformation. You will need to find your own path, happily so, you are unique. May your travels be beneficial!

References

Bruner, J. (1999). The narrative construction of reality. *Critical Inquiry, 18*(1), 1-21.

Krippner, S. (2016). Remembering Salvador Roquet. (This volume)

Lebedev, A. V., Lövdén, M., Rosenthal, G., Feilding, A., Nutt, D. J., & Carhart-Harris, R. L. (2015). Finding the self by losing the self: Neural correlates of ego-dissolution under psilocybin. *Human Brain Mapping, 36* (8), 3137–3153.

Lee, M. (1994). *Acid dreams: The complete social history of LSD: The CIA, the sixties, and beyond.* New York, NY: Grove Atlantic.

Shulgin, A., & Shulgin, A. (1991). *Pihkal: A chemical love story.* Berkeley, CA: Transform Press.

Stevens, J. (1998). *Storming heaven: LSD and the American dream.* New York, NY: Grove Atlantic.

Wolfson, P. (2016). Psychedelic experiential pharmacology: Pioneering clinical explorations with Salvador Roquet—An interview with Richard Yensen. (This volume)

Index

Winkelman, Michael 64
World Health Organization 106

Y

yage 378
Yensen, Richard 14, 59, 60, 64, 67, 69,
        86, 379
Young Mania Rating Scale (YMRS) 212

Z

Zarate, Carlos 156
Zung Anxiety Scale 293, 300

About the Publisher

Founded in 1986, the Multidisciplinary Association for Psychedelic Studies (MAPS) is a 501(c)(3) non-profit research and educational organization. Since our founding in 1986, MAPS has raised over $36 million to develop psychedelics and marijuana into prescription medicines and to educate the public honestly about the risks and benefits of these substances. **Learn more about our work at maps.org.**

MAPS works to create medical, legal, and cultural contexts for people to benefit from the careful uses of psychedelics and marijuana. MAPS furthers its mission by:

- Developing psychedelics and marijuana into prescription medicines
- Training therapists and working to establish a network of treatment centers
- Supporting scientific research into spirituality, creativity, and neuro-science
- Educating the public honestly about the risks and benefits of psyche-delics and marijuana.

Our top priority is developing MDMA-assisted psychotherapy into an approved treatment for posttraumatic stress disorder (PTSD). MAPS has completed six Phase 2 clinical trials into the safety and efficacy of MDMA-assisted psychotherapy for PTSD, and is beginning Phase 3 clinical trials in 2017. Data from Phase 3 clinical trials will be submitted to the U.S. Food and Drug Administration (FDA) and European regulatory agencies, with approval anticipated as soon as 2021. With promising results and growing support from medical and therapeutic professionals, the main challenge is to raise the funds necessary to support this vital research. **For more about how you can help make psychedelic therapy a legal treatment, visit maps.org.**

At the time of this publication, there is no funding available for these studies from pharmaceutical companies or major foundations. That means that—at least for now—the future of psychedelic and medical marijuana research rests in the hands of individual donors.

Please join MAPS in supporting the expansion of scientific knowledge in the promising area of psychedelic research. Progress is only possible with the support of those who care enough to take individual and collective action.

Learn more and sign up for our monthly newsletter at **maps.org**, or write to us at **askMAPS@maps.org**.

Why Give?   maps.org/donate

Your donation will help create a world where psychedelics and marijuana are available by prescription for medical uses, and where they can safely and legally be used for personal growth, creativity, and spirituality.

Every dollar we spend on this work has come from visionary individuals committed to our mission. For-profit drug companies don't invest because there is no economic incentive to develop these drugs; these compounds cannot be patented and are taken only a few times. We're encouraging government agencies and major public foundations to support our research. For now, however, it's up to individuals like you to support the future of psychedelic medicine.

To thank you for your contribution to MAPS, we offer these benefits:

Give $50 or more ($60 for international donors): Receive the tri-annual *MAPS Bulletin*

Give $100 or more ($120 for international donors): Receive a free MAPS-published book

Give $250 or more: Receive a copy of *Modern Consciousness Research and the Understanding of Art* by Stanislav Grof, or another MAPS-published book. We'll also send a one-year *Bulletin* subscription to a friend or colleague.

Give $1,000 or more: Receive invitations to attend special interactive webinars with MAPS' executive staff, and a silver MAPS logo pendant.

Each giving level includes the benefits for the levels listed above.

Donations are tax-deductible as allowed by law, and may be made by credit card, or by personal check made out to MAPS. Gifts of stock are also welcome, and we encourage supporters to include MAPS in their will or estate plans (**maps.org/bequests**).

MAPS takes your privacy seriously. The MAPS email list is strictly confidential and will not be shared with other organizations. The *MAPS Bulletin* is mailed in a plain white envelope.

Sign up for our monthly email newsletter at **maps.org**.

MAPS
PO Box 8423, Santa Cruz CA 95061 USA
Phone: 831-429-MDMA (6362) • Fax: 831-429-6370
E-mail: **askmaps@maps.org**
Web: **maps.org** | **psychedelicscience.org**

More Books Published by MAPS   maps.org/store

Ayahuasca Religions: A Comprehensive Bibliography & Critical Essays
Beatriz Caiuby Labate, Isabel Santana de Rose, and Rafael Guimarães dos Santos
translated by Matthew Meyer
ISBN: 978-0-9798622-1-2 $11.95

The last few decades have seen a broad expansion of the ayahuasca religions, and (especially since the millennium) an explosion of studies into the spiritual uses of ayahuasca. *Ayahuasca Religions* grew out of the need for a catalogue of the large and growing list of titles related to this subject, and offers a map of the global literature. Three researchers located in different cities (Beatriz Caiuby Labate in São Paulo, Rafael Guimarães dos Santos in Barcelona, and Isabel Santana de Rose in Florianópolis, Brazil) worked in a virtual research group for a year to compile a list of bibliographical references on Santo Daime, Barquinha, the União do Vegetal (UDV), and urban ayahuasqueiros. The review includes specialized academic literature as well as esoteric and experiential writings produced by participants of ayahuasca churches.

Drawing it Out
Sherana Harriet Francis
ISBN: 0-9669919-5-8 $19.95

Artist Sherana Francis' fascinating exploration of her LSD psychotherapy experience contains a series of 61 black-and white illustrations along with accompanying text. The book documents the author's journey through a symbolic death and rebirth, with powerful surrealist self-portraits of her psyche undergoing transformation. Francis' images unearth universal experiences of facing the unconscious as they reflect her personal struggle towards healing. An 8.5-by-11 inch paperback with an introduction by Stanislav Grof, this makes an excellent coffee table book.

Healing with Entactogens: Therapist and Patient Perspectives on MDMA-Assisted Group Psychotherapy
Torsten Passie, M.D.; foreword by Ralph Metzner, Ph.D.
ISBN: 0-9798622-7-2 $12.95

In this booklet, Torsten Passie, M.D., a leading European authority on psychedelic compound, explores MDMA and other entactogens as pharmacological adjuncts to group psychotherapy. It presents intimate insights into entactogenic experiences from first-hand accounts of clients who participated in group therapy sessions, and crucial background on the neurobiological and psychospiritual components of those experiences. The word "entactogen" refers to compounds that "produce a touching within," and is derived from the roots *en* (Greek: within), *tact's* (Latin: touch), and *gen* (Greek: produce. Entactogen is used to describe a class of psychoactive substances that decrease anxiety; increase trust, self-acceptance, and openness; and allow easier access to memories, providing fertile ground for transformative healing.

Honor Thy Daughter
Marilyn Howell, Ed.D.
ISBN: 0-9798622-6-4 $16.95

This is an intimate true story by Marilyn Howell, Ed.D., about her family's search for physical, emotional, and spiritual healing as her daughter struggles with terminal cancer. The family's journey takes them through the darkest corners of corporate medicine, the jungles of Brazil, the pallid hallways of countless hospitals, and ultimately into the hands of an anonymous therapist who offers the family hope and healing through MDMA-assisted psychotherapy. The story was originally featured in a 2006 Boston Globe article entitled "A Good Death" in which Howell's identity was concealed. With psychedelic medicine increasingly a part of the mainstream vocabulary, in this poignant new book Howell comes out of the closet and shares with us how psychedelic therapy helped heal the bonds ripped apart by illness.

Ketamine: Dreams and Realities (out of print)
Karl Jansen, M.D., Ph.D.
ISBN: 0-9660019-7-4 $14.95

   London researcher Dr. Karl Jansen has studied ketamine at every level, from photographing the receptors to which ketamine binds in the human brain to observing the similarities between the psychoactive effects of the drug and near-death experiences. He writes about ketamine's potential as an adjunct to psychotherapy, as well as about its addictive nature and methods of treating addiction. Jansen is the world's foremost expert on ketamine, and this is a great resource for anyone who wishes to understand ketamine's effects, risks, and potential.

LSD: My Problem Child
Albert Hofmann, Ph.D. (4th English edition, paperback)
ISBN: 978-0-9798622-2-9 $15.95

   This is the story of LSD told by a concerned yet hopeful father. Organic chemist Albert Hofmann traces LSD's path from a promising psychiatric research medicine to a recreational drug sparking hysteria and prohibition. We follow Hofmann's trek across Mexico to discover sacred plants related to LSD and listen as he corresponds with other notable figures about his remarkable discovery. Underlying it all is Dr. Hofmann's powerful conclusion that mystical experience may be our planet's best hope for survival. Whether induced by LSD, meditation, or arising spontaneously, such experiences help us to comprehend "the wonder, the mystery of the divine in the microcosm of the atom, in the macrocosm of the spiral nebula, in the seeds of plants, in the body and soul of people." More than sixty years after the birth of Albert Hofmann's "problem child," his vision of its true potential is more relevant—and more needed—than ever. The eulogy that Dr. Hofmann wrote himself and was read by his children at his funeral is the forward to the 4th edition.

LSD Psychotherapy
Stanislav Grof, M.D. (4th Edition, Paperback)
ISBN: 0-9798622-0-5 $19.95

   LSD Psychotherapy is a complete study of the use of LSD in clinical therapeutic practice, written by the world's foremost LSD psychotherapist. The text was written as a medical manual and as a historical record portraying a broad therapeutic vision. It is a valuable source of information for anyone wishing to learn more about LSD. The therapeutic model also extends to other substances: the MAPS research team used *LSD Psychotherapy* as a key reference for its first MDMA/PTSD study. Originally published in 1980, this 2008 paperback edition has a new introduction by Albert Hofmann, Ph.D., a forward by Andrew Weil, M.D., and color illustrations.

Modern Consciousness Research and the Understanding of Art; including the Visionary World of H.R. Giger
Stanislav Grof, M.D.
ISBN: 0-9798622-9-9 $29.95

   In 200 spellbinding pages—including over 100 large, full-color illustrations—*Modern Consciousness Research and the Understanding of Art* takes readers on an enchanting tour of the human psyche and a visual tour of the artwork of H.R. Giger. In this book, Grof illuminates themes related to dreams, trauma, sexuality, birth, and death, by applying his penetrating analysis to the work of Giger and other visionary artists.

The Secret Chief Revealed
Myron Stolaroff
ISBN: 0-9669919-6-6 $12.95

The second edition of *The Secret Chief* is a collection of interviews with "Jacob," the underground psychedelic therapist who is revealed years after his death as psychologist Leo Zeff. Before his death in 1988, Zeff provided psychedelic therapy to over 3,000 people. As "Jacob," he relates the origins of his early interest in psychedelics, how he chose his clients, and what he did to prepare them. He discusses the dynamics of the individual and group trip, the characteristics and appropriate dosages of various drugs, and the range of problems that people worked through. Stanislav Grof, Ann and Alexander Shulgin, and Albert Hofmann each contribute writings about the importance of Leo's work. In this new edition, Leo's family and former clients also write about their experiences with him. This book is an easy-to-read introduction to the techniques and potential of psychedelic therapy.

The Ultimate Journey: Consciousness and the Mystery of Death
Stanislav Grof, M.D., Ph.D. (2nd edition)
ISBN: 0-9660019-9-0 $19.95

Dr. Stanislav Grof, author of *LSD Psychotherapy* and originator of Holotropic Breathwork, offers a wealth of perspectives on how we can enrich and transform the experience of dying in our culture. This 356-page book features 40 pages of images (24 in color) and a foreword by Huston Smith. Grof discusses his own patients' experiences of death and rebirth in psychedelic therapy, investigates cross-cultural beliefs and paranormal and near-death research, and argues that contrary to the predominant Western perspective death is not necessarily the end of consciousness. Grof is a psychiatrist with over forty years of experience with research into non-ordinary states of consciousness and one of the founders of transpersonal psychology. He is the founder of the International Transpersonal Association, and has published over 140 articles in professional journals. The latest edition of *The Ultimate Journey* includes a new foreword by David Jay Brown, M.A., and Peter Gasser, M.D.

Shipping and Handling

Shipping varies by weight of books.

Bulk orders are welcome. Please contact MAPS for details.

Books can be purchased online by visiting **maps.org** (credit card or Paypal), over the phone by calling +1 831-429-MDMA (6362), or through your favorite local bookstore.

You may also send orders by mail to:

MAPS

P.O. Box 8423

Santa Cruz, CA, 95061

Phone: +1 831-429-MDMA (6362)

Fax: +1 831-429-6370

E-mail: **orders@maps.org**

Web: **maps.org** | **mdmaptsd.org** | **psychedelicscience.org**

About the Editors

Phil Wolfson, M.D., is Principal Investigator for a Phase 2, FDA approved 18-person study of MDMA Assisted Psychotherapy for individuals with significant anxiety due to life threatening illnesses. His clinical practice with ketamine has informed his role in the development of Ketamine Assisted Psychotherapy. Phil is a sixties activist, psychiatrist/psychotherapist, writer, practicing Buddhist and psychonaut who has lived in the Bay Area for 38 years. He is the author of *Noe: A Father-Son Song of Love, Life, Illness, and Death* (2011, North Atlantic Books). In the 1980s, he participated in clinical research with MDMA (ecstasy). He has been awarded five patents for unique herbal medicines. He is a journalist and author of numerous articles on politics, transformation, psychedelics, consciousness and spirit, and was a founding member of the Heffter Research Institute. Phil has taught in the graduate psychology programs at JFK University, CIIS and the UCSF School of Medicine Department of Psychiatry.

Glenn Hartelius, Ph.D. is Founding Director of the Ph.D. in Integral and Transpersonal Psychology at the California Institute of Integral Studies (CIIS) in San Francisco, where he serves as Associate Professor. He is also leading an initiative to develop a new research facility at CIIS for research in whole person neuroscience. Glenn is main editor for the *International Journal of Transpersonal Studies,* a peer-reviewed academic journal. He is co-editor of *The Wiley-Blackwell Handbook of Transpersonal Psychology,* and Secretary of the International Transpersonal Association. His research on the definition and scope of transpersonal psychology has helped to define the field. He is developing a model of attention and how to manage it in lived experience that is designed to simplify complex skills such as meditation, sustained focus, and leadership presence. He has also taught at the Institute of Transpersonal Psychology, Naropa University, Saybrook University, and Middlesex University in the UK.

"Ketamine offers a powerful and beneficial new approach, and is worth more scientific study."
—Jack Kornfield, Ph.D., founder of Spirit Rock Meditation Center
and author of *A Path With Heart*

"Taking in all the information about ketamine in this book will not fully satisfy your curiosity, nor completely subdue your concerns, but you will know far better how it is that this substance has so many different uses and effects, depending on set and setting, dose, method of ingestion, and intention of the patient as well as the practitioner. Here are wonderful first-person stories, both inspiring and cautionary, technical papers detailing specific results, and both sides of the major controversies between therapist/researchers—each committed to the best ways to maximize ketamine's benefits. The book is an invaluable resource."
—James Fadiman, Ph.D., psychedelic researcher and
author of *The Psychedelic Explorer's Guide: Safe, Therapeutic and Sacred Journeys*

"Here is an extraordinary collection of essays demonstrating that ketamine is more than just another molecule. If you are interested in the promise of ketamine as a tool of value in psychiatry, and/or you are interested in ketamine as a tool in exploring the nature of mind and the nature of what we call reality, then this book is for you!"
—David E. Presti, Ph.D., author of *Foundational Concepts in Neuroscience: A Brain-Mind Odyssey*

"Easing the pains of our campmates is what makes us human. These explorations of the use of ketamine for depression are drawn from the most ancient and noble of human traditions. Even if the mechanisms are not yet well understood, the results are promising."
—Dale Pendell, author of *Pharmako/Gnosis*

"The first time I heard of ketamine used in a therapeutic context was when it was administered by an emergency room doctor when he set my six-year-old daughter's broken arm. What I remember from that moment is only the near-bliss I experienced when her pain was finally relieved. To read in this fascinating book that the drug is useful as an aid to psychotherapy is tremendously exciting."
—Ayelet Waldman, author of *A Really Good Day*

"At a time when ketamine is the subject of increasing psychiatric research and now clinical use as an antidepressant, *The Ketamine Papers* provides useful summaries of the published data and information about skillful administration practices. It also takes us beyond the limits of a reductionist focus on ketamine's glutamatergic effects. With contributions from leaders in the field of consciousness research and depth psychology, combined with reports of extensive clinical experience using ketamine in conjunction with psychotherapy, Wolfson and Hartelius present fascinating accounts of the intimate relationship between healing and the richness of direct experience."
—Michael C. Mithoefer, M.D., Psychedelic therapy researcher